Supreme
Discomfort

Supreme Discomfort

The Divided Soul of
CLARENCE THOMAS

Kevin Merida and
Michael A. Fletcher

Broadway Books
New York

For Stanley and Beryl Fletcher
In memory of Jesse J. and Jesse E. Merida

PUBLISHED BY BROADWAY BOOKS

A hardcover edition of this book was originally published
in 2007 by Doubleday.

Published in the United States by Broadway Books, an imprint of
The Doubleday Broadway Publishing Group, a division of
Random House, Inc., New York.
www.broadwaybooks.com

BROADWAY BOOKS and its logo, a letter B bisected on the diagonal,
are trademarks of Random House, Inc.

Book design by Michael Collica

Library of Congress Cataloging-in-Publication Data
Merida, Kevin.
Supreme discomfort : the divided soul of Clarence Thomas / by Kevin
Merida and Michael A. Fletcher.
p. cm.
1. Thomas, Clarence, 1948– 2. Judges—United States—Biography.
3. United States Supreme Court—Officials and employees—Biography.
[1. African American judges—Biography.] I. Fletcher, Michael A.
II. Title.
KF8745.T48M47 2007
347.73'2634—dc22
[B]
2006036435

ISBN 978-0-7679-1636-3

PRINTED IN THE UNITED STATES OF AMERICA

1 3 5 7 9 10 8 6 4 2

First Paperback Edition

CONTENTS

PROLOGUE

I t was 8 a.m. when the phone rang in his Westin Hotel room. Done with breakfast, Associate Supreme Court Justice Clarence Thomas still had an entire morning to spend before his luncheon speech to the Savannah Bar Association. Lester Johnson was on the line.

"What're you doing?" Johnson asked.

"I'm just coolin' out," Thomas replied.

Johnson, an old friend and prominent local attorney, figured Thomas would enjoy a quick tour of the renovated Bull Street Library, the main branch in Savannah's Victorian district, which wouldn't admit blacks until 1963. When Thomas was growing up here, he spent most of his free time in the Carnegie Library, on the black side of town. It wasn't until he was a teenager that integration gave him access to the Big Library, as he called it, but once access was granted Thomas became a Bull Street regular.

Thomas notified his security detail and met Johnson in front of the library. Not wanting to monopolize Thomas's time, Johnson had promised the tour would take just fifteen minutes. But once Thomas planted himself among the historical texts and old city maps, once he started reminiscing about "story hour," once he started introducing himself to the genealogy specialist and the security guard and posing for photos, it was hard to drag him away. He stayed for two whole hours.

He spotted a group of black fourth and fifth graders from a private academy and, hoping to inspire them, sidled over. This was vintage Thomas, always drawn to the children in a room. When he was a kid, Thomas told them, the library was how he expanded his world, using books to visit places that were beyond his reach. The kids, however, were having too much fun on the computers to pay close attention to this VIP they didn't recognize. Johnson seemed more bothered than Thomas by the lack of recognition. He had a library staffer make twelve copies of Thomas's bio and instructed the students to tell their parents whom they had met—not only the sole African American on the nation's highest court but arguably Savannah's most famous son.

Johnson, a soft-spoken man of slight build, had long admired Thomas, who is five years his senior. Both came up through the Catholic school system in Savannah during Jim Crow's reign. Thomas, in fact, spent little time in public education, snatched out by his grandfather, who figured he'd get superior, more disciplined instruction from the Franciscan nuns and perhaps one day become the city's first black priest. Thomas and Johnson both ended up at College of the Holy Cross in Massachusetts, though not at the same time, and pursued legal careers. While at Yale Law School, Thomas became something of a mentor to Johnson, imploring him to avoid easy courses as an undergrad and prepare for life's later competitions. ("Let them white boys go out and get drunk," he told Johnson. "You need to be staying on campus and hitting those books.")

Upstairs, the Bull Street Library tour continued. Thomas and a childhood acquaintance, W. John Mitchell, were giddily recalling youthful pastimes such as "pluffer," a game that involved shooting chinaberries at each other through a tube of cane. But the good cheer was interrupted when Abigail Jordan, a retired educator and local black activist who just happened to be in the library, spotted Thomas.

There was something in the spectacle of the burly justice, with his booming laugh and broad grin, yukking it up with his friends that compelled Jordan to move toward the group, close enough, as she would later say, "to be kissed" by Lester Johnson. She stood before them, glared, and abruptly said, "I just wanted to see what a group of Uncle Toms look like." Then she walked away.

To some people, just being in the company of Clarence Thomas is enough to damn you.

That episode occurred on May 11, 2001. To us, as chroniclers of Thomas's life, the tale remains vivid. It represents an awkward convergence of what both inspires and haunts him most.

"Uncle Tom" is the most searing insult a black American can hurl at a member of his or her own race, a synonym for sellout, for someone subservient to whites at the expense of his own people. No black man wants that label. That the lone African American on the Supreme Court would provoke such a cutting slur should be astounding—and yet it has become part of mainstream discussion.

But not among children. No *child* would call Clarence Thomas an Uncle Tom. In children, Thomas sees uncluttered minds, fresh possibilities, hope —the hope that maybe they won't prejudge him, won't view him through the lens of their elders, some of whom he believes are stuck on old ideas. Maybe they will grow up to become independent thinkers, which is how Thomas sees himself. So he's never too busy for the kids. Sometimes he'll spy a touring school group at the court and invite the students up to his chambers. For Thomas, being a kid at the library, alone with his books, is among his happiest memories.

But then there's always the prospect of an Abigail Jordan appearing out of nowhere, if not literally then metaphorically. While it may be unusual for a Supreme Court justice to be publicly confronted in such a provocative way—Thomas's wife, Ginni, says her husband rarely encounters anything but polite receptions—the an-

tipathy toward Thomas among African Americans is wide and deep
and persistent. It surfaces at corporate water coolers, in beauty
shops, gymnasiums, faculty dining rooms—wherever blacks con-
gregate and Thurgood Marshall's successor happens to be mentioned.

This book grew out of such an occasion. We were attending a
party of black professionals some years ago when Thomas's name
was harmlessly invoked. The conversation started small and quiet,
but soon people overhearing it came from the other side of the
room to participate. Almost instantly, a roaring, improvisational debate was taking place. Did Thomas deserve the harsh judgments?
How is it decided who qualifies for black legitimacy? As we saw it,
no other public figure in American life had the ability to spark such
intense passions among blacks—if not seething anger, then the restless need to analyze him, to come up with some piece of sideline so-
ciology to explain the vast gulf between arguably the most powerful
African American in the land and so many members of his own race.

A 1998 poll conducted by the Joint Center for Political and Economic Studies, which specializes in research on African Americans,
showed Thomas had a favorable rating of just 32 percent among
blacks. "These are the worst numbers of any prominent black figure
I've ever asked about," said David Bositis, the center's longtime political analyst. That roster would include Condoleezza Rice and Jesse
Jackson, Colin Powell and Al Sharpton.

On August 4, 2002, the *Washington Post Magazine* published a cover
story by us, "The Lonely Stand of Clarence Thomas." It was our first
crack at exploring both the racial vehemence that has hounded
Thomas and the roots of his ascension to the judicial mountaintop.
This book is the product of a more far-reaching journalistic mission
to understand and explain Thomas. We were guided by a simple
notion—that all lives are complex, that there is no singular, overrid-
ing truth about any of us. Which is the most authentic portrait: The
magnetic Clarence Thomas who strikes up friendships in RV parks
as he drives his forty-foot motor coach around the country? The

ideological Clarence Thomas who is a hero of the conservative right and officiated at Rush Limbaugh's wedding? Or the despised Clarence Thomas, the mere sight of whom kindles an epithet in the hush of a public library?

Aubrey Immelman, a psychology professor at Saint John's University in Minnesota, is an expert at developing personality profiles of public figures, including George W. Bush, Bill Clinton, and John McCain. After conducting a study of Clarence Thomas based on published accounts of his life, Immelman concluded: "I find him to be a shy and insecure person who is very sensitive to rejection."

Immelman sees in Thomas a discontented man who "views himself as misunderstood." He wants to reach out to those who don't understand him, according to Immelman, but fears getting hurt, and fears failure and humiliation. So he avoids confrontation. Thomas holds himself to high standards, Immelman found, and has a tendency to be judgmental and inflexible. "He's a very critical individual, not that accepting of others' flaws or shortcomings."

For nearly sixteen years, people have been searching for clues to the mystery that is Clarence Thomas, a man who seems to embrace the mantle of enigma. It has been that long since he was confirmed to the high court by the smallest margin—four votes—in more than a century. His bitter confirmation battle became a cultural touchstone, a transforming political event that pulsated long after it was over. It tarnished the image of the white-male-dominated U.S. Senate, inspired the successful campaigns of women running for Congress, reignited the uneasy debate about black male-female relationships, and added kerosene to the partisan wars over judicial nominations. Those wars have seen no truces.

For Thomas, it was the worst possible humiliation, a televised nightmare from which he may never fully recover. Long Dong Silver? Pubic hair on a Coke can? Though he often tries to act like a healed man, his private demeanor, according to intimates, suggests that torment and anger live on inside him.

"I think it is very painful to Clarence that there are large numbers of people that think badly of him and think him to be a bad person," says Dick Armey, the former U.S. House majority leader and a personal friend. "That bothers him immensely."

Armey still recalls a soul-searching night around the Thomas kitchen table—Dick and Susan Armey, Clarence and Ginni Thomas. The discussion was about labels, the way you can get branded in Washington with an image that is unshakable. Tattoos, Armey called them. He would remember the conversation for a book he later wrote, *Armey's Axioms*. One of those axioms is: Tattoos last forever. What anguished Thomas that night and anguishes him now, according to Armey, is that when he dies his obituary will mention prominently that he was accused of sexual harassment by a former employee and protégé he was once close to, Professor Anita Hill. He will never be able to live that down. Never.

The Anita Hill–Clarence Thomas drama remains a subject of debate and puzzlement, even today. Time has only hardened loyalties. And no definitive truth about what happened between them has emerged since the hearings, though there has been no shortage of speculation and prose on the subject. Some will always believe Hill's account of lewd behavior and unwelcome sexual advances by Thomas; others will always believe Thomas was the victim of a smear campaign that permanently damaged his reputation.

What seems undeniable, though, is that the episode has framed the rest of Clarence Thomas's life. He has not been the same man since. Some, in fact, believe the scars of that ordeal have affected his judicial judgment, making him more rigid in his deliberation of cases than he might otherwise have been.

Those searching for easy conclusions about his life will be disappointed here. Thomas can be surprising and predictable, warm and icy, generous and unmerciful, confident and insecure. He is, in essence, a welter of conflicting personas.

Thomas once said he would never accept a race-based job, and yet he spent an entire federal career in such positions, including a stint as the longest-serving chairman of the Equal Employment Opportunity Commission in the agency's history. Was he a shrewd calculator of what it took to fulfill his greatest ambitions? Or a promising black bureaucrat who allowed himself to be pushed and pulled and sponsored all the way to the Supreme Court? The irony is that the career path that led him to the most prestigious tenured position in America is one he discourages other blacks from following.

Thomas often talks about his distaste for the media. Print and broadcast outlets have treated him poorly, he says, or just flat out gotten his story wrong. "You've got some scoundrels in your business," he told one of us at a judicial conference. "Why do you have so many scoundrels?" And yet he has cultivated and maintained relationships with journalists of varying ideological bents—from National Public Radio correspondent Juan Williams to former *Washington Post* deputy editorial page editor Colbert King to columnist George Will, with whom he goes to baseball games. Last year, the same man who sees "so many scoundrels" in the media was out late hobnobbing at the preeminent media social event of the year, the annual White House Correspondents' Association dinner.

One of the myths that have grown up around Thomas is that he doesn't pay attention to the critiques of him as a justice. In fact, it has been widely reported, he rarely even reads newspapers and periodicals, except for the *New York Post* sports section and the *Wall Street Journal* editorial page. But those on the receiving end of one of his surprise phone calls know better. Contrary to popular belief, he is hardly a disengaged justice.

Some are stunned to see Thomas strolling over to the Dirksen Senate Office Building for the hot buffet lunch, stopping several times along the short route from the court to gladhand and backslap with people whom he recognizes or who recognize him. Clerks sometimes joke that the only problem with going to lunch with Thomas is it might take thirty minutes to cross the street.

It's intriguing that Thomas has found a lunch home of sorts in the U.S. Senate, scene of his "high-tech lynching," as he bitterly put it during his confirmation hearings. The institution that robbed her husband of his dignity, according to Ginni Thomas, is now where he loves to take his meals—eating among Senate staffers, chatting with the black women who cook and waitress, occasionally even break-fasting with the senators themselves in their private dining room.

Any close inspection of Thomas's life will sooner or later lead to a conundrum. The man who relishes his privacy, for example, is also remarkably revealing in public. One part of him pines for anonym-ity, and another part of him has an almost cathartic need to turn a microscope on himself. Thomas delivers some of the most emo-tional, self-examining speeches in public life. His best material is his own lingering pain—the hurt, for instance, of graduating from a top-flight law school and barely getting any job offers. For three decades, he has kept a stack of rejection letters. He tries to act tough, wants to be brave. "Judges do not need protection from the slings and arrows of mere words," Thomas once said. "We are not that fragile." But fragile is what you sometimes see when you look at him.

In assessing Thomas, we are reminded of W. E. B. Du Bois's thought-provoking analyses of race issues a century ago. A co-founder of the NAACP and the first African American to earn a doc-torate from Harvard, Du Bois led a transcendent life and was never predictable. In his most famous work, *The Souls of Black Folk*, pub-lished in 1903, Du Bois wrote: "It is a peculiar sensation, this sense of always looking at one's self through the eyes of others. One ever feels his two-ness—an American, a Negro; two souls, two thoughts, two unreconciled strivings; two warring ideals in one dark body, whose dogged strength alone keeps it from being torn asunder."

A century later, race remains an inescapable factor in most black lives, no matter how successful or disappointing they have turned out to be. Even in his cloistered, rarefied world as a member of the most important judicial body in existence, Thomas will always be black and he knows it. Not just black, but black before everything else.

On the court he is known as an unwavering proponent of the Constitution's original text. For popular consumption, he is an ideological conservative. For someone who spent a decade navigating the treacherous political waters of Washington, Thomas isn't much of a politician in this body. Rarely willing to compromise, he's not often tapped to write opinions that require a delicate touch in order to hold a 5–4 majority. Nobody fusses over him, as they did over retired justice Sandra Day O'Connor, whose swing-vote throne now has been assumed by Justice Anthony Kennedy. Thomas is, consequently, not much of a player in his workplace—at least not as measured by the weight of his scholarship or his ability to sway colleagues to his point of view. In fact, his body of opinions is notably thin on constitutionally significant cases. Not that Thomas really cares. He seems happiest when playing the lone wolf, drafting provocative dissents that he hopes—believes—might one day become law. He has amassed quite a team of loyal former clerks, who gather monthly for lunch with their old boss, trading gossip and sharing stories about their children. Some have become missionaries of sorts, writing law journal articles and appearing at forums to defend and bolster Thomas's image. Some even quietly pushed the idea of Thomas as chief justice.

When it became apparent in early 2005 that Chief Justice William H. Rehnquist was seriously ill from thyroid cancer and might not last much longer on the court, President George W. Bush briefly considered Thomas as a replacement. But the consideration never went far. The president didn't talk to Thomas, and no Oval Office surrogates were dispatched to sound him out. Though he liked Thomas, Bush couldn't get past his own wariness of "re-litigating old fights from his father's administration," according to a senior White House official. The president worried that nominating Thomas would energize the opposition and spark another heated confirmation battle of the kind seen in 1991. He also was determined "to put his own stamp on the court," as the White House official put it, a process that ultimately led Bush to nominate federal appeals court judge John G. Roberts Jr. as chief justice.

Thomas remains a puzzle to many who watch the court, and to

those who don't. He is routinely silent at oral arguments, the quietest justice, giving no hint of how he thinks or what he's thinking. Those wondering about Thomas's mind can find clues in the texts of some two hundred speeches he has given—on subjects from civility to character. Those lucky enough to get an invitation to "drop by" his chambers will be there for hours and find themselves canceling other meetings, as Thomas discusses everything from his friendship with Bobby Knight to racism in the Missouri seminary he abandoned.

He is not an uninteresting man. Maddening sometimes, but not uninteresting. Even as Thomas goes about his work, perhaps the purest conservative on the court, it's his racial identity that most defines him. Would he even be on the court if he were not black? Would his silence at oral arguments be cause to question his intellect if he were not black? Would he be the subject of such public scrutiny if he were not a black conservative? And if he were not a black conservative would his white ideological comrades view him as so courageous and be so in love with him? Thomas tosses around such questions in his head more than most think.

"People say that because I am black, Justice Scalia does my work for me," he told students at the University of Louisville in 2000. "But I rarely see him, so he must have a chip in my brain."

This book examines Thomas's entire life, but it relies heavily on the racial prism. For that is the prism through which Thomas often views himself. He is in constant struggle with his racial identity—twisting, churning, sometimes hiding from it, but never denying it, even when he's defiant about it.

"It pains me deeply—more deeply than any of you can imagine—to be perceived by so many members of my race as doing them harm," he told a national organization of black lawyers and judges in 1998. "All the sacrifice, all the long hours of preparation were to help, not to hurt. But what hurts more, much more, is the amount of time and attention spent on manufactured controversies and media sideshows when so many problems cry out for constructive attention. I have come here today not in anger or to anger. . . . Nor have I come to defend my views, but rather to assert my right to think for myself, to refuse to have my ideas assigned to me as though I was an intellectual slave because I am black."

As black journalists, we understand Thomas's desire to escape limitation. When we were roommates at Boston University in the late 1970s, we published an alternative student newspaper and brought some of the nation's leading journalists to campus. We didn't consider our newspaper inferior because it was targeted to black students, and we didn't think our speakers were less worthy of being heard because they were black. And yet we came to realize that some students, faculty, and administrators had placed a box around us that we had not placed around ourselves—a black box. To us, we were just experimenting with our promise, chasing our dreams.

Thirty years later we have reported on every level of politics and government, traveled on Air Force One, interviewed presidents, and we now make our living at the *Washington Post*. During our careers, some have expected less of us than of our white colleagues, and some have expected more. Being black journalists has cut both ways. That we are, to our knowledge, the first black journalists to write a book about Thomas carried no weight with him—not even in getting an audience. Despite being urged to meet with us by some of his African American friends—as well as by some of his white friends— Thomas decided against it. That we worked for the *Post* (considered a liberal organ by many conservatives), *and* were black, *and* were interested in exploring with him the complexities of race seemed to be too unsavory a combination for the justice.

Always pleasant and cordial when he saw one of us in public ("It's nothing personal, buddy," he said on one occasion. "Wish you the best of luck."), Thomas was influenced greatly by the wariness of his wife, we are told, and perhaps by his own insecurity. Fortunately for us, many of Thomas's closest friends, family members, former law clerks, and other employees lent their insight into the justice. We also searched widely for others who had experiences with Thomas and discovered many who had never before commented on their interactions or shared their observations about the justice.

After Abigail Jordan created her stir at the Bull Street Library—she says she was there for a meeting and just happened to bump into the Thomas entourage—Lester Johnson asked the marshals to keep an eye on her. He was infuriated. But there was nothing really to do about it. The embarrassment had been caused. All Johnson wanted to ensure now was that Jordan, whom he had clashed with before on city issues, left it at that. Thomas, meanwhile, didn't remark on the incident right away, but as he was leaving the library he turned to Johnson and quipped: "Was that one of your irate clients?"

Who knows how often Thomas sits alone wondering how he became so estranged from people who look like him and grew up like him? After all he overcame—his father left him when he was two, he was chastised by teachers for his Gullah dialect—Thomas can't buy a soda pop in some black neighborhoods without risk of being hissed at. Or, perhaps worse, going unrecognized and ignored. The pinnacle of achievement isn't supposed to look like this.

In Thomas's hometown of Savannah, even his elderly mother worries about his image. Why does there seem to be more criticism than celebration of her son by African Americans? "I don't tell him anything back here because I don't want him to worry," Leola Williams told us, "but he knows that the black people is against him. He knows that."

We were sitting in her living room in the house Thomas grew up in, listening to a prideful mother's agitation build. She recalled how her father would get her out of bed to attend NAACP meetings with him, how committed her family was to supporting the organization. But then the organization turned its back on her son, she says.

Thomas tells her not to worry, but their phone conversations—sometimes he'll call at 4 a.m., before her work shift—reveal what he tries hard to mask. The longer they talk on the phone the more she can tell he's pained by his black-pariah circumstance.

"Yes, it hurts," she said. "It really hurts."

1

COURTING VENOM
Being Clarence Thomas

Dallas attorney Eric Moye received his copy in the mail from a fellow Harvard Law School alum. He started reading it but stopped to make a copy of the copy for a friend. He continued reading, absorbed, enchanted, depressed, exhilarated. Couldn't put it down—except to make more copies.

It wasn't a John Grisham thriller, but it might as well have been. "An Open Letter to Justice Clarence Thomas from a Federal Judicial Colleague" created an enormous buzz when the *University of Pennsylvania Law Review* published it in January 1992. Written by A. Leon Higginbotham Jr., chief judge emeritus of the U.S. Court of Appeals for the Third Circuit, it was part history lesson and part admonition. Crafted with scholarly precision, it contained eighty-five footnotes and numerous citations of important court cases. But the essence of it read like a stern grandfather lecturing his bull-headed grandson: *Don't forget the roots of your success, boy, and the responsibilities you have to those who paved your way*.

"You . . . must try to remember that the fundamental problems of the disadvantaged, women, minorities, and the powerless have not all been solved simply because you have 'moved on up' from Pin

Point, Georgia, to the Supreme Court," Higginbotham wrote in the conclusion of his twenty-four-page set of instructions to Thomas. Reciting a roster of notable names from the past, Higginbotham urged Thomas to see his life as connected to "the visions and struggles of Frederick Douglass, Sojourner Truth, Harriet Tubman, Charles Hamilton Houston, A. Philip Randolph, Mary McLeod Bethune, W. E. B. Du Bois, Roy Wilkins, Whitney Young, Martin Luther King, Judge William Henry Hastie, Justices Thurgood Marshall, Earl Warren, and William Brennan, as well as the thousands of others who dedicated much of their lives to create the America that made your opportunities possible."

The "open letter" read at times like a personal letter and was dated November 29, 1991, which was shortly after Thomas took his seat on the high court. Higginbotham felt ambivalent about making his letter public but did so, he said, to help this generation and future ones better evaluate Thomas. Because it was so well sourced and because it was penned by a black twenty-seven-year veteran of the federal bench, the letter as law review article carried an authority that most Thomas critiques did not.

As such, it received considerable attention. The University of Pennsylvania received more than seventeen thousand requests for reprints, and law offices around the country busily churned out photocopies.

"Sometimes chain letters circulate all over the place," recalled Moye, "and this was kind of like one of those." Nowhere was the interest greater than in black legal circles, where a robust debate was unfolding about what kind of justice Thomas would become. Moye, a former state district judge with a weakness for Cuban cigars and the finest steaks, acted as if he'd reached nirvana. After he made his first copy of the Higginbotham treatise and got his secretary to make five more copies, he bought the bound version to put on his office shelf. So many photocopies were in circulation that another one even came back to Moye—just like a chain letter.

"It was spreading like fire across the dry prairie," Moye recalled.

"Folks were calling one another speculating on whether Thomas would ever respond to Judge Higginbotham's open letter."

The showdown marked the beginning of a transition in the way African Americans came to view Thomas, a shift that helped harden his image nationally. Gradually but inexorably, wariness supplanted wait-and-see as the predominant state of mind among blacks. Wariness became distrust, which blossomed into contempt.

"I'll put it like this," said basketball legend Kareem Abdul Jabbar. "If he let people know that he was going to be at some public destination, let's say in Harlem, at a certain hour on a certain day, let's see how many supporters would show up and how many detractors would show up." The National Basketball Association's all-time leading scorer was another who had discovered Higginbotham's law article and wondered: How can someone who benefited so richly from affirmative action not support the same remedy for those in similar circumstances?

Though his confirmation hearings left Thomas wounded and enraged, the good news should have been that initially, at least, more than twice as many African Americans, according to polls, believed him as believed Anita Hill. But Thomas couldn't find the resolve to embrace that reassuring fact. He was shell-shocked by his ordeal and retreated into his work, which was difficult enough, and he was already behind. The court's term began in October 1991. Because of his drawn-out confirmation process and the death of Chief Justice William Rehnquist's wife, Nan, Thomas wasn't sworn in until the first day of November. He arrived with no staff, his law clerks weren't up to speed, and he was hamstrung by his inexperience as a judge—he'd spent just nineteen months on the D.C. Circuit of the U.S. Court of Appeals. Plus he was bone tired.

Higginbotham was certainly no help. He became a more formidable nemesis, shedding the reproving grandpa role for the part of public castigator. In an attention-getting 1994 lecture at the Hastings College of Law in San Francisco, Higginbotham used his hour-long remarks to issue a stiff condemnation of Thomas's jurisprudence. In one pointed comparison, he said he had studied every opinion written by Thomas and every one composed by his predecessor Marshall, and the difference between the two jurists was "the difference between zero and infinity."

Then he dug the knife in even deeper.

"I have often pondered how it is that Justice Thomas, an African American, could be so insensitive to the plight of the powerless. Why is he no different, or probably worse, than many of the most conservative Supreme Court justices of this century? I can only think of one Supreme Court justice during this century who was worse than Justice Clarence Thomas: James McReynolds, a white supremacist who referred to blacks as 'niggers.' "

Those in the packed auditorium couldn't help but notice how emotional Higginbotham had become, his voice trembling, tears flowing. Removing his glasses, he wiped his eyes with a handkerchief. During Democratic presidencies, Higginbotham's name often surfaced on short lists of potential Supreme Court nominees. But it never rose to the top. (In 1995, he would be awarded the Presidential Medal of Freedom, the closest thing a president can muster to a consolation prize.) The hard part was that Higginbotham was sixty-five and now retired, and not only had he been passed over for a position he had long coveted, he saw it snatched by a junior he felt had not earned it. Detractors attributed Higginbotham's behavior to some combination of bitterness, jealousy, and a broken heart. But whatever his reasons, the blasts were effective. And the judgment that Thomas was the kind of black man no black person should admire mushroomed.

The catalog of Thomas-targeted insults is fat and brutal, and today the estrangement between the justice and broad swaths of his own people seems almost irreconcilable. *Emerge*, a since-departed African American–oriented news magazine owned by the country's first black billionaire, Bob Johnson, twice parodied Thomas on its cover—once wearing an Aunt Jemima–style headscarf and another time as a lawn jockey. The editions were among the magazine's best sellers. *Ebony* magazine, which annually publishes a list of the nation's hundred most influential African Americans, routinely leaves Thomas off its tally. A former Kansas City mayor can make it, but not the nation's only black Supreme Court justice?

Invitations for Thomas to speak are now carefully vetted. He has discovered that saying yes to an offer also could mean signing up for public humiliation: name-calling, pickets, boycotts. The mere announcement of a Thomas visit is apt to trigger a controversy. In the most famous such episode, the superintendent of the Prince George's County, Maryland, school system disinvited Thomas from speaking at a middle school in 1996 after several black school board members complained and threatened protests. The school board overruled its schools' chief, and the show went on—demonstrations and all. (Later, a law clerk gave Thomas a placard that he proudly displayed in his chambers as a kind of combat medal. It read: "Banned in P.G. County.")

Thomas has become more intimate with his opposition than he ever thought would be possible in the relatively isolated life of a Supreme Court justice. No venue is sacred. The Reverend Al Sharpton took his beef straight to Thomas's home. He led four hundred demonstrators, who stepped off chartered buses, to a public road outside the justice's secluded suburban Virginia subdivision. There they denounced Thomas as a traitor. Nearly a decade later, Sharpton would campaign for president and continue his bashing of Thomas in a nationally televised debate, claiming, "He is my color, but he's not my kind." Even in academia, where philosophical debate is encouraged, five black University of North Carolina law professors boycotted a visit by Thomas in the spring of 2002.

Racial disillusionment is the common theme in all these demonstrations—not ideology, not politics, but the seething sense that one of the potential bright lights of the race has rejected his chance to shine. Otherwise, the black North Carolina professors would have howled about the appearances of Justice Antonin Scalia and Justice Sandra Day O'Connor in preceding years. But they didn't. As the professors wrote, explaining their position, in a nation "in which African Americans are disproportionately poor, undereducated, imprisoned and politically compromised, identity—racial identity—very clearly matters. Were that not the case, Justice Thomas, for all his claims to the contrary, could not have declared himself the victim of a 'high-tech lynching' during the heated opposition to his appointment to the Supreme Court."

A special strain of animus seems reserved for Thomas. When the American Civil Liberties Union of Hawaii proposed inviting Thomas to a debate on affirmative action in 2003, black board member Eric Ferrer was furious. That would be tantamount to "inviting Hitler to come speak on the rights of Jews," he fumed. Thomas didn't accept the invitation, but Ferrer ended up resigning from the board over the mere fact that an invitation had been extended. "The appropriate word is venom," said conservative media critic Brent Bozell, assessing what has happened to Thomas. "I would challenge you to find anyone on the left who has been the target of such a vitriolic character assassination campaign as has Clarence Thomas. I even challenge you to find anyone on the right who has. This man is in his own league."

A league of his own, but one he has helped create, as far as Eric Moye is concerned. Moye, active in Democratic politics, was up for a federal appeals court judgeship during the Clinton administration. He still remembers some of Thomas's harsh critiques of civil rights groups during his years as Ronald Reagan's chairman of the Equal Employment Opportunity Commission. Thomas once told an interviewer that there was not a single area in which the NAACP was doing good work—"I can't think of any"—and another time complained that all civil rights leaders do is "bitch, bitch, bitch, moan and moan, whine and whine." Moye wonders if Thomas ever stops to think when he dons his robe: Where would I be if these civil rights figures had not carried the fight to statehouses and courthouses, had not taken the beatings, gone to jail, refused to wilt under exhausting oppression, and even been willing to die for equality?

(Actually, Thomas has answered that question. He doesn't credit civil rights leaders for his opportunities. "My grandfather—that's the guy that got me out," he once told an interviewer. "It wasn't all these people who are claiming all this leadership stuff.")

As Moye sees it, Thomas has tilted so far away from his heritage that there is no longer any real debate about him. "I think there is a profound sense of despair," Moye says. "In order to have disappointment you have to have high expectations. I think there were those who hoped he was going to blossom and develop. But I don't think you know many African Americans, other than those who know him personally, who think he turned out all right."

Comedians now use him as material. Rappers turn him into lyrics. This, from the song "Build and Destroy," by KRS-One:

> *The white man ain't the devil I promise*
> *You want to see the devil take a look at Clarence Thomas.*

Essayists have taken the Thomas-dissecting cottage industry to new heights. Michael Thelwell, an Afro-American studies scholar, writes: "Perhaps black people ought to give serious thought to retiring Clarence from general use as a name in our communities."

This is what Moye was talking about—Thomas has become an infamous cultural symbol. The Notorious C.T.

In September 1997, Moye happened to be seated next to Judge Higginbotham at a Harvard Law School dinner at Legal Sea Foods in Cambridge, Massachusetts. At one point, still curious after all these years, Moye leaned over and asked if Higginbotham had ever received a private reply to his letter. No, the judge said, he hadn't. It was the last time Moye would see Higginbotham.

Thomas was terribly bothered by Higginbotham's criticism, he confided to friends, for it seemed to defy customary judicial decorum and was so unsparing. In 1998, Higginbotham opposed having Thomas speak to the National Bar Association convention in Memphis, saying it was like inviting George Wallace to dinner after he stood in the schoolhouse door and promised to maintain segregation forever. After the usual controversy over his appearance and much hand-wringing, Thomas did speak to the group. In remarks that veered from self-pitying to combative, he maintained that the "principal problem" he faces could be summed up in one succinct sentence: "I have no right to think the way I do because I'm black." When Higginbotham was asked about this comment later in a television interview, he shot back: "He's got a right to think whatever he wants to, but he does not have a right to be free of critique."

Early in his tenure as a justice, Thomas arranged for a modernization of the court gym. He's bigger than you'd expect for someone who is five foot eight and a half. He has a running back's legs and a lineman's chest, a body that always seems stuffed into his suits. He likes lifting weights. The court's gym was freighted with outdated equipment, but Thomas turned the renovation into something defiantly delicious. In public and in private, he loved telling people that he planned to work out vigorously so that he could live a long life, stay on the court for forty or fifty years, and outlast all his critics. The story would sometimes be accompanied by that booming guttural laugh of his, but his intention was clear. He was sending a message to his tormentors: No matter how many shots you take at me, I'll still be here.

It's been sixteen years now and, indeed, some of his critics have passed on. A. Leon Higginbotham Jr. died on December 12, 1998, from a stroke. He was seventy.

Thomas never responded to his open letter.

The audience cheered with pride, laughed at his stories, urged him on. And when he choked up—by mentioning Gil Hardy, his best friend, who tragically drowned in a scuba diving accident in 1989—they let Clarence Thomas know that it was OK, that he was among good friends. He grabbed a pink napkin, dabbed his eyes, and kept going. Hardy, ironically, had introduced Anita Hill to Thomas and urged his pal to help her out. Many believe Hardy is the one person who knew what really happened between them.

The setting was a national leadership conference in Washington sponsored by *Headway*, an obscure Houston-based magazine run by Republican entrepreneurs Willie and Gwen Daye Richardson. But the important thing was the audience—chiefly black and conservative, the people with whom Thomas is most comfortable. Nowhere in public will you see him more alive, more rebellious, less cautious, more at ease than in a roomful of black conservatives.

Here, he can scan the crowd and see people like himself. Here, he can promote his views to an amen chorus, still be black and not scorned. "It is hard to be disliked," he said. "It is hard to walk into a room and know you're going to always be beaten up." Sometimes less confident blacks approach him in dark corners and whisper, "I'm with you, but I'm not going to say that." It takes courage, he continued, to stand up for your personal beliefs, to take the blows and not retreat.

Heads nodded. This group knew exactly what Thomas meant.

The words themselves were succor for Thomas. The courageous underdog is one of his favorite personas, adopted by him in countless speeches and observed by friends in private conversations. Putting on his battle armor—seeing himself as a man under attack for his ideas—is one of the ways Thomas copes with the ostracism he endures from blacks who disagree with him.

"Life is not worth living without principles," he said. "It's not worth living without backbone. If you don't have a backbone, you slither. You don't walk upright."

And yet there is an inescapable irony in his message. The man who abhors the "crisis of victimhood," as he once described the self-inflicted predicament of too many blacks, has turned himself into the most successful victim in America. On the one hand, he wants you to know he has a racial identity. He sometimes mentions, for instance, that he gave his only son, Jamal, an Afrocentric name. "So you know where my head was when I named my child." On the other hand, he makes it clear that one's racial identity should not come into play when judging cases.

He is a favorite of the court's black cooks, janitors, and elevator operators, in part because he takes time to have meaningful conversations with them. Yet, he rarely speaks to black organizations and never attends the reunions of his black classmates at Holy Cross, where he is a trustee.

Sometimes, he dismisses the harsh appraisals as unworthy of his brain power. And other times he sounds so beaten down by the constant denigration that he seems in need of therapeutic comfort, or at least commiseration.

Debra Dickerson, a gifted writer who often pens unconventional essays and commentaries about race, received a call from Thomas after an op-ed she wrote for the *Washington Post* in 2001. The column was about the "conundrum" Colin Powell and Condoleezza Rice present as powerful African Americans whose achievements merit admiration but whose Republican affiliation often puts them at odds with most other blacks. Thomas liked the column, he told Dickerson, and he talked about how difficult it is for blacks in public life who don't conform to traditional views. He talked and talked and laughed and talked some more, keeping her on the phone so long that Dickerson concluded: "He's a lonely guy."

"I think he would clearly love his relationship with the black community to be different. . . . There is a wistfulness there," she said. "You can't be outside of the fold and not feel it. He is the lowest of the low in sort of official blackdom. It's unfair, and it's got to hurt."

Of all the slights since his confirmation ordeal, none has been more depressing to him than the protests that preceded the construction of a Clarence Thomas wing in the renovated Carnegie Library in Savannah. This was the once all-black library Thomas frequented as a kid, the place where he learned to dream big dreams through literature. It seemed like a no-brainer in 2001 when Texas development magnate Harlan Crow offered the Savannah library board a substantial donation to complete Carnegie's long-stalled

renovation. Crow had met Thomas many years earlier at a conservative policy forum and the two had become fast friends; their families sometimes camped out together on Crow's farm in East Texas.
A collector of historical memorabilia, Crow generated some attention in Washington when Thomas reported on his financial disclosure form a $19,000 Bible once owned by Frederick Douglass—a
gift from Crow.

Crow was hoping to have the entire Carnegie Library renamed in
honor of his friend. But that would not be possible, Crow was told.
Something more modest might be.

What transpired next was a three-month protest of the proposed
gift that divided the Savannah community and put the expansion under a dark cloud. In the end, the library board accepted a $175,000
contribution from Crow in exchange for naming a wing of the facility after Thomas. Even so, some continued to balk at the terms of
the gift. "We didn't want him held up as a role model," said Robert
Brooks, who led the protests and resigned from the library board
over the matter.

Thomas followed the flap from afar, incredulous. He couldn't believe grown men and women would be willing to turn down a generous donation to help a neighborhood library. "It's ridiculous that
so-called black leaders in Savannah would jeopardize the future of
young black children because they don't like me or my political
leanings or my decisions," he told his friend Savannah attorney Lester
Johnson. Johnson agreed but was even more pointed. "We still have
these folks who have never left Savannah and who believe that to be
black you've got to be a Baptist, you've got to eat fried chicken,
you've got to believe in the civil rights movement, you've got to
support Jesse Jackson and Al Sharpton and believe in everything
they do, and you've got to be liberal."

Out in the broad expanse of the country, in big cities and ham-
lets, Thomas says, he doesn't encounter hostility from workaday
African Americans. His conflict is with activists, he says, professional critics who launch their attacks from a distance. As Thomas

sees it, liberal elites—the media included—drive the negative por-
trayals of him. He gets along fine with regular folk, he says, just not
with the leaders. Of course, not many workaday Americans of any
race are going to approach a Supreme Court justice and give him a
tongue-lashing. But his point is worth exploring.

In May 2003, Thomas met Keith Burchfield in a restroom and
struck up a conversation. Burchfield was banquet manager for the
Holiday Inn in Athens, Georgia, where Thomas was scheduled to deliver the University of Georgia Law School commencement address
the next day. By the time the two had finished drying their hands,
Thomas knew Burchfield's bio: He grew up in a middle-class family
in Greenville, Mississippi, ran a store there, fell on hard times. He
couldn't pay his bills, couldn't find work, and eventually moved
to Athens, where he took a job as a server at the Holiday Inn. In
three months, he was promoted to banquet supervisor, then assistant manager, then banquet manager. And now he was catering a
private dinner for a Supreme Court justice. Thomas didn't budge.
The poached salmon and tabouli could wait—he was enjoying Burchfield's story. "It's funny how life goes that way," Thomas said, adding
that he had never expected to end up in D.C. and certainly not at the
Supreme Court. "Yeah, life is funny like that," said Burchfield, impressed that someone of Thomas's stature would be so earthy and accessible.

Thomas can be charming and warm in person; he radiates humil-
ity. His manner surprises the uninitiated and sometimes softens even
those not predisposed to like him. Ben Carson, a renowned brain
surgeon at Johns Hopkins Hospital in Baltimore, became friends
with Thomas through their mutual involvement in the Horatio Alger
Association of Distinguished Americans. Named for the prolific
nineteenth-century author who wrote novels about boys rising from
poverty to wealth and fame through "pluck and luck," the association includes some 250 prominent people whose lives parallel the
subjects of Alger's books. It annually awards more than $5 million
in college scholarships. The group is very dear to Thomas.

Before meeting the justice, Carson had the impression that Thomas was not especially concerned about his own people. "I had heard what everyone else had: 'This guy is a sellout. He doesn't care about black issues.' But as I got to know him, I saw this was a complete lie." Carson decided to confront Thomas about some of his ideas. The first issue he raised was school busing. Why did Thomas oppose it, since busing had been the way to desegregate schools and desegregation had been an avenue for blacks to get better educations? Thomas said that huge amounts of money had been spent on busing black children out of their neighborhoods to schools where they weren't wanted. "I don't want these kids thinking they have to go somewhere else to be successful," he told Carson, who ultimately concluded that Thomas's argument "made a lot of sense." Noting that Thomas "is mesmerizing when he speaks to young people," Carson adds: "The public persona of him that now is set in place is extraordinarily inaccurate. I guess he figures that the amount of energy it would take to alter that is more than he has."

Thomas is not naïve. He is so acutely aware of his radioactivity that he sometimes tries to shield other promising African Americans with like-minded views from fallout. Ralph Boyd Jr., the former assistant attorney general for civil rights in George W. Bush's administration, had met Thomas on several occasions. Boyd, now an executive with Freddie Mac, thought it was curious that Thomas always seemed to keep his distance. Later, he heard this was intentional.

"He was trying to protect me," recalled Boyd, who had come under fire himself from civil rights groups during his time at the Justice Department. Thomas thought it would undermine Boyd's credibility in some circles to be publicly associated with him. Thomas's dilemma reminds Boyd of a conversation he once had with his parents. "It must take so much courage to be Jesse Jackson," they told him. Wherever he goes, whenever he speaks out, he faces criticism, they said. Boyd scoffed. "Jesse Jackson is getting criticized by people he *wants* to be criticized by," Boyd replied. "The problem for Justice Thomas is that he gets attacked often by his own people.

It is harder for him to go home. Jesse goes home and he's a hero. Where does Justice Thomas go?"

Early in Thomas's tenure on the court, Harvard law professor Charles Ogletree approached Eddie Jenkins, a Boston attorney and a classmate of Thomas's at Holy Cross. "Tree," as he's called by his friends, is a peripatetic activist lawyer who always has sixteen projects going at once—from organizing a conference of Stanford's minority alumni to representing the survivors of the 1921 Tulsa race riot in a reparations lawsuit. He can barely make time for a sandwich.

But after his most famous turn in the spotlight—as Anita Hill's chief counsel when she testified before the Senate Judiciary Committee—Ogletree wondered if a line of communication could be established with Thomas. "You guys were close," Ogletree told Jenkins. "We've got to get to him, get a meeting."

Given Ogletree's role in the most hurtful episode of Thomas's life, it was unlikely that the Harvard professor would get a meeting. But the attempted overture reflected the realization that Thomas, then the youngest justice, would be on the court for a long, long time and possibly as the only *black* justice. There was no getting around that. While many African Americans were too embittered to reach out, Ogletree figured: Why not?

Jenkins saw Thomas in his chambers in 1997, but he didn't raise Ogletree's idea to establish a line of communication. He had some unfinished business of his own. There had been tension between Thomas and Jenkins, too, dating back to Thomas's confirmation hearings. Jenkins, a football star at Holy Cross who later played for the 1972 Super Bowl champion Miami Dolphins, is a raconteur with a healthy opinion of himself. He also happened to introduce Thomas to his first wife, Kathy Ambush, when they were all students in Worcester, Massachusetts. So after Thomas was nominated to the Supreme Court, journalists sought out Jenkins for interviews about what Thomas had been like then. Apparently, some of what he told them—about drinking wine and horsing around—did not sit well with Thomas, who sent word through mutual friends that he no longer wanted Jenkins to speak about him to the press. Jenkins was both hurt and puzzled.

"He was now trying to refine even the drinking of wine," Jenkins recalled. "I started thinking, Something is wrong with this brother."

But several years later Jenkins wrote Thomas an impassioned letter, his way of extending an olive branch. He talked about Gil Hardy, their mutual friend who had died in the scuba diving accident and was sorely missed. Hardy had attended Holy Cross and then accompanied Thomas to Yale Law School. He had been the linchpin of their three-way friendship, and his death was crushing. Jenkins went on to say in his letter that he meant no harm to Thomas in those interviews—he was only trying to help humanize him.

Apparently softened by the letter, Thomas invited Jenkins to the court. When Jenkins arrived, one of the first things Thomas brought up was his vilification by African Americans. "It's unfair how black America criticizes me," Thomas protested. "I'm trying to help black America." Whether there could be a reconciliation with African Americans was one of the things Jenkins pondered. It wasn't going to happen through Ogletree, but maybe through others it might.

William Coleman, who was the first black law clerk in Supreme Court history when he worked for Justice Felix Frankfurter in 1948, remembers how disputes got ironed out in the old days. A former Transportation Department secretary in the Ford administration, Coleman points out that, for all the street agitation over civil rights, no civil rights legislation would have passed without the friendship President Lyndon Johnson had with Republican Senate leader Everett Dirksen. "After all the yelling and screaming, you have a drink and cut a deal. We've gotta do that. The whole thing is to get to know people." It would take more than a drink and some back slaps to alter the relationship between Thomas and many African American leaders, and not even the formidable Bill Coleman was up to that challenge.

In 1994, though, a curious thing happened. Armstrong Williams, the conservative commentator and a Thomas protégé, arranged for a small group of African Americans to meet with the justice in his chambers. One of those invited was Donna Brazile, a Democratic congressional staffer and campaign organizer who would become one of her party's most influential strategists. It was the beginning of one of Washington's oddest but little-known friendships.

This is the same Donna Brazile who carried a sign during Thomas's confirmation ordeal: "Hill told the truth; Thomas lied." When her friends and political allies found out that Thomas had sent her a photo and she had hung it on her wall, that she had sent him a birthday card, that they had shared experiences of raising relatives and growing up in the South, some thought Brazile had lost her mind. But she hadn't. She was not trying to play strategist and help Thomas get back into the comfortable fold of his race. She was just trying to connect with him as a human being.

Brazile went on to manage the presidential campaign of Al Gore, who lost the 2000 election by a whisker, his fate sealed by the Supreme Court, whose 5–4 majority against continuing a Florida recount included Clarence Thomas. "I mean, I can't tell you how disappointed I was after Bush beat Gore," she says. "It was bad enough I had to pass the Supreme Court because I lived close to there." Despite that, she maintained her relationship with Thomas. "I'm sorry. I'm not going to tell some little black boy or girl in Louisiana that they can't grow up and be a Supreme Court justice like Clarence Thomas. We have given a whole bunch of other people redemption. We have prayed for people to come home. I don't know why that same kind of prayer can't be given for Clarence Thomas."

The problem is, many African Americans think Thomas is beyond the reach of prayer. They know him all too well, which is to say, it is hard to get past his record. Thomas's opinions on voting rights, prisoners' rights, affirmative action, and limiting the power of the federal government to correct injustices have curbed in many the appetite for entreaties.

The enmity for Thomas in the black community is now so in-grained that a reversal may be next to impossible—at least in the foreseeable future. "It's never too late," says former congressman and ex-NAACP head Kweisi Mfume, "but it gets later every day." Even Fred McClure, a stalwart Republican who shepherded Thomas's nomination through the Senate as a senior White House staffer, is not hopeful. "I don't know if twenty years from now it's going to be any different," says McClure, who is black. "I don't know how you can get out from under it."

Every now and then there are moments that signal an opening. In 2005, Thomas spoke at the swearing in of Leah Ward Sears, the first black woman elected chief justice of the Georgia Supreme Court. During his remarks, Thomas made a point of thanking former United Nations ambassador Andrew Young and other civil rights stalwarts for making such achievements possible. Later, Young said he had come away with a better understanding of the justice following a private chat and predicted the two would develop a closer relationship.

It seemed to many that the greatest opportunity for Thomas to improve his relationship with blacks was through the preeminent organization of black lawyers and judges, the eighteen-thousand-member National Bar Association. Even with all the controversy surrounding Thomas's appearance at the 1998 convention in Memphis—Judge Higginbotham's formidable opposition, threats of a walkout—Thomas came, spoke, and had a good time.

He made himself available. The day before the speech he met in his suite with a contingent of black state supreme court judges. The man most responsible for the appearance, the chair of the luncheon, was a Memphis circuit judge, D'Army Bailey. A longtime activist, Bailey was a driving force in converting the Lorraine Motel, where Martin Luther King Jr. was assassinated, into a civil rights museum. He hoped Thomas would change one day and felt it was important to develop a relationship with him.

"If we just isolate him, we would have no hope," said Bailey, who came up with the idea of inviting Thomas to the national bar gathering a year before, after listening to so many black lawyers and judges speak of him derisively. "When he goes before those conservative crowds, they treat him like a king."

The black bar association's version of kingly treatment was to take Thomas on a boat ride that evening after the speech. That's where the serious partying was done. When Bailey went to Thomas's room to pick him up, the justice was wearing a suit. Bailey urged him to dress down, and Thomas put on a casual shirt and slacks—except he had no belt. Only suspenders for his suit. So Bailey took off his belt and loaned it to him. That night, Thomas mingled freely and danced so hard that he later joked about pulling a muscle in his back.

Whenever Thomas is asked about his National Bar Association appearance, he plays down the controversy and plays up how well he was treated. For Bailey's part, he thought he had developed a rapport with Thomas—both for himself personally and for the organization. Sometime later in 1998, Bailey was in D.C. and stopped by Thomas's chambers. Thomas was scheduled to leave town, but he pushed back his departure to chat. They talked about civil rights and discussed the best avenues for pursuing civil rights claims. "If there is ever anything I can help you on," Thomas told Bailey, "let me know."

The name Ronnie White, a black Missouri Supreme Court judge, was brought up. White's nomination to a federal judgeship had been stalled in the Senate and was ultimately killed. His leading opponent happened to be John Ashcroft, then a Republican senator from Missouri and a Thomas friend.

"Nobody asked me," Thomas said. "If they had, I would have helped him."

Bailey left the meeting feeling good. He and Thomas began corresponding from time to time. But then one night in February 2001, Bailey was channel surfing and caught Thomas on C-SPAN giving the keynote Francis Boyer lecture at the American Enterprise Institute's annual black-tie dinner.

The sixteen hundred guests included some of Washington's most powerful luminaries, from Vice President Dick Cheney to Justice Antonin Scalia. Thomas received an award from the conservative think tank, a bust of Abe Lincoln, and then launched into a long articulation of the perils of a civil society and the need for public servants to be morally courageous. "It does no good to argue ideas with those who will respond as brutes," Thomas said, adding: "Even if one has a valid position, and is intellectually honest, he has to anticipate nasty responses aimed at the messenger rather than the argument."

Thomas extolled the work of leading right-wing intellectuals— Gertrude Himmelfarb, Michael Novak, Michael Ledeen—and seemed to remove his judicial robe for the night and take up arms as a conservative movement combatant. He recounted his personal experience as a newcomer to Washington in 1979: "It became clear in rather short order that on the very difficult issues such as race there was no real debate or honest discussion. Those who raised questions that suggested doubt about popular policies were subjected to intimidation. Debate was not permitted. Orthodoxy was enforced. When whites questioned the conventional wisdom on these issues, it was considered bad form; when blacks did so, it was treason." Though these "rules of orthodoxy" still apply, Thomas continued, he urged his fellow conservatives to fight back. "Often the temptation is to retreat to complaining about the unfairness of it all. But this is a plaintive admission of defeat. It is a unilateral withdrawal from the field of combat." As David Skinner, an editor at the conservative *Weekly Standard*, later wrote for Salon.com: "It was truly something to behold. In a roomful of conservatives, Thomas proved more conservative than the vast majority. In a roomful of outspoken people, he seemed the boldest."

The speech incensed Bailey, for it seemed designed to play up to the under-siege mentality of the predominantly white conservative crowd—not to mention that it seemed awfully self-pitying. Bailey thought the speech was inconsistent with the Thomas he had come to know. Was this the same justice who seemed interested in more give-and-take, who wanted to develop relationships with those he felt had misjudged him? Bailey was baffled.

He stayed up late and banged out a letter to Thomas, angrily complaining that the justice's speech did no more than offer relief to the contented. "What in one context could be seen as the healthy remarks of a brother challenging his people, could, among the powerful and well-heeled white audience of AEI, be viewed as a divisive and immoderate call to arms of the haves against the have nots," Bailey wrote.

Thomas never wrote back, and the two have not spoken since.

2

THE PIN POINT MYTH

It's possible to miss this speck of a place as you're driving south on the Diamond Causeway, eleven miles from downtown Savannah. Most people cruising this stretch of highway are headed across the bridge to Skidaway Island, where the rich reside in a privately patroled community the uninvited can't access. But all of a sudden there it is, off to the right, a flimsy blue metal sign beckoning you down a back road: WELCOME TO PIN POINT. BIRTH PLACE OF SUPREME COURT JUSTICE CLARENCE THOMAS.

Pin Point, population 275, was a plantation site before being carved up and sold to blacks in the late 1890s and early 1900s. Many of the original lots are held by the heirs of the former slaves who bought the parcels more than a century ago. Pin Point is just seven-tenths of a mile from one end to the other, but getting your mind around it takes some time.

This is where Clarence Thomas was born *twice*—first physically on June 23, 1948, as the second child of M. C. and Leola Thomas; then symbolically in the summer of 1991 as the humble young judge who rose from poverty and was tapped by President George H. W. Bush to replace Thurgood Marshall. This last birth turned Thomas into an emblem of America's progress and made Pin Point a fabled corner of the South.

White House advisers were so enraptured by the idea of Thomas as a Jim Crow–era child of deprivation—his family's wooden shack insulated only with newspapers, the kerosene lamps, the outhouse shared with neighbors—that they decided the road to confirmation led straight through Pin Point. The "Pin Point strategy," some advisers dubbed it: file down the sharp ideological edges and keep emphasizing Thomas's personal story of triumph over adversity.

A skeptical Vernon Jordan called the strategy a "bootstrap myth," but Hollywood couldn't have produced better imagery. Without Thomas's '91 rebirth, Pin Point would never have been known to the nation. And without Pin Point, Thomas would never have made it to the Supreme Court.

What the White House advisers didn't know—or, perhaps, just ignored—was that Thomas's connection to his birthplace was tenuous at best. His family's house had burned down when he was six, and for most of his young life he was raised comfortably in Savannah by his grandfather Myers Anderson, one of the black community's leading businessmen. Thomas never maintained strong ties to Pin Point. Though his older sister, Emma Mae Martin, is still there, they are not close. According to Martin, Thomas has never even been inside her home. "No, I don't think so," she said.

When Thomas does return to Pin Point, he comes quietly and leaves quickly; there is little fuss over his visit. But he doesn't come back often. In the summer of 2004, in fact, Pin Point's quadrennial reunion was held without its most renowned ex-resident. "That's one of his busiest times," explained his childhood friend Abe Famble. But the reunion was held in July, after the court issued its final opinions for the term. Thomas wasn't there for the 2000 reunion, either. "He says he'll try to make it one of these times," offered Famble. Maybe in 2008?

"The truth is," said Charles Harris, president of the Pin Point Betterment Association, "we don't ever see him."

Pin Point is neither city nor town nor municipality. It is a rural settlement of mostly trailer homes sitting on cinder blocks. It is beautiful, in a sleepy, antebellum way—the tall oak trees draped with Spanish moss, the gentle summer breezes. The community's valuable waterfront property looks out on Shipyard Creek, where commercial crabbers still ply their trade and high tides overtake the marsh in the middle of the day. Just beyond the creek and the marsh is the real Moon River, romanticized by Johnny Mercer's 1961 ballad.

Virtually all the residents know one another—if they're not friends, they're cousins. Families sit around picnic tables on summer Saturday afternoons and enjoy their "low-country boils"—crabs, spiced shrimp, sausages, corn on the cob. They drink fruit punch and beer. They trade gossip. Everybody has a nickname. John Henry Haynes is "Pig." Bill Haynes is "Bubba." Abe Famble is "Nerve." Clarence Thomas was "Boy" when he was growing up.

Old-timers turn wistful talking about Pin Point's charmed history of play and struggle. Some remember when there was no running water, no locks on doors (just a nail and a piece of wire), and payments for the life insurance collectors would be left for pickup without fear of theft. Neighbors spanked one another's children and got gratitude instead of grief. Whenever Joe Louis fought, everyone gathered with pride around the nearest radio. So idyllic was Pin Point that many residents never even considered leaving.

"This is paradise here," said Famble.

But Pin Point is not just quaint; it's also tragic. It has no gym, no public swimming pool, no convenience store, no school—kids attend schools in a nearby jurisdiction—and 80 percent of its inhabitants live below the poverty line. The lone church is next to a cemetery where the weeds are often taller than the headstones. Paved roads are a relatively recent improvement, and not all the roads are paved. The one business in Pin Point—A. S. Varn and Son's oyster-and-crab company—shut down in 1985. This was where generations of Pin

Point residents, including most of Thomas's family, picked crabs and earned five cents a pound. At one time, Varn's crabs and oysters were served in the nation's finest restaurants and eaten by presidents. But now the shuttered, decaying factory is just another Pin Point relic.

Today, Pin Point claims a U.S. Supreme Court justice as its most noted commodity but can't muster enough political clout—or wherewithal—to get a historical marker to celebrate this fact. Delroy Lindo, the actor who played Clarence Thomas in a Showtime movie, spent more time in Pin Point studying his role than most politicians have spent studying Pin Point.

Sadly, much of Pin Point simply looks disheveled. Or forgotten. For every well-kept cottage and manicured lawn there is a run-down trailer with a rusted roof. Too many idle cars—even one vending truck—have been put to rest in front yards, and not enough trash has been taken away. Recently, across from Pinpoint Hall, the community's main social gathering place, there was a dilapidated house on the verge of collapse. This is the same block that was roped off by federal marshals and spiffed up for the national media when Clarence Thomas returned home in 1993, bruised but victorious, to thank Pin Point for his ascendancy.

Drugs—whatever kind you want—have been a persistent problem. A neighborhood march called attention to the scourge, but the drug dealers didn't leave. A warning sign was erected along the community's main drag: "Our Neighborhood Will Be Drug Free. You Buy—We Spy. You Sell—We Tell." But the illegal commerce continued. Bishop Thomas J. Sills of Sweet Field of Eden Baptist Church had hoped to shame the drug boys away one Sunday morning by leading his congregation to sing and pray before them. Sills is a young thirtyish minister, and his church is hip enough that one morning a deacon preached a sermon in an oversized Phat Farm shirt. But dealers are hard to shame. "The guys who were on the corner just walked away," said Sills, but they didn't stay gone. As Sills pointed out, the dealers have a complicated profile in Pin Point, as they do in many other poor communities. Yes, they deal drugs, and nobody endorses that. But they also helped finance the renovation of Pinpoint Hall and have paid so many residential utility bills that they've engendered some ambivalence.

One of the dealers was Clarence Thomas's nephew, the nephew Thomas no longer talks about. Until he was sentenced to thirty years in prison on federal drug charges in 1999, Mark Elliot Martin, the second-oldest son of Thomas's sister, had been part of Pin Point's drug problem. He had been in and out of trouble—arrested at least twelve times, according to court records—and in and out of jail. In 1997 he was convicted of pointing a pistol at another person. In court papers, a federal magistrate judge depicted Martin as "a principal figure in a drug organization that has routinely distributed multi-kilogram quantities of crack and powder cocaine." The court documents described him as someone with "a history of violence."

Martin also is good with his hands and worked for a time repairing piers at a nearby marina. But he injured himself and lost that job. And because he was illiterate, according to his attorney, he had little means of supporting himself. He was on probation and out of work when the worst happened.

On August 19, 1998, thirteen suspected drug dealers—all from Pin Point and neighboring Sandfly—were arrested by authorities in a 6 a.m. raid and charged with conspiracy to distribute crack cocaine. More arrests and warrants followed. And soon everyone in Pin Point had an immediate family member, distant cousin, or close friend brought down by "Operation Pin Drop," as it was called. Some suspects snitched on others, affecting relationships in the community.

Martin was convicted of selling 17.2 grams of cocaine to a government informant in two transactions. The informant turned out to be Martin's cousin Rufus Anderson, a recovering crack addict who was a key figure in the sting. Investigators had sent Anderson out to make drug buys from his friends and family, and most of the transactions were captured on video- or audiotape. Martin's defense was entrapment. His only reason for selling coke to Rufus, he claimed, was because his cousin had badgered him into doing so at a time when he was broke, out of work, and in need of money to support his children.

One of Martin's kids, it turns out, was being raised by Clarence Thomas. Thomas had taken custody of Mark Elliot Martin Jr.—"Marky," they called him—around Thanksgiving of 1997. Thomas was hoping to give him opportunities to succeed beyond what the boy had in Pin Point. But his father was another story. He had become such a disappointment to Thomas that, when the drug bust went down, Uncle Clarence offered no legal advice, no pep talk, nothing.

In defense of her son's behavior, Thomas's mother said Clarence had tried in vain to reach his nephew many times. "Mark, please, you got them pretty little kids. Please," she recalled her son pleading. But he couldn't get through, and now he really was through. This time, Uncle Clarence just kept his distance. And Emma Martin didn't say a word, "just left it alone," as she put it. She didn't even bother asking her well-connected brother for help. "Nope, nope, no, no," she said emphatically, signaling the strain in their relationship.

"He didn't want to get involved anyway," she added. Not only is Emma convinced that her son had "one of the best attorneys," as far as court-appointed lawyers go, she believes her brother's name and position actually hurt her son's quest for leniency. When asked why she didn't tap her family's finest legal mind with the stakes so high, Emma replied: "What good is that? What good is that? By mentioning him, that's why Mark got so much time. Mark's lawyer mentioned that Clarence was Mark's uncle and got him thirty years."

Reached at the Federal Correctional Institution in Coleman, Florida, Mark Martin was doing the kind of long, difficult stretch that saps one's spirit. "Down here it's hard," he said. "Any given day you can die." And being Clarence Thomas's nephew has no benefits.

"I try to avoid letting people know who he is to me because they might want to do something to me because of him," Martin said.

Thomas is not popular among the other inmates, Martin emphasized. Most consider the justice a sellout, someone who supports draconian penalties that unfairly punish those deserving better consideration. (On the court, Thomas has largely backed the government's position on drug crimes and incarceration, including on questions of inmate property forfeiture, visitation rights, and maximum sentences for repeat offenders.) The nation's drug laws, which hit low-level dealers and African Americans disproportionately hard, were a special source of ire among those who served time with Martin. Some wondered why Justice Thomas was not affected by the circumstance of a blood relative.

Said Martin: "They always asking, 'Why he ain't got you out of this stuff?' . . . They say he could help change the law and he doesn't." Not long ago, Martin decided to try to help himself. He figured he'd study up on the law, so he asked Thomas if he would mind sending him some law texts. "He said he would try to get some books to me as soon as he can."

Most people in Pin Point thought the twenty-month local, state, and federal undercover drug investigation that nabbed Mark Martin— and also the son of Thomas's favorite cousin, Isaac Martin—would put an end to the drug trade. It was just the kind of sad, sobering episode that unites communities, even though it tore families apart. It didn't take long to discover the drug dealing wasn't over.

Charles Harris recalls conducting a Pin Point Betterment Association meeting a few years ago and proudly reporting that the drug problem had been cleaned up. But then hands were raised, and voices cried out: It ain't so. Harris was surprised. Maybe it was time for another neighborhood march. Though the main dealers were in prison, "I guess the younger people have taken over," he surmised.

Harris, sixty-two, is a big man who walks slowly with a cane— he suffers from arthritis. He lives down a lumpy dirt road that has no right to be called an avenue. It's just another of Pin Point's ironies that the man who holds the only leadership position in the community can't even get a paved street for himself. "We're working on it," Harris says. The Pin Point Betterment Association is something of a family franchise. Harris has been president since the early 1990s. His wife, Ethel, was president before him. Harris's father was president before her.

As kids, Harris and Thomas were friends—"I used to beat him up," Harris quips. But now, like many others in Pin Point, he mostly just wonders about the justice. Why isn't Thomas more involved? Why doesn't he try to influence the kids here? Why doesn't he walk the streets and visit folks, let people see him when he's in town?

"When he comes home," says Harris, "he's left before we even know he's been here."

Moved by the support of Pin Point residents during his confirmation struggles, Thomas agreed to serve on the board of the Betterment Association. Harris issued the invitation through Thomas's sister, Emma Martin. But the justice is not active, and never was— the association doesn't reach out to him, and he doesn't reach out to it. Certainly Thomas's advice and connections could help improve the quality of life here.

"I think if our people took more time to encourage him," admonishes Bishop Sills, "he'd do more."

The association's activities include things like buying flowers for the families of the deceased, cleaning up the cemetery, and sponsoring youth sports teams. When residents can't help themselves— with bills, house repairs—the association tries to lend a hand, raising money through chicken dinners or fish fries at Pinpoint Hall. The group meets every fourth Monday and asks each resident to pay $50 in annual dues. Only six or seven actually pay. Some just don't have it to give.

In 2001, Pin Point and the nearby communities of Sandfly and Montgomery were jointly awarded a three-year grant by the Casey Foundation that was worth $1 million. Some ideas for using the money were wonderful—an after-school tutorial program, for example. But other ideas flopped. Only two families ended up using the free tax-return assistance, and one of them was the Harris family. And then there was Senior Citizens Day, the highlight of which was a limousine ride to and from the new downtown Savannah convention center. Because there weren't enough seniors to fill the limos, kids, parents, anybody who happened to be around got lifts.

Ethel Harris gets riled at her husband just thinking about that one. Surely we could've done something better for these old folks than give them a limo ride downtown, she tells her husband as she cooks his dinner and swigs a Mountain Dew. Pay a utility bill, buy some medicines. But a long ride in a fancy car? "Wasn't nobody there to explain nothing," she says. "We just rode and looked."

Charles is offended. "Ain't nothing wrong with the limousine ride," he retorts. He puts it in perspective for his wife. "Half of those who went . . . they died. So at least they got to see something before they died."

This is the kind of discussion about Pin Point that never reaches Thomas's consciousness. His life as a justice is too far removed from the day-to-day struggles of this community, even though his sister remains there, cousins remain there, his close friend Abe Famble remains there, his mother attends church there and brings the pastor supper every Sunday. Not even in speeches does Thomas remark much on the Pin Point part of his childhood. Most of his boyhood remembrances are centered in Savannah and anchored on the lessons learned under the direction of Grandpa Myers Anderson. Pin Point today? Thomas is curious, but from a distance.

Sometimes Thomas will ask his old friends about Pin Point's youth. Why are so many of them throwing their lives away? Sometimes he'll talk about the need to sit with some of Pin Point's seniors before they all die and that living history is gone. But he never seems to get around to it.

As president of the Betterment Association, Charles Harris is struggling every day to get a handle on Pin Point's problems. Like

Thomas, he is concerned about the old people dying. But his concern runs even deeper—he fears that Pin Point is on the verge of losing its soul and character. "People come through here every day trying to get property," Harris says. By people, he means white people: developers, real estate agents, schemers with dreams of turning Pin Point into the next Hilton Head. "They're trying to get us out bad," Harris believes. "They want this."

As evidence to fuel his suspicious mind, Harris brings up the most magnificent spread in all of Pin Point. This Mediterranean-style home, built from scratch, is surrounded by a fence and has a gated paved drive. It has a screened-in back porch, a gazebo with a bar, a brick swimming pool—nobody else in all of Pin Point has a pool—and a dock on the creek for the boat. The house is airy and modern and decorated in pastel colors. It looks like some kind of celebrity pad, for there is not another one remotely like it in Pin Point.

And it is owned by a white couple with two children.

"Unfortunately, our society tends to keep people away from each other because of racial differences," says Beth New, an attractive blond with a French manicure who welcomes visitors with pitchers of sweet tea and lemonade. She knew about Pin Point because of her brother, a commercial crabber who used to get one of the Pin Point women to pick his crabs. "I get highly upset when people ask, 'Why did you all move out here?' " New continues. "I drove up and saw the lot and nothing else mattered."

In 1999, for just $65,000, Ike and Beth New bought themselves two acres of high ground and two acres of marsh that stretch to Moon River. Before they could build on their property, they had to haul away twenty-two tractorloads of trash. They had to renovate the grounds. The neighbors watched this yearlong project with kindness—they let the News use their electricity and water and watched the property and equipment at night.

Still, they know some Pin Point longtimers view them with suspicion. "I've been told, 'You're going to ruin the neighborhood,' "

Ike says. At the same time, some of his white friends think he's nuts for living in Pin Point. They tell him: "You live in crack heaven."

Ike admits there's something to that. For those who whisper about the News' gated entrance—Are they just trying to wall themselves off from the rest of us?—Ike has a quick explanation: "Keep the crackheads out." Ike usually spots the dealers first, driving through in their Navigators and Land Rovers, conducting transactions on the street. One night a man on crutches knocked on his door begging for money, said he was in the federal Witness Protection Program after cooperating with authorities in the 1998 drug bust in Pin Point. Turns out that ratting on the dealers wasn't such a good move. They burned down his house as revenge, or so his story went. And the thing is—elements of his story checked out.

Pin Point can be so strange, and yet Ike would live nowhere else. Though he runs a swimming pool company now, he used to dance and travel with the late James Brown before Brown became a recording superstar. Ike grew up poor in Alabama and has but an eighth-grade education. Clarence Thomas, he relates to. In fact, he is thinking of writing the justice a letter inviting him to stop by the next time he is in Pin Point. Ike never anticipated such a life for himself, sitting by his big window watching sunsets over Moon River.

"If there's something better than this," he says, "it must be heaven."

All Charles Harris knows is that Ike attended one meeting of the Betterment Association and stopped coming. To Harris, he's just the mystery man living on the gated property, an uncomfortable symbol of the changing Pin Point. "If ever there was a time to stick together it's now," says Harris. He only wishes Thomas would take more of an interest in this place that catapulted him to the Supreme Court. "It looks like to me a person of his status could tell us something or give us some advice on how to save it."

Clarence Thomas was born to teenage parents who had little education and little commitment to each other. M. C. Thomas, who dropped out of school after fifth grade, worked with other family members doing chores and tending the land at nearby Bethesda Home for Boys, one of the nation's oldest orphanages. M. C. was from a family of sharecroppers who had bounced from one Georgia farm to another, and his father, Norman "November" Thomas, had finally settled the family in the shadow of Pin Point, where they lived on the grounds of the boys' home. Because Pin Point was within easy walking distance, meeting Leola Anderson was not hard to do. The children of the people who worked at the boys' home often hung out with the children of Pin Point.

Leola was in Pin Point because she had been abandoned. Her mother, Emma Jackson, died when Leola was five years old, after a complicated childbirth. Her father, Myers Anderson, was something of a wanderer. He had grown up in rural Liberty County, had farmed, fished, and worked for a white contractor, and was now living in Savannah running his own business delivering coal, wood, and ice to people's homes. Leola was his second child. Having never married Leola's mother, he left his daughter to be raised by her aunt Annie Devoe Jones, her mother's sister. In Pin Point, Leola started picking crabs at age nine and dropped out of high school after the tenth grade.

She met M. C. Thomas at a community dance. Soon the two were romantically involved and Leola was expecting her first child. She was sixteen. In the close-knit Pin Point community, Leola's out-of-wedlock pregnancy posed a problem. The Baptist Church expelled her, and her strict, embarrassed absentee father, Myers Anderson, decided to insert himself back into her life by insisting that she get married. Never mind that Anderson himself had fathered two children out of wedlock by the time he was seventeen—Leola and another daughter, who had a different mother. For Myers Anderson, it was: Do as I say, not as I do. Leola complied. She gave birth to Emma Mae on November 17, 1946, and married M. C. two months later.

It wasn't long before the marriage unraveled. In the soap opera atmosphere of Pin Point, it was sometimes difficult to separate fact from rumor. Even on the most basic things. Their marriage license, issued January 6, 1947, put Leola's age at seventeen and M. C.'s at twenty-one. But information compiled by M. C.'s family when he died, had him much younger, younger even than Leola.

If that was true, M. C. would have been not yet sixteen when Emma Mae was born, not yet eighteen when Clarence was born, and only nineteen when the couple's third child, Myers, was born. In short, too young—and too rambunctious—to be raising three kids. By the time little Myers entered the world, M. C. had fled Pin Point for Philadelphia, never to return meaningfully to his children's lives.

"I just wanted to get out of the country," he told an interviewer more than fifty years later. It was his only explanation for why he had abandoned his family. In Philly, with only a fifth-grade education, he earned a respectable living as a manual laborer, digging ditches and installing pipe. He remarried twice, had three other sons and two other daughters, and became a block captain of his South Opal Street neighborhood. He was known fondly as "Mr. Tom."

M. C. had been a restless soul anyway when he was living in Pin Point, so the fact that he bolted for Philly was no surprise to some of the Georgia locals. Leola was his wife, but not his only girl.

"He took off when they were babies in diapers, but I forgive him," says Leola, who is now in her fourth marriage, to David Williams. "In order to try to be a Christian you got to forgive."

Maybe that's how she feels now. But that's not how she felt in January 1951 when M. C. filed for divorce, claiming Leola was the wild one—an absentee mother and wife who cavorted at all hours of the day and night "in the company of people with whom she should not be." According to M. C.'s divorce petition, the couple broke up "on or about" July 4, 1949, when he was "forced to separate from said defendant on account [of] the many acts of cruel treatment practised [sic] by her unto him." Clarence was just a year old.

M. C. went on to accuse Leola of neglecting "the care, welfare and cleanliness" of their children, of allowing the kids and their home "to remain dirty and untidy." And when he tried to discuss these matters with her, the petition said, she "scorned him and would abuse and curse him." So he left.

In the petition, M. C. said he contributed $10 of his $25-a-week salary to Annie Devoe Jones for child support. He asked the judge to award Aunt Annie custody of the Thomas children, and she took them. Leola never answered the complaint. But many years later, she told an interviewer that the reason M. C. had deserted the family was because he had impregnated another woman, whose father had threatened to shoot him if he didn't marry her.

In March 1951 a judge, indeed, awarded custody of the children to Leola's aunt Annie. M. C. was ordered to pay $10 a week in child support until the youngest, Myers, was eighteen. Young Clarence Thomas could hardly have known what was going on. When the divorce became final, he was not yet three years old.

As a boy in Pin Point, Clarence didn't have two pennies to rub together, as the old folks like to say. His earliest memories, as he would testify during his confirmation hearings, are of simple pursuits in Pin Point. "As kids, we caught minnows in the creeks, fiddler crabs in the marshes, . . . and skipped shells across the water." David McKiver, who is twelve years older than Thomas and still lives in Pin Point, recalls shooing him home when dusk turned to dark. In those days, the older kids looked after the younger ones and taught them lessons like "how to stay out of trouble, work for what you want, and don't take no wooden nickels from nobody," he says.

The kids growing up in Pin Point in the 1950s were ingenious. With no money for toys, they created their own fun, kicking juice cans and making boats out of watermelon rinds. They wrapped aluminum foil around wads of moss and called it a baseball, picked up a stick and called it a bat. "Anything to play ball," recalled Thomas's cousin Isaac Martin. They'd cut grapevines and swing out of trees hollering as if they were Tarzan.

In summer, it was so hot the kids often wore nothing but short

pants. No shoes, no underwear, no shirt. Just shorts. Thomas liked
to wrestle in the dirt and race barefoot through the woods against
his younger brother, Myers, cousin Isaac, and friend Abe Famble.
But though he enjoyed playing outdoors, he developed an early interest in reading and soon that became his activity of choice.

"Sometimes Clarence would be in there reading books and you
couldn't get him to come out," recalled Famble. That alone set him
apart from most of Pin Point's youth—he was reading at the age of
five or six, according to childhood friends. There was something
about the solitude of reading, and also the adventure of it. Through
books, Thomas could lose himself in his imagination.

Perhaps the key figure in nurturing this early interest was someone Thomas rarely mentions when recounting his family narrative—
his great-aunt Maggie Devoe. Aunt Maggie was better educated
than most in Pin Point—she could read and write—and she pushed
Thomas to learn. She also was light-skinned. Ironically, Thomas
would come to dislike blacks who looked like Aunt Maggie. A string
of slights and taunts—some incurred by him as a child, others meted
out against his grandfather, Myers Anderson—would harden Thomas
against some of the most successful products of his race. To him,
most blacks of a lighter hue were snobs, the self-annointed superior
class of the race who considered themselves a cut above dark-
skinned blacks with broad noses and thick lips, like himself. This
class-and-color consciousness, not uncommon in the South, would
become an obsession with Thomas in his adult life, and that obsession remains with him on the Supreme Court.

But Aunt Maggie and her husband, Charlie Devoe, were not
snobs. They were young Clarence's first true parents, displaying the
devotion to him that his biological mother and father couldn't manage. Perhaps they understood, better than most at the time, that Pin
Point was not exactly the kind of place that built ambition. Many of
the kids in Pin Point never had the opportunity to graduate from
high school, because their families needed them to work.

"When a young black man became a teenager, he was expected to ply the river to bring food into the house," said Ella Washington, who was born in Pin Point four years before Clarence Thomas. Her mother, Maebell Thomas, ended up marrying Clarence's paternal grandfather, November. "There was a lot of alcoholism out there at the time because it was a hard life," Washington continued. "And if you didn't have a trade it was even harder. I look at a lot of people who grew up in Pin Point at the same time [as Thomas] and they are stuck."

The Thomas family lived in a two-bedroom house with a corrugated tin roof and wooden siding. It was built by Uncle Charlie and owned by his sister, Annie Devoe Jones. Uncle Charlie would bring home books discarded by the children of white employers. Aunt Maggie would then use those books to tutor young Clarence, whose own mother was ill-equipped and preoccupied. Leola had gone back to picking crabs after Clarence was born. Sometimes, when there was no relative available to watch him, he'd be in a playpen next door to Varn's cannery. That way Leola could look in on him, and so could others, including old man Varn himself. But after Myers was born, and M. C. had run off, the pressure of raising three small children overwhelmed Leola. It was difficult to make ends meet and juggle her responsibilities. She delegated more and more of her parental duties to relatives and even to neighbors.

As the years wore on and Thomas came to realize just how dysfunctional his early family life had been, it gnawed at him. He resented his mother, his father, even his sister, who he felt had not worked hard enough to better herself. For a long time, the only immediate family member he respected—or even had something in common with—was his younger brother, Myers.

But Clarence wouldn't spend very long in Pin Point. And that singular fact would become his salvation. In fact, says Bill "Bubba" Haynes, one of the community's oldest residents, it would be hard to argue that Pin Point molded Thomas. "I personally don't think so," he says.

In the fall of 1954, four months after the Supreme Court's ruling in *Brown v. Board of Education* mandated that public schools be desegregated, Thomas began first grade at the segregated Haven Home School. The school bus he caught on Pin Point Road was driven by his grandfather, November Thomas, who drove it for thirty-two years, raised hogs, and also became a Baptist preacher. The neighborhood kids all liked him. They called him "Mr. November."

Clarence was just settling into first grade when a tragedy occurred that would reshape his life. Walking home from school with Emma, he discovered his house ablaze. The siblings ran frantically toward the smoke and flames, along with other children. The fire had been started accidentally by Clarence's little brother, Myers, and another boy. Home alone, they were attempting to light a stove heater with matches when a curtain caught fire. Residents, carrying buckets of water back and forth, tried their best to save the house. But it was destroyed.

"We lost everything," Leola recalled. "I don't even have a baby picture of Clarence or me or my other two children, because everything was burned up." The fire split the Thomas family further. Leola decided that Emma, eight, would remain in Pin Point and live with Aunt Annie in another house. Six-year-old Clarence and five-year-old Myers would move to Savannah with her. Leola found work as a maid earning $15 a week and rented a shabby one-room tenement with an outdoor toilet.

For Clarence, it was good-bye Pin Point, hello Savannah.

3

THE SAVANNAH
REALITY

The 500 block of East Henry Street was roped off for the occasion. More than a hundred plastic chairs had been arranged in front of the refurbished Carnegie Library, and all of them were filled. Counting those standing and milling about, the crowd topped 250. The oak trees provided partial shade from the summer sun, but it was hot and steamy nonetheless.

Clarence Thomas was wearing a dark suit that he never unbuttoned and a red tie that he never loosened. But somehow, on August 21, 2004, Clarence Thomas seemed as relaxed—and happy—as he has ever been at a public event.

"I do feel at home," he said, beaming.

Thomas's disposition was striking, for he so often seems burdened by the childhood he was on East Henry Street to commemorate. His reflections are typically punctuated with tales of struggle, hardship, pain, abandonment—or a longing for the good ol' days of high morality and incorruptibility. In this oversimplified version of his upbringing, his grandfather was the epitome of righteousness and principle, and he was the little boy who was battered by slights and taunts but who absorbed the lessons of Myers Anderson to make something of himself.

"I got teased about my hair, because it's Negroid," Thomas once said of his childhood. "My lips, because they're Negroid. My nose, because that is Negroid. My feet, because they are Negroid and they don't fit in Italian shoes. My complexion, because it is definitely Negroid. Friends on the corner used to laugh when I'd go into the library. I used to have to sneak into the library, into the Carnegie Library. It wasn't cool to go into the library. You weren't a man."

But on this Saturday afternoon there was none of that. Thomas was just another regular guy from the community, not some wounded warrior who had beaten long odds. He had returned to the largely black Dixon Park neighborhood of Savannah—his neighborhood—to help rededicate the library of his youth. Built in 1914 with a donation from philanthropist Andrew Carnegie, the library had been shuttered in 1997 because of widespread disrepair. Now, after a $1.3 million renovation, the 7,000-square-foot Carnegie was back in business.

Just two blocks away on East Thirty-second Street was the home in which Thomas was raised by his grandparents. It is now occupied by his mother, who was seated in the front row of the audience. As Thomas recalled, his grandfather steered him to the small brick library for the first time in 1955. He was just seven then, and it was the only library for blacks in Savannah until Mayor Malcolm McLean ended segregation in public libraries in 1961. On Saturday afternoons, Thomas could usually be found in the basement children's room listening to the librarians read Dr. Seuss. As he got older, the Carnegie began "opening a door to another world," as he put it. Thomas told of leafing through "every single page of every single encyclopedia" on the shelves, of absorbing the adventures of *Crazy Legs McBain* and roaming the Old West with *Two-Gun Kid* and *Kid Colt*. He sailed the seas with *Horatio Hornblower*. He'd sit for hours reading periodicals about black life—the *Pittsburgh Courier*, *Ebony*, and "what some people called the *Jet* book."

Speaking from the landing to the library's main entrance, Thomas was able to peer down on the crowd in the street—the library board types, the city officials, the area children, neighborhood folk who had just wandered by. Though he had a written script, he didn't seem much interested in it. Instead, he spoke off the cuff, in a kind of conversational reminiscence.

He remembered scooting over to the library from the park across the street, still sweaty from playing touch football. Sometimes his grandfather, whose business was supplying fuel oil to people's homes, would drop Clarence off after making deliveries. "This was the one place my grandfather would let me come and get out of work," he quipped. "So I came often."

Inside the library, Thomas said, nothing was beyond reach. Neither the shackles of segregation nor neighborhood cynicism—"The Man ain't going to let you do nothing"—could limit one's dreams. "I can remember being told . . . that we could be president, that there was a hope and a possibility," Thomas recalled.

Nowhere in sight were the protesters who didn't want Thomas's name attached to the library renovation. They lost that battle. Thomas now has his own Carnegie wing, thanks to the controversial $175,000 put up by Texas developer Harlan Crow and $25,000 donated by Miami Dolphis owner Wayne Huizenga, another close Thomas friend, through the Huizenga Family Foundation.

In the end, the fuss over whether Thomas was a proper role model who deserved a place of esteem at the neighborhood library wasn't about any monument of grandeur. The newly constructed Thomas annex is marked by an underwhelming bronze plaque mounted at fourth-grade eye level. It reads: "East Addition Dedicated to the Honor of Supreme Court Associate Justice Clarence Thomas." But for Thomas, it hardly mattered. He was clearly thrilled just to be home, saluting the neighborhood library. Jean McCorkle, the library board chairwoman, said the justice "gives new meaning to the term *hometown success*."

Yet, he was certainly not the only Carnegie alum to do well. George Atkinson became an all-pro defensive back for the Oakland Raiders, Orion Douglass a state judge in Georgia. Another Carnegie denizen became a master sergeant in the military, and another a surgeon. Then there was W. John "Butch" Mitchell, a corporate executive turned local community leader. He was the one who battled hardest to save the library from annihilation. Like Thomas, they all had buried themselves in Carnegie's stacks. However uncool it was to frequent the library, as Thomas has explained this childhood experience, he was hardly alone in daring to be uncool. Maybe the teasing just got to Thomas more than it did to the others. Because, according to Mitchell, spending time at the Carnegie was a more common occurrence for neighborhood youth than Thomas lets on.

At the end of the celebration, a group of kids stood on the lower steps holding placards of picturesque scenes from around the globe while a grown-up sang "What a Wonderful World." Thomas smiled, looking down on the children from the landing. Leaning on the brick bannister, he softly sang along.

For Clarence Thomas, it had been a perfect day. No hecklers. No drama. Only reminders of the best part of his childhood, of being a boy lost in his books.

Thomas's youth was defined more by the advantages afforded him than by the hard times he had to bear—a point often skirted in the telling of his story. His was not the kind of privilege that the wealthy enjoy. What he had were opportunities—nine years of parochial school education, for example—that most blacks of his generation in Georgia had to get by without. Looking back on their shared lives in Savannah, some of Thomas's former classmates saw him differently from the way he apparently saw himself.

"His life wasn't no struggle," says Charlie Mae Garrett, a classmate of Thomas's at St. Pius X High School. "He had a good life. I think all of us who went to Catholic school were somewhat privileged."

Garrett recalls watching Thomas's confirmation hearings, listening to the emphasis placed on his hardscrabble Pin Point beginnings, and wondering: Is this the same Clarence we knew? "I was like, 'When did he live in Pin Point?'" The defining part of his childhood was anchored in Savannah, she knew, and it was far from impoverished. "He always had money to go to the store to buy ice cream and candy," Garrett remembered.

She telephoned her friend Marion Poole (formerly Marion Blount), whom she always thought Thomas had a crush on in high school. Poole was just as perplexed as Garrett. "Personally, I thought he was rich," at least by the standards of the neighborhood, said Poole. She remembered how successful Clarence's grandfather was as the primary fuel oil provider in the black community.

Not that young Clarence was unacquainted with misfortune. In the beginning the move from Pin Point to Savannah in 1954 hardly looked like an upgrade. Clarence, a first grader at the Florance Street public school, usually found himself unchaperoned after school let out. He remembers eating cornflakes several times a day and aimlessly roving the streets while his mother struggled to pay the bills on a maid's wages.

In the summer of 1955, Thomas's mother met Richard Dykes, who would become her second husband but would play no role in Clarence's life. First his biological father had ditched him; now his stepfather had no use for him. This sequence of events would begin to shape the bitterness Thomas felt toward his mother for many years.

"Why did my mother choose to marry someone who did not want two little boys?" Thomas asked during a speech many years later. For his part, Dykes would be virtually erased from the Thomas family history. Justice Thomas never utters his name, and Leola acts as if her second husband didn't exist. When detailing the difficulty of raising Clarence and Myers after the family left Pin Point, she speaks like a single mother, never mentioning where Dykes was or what he contributed—if anything—during this critical period.

Written testimony contained in the court files of her 1974 divorce of third husband, Perry Ling, indicates that Leola's memory of her second husband already had faded by then. She couldn't remember if her divorce to Dykes was granted in New York or North Carolina and couldn't be precise about the year—"approximately 1960."

As it turned out, with or without the support of Richard Dykes, Clarence Thomas caught perhaps the luckiest break of his life in the summer of 1955. Realizing that "things were getting hard" trying to raise Clarence and his little brother, Leola went to her father to ask for help. Clarence was with her, she said. "And my daddy looked at me and told me no," Leola recalled. "Those were his words to me: 'No!' And I got on the back porch and I started crying." The emotion of the moment had much to do with Leola's own upbringing and her unsettled relationship with her father, Myers Anderson. She could never understand why he didn't insist on having custody of her. On the back porch, with nowhere else to turn, Leola sobbed. Her stepmother, Christine, spoke up. "Myers, I think you'd better pack your clothes. Get your suitcase and pack your clothes because these are my grandchildren . . . and I'm going to have to take care of these kids."

Anderson walked off the porch and didn't say a word. He went to talk things over with his buddy who ran Wise's Café, a popular neighborhood hangout. When he returned, nothing more was said. "Not another word," recalled Leola. The boys began living with their grandparents. It's unclear what, if anything, Clarence heard of the porch exchange or whether he was even aware of his grandfather's initial rejection of him and his brother. But from then on, Myers Anderson would be the most important figure in Clarence's life.

"Imagine, if you will," Thomas reflected many years later, "two little boys with all their belongings in two grocery bags."

Young Clarence's circumstances improved quickly. Home-cooked meals awaited him every day; he had all the clothes he needed and even a little money in his pocket. And he was given an ongoing lesson in hard work, generosity, and sacrifice from an illiterate man with a third-grade education who happened to be one of Savannah's most respected black entrepreneurs.

"He got to be pretty big here," recalled Myers Anderson's best friend and business partner, Sam Williams. "He was probably the biggest ice and wood man, black, in the whole city."

Myers Anderson started with a wood-delivery business, then added coal, then ice, before switching to fuel oil. He bought his supplies from white folks but had his own truck, and he sometimes put his grandsons to work helping him. He'd rise at two or three in the morning to start work, sometimes on two or three hours of sleep, Thomas has said. He had built a bungalow on East Thirty-second Street with his own hands and then acquired rental properties in the area, which brought in more income. Anderson didn't have the swagger of success, but he had the means to provide a comfortable existence for his family.

"Oh, Myers was middle-class," says Prince Jackson, a longtime friend of the Thomas family who delivered Anderson's eulogy in 1983. "He was definitely middle-class."

It's likely, though, that Anderson never considered himself middle-class. He was a self-made man who pored over the Bible in order to pass a literacy test required to vote and learned to rebuild an engine by taking one apart. And this was one of the prime messages he drilled into Clarence's head: *Make a way out of no way. Let no obstacle be insurmountable.* Having created his own way, Anderson was able to set his daughter up in a nice house on East Duffy Street even as he was raising his grandchildren on East Thirty-second Street. He also was able to afford the $40 a year it took to send both Clarence and young Myers to St. Benedict the Moor School, where they would benefit from the rigorous tutoring and strict discipline of Franciscan nuns.

"My grandparents weren't educated," Thomas recalled, "but they insisted that my brother and I be educated. My grandfather used to tell us that if we were to die, he would take us to school for three days just to make sure."

The school was across the street from St. Benedict the Moor Catholic Church, which was known as the "Mother Church" for Savannah's black Catholics. Because Anderson himself attended, he received a break on his grandchildren's tuition. Anderson had grown up Baptist. Before moving to Savannah at age twenty, he was a member of Palmyra Baptist Church in Liberty County, where he now owned a farm. But he had become dissatisfied with his local church and was introduced to St. Benedict the Moor by Sam Williams. Anderson was impressed by the visibility of the Catholic Church in the black community, especially by its nurturing attitude toward black youth. Anderson decided to convert. He was baptized at St. Benedict, attended mass regularly, and gave back to the church in time and manpower. He got to know the nuns, and they helped him learn to read. The relationships he developed through St. Benedict's were important to him, and he would always feel a debt to the Catholic Church.

St. Benedict operated one of three black Catholic elementary schools in Savannah, an eight-block walk from Anderson's home. While the Catholic schools also were segregated, they were far superior to the public schools. "Segregation had really ruined the [public] schools," said Bill Haynes, who grew up with Thomas's mother in Pin Point and managed to become a successful architect despite his public school education. "You always got books that were torn or marked up. Some of them didn't have pages in them." Many black families coveted the kind of education Thomas received, but few could afford it. Established in 1915, St. Benedict's was a spacious school with an enrollment of four hundred in grades one to eight. When Clarence started there in second grade, he was just a C student. In third grade, he raised his average to a B. And by eighth grade, he was earning straight As.

Clarence thrived under the Franciscan sisters' tough-love approach, and he would never forget them. He later wondered why these white sisters, derided by Georgia racists as "nigger nuns," had taken such an avid interest in pushing black kids like him. He was especially fond of his eighth-grade teacher, Sister Mary Virgilius Reidy, whom he singled out during his confirmation hearings and who testified on his behalf. "The nuns gave us hope," Thomas said in 1991, "and belief in ourselves when society didn't."

His experience with the nuns marked the first time anyone white had had a significant impact on his life. But it would hardly be the last. After Myers Anderson, observed Floyd Adams Jr., who grew up with Thomas and went on to become Savannah's first black mayor, "most of his influences were white folks."

In his black neighborhood, Clarence saw both models of inspiration and sources of denigration. Those he looked up to were mainly his grandparents and their friends, the people he knew who worked hard, stayed sober, kept out of jail, and persevered through segregation with their dignity intact. From them, he learned how and how not to behave, what and what not to believe in.

"Yes, we were to be what they called mannerable. Period," Thomas recounted. "We did not dare walk down the street without saying good morning to Miss Gladys, Miss Mariah, Miss Bec, and especially Miss Gertrude. . . . We would never refuse to take a trip to the store for an adult who asked. . . . And I remember the 'dos' maybe even better than the 'don'ts.' Church on Sunday. Tend to property on Saturday. Wash the car. Cut the grass. Polish your shoes. And all of us—especially my brother and I—were expected to work."

No work, no eat. That was his grandfather's rule. In Thomas's nostalgic retelling of his upbringing, God and school were central, knowing right from wrong a priority. Crime, welfare, slothfulness, and alcohol were not tolerated.

Rarely would Thomas mention the unsavory aspects of his neighborhood. As Butch Mitchell, who grew up not far from Clarence, put it: The area was hardly idyllic. Even though there were many adults doing the right thing, there also were shootings, ice pick stabbings, and an abundance of "shot houses," which were basically illegal bars operated out of private homes on weekends.

Thomas took his cues from the pillars of the neighborhood. But whatever lessons he learned from them, he seemed to internalize more deeply being belittled by kids who were doing what kids do everywhere—picking on one another. Thomas, however, went beyond being angry and hurt. He personalized the teasing, absorbing it into his psyche. In Thomas's mind, there was a direct connection between the elitism he ascribed to the families of Savannah's black professionals—a good number of them fair-skinned—and the barbs directed at him as a jet-black boy with Negroid features and a bow-legged gait who spoke with a Geechee/Gullah accent. This patois, whose roots were in Africa, had survived along the coasts of Georgia and South Carolina, and Thomas absorbed it during summers in Liberty County with his grandfather. For a young, sensitive boy, this was not a dialect to be proud of, as his speaking manner was often derided as that of uneducated country folks.

By the time he began St. Pius X High School in 1962, a scrawny boy, five foot two and not yet a hundred pounds, the sum total of the needling, as he recalls, had become merciless. "Back then they used to call it 'checking,'" Thomas remembers. "And before it was popular for all of us to be black and proud, as James Brown used to cheer us on, having Negroid features was not exactly popular. It provided a rich source of insults."

While Clarence was struggling with being called names, Savannah was in a struggle over how far to go in granting civil rights to blacks, who were 35.5 percent of the population. Led by W. W. Law, president of the local NAACP, blacks were aggressively—but nonviolently—combating segregation. Law held weekly mass meetings at black churches. Myers Anderson, though not an activist, attended those meetings and supported the NAACP's efforts financially. Beginning in 1960, blacks staged "wade-ins" at whites-only Tybee Beach and lunch counter sit-ins at Woolworth's, Levy's Department Store, and other high-profile targets. They held "kneel-ins" at downtown white churches. A fifteen-month boycott of white merchants sent five small stores into bankruptcy and caused several supermarkets to close.

The impact on the economy of Savannah was substantial, acknowledged Harry Goldberg, president of Levy's, and it wasn't long before white businesses began integrating their workforces. Though some of the protests grew tense, there was never violence. In the fall of 1963, segregation in Savannah ended in most public places—and without the ugly scars that marked many Southern cities' transition to equal access for all citizens. Impressed by Savannah's progress, Martin Luther King Jr. later called it "the most integrated city south of the Mason-Dixon line."

Clarence Thomas was a fifteen-year-old sophomore at Pius in 1963 and still grappling with his own doubts. Over and over again as an adult, Thomas would recount how schoolmates ridiculed him. He rarely offered details. One example, however, has become part of the Thomas lore, working its way into countless newspaper and magazine profiles and dropped into biographies: Thomas said he was given a cruel nickname in the schoolyard—"ABC: America's Blackest Child."

Apparently that moniker struck a nerve that permanently injured Thomas. But it's difficult to find a childhood friend or acquaintance with a recollection of the nickname or its origin. Thomas's mother also has no remembrance of the "ABC" tag and has given conflicting accounts of the seriousness and source of the teasing in general. Leola told us that she didn't know about any taunts at the time Clarence was growing up, saying her father—Clarence's primary caretaker—shielded her from such things. She later learned that her son was jeered by students at the all-white St. John Vianney Minor Seminary, where Clarence transferred after two years at Pius.

"But no," she emphasized, "he wasn't teased by blacks."

Whatever hurtful things were said about him, and whoever said them, Thomas has carried the memories with him all the way to the Supreme Court.

Philip W. Cooper Jr., a Savannah dentist who attended Pius with Thomas, says *everybody* was teased in high school. Marion Poole, for example, says she was called "Bony Marony" because she was so skinny, and "Big Nose."

"Some people may have made jokes," Cooper said, "but I don't really think we were that sensitive about another person's features. Our school was full of Negroid-featured people." When Cooper heard that Thomas was scarred by ribbing related to his skin color, he was puzzled. "There was a time somebody might say to you, 'You so black, you're the blackest nigger in the house.' Who cares? It was not, You're black, you're no good. You're just black." Raised in an upper-middle-class family as the son of a dentist, Cooper says he, too, was teased, for being light-skinned and a kid of privilege. People called him "Dr. Cooper's boy."

Orion Douglass, who also grew up in the city's Catholic schools but was older than Thomas, says there was, indeed, a "de facto caste system" in black Savannah. But he says it was based not on skin color but on career status, which fed into social standing. Mailmen, government workers, teachers were considered part of the upper strata. Small businessmen like Myers Anderson, who drove a truck and didn't learn to read until late in life, were not. "As you went down the caste system in Savannah, because the communities were segregated, black entrepreneurship was not assigned a special premium in and of itself," recalls Douglass. "We had black movie theaters. We had black drive-in theaters. Black restaurants. Wherever black people did commerce in a segregated society you could pretty much expect a black entrepreneur providing the service."

Some of those black businesses, while vital, were hardly major enterprises. Mr. Dixon, for instance, ran a corner store that had a raggedy screen door and a low overhang that forced anyone taller than six feet to duck to enter. The store sold loose cigarettes (three for a nickel), five-cent sodas, Spic & Span. The shelves were always neatly stacked. A jar of pickles sat on a chest. When a customer arrived, a cow bell would ring notifying Mr. Dixon, who might be upstairs in his living quarters. Mr. Dixon put his kids through college running this store, but businessmen like him were not part of the black elite.

Douglass, however, *is* from one of those crème de la crème families of black Savannah. Both his parents were educators—his mother a teacher, his father a high school principal with a master's degree. The Douglass family lived in a beautiful split-level house with hardwood floors and an underground garage. Douglass's mother ran a club for boys called the Gigolos, which met on Saturdays. They roasted hot dogs on wire hangers over an open fire. They played cowboys and Indians, studied geography and chemistry, and learned about the social graces.

Thomas was not part of the Gigolos.

"We were looking at the same community from different rungs," said Douglass, who preceded Thomas at Holy Cross College and remains friends with him. "Whereas maybe Clarence would see it as a reflection on his complexion or a reflection on his clothes, from my perspective it was more what rung his family came on in the caste system. . . . So it wasn't clothes, it wasn't complexion—because there were many, many very dark-skinned physicians, for example. I think it broke down more in terms of education and employment."

But as far as Thomas is concerned, snobbery was snobbery and he still holds a grudge. "You had the black elite, the schoolteachers, the light-skinned people, the dentists, the doctors," he has said. "My grandfather was down at the bottom, an uneducated man who had money in the bank and took care of himself. And . . . they would look down on him. Everybody tries to gloss over that now, but it was the reality. It was the reality."

It's ironic that the most prominent African American Savannah has produced speaks sneeringly of the leading lights in his community—the educators, physicians, and other professionals. He appears to reserve a level of contempt for these high achievers that he doesn't hold for whites who maintained the laws that thwarted black progress. Families like Orion Douglass's and social organizations like Jack and Jill of America—founded in 1938 by a Philadelphia concert pianist to provide black children with the cultural experiences often denied them under segregation—may have been guilty of forming exclusive cliques. But they weren't the perpetuators of the racist notion that blacks were inferior.

Years after he left Savannah, Thomas would become a loyal Republican, aligning himself with the Strom Thurmonds and Jesse Helmses of the South. And he was willing to cut these former segregationists the kind of slack he wouldn't cut the families of Savannah's black elite. In a 1994 speech, Thomas warmly recalled how friendly Helms had been when Thomas was a junior aide on Capitol Hill. "When he saw you, he always had a good word," Thomas said of the longtime Republican senator from North Carolina, who has since retired. "I said to myself, 'Oh, my goodness. He's supposed to be a mean man. Why is he always talking? Why does he say good morning? Why does he say good afternoon?' You'd get in the elevator and he would ask you how you're doing or who do you work for. . . . I have always been taught that on a personal level you judge a person by the way he or she treats the least among us."

This was the same Jesse Helms who stated in 1979—the year Thomas went to work on Capitol Hill—that segregation wasn't wrong. "Not for its time," he told reporters. This Jesse Helms said the legacy of Martin Luther King Jr. "was really division—not love," and once declared: "It is time to face, honestly and sincerely, the purely scientific statistical evidence of natural racial distinctions in group intellect."

These are hardly views Thomas would embrace. Yet he embraces the man who holds these views. (There is no record of Thomas ever criticizing Helms for his racial attitudes.) To Thomas, it was his personal interaction that endeared Helms to him, and the rest he apparently could overlook. He has not been so generous in his appraisals of blacks whom he felt snubbed him and his family.

"People love to talk about conflicts interracially," Thomas has said. "They never talk about the conflicts and tensions intraracially. The ones we had to deal with most often and most frequently were the intraracial ones. And it gives you a different perspective on life and the things that are happening to you."

What Thomas rarely mentions is how much he actually had in common with the black kids he grew up with—their family's circumstances were more like his than not. According to a St. Pius survey conducted in the late 1960s after Thomas had left, only 5 percent of the students' fathers had completed college and 35 percent hadn't finished high school. Half the students' parents were skilled or unskilled workers; a third were dead or not living at home.

Butch Mitchell, who sat on the podium with the justice at the Carnegie Library rededication, says the divisions within the black community when Thomas was growing up were more complicated than Thomas portrays. The kids attending Catholic schools, for instance, were considered by most to be a cut above those attending public schools. "We never played with the Catholic school kids," says Mitchell. In the neighborhood, the Catholic school kids stood out. Walking home from school, they were easily identifiable in their uniforms—gray slacks, gold ties, and burgundy jackets at Pius. They went to school late every first Friday because they had 8:30 a.m. Mass. They didn't eat meat on Fridays. They hung out together. And Thomas was as Catholic as a Catholic school kid could be—he was an altar boy, someone who would volunteer when the priests needed help serving Mass, and later a recruiter sent to the elementary schools to talk up the seminary. In this insular world, Thomas had status.

"Clarence was a legend around here, in the black Catholic community," recalled Lester Johnson, who is five years his junior and followed him up the Catholic school chain. "Everybody thought he'd be our first black priest."

After two years at St. Pius X High School, Thomas set out to become just that. It was one of his grandfather's dreams for him, one that Thomas promised he'd fulfill. He left behind his all-black school for St. John Vianney Minor Seminary on the Isle of Hope, less than six miles from Savannah. St. John's, a boarding school, was where boys preparing for the priesthood went.

Thomas would later reflect on his time at St. Pius with a mixture of anger and remorse. The school, which opened in 1952 and closed in 1971, became a casualty of integration. After a study of the city's Catholic schools by Notre Dame University, diocesan school officials announced that Pius's student body and faculty would be "amalgamated" with Savannah's two white high schools. In outlining the benefits of Pius's closure, the headmaster of Benedictine, one of the white schools, explained "that in America today, quality education includes the growth in knowledge and maturity that can only come when people whose lives are oriented by the same spiritual and moral values are able to share them with one another. Such sharing, of course, is not possible when they are kept apart by such artificial barriers as the color of their skins."

As a practicing Catholic, Thomas would find it difficult to disagree with that ideal. But he would spend his career battling such logic as it related to education. Even though he didn't graduate from Pius, its closure—and the closure of other black Catholic schools—helped sour him forever on integration. "It broke my heart to see St. Pius close," he told fellow Savannah Catholics after he was on the Supreme Court, adding: "Some people think that the solution to all the problems of black people is integration. I never worshipped at the altar [of integration]. . . . The poor education for blacks that resulted from some of these decisions deeply saddens me. It was very harmful."

Leaving St. Pius in 1964, Thomas plunged into the whitest environment he had ever been in, competing against kids who had no experience with blacks as peers. Some of them, it seemed to Thomas, doubted his abilities and tried to make life at the school miserable for him.

"I was a stray dog," he said.

Clarence arrived as one of only two black seminarians—the other was Richard Chisholm, who entered as a freshman. Clarence entered as a sophomore, held back, he was told by St. John's officials, because he did not meet the Latin requirements and would need an extra year to graduate. While many of Thomas's memories of St. John's would center around the alienation and insecurity he felt, what struck Chisholm back then was Clarence's confidence. He was outgoing, not shy. "Which, to me, took a lot of courage," Chisholm said.

Physically, Clarence was short but sculpted. He had closely cropped hair with a part on the left side. He had the carriage—"the streetness," as Chisholm put it—of someone who didn't plan to take any guff off anyone. In the school's common settings—the dining hall, the study hall, the athletic field—the Clarence Thomas observed by Chisholm was independent and opinionated, just like he is today. It wasn't a matter of trash-talking, but rather, " 'I can do this, I can do that,' and then he would go out and show them," Chisholm recalled.

Meanwhile, Chisholm struggled. He felt left out of plans and conversations. He began to wonder: How could his fellow seminarians, who were supposed to be future spiritual leaders, not accept one of their own? The priests, he thought, seemed to be oblivious to the racial dynamic created in a school that had twenty white boys and two black boys. Chisholm, like the other students, was assigned a counselor. But he was thirteen and didn't know quite what to tell the priest. "What do you do, go in there and say, 'Nobody likes me?' " Oddly, Chisholm and Thomas never discussed what it felt like to be at St. John's as black seminarians. "He always had a jovial disposition about him," recalled Chisholm, "so it was hard to know if he was experiencing the same things."

Though both had attended St. Benedict's, had been altar boys to
gether, and lived on Savannah's east side, at St. John's they were just
two kids separately trying to fit in. Chisholm says there was little
time in the school schedule to huddle privately. But that doesn't explain why he and Thomas never got together at home and, as adults,
never discussed their shared experience. "For the life of me,"
Chisholm said, "I don't know why we never talked about it. I guess
our lives just took different paths."

On Thursday afternoons, Myers Anderson would pick Clarence
up for a home break, and Chisholm sometimes hitched a ride. But
the car conversations were always cordial, with neither boy offering
any hint of St. John's difficulties. "You kind of suffered in silence,"
Chisholm recalled. Finally, though, Chisholm knew he had to tell his
parents that St. John's was not working out. He was homesick, disillusioned, and "didn't want to continue." He also remembered what
his mother had always told him: Don't go where you're not wanted.
So Richard Chisholm did not go back. He ended up graduating from
Pius.

Now, Clarence was really alone.

"I cannot begin to tell you how difficult and lonely it was," he reflected in a 1986 tribute to the Franciscan sisters he so admired.
"But my training by the nuns and my grandparents paid off. I decided then, at the ripe old age of 16, that it was better to be respected than liked. Popularity is unpredictable and vacillating." As
it turned out, Clarence apparently was feeling the same emotional
stress that had sent Chisholm packing—except Clarence wouldn't
talk about it until many years later. The St. John's anecdotes he tells
as an adult are mostly about an unpleasant time in his life.

Several of those tales involve nights in the dormitories, which
were low-slung cinder-block buildings with brown tile floors. The
boys slept in open rooms on metal bunk beds. One night after the
lights were turned off, Thomas recalls, somebody called out from
the darkness, "Smile, Clarence, so we can see you." On another occasion, he won a Latin spelling bee and was honored with a statuette

of St. Jude, patron saint of hopeless causes. He put the statuette on the bureau by his bed, only to discover a few days later that the head had been broken. He glued it back on, and somebody broke it off again. This time, in reassembling St. Jude, he put the glue on real thick. And, as Thomas has told the story, the culprit apparently got the message: He, Clarence Thomas, could not be broken.

Thomas's white classmates don't remember Clarence as being traumatized by his St. John's experience, though surely they were viewing the school through a different lens than Thomas. To classmate Steve Seyfried, the racial conflicts "seemed like something he blew off."

"He was essentially one of the guys, as far as I was concerned," said Seyfried, who was coeditor of the school newspaper with Thomas. But Seyfried adds: "As my wife always points out, there's a lot of stuff that happens in front of my eyes that I miss."

An opinion piece Thomas wrote for the school newspaper is the only known written record of how he felt about the volatile issue of race as a high school teenager. The following appeared in the November–December 1966 issue of the *Pioneer*:

Is it disastrous or auspicious? Well, looking back, I notice that the violence and hatred which developed from the acquisition of equality of all races seem to indicate that a disaster has gripped our country. Just to keep the records straight, I don't believe that one race is more to blame than the other. There are times when one ethnic group provokes the other until there is a violent eruption of anger and, consequently, more melees, picketing, and rioting.

But why can't black and white live in harmony? This is quite a question. I am sure that some Stokely Carmichaels would quite readily assert that if there were fewer George Wallaces, race could live together with no friction, while the George Wallaces would, of course, pay the same compliment to their accusers. These conclusions do not offer a solution, but on the contrary, make matters worse.

I think races would fare better if extremists would crawl back into their holes, and let the people, whom this will really affect, do just a little thinking for themselves, rather than follow the Judas goats of society into the slaughter pens of destruction. True, the intellectuals must start the ball rolling, but ignorance in the intelligentsia is not unheard of.

It's about time for the average American to rise from his easy chair and do what he really and truly believes God demands of him—time to peel off the veil of hate and contempt, and don the cloak of love (black for white and white for black).

Clearly, the young Clarence was no militant. It's striking that he blamed both races for the turmoil that accompanied the struggle by blacks to gain the same rights whites were born with. The comparison of George Wallace to Stokely Carmichael—both apparently extremists in Thomas's eyes—is particularly intriguing. One was the governor of Alabama who wielded the power of his office to uphold segregation; the other was a fiery street activist who called for "Black Power" to combat what the George Wallaces of the country were determined to preserve. Without a George Wallace, there would have been no Stokely Carmichael.

Even then, as the lone black boy among white seminarians, Clarence wouldn't line up on the side of blacks. Maybe he was self-conscious about fitting in among his peers. But this reflex—despite a brief flirtation with black nationalism—would remain with him into adulthood. His approach to racial problems—notably a willingness to hold blacks more accountable than whites—would earn him a roster of committed critics.

Long after he left St. John's, however, Thomas would cite his experiences in both all-black and all-white schools as evidence that he

was comfortable in his black skin. "Having had to accept my blackness in the cauldron of ridicule from some of my black schoolmates
under segregation, then immediately thereafter remain secure in
that identity during my years at an all-white seminary, I had few
racial identity problems."

Judging from snapshots in the St. John's yearbook and newspaper,
Clarence was hardly a loner or social misfit. He was business editor
of the *Grail*, the school's yearbook. He was among a group of six
seminarians who tutored kids in the black community of Sandfly.
The *Pioneer* did a whimsical page on the senior class in 1967, and
Clarence's picture appeared with this caption: "Faster than a speedy
spitball . . . more powerful than home brew . . . able to leap . . .
able to . . . able to . . . and then there's . . . nicotine fiend." He
played for the Three-L Lllamas, as the school's basketball team was
known, named after an Ogden Nash poem. In the school yearbook
are photos of him dunking a basketball, leading a fast break, and fading back to pass a football. "He was the best athlete in the school,"
recalled classmate Mike Dillon. "Without a doubt. Beyond anybody. . . . He had muscles, he had shoulders and arms. He was
strong as an ox and fast as lightning."

These are the kind of descriptions that make blacks cringe, and
Thomas may have felt sensitive about being best known for what he
could do athletically. However dominant he was as an athlete, his
one enduring St. John's sports memory is not a happy one. One
spring evening after dinner, a group of boys went to the basketball
court for a pickup game, as was the practice if you didn't have kitchen
duty. As was the practice, they lined up to shoot for sides. Thomas
shot first and made the basket, but as he got ready to pick his team
the other six boys went to the other end of the court and played
their own three-on-three game. Thomas, crushed, left the court and
headed toward the school's main building in what he later described
as the "loneliest walk" of his life. "I vowed then and there never to
let those kids, their slights, disturb me," he recalled. "I think I went
into the chapel to pray. Never again would I let rejection hurt me."

This would prove untrue. Time and again, Thomas has returned to the pain of other rejections, including his failure to obtain coveted job offers after graduating from Yale Law School and the sting of being treated as an outcast by many African Americans. Thomas graduated from St. John's with an A average, having quietly mastered a curriculum that included Latin, English, algebra, geometry, German, history, religion, music, physics. But one anguished moment after another seems to be what's etched in his mind.

One of the explanations Thomas has given for why he typically doesn't speak during oral arguments at the Supreme Court is tied to one of those anguished St. John's moments. During his first semester at the school, Clarence was told by Father William Coleman, the rector and dean of studies, that his spoken English was poor. Unless he got rid of his Geechee/Gullah dialect, Coleman told Clarence, he wouldn't make it at the school and wouldn't reach his goals when he left. Already sensitive about his speech, having been teased about his accent even in black Savannah, Clarence was now shattered.

As he later explained, "I just developed a habit of listening." And so when advocates appear before the robed justices to make their case, Thomas rarely asks questions, even though he long ago dropped his coastal accent and now has one of the most eloquent speaking voices on the court. He'd rather just listen, he has said.

The irony is that after all his suffering at the minor seminary, recounted in numerous speeches, he returned to the Diocese of Savannah headquarters in 1997 to say of St. John's: "I would go there all over again. I had no complaints."

When Clarence graduated from St. John's in 1967, he was on a course to become Savannah's first black priest. Leaving the South behind, he caught a plane to Kansas City, Missouri. From there, it was a ninety-mile drive to Conception Seminary in the northwestern boonies of the state. Another white seminary in another white community. But for Clarence, Conception would prove to be an even tougher challenge than St. John's.

Some of his old friends couldn't understand why Clarence was putting himself through such an ordeal. "I said, 'Man, you're going into the priesthood? Shit, that's not for me,' " Abe Famble recalled telling his boyhood pal from Pin Point. "I know what those people are all about. They talk you *out* of sex. I want to be talked *into* sex."

Thomas just laughed; Famble was so crazy. But Nerve, as everybody called him, was seriously concerned. He thought his friend was messing up his life.

"When he made that choice," Famble recalled, "I said to myself, 'That's a bad one.' "

Clarence clearly wanted to please his grandfather, who hoped his grandson would become Savannah's first black priest. But weren't there other ways to show Myers Anderson gratitude? That young Clarence was willing to endure the taunts and take on the challenge of making it to the priesthood proved something others around him could plainly see: Myers Anderson had become the father he never had, and he didn't want to let him down.

4

MYERS, LEOLA, AND EMMA

Few photos of Myers Anderson exist. The one reproduced countless times for public consumption is undated. It shows Anderson in a white T-shirt, unsmiling, with piercing eyes and thin white hair around the temples. He is standing in front of a mantel. His face, shiny and etched with lines and crevices, conveys a man who didn't make his living sitting in an easy chair. He toiled, sweated, got dirty. He is old in this photo but doesn't look old. He looks wiry-strong, stern, and unyielding.

Clarence Thomas took this photo. He snapped the picture and ran, according to his mom, for Myers Anderson didn't believe in posing for photos. Just refused to do it. So the daring grandson took his grandfather's picture and had copies made for the rest of the family.

Today, Thomas needs no visual reminder of his late grandfather. Anderson's image is engraved in his mind. No human being—alive or dead—has been cited more, quoted more, deified more by Thomas than his grandfather.

Thomas has chosen Myers Anderson to exalt, the family member he views most worthy of public embrace. In Anderson, whom he called "Daddy," Thomas sees himself. "My grandfather would be an anachronism in today's world. He would be looked upon as an insensitive brute. I know that many view me that way."

Thomas hails from a family in which he has no peers—no one educated at a leading university, no one who eats out at Morton's steakhouse, no one who travels to Italy to lecture or commands $1.5 million for a memoir. It is a family well acquainted with many of society's most challenging problems—poverty, illiteracy, inadequate education, divorce, child abandonment, drugs, crime, imprisonment. Somehow Thomas emerged barely nicked. Given a generous boost from his grandparents, he flourished.

And in flourishing, Clarence Thomas became virtually an outsider in his own family. He can't—or won't—talk to any of them about the Constitution's pillars or his loneliness on the court or even his estrangement from vast sectors of his race. Those discussions are saved for others.

The ambivalence—at times, shame—he felt about some members of his family has been hard to shake. His sister, a dropout who later earned her high school diploma as an adult, lives in a rundown house in Pin Point and is a disappointment to Thomas; she doesn't pay him any mind. His father deserted him and is now dead. His mother had a string of men who didn't pan out. Though she's now happy in her fourth marriage, she was more like a sister to Clarence when he was growing up—shooting marbles and wrestling with him—than a parent. His grandmother was important but resided in the shadows, as many women did in those days; she doesn't get the outsize credit Thomas heaps on Myers Anderson. The one who was most like Clarence, younger brother Myers, died suddenly in the prime of his life. And even Myers, though he served in the air force and did well in business, was not as driven as Clarence.

In Thomas's eyes, Myers Anderson stood tallest. Alone among black men he showed Thomas love—even if it was tough love. So it was easy to make Anderson a hero. He is the one memorialized with a bronze bust that rests prominently on a shelf in the justice's chambers. Anderson poured into his grandchildren what he had failed to give his own kids. He embodied, to Thomas, grit and resolve—the determination to defy expectations. Which is what Thomas most values in his own life. Never is Thomas without a Myers Anderson adage: *Old Man Can't is dead; I helped bury him.* Or: *If you make your bed hard, you lay in it hard.* The Thomas translation: "Simply put, we would suffer the consequences of our actions."

Thomas loves to share long, flowing anecdotes that speak to his grandfather's wisdom and generosity—and his absorption of it all:

A few years before he died, I asked my grandfather why he insisted on working for himself. It all seemed so pointless. There wasn't much money to be made, and it required him to work all the time rather than just forty or fifty hours per week. It seemed to me that there was more security in having a job rather than owning an ever declining business. His response was simple: It's mine. That trumped security. Secretly, I think he just couldn't stand the idea of anyone telling him what to do or where to go. For that, he was willing to accept the anxiety and the work. In fact, he seemed to relish the challenge of being successfully independent—and thus, free.

What was so interesting is that in assuming responsibility for himself, my grandfather also accepted responsibility for the community in which we lived. He was especially fond of saying that because he was so fortunate to have produced more than he needed, he could now provide for those who could not do for themselves. I can still see him taking produce or groceries to the doors of those who were destitute or elderly. He would just leave it there (at the door or on the porch), without saying a word and without accepting a word of thanks. It was clear that he didn't do it to be appreciated. He was simply once again accepting responsibility to help those in the community who could no longer help themselves. Gratitude was not necessary.

Thomas's recollections of his grandfather are notably vivid and specific; time and distance haven't dulled his memory. He remembers Anderson railing about rock 'n' roll and R & B music: "He would actually go so far as to take the fuse out of the car so we couldn't play that awful radio and run his battery down."

Anderson was so addicted to work that "spare time" didn't even merit an entry in his lexicon. Occasionally, he'd catch a minor league baseball game at Grayson's Stadium. But he wasn't much for games— and play was not something Myers Anderson did with his grandsons. He was more comfortable barking out orders.

Unimpressed with scholarship and theory, Anderson would delight in verbally kicking Clarence's collegiate butt when he returned home from Holy Cross and tried to debate him about value and principles. "He seemed totally unmoved and undaunted by my citation to philosophers or professors," Thomas recalled. Anderson had his own philosophy. In Thomas's memory, his grandfather was a cross between Booker T. Washington and Confucius. And yet much about Myers Anderson's life gets left out of the storytelling.

Anderson was the product of an adulterous liaison between a married Baptist minister and a young farmworker who avoided scandal by quickly wedding another man months before Myers was born. Both parents died when Anderson was a young boy, and he was raised next by his grandmother and then by uncles in rural Liberty County, Georgia, thirty-three miles from Savannah. As was mentioned earlier, by the time Anderson was seventeen he had fathered two daughters with two different women, neither of whom he married.

One of those daughters was Clarence Thomas's mother, who didn't even meet Anderson until she was twelve, and that happened when she was brought to a family funeral. "In Savannah, all you hear is, 'Oh, Mr. Anderson, oh, he was so great,'" Leola said, with bitterness in her voice. "What did he ever do for me? Nothing." In fact, he did a great deal for her later in life—taking over the raising of her sons, setting her up in houses he owned when she was down on her luck. But as a father, he was absent in her upbringing. "My dad didn't have anything to do with me too much when I was growing up," Leola said.

How Thomas reconciles Anderson's irresponsibility as a father with his otherwise sterling image is unclear. It is the kind of behavior Thomas himself has derided in public speeches. For someone who has detailed the crippling psychological wounds of his own childhood, he has displayed remarkably little sympathy for his mother, who was forsaken by her dad. Thomas has lifted Anderson to a height that leaves little room for consideration of his failings.

He was not an absolute ace at everything. Take his cinder-blocks enterprise. Anderson was something of a local pioneer, at least in the black community, in manufacturing the concrete blocks. As the story goes, only Jim Crow—era racism prevented him from getting a fat contract with the city. That may have been true, but according to Bill Haynes, a Pin Point architect who knew Anderson, his blocks "weren't the best quality." Haynes recalls Anderson's blocks being used to build an outhouse for Pin Point's Baptist church. "You'd try to cut them up and they'd break."

This critique doesn't diminish Anderson. His resourcefulness was amazing—he taught himself plumbing, bricklaying, carpentry. He knew the Bible by heart. "He was one of the smartest men without an education that you've ever seen," said his best friend and business partner, Sam Williams. Even Anderson's difficulties with numbers proved surmountable. With Williams's help, he learned a system of counting that relied on even numbers.

Anderson, known as "Mike" to his friends, had more dimensions than Thomas has given him. He was not as rigidly predictable, for instance, as he is sometimes portrayed. He briefly went into the nightclub business with Williams, a decidedly un-Anderson-like venture. The club wasn't his kind of scene. The patrons were sometimes rowdy, loose, and drunk, and he saw himself as a serious, hardworking, religious man. But the New Derrick Inn was a favor to Williams, who got Anderson a license for a gun, "and he took care of all the outside," Williams recalled. "Anybody that got into trouble, he was right there."

It's puzzling that Thomas sometimes treats his grandfather's business success as more modest than it actually was. James Millet, a Holy Cross classmate, was surprised to learn from us that Anderson actually *owned* a fuel oil business. "I thought he worked for the fuel oil people," remarked Millet, who said Thomas always emphasized "the sharecropper thing."

Sharecropper thing? Anderson was a descendant of slaves, as most other Southern blacks of his generation were. He also worked long hours as a boy farming with his uncle Jim—but he was never a sharecropper. Long before Clarence arrived at Holy Cross in 1968, his grandfather owned a sixty-acre farm in Liberty County. The property had been in the family since 1892. Anderson loved to escape to his farm, where he'd hunt squirrel and turkey. He raised chickens and hogs and harvested enough vegetables—corn, okra, butter beans, sweet potatoes—to give plenty away to the needy.

So committed is Thomas to preserving his up-from-poverty narrative, he seems reluctant to trumpet Anderson's prosperity, which was considerable for an independent black businessman of his era. Anderson was well-off enough to be a sponsor of Clarence's high school yearbook, taking out an ad just like the white-owned businesses.

In public, Thomas has carefully chiseled his grandfather's image. In private conversation, however, some have glimpsed sides of the Thomas-Anderson relationship that the grandson rarely discusses publicly. Tony Califa, a Yale Law School classmate, recalls Thomas talking about how harsh his grandfather could be. According to Califa, Thomas said that he and his brother would have "the shit beaten out of them" if they so much as slept too late. Myers Anderson didn't have to work hard to intimidate. "Daddy had some eyes would make the water come out of yours," daughter Leola explains.

His wife, Christine, was a different personality. The two met not long after Myers moved to Savannah, marrying in 1933. Christine

Hargrove was six years younger than Myers, had grown up in nearby Bryan County, and had attended school through sixth grade. Because she could read and write, she kept the books for Anderson's businesses. She also became a surrogate mother to Clarence and his brother, Myers, not to mention a calming influence in the house. Whereas Myers was determined to teach his grandsons hard lessons, "Aunt Tina," as she was called, doted on the boys and was more merciful with punishment. She made aprons and sold them to help pay for Clarence's schooling. She baked pies and sold them to help pay for the trip to Clarence's Holy Cross graduation, which Myers intentionally skipped. She washed Clarence's clothes, ironed his shirts, took care of him when he was sick. And at the dinner table, she even protected Clarence's favorite piece of fried chicken—no one else was to touch the drumstick. She was a full partner in the rearing of Clarence, but it's not often you'll see Tina mentioned separately by name in a Thomas speech. Perhaps that is because Myers Anderson had such a dominant persona—a strong *man* at a time when Thomas had no men in his life.

"That's the part you don't hear about," said Sam Williams. "She was the one who did so much for those boys."

But perhaps the most significant omission in Thomas's nostalgic reflections is Anderson's disappointment in how his grandson turned out. It wasn't just that Clarence abruptly dropped his pursuit of the priesthood—that was enough to get him kicked out of the house—or never returned home to Savannah to practice civil rights law, all of which pained his grandfather. It was more complicated than that.

Though he was proud Clarence had worked hard to advance up the ladder of government, Anderson wasn't happy with his grandson's choices. All those opportunities growing up, all that formal education, and Clarence ends up a prominent Republican, one of the few black faces of the Reagan administration?

"Yes, I think that's what caused Myers to turn against him," said Williams, "the way he accepted politics." As Williams put it, the GOP "was not in our corner at that time." Not that Southern white

Democrats had a great legacy with blacks. But by the time Thomas had gotten on his professional track, just several years before Anderson died, it was the Republican Party that was anathema to blacks.

To Prince Jackson, a family friend, it seems that Thomas has his grandfather's earn-your-own-way philosophy but lacks his compassion. Myers Anderson never refused people fuel oil because they couldn't pay. He'd just fill up their tanks, not wanting them to suffer in winter. The grandson, said Jackson, appears to have less empathy for those who can't find a way to make it. That Thomas was becoming a prominent figure in an administration not known for its compassion was tough for Anderson to swallow. And yet there were other things about Clarence that apparently bothered Anderson even more.

"I detected there might have been some strain," said Jackson, who delivered the eulogy at Anderson's funeral, which was held at St. Benedict Catholic Church in Savannah on April 4, 1983, with Thomas in attendance. As Jackson sees it, the tension between grandfather and grandson had more to do with Thomas's drift away from the church and the dissolving of his marriage than to politics or career decisions. Anderson liked Thomas's first wife, Kathy, very much. Their breakup not only went against Catholic orthodoxy but personally "hurt him very badly," according to Williams. It deepened Anderson's sense that Clarence had lost his way spiritually, and faith was very important to Anderson.

Family friends and relatives say the distance between Thomas and Anderson never really closed. Thomas, though, has taken comfort in his final meeting with his grandfather, citing it in speeches as evidence of Anderson's blessing of his life, however grudging. As Thomas tells the story, he was being deluged with criticism early in his tenure as President Reagan's chairman of the Equal Employment Opportunity Commission (EEOC) and went to see his grandfather. "It was the last time I saw him alive," Thomas recalled, "and he told me, 'Son, you have to stand up for what you believe in.' "

The following month Anderson died from a massive stroke, two days before his seventy-sixth birthday. A month later Tina died. The twin deaths left Thomas inconsolable. He lapsed into a long, sad period of introspection, one he has described as "the dark night of my soul."

"He was devastated," remembers Jackson. "It was almost like he lost everything in the world. He knew they were responsible for everything he had." Thomas sought salvation by renewing his faith. "I turned where the hopeless and the lonely turn," he recalled years later. "To God."

Myers and Christine Anderson are buried in the cemetery adjacent to Palmyra Missionary Baptist Church, a white brick building on a rural dirt road in Midway, Georgia. This is where Anderson wanted his body to rest—in the county where he had grown up, near the farm to which he escaped during summers well into his senior years. Thomas returns there from time to time to pay his respects and reminisce. The farm Anderson owned down the road, Thomas inherited. A tenant lives on the property, but there's no farming being done anymore—the grass is tall, the crop fields untended. All that could be observed one recent summer day was a barking hunting dog, a satellite dish, and a couple of boats. A pickup truck was in the yard, parked next to the cinder-block house where Anderson once lived.

Myers Anderson, whose name was invoked so much during Thomas's confirmation hearings, never got to see his grandson ascend to the highest court in the land. Asked if he would have been proud of Clarence on the Supreme Court, Anderson's best friend Sam Williams replied: "I don't believe he'd have an answer for it. I don't believe he'd answer you."

Leola Williams has a small office at Candler Hospital, where she has worked since Jimmy Carter was president. The space was once a supply closet, but it's more than sufficient for her. She has a chair, a tiny refrigerator, the Holy Bible, and a radio, which is always tuned to WSOK-AM, the gospel station. Every morning E. Larry McDuffie plays her favorite song, "Too Close to the Mirror."

Williams is Candler royalty. She has a desk (adorned with family photos, including of her famous son) out in the lobby. From there she directs patients, in her green scrub pants and flowered smock. That's her job—she's a greeter. The doctors and nurses all love her. The old folks, especially, depend on her to help navigate hospital bureaucracy or procure an appointment with an unreachable doctor. She is well into her seventies but still rises at 3 a.m. and gets to work at 4:30. The seniors see her as a remarkable wonder of their own. Only arthritis slows her down. Everyone, naturally, knows she is the mother of a Supreme Court justice. And that fact is a source of hospital pride.

Much less well known is this: her favorite son, the one who lives in her heart, was Myers Thomas, Clarence's younger brother. Pinned to the bulletin board in her office is the January page from a 2000 calendar. The date January 23 is marked in ink, for that was the day Myers went for a Sunday morning jog in New Orleans and collapsed from a massive heart attack. Dead at age fifty, a husband who was adored, a father loved by two children.

"I think about Myers all day," Williams confides. The relationship between Clarence and his mother is best seen through the prism of Myers Thomas. He was everything Clarence was not—notably, attentive. "Myers was the kindest-hearted one," Williams says. He called often, came to visit when she was lonely, took her for rides. He was protective of her, never judgmental like Clarence. And never too busy to help her sort out a problem. When her first Social Security check came in the mail, Williams didn't believe she was entitled to it. To her, it was free, unexpected money from the government. She was suspicious of it, didn't want a handout. She talked to her cousin Gertrude about the check, phoned the Social Security office, conferred with coworkers. Everyone told her she had earned the money. Still, she didn't believe them until she called Myers, who told her: "That is yours, and don't you dare take it back to those people."

Myers she trusted like no one else.

On a scorching August day in 2003, the front porch of Williams's home on East Thirty-second Street is still adorned with the three-year-old plants from Myers's funeral. Leola Williams invites a pair of visitors inside. She shows off her fish tank. The living room walls are painted sea blue. A portrait of a black Christ cradling a black man hangs on one wall. Her tables and mantels are crammed with family photos. The pictures of Myers are forever being reviewed. She keeps Myers in her wallet, in her bedroom. He's never far away.

"I had more dealing with Myers," she explains. "Me and Myers were more really open and close together." Through their closeness she learned how much Myers truly despised his father, M. C. Thomas. The quiet sibling, he had kept his anger bottled up inside since childhood. But when he returned home after serving in the air force, it became clear that he wanted nothing to do with his dad—ever.

M. C. had phoned Leola, saying he wanted to reconnect with his son, but Myers had not returned his calls. She knew Myers was at the filling station getting his car serviced, so she directed her former husband there. He hadn't seen his son since Myers was nine years old. According to the account Myers gave his mother, the reunion didn't go well. "Hey boy, hey boy, I'm your daddy," M. C. said when he saw Myers. "And Lord have mercy, Myers went off on him," Leola remembers her son telling her.

That was not the worst of it. When Myers found out from his mother that M. C. had blamed her for the outburst, he picked up the phone and berated his dad even more vociferously. Myers was loyal to his mother. He blamed his father for her struggles as a parent. He even told him that he wished he could change his last name—he no longer wanted to be a Thomas.

Clarence was harder for his mother to figure out. He didn't confide much. Ambition often seemed to drive him. They didn't speak the same language. His mother wasn't certain how he felt about his father, for he didn't say. Unknown to her, he was curious about his father's family. He wrote letters to his relatives and to this day stays in touch with some of his half brothers and sisters. Though he never forgave his father, unlike Myers he didn't cut off contact with him. He invited M. C. to the White House ceremony celebrating his Supreme Court confirmation, calling him up to the South Lawn stage to meet President Bush. And when his father died in 2002, he attended the funeral in Philadelphia.

But the tension between his mother's family and his father's is palpable, and Clarence is the high-profile conduit for it. "He only stays in touch with us because he wants the missing pieces filled in, but we ain't got time for him," fumes Ethel Thomas, a niece of M. C.'s who lives in Savannah. She questions Clarence's sincerity and notes he has said unkind things about M. C. publicly. "He don't want to know the Thomas side of the family, and the Thomas side of the family don't want to know him," Ethel says. "He's a sellout."

Whatever burdens Clarence carries about the splits in his family, he hasn't shared them with his mother. While his brother was alive, his relationship with her was limited. He did, however, give her away when she married for a fourth time in 1983. He came down from Washington, and the marriage took place right there in the house where Clarence and his brother had been raised by their grandparents. It was now his mother's home. In giving her away, Clarence quipped to his new stepfather: "If you can put up with my momma, you can have her. . . . My momma is set in her ways."

Thomas certainly knows something about being set in one's ways. Comparing Clarence and his brother, Lester Johnson, a friend and lawyer for the family, said: "Myers was very businesslike but in my view a little more flexible. . . . If Clarence believes in something, I don't know if anybody can get him to change his mind. . . . He will dig in. . . . Myers was not that way." An accountant by training, Myers worked for years in the hotel industry and later for an organization doing revitalization work on New Orleans's waterfront. But he didn't take himself so seriously. "Myers was a little more relaxed than Clarence in terms of personality," Johnson added.

After Myers died, Leola Williams wanted to stop working—"I

just couldn't take it"—but the doctors at the hospital convinced her that returning to work would be best for her mental health. But Myers's death didn't tear just Williams apart, it tore Thomas apart as well. It caused him to reexamine how he was living his life. "When my brother died," Thomas said later, "it showed me the other perspective that not only do we do things in our professional life, but there is the family side of life—the things that really matter." Myers was his "stabilizing force," as he sometimes put it to Johnson. "If I ever get the big head about anything, you know, Myers will make sure that he brings me back down to earth."

Thomas depended on his brother to look after their mother—whatever she needed Myers arranged. When he died, Thomas had to step into that role. He knew he had not always thought the best of his mother. He had even disparaged her before friends and colleagues. One former Thomas aide, Michael Middleton, recalled his boss saying that "his mother dumped him and his brother on the grandfather because she'd met some man." Thomas carried his resentment of his mother for a long time, according to friends. But now he was the only son she had. Gradually, perhaps out of guilt, perhaps in tribute to his brother, he inched closer to her, and she to him.

In one particularly poignant moment for her, Clarence readied her for something that he had long intended to tell her. "And I'm just sitting up, now I want to hear what it is," Leola recounts from her living room. And Clarence told her: "I just want to let you know that I love you. Hadn't been for you, I wouldn't have been here today. Hadn't been for you having me, I wouldn't be where I am today. So I give it all to you."

Now they talk on the phone all the time. Sometimes Clarence calls at 4 a.m., when she is just about to leave for work. "Hey, Leola, what are you doing?" She is not a phone person, but he is. "I fuss at him because he run his mouth," she says. "He be running his mouth to me." This she can indulge, so clearly happy is she to have her son more involved in her life.

"I thank God for Clarence . . . helping me now," she says, "and he keeps up with my doctors and see that everything is paid up. And I can't ask for no more."

Williams notices that she has even started laughing like her son— after all these years.

In December 1980, Clarence Thomas introduced his sister to the nation. He was not kind. Attending a conference of black conservatives, he gave an interview to Juan Williams of the *Washington Post* in which he singled out Emma Mae Martin as an example of the debilitating effects of welfare dependency. "She is so dependent," Thomas claimed, "she gets mad when the mailman is late with her welfare check. . . . What's worse is that now her kids feel entitled to the check too. They have no motivation for doing better or getting out of that situation."

At the time, Thomas was an unknown junior aide to John Danforth, the Republican senator from Missouri, and Ronald Reagan had just been elected president. Thomas's insensitivity to his sister— not to mention his failure to accurately reflect her circumstance— has dogged him ever since. When he was nominated to the Supreme Court in 1991, critics recycled the interview as evidence that he lacked compassion. For many blacks, irrespective of the facts, he had violated a cultural taboo: You don't put your family's business in the street. "He should have gotten some bad press on that," said Prince Jackson, a family friend.

Thomas apologized to his sister, but his recollections are not consistent with hers. According to what he later told Armstrong Williams, an aide at the EEOC, he was so upset by the sudden realization that he had hurt and embarrassed Emma that he drove all night to Georgia in the snow to make amends personally. Emma remembers no such trip. In a recent dissection of the controversy, Thomas suggested his sister had endorsed his critique of her reliance on welfare. He told journalist Ken Foskett that he talked to his sister when he went home for Christmas "and she said, 'It's true. It does have these negative effects.' She agreed with me. I still didn't feel better. I was mollified but didn't feel that much better."

Whatever Martin may have told Thomas privately, she has consistently let interviewers, including us, know that she was off welfare when her brother made his comments. Furthermore, during part of the time she was on welfare, Martin said, she was looking after not only her kids but an elderly aunt, who had raised her, and an uncle. "I had a choice of taking care of these old people or keeping a job."

Martin said she was on welfare for a total of eight years. But precisely when she was on and when she got off is difficult to nail down. The best judgment, based on her sometimes fuzzy chronology of her life, is that those eight years of public assistance were sometime between 1969 and 1980. As for the stigma of welfare, she doesn't share her brother's view, "because I knew I had to raise my children," she explained. "I didn't have nobody to help me, I mean."

She had her first son, Clarence, in 1967, two weeks shy of turning twenty-one. She married his father, Paul Martin, in 1968. In two years, they separated. By that time, a second son, Mark, and a daughter, Christine, had been born. Emma was living in an apartment in Savannah at the time, raising her children alone. In 1973, Paul and Emma officially divorced, at which time Paul was ordered to pay $25 a week in child support. But by 1976, Emma, describing herself as indigent, was in court seeking back payments her former husband owed, according to court records. The court ruled Paul was $3,000 in arrears. It was also in 1976 that she had another son, Leon, by another man and moved back to Pin Point, where she has remained. She has never remarried.

"I can do bad by myself," she said matter-of-factly.

What Clarence left out of his anecdote about her welfare dependency, she said, is that she always wanted to work—and did work—even during periods when she struggled. She started picking crabs at age seven in Pin Point and ended up picking for thirty years. She worked at a nursing home. At times she held down two jobs. She wasn't ambitious like her brother, she admits, had no big aspirations. But she did go back and get her high school diploma after dropping out. She finished at night school. She was twenty-seven. She never thought about college but did take cooking classes for several years. That helped her get a job preparing meals at the Bethesda Home for Boys, the nation's oldest existing children's home. That is where she works today.

Another thing Clarence left out of his anecdote about her welfare dependency, Martin suggested, is that she was often resourceful. She bought clothes on layaway and resoled her kids' worn-out shoes to save money. And even with welfare, it was hard to get by. "So when I got two jobs I got off welfare," she said.

Thomas may have felt stung by the public exposure of his thoughtlessness. But his comments reflected his true feelings about his sister, sentiments he shared with others before 1980 and has since repeated. "He was pretty disgusted with his sister for being on welfare," recalled Fletcher Farrington, whose Savannah law firm employed Thomas in the summer before his final year in law school. According to a close friend, Thomas still occasionally talks, even at the Supreme Court, about how his sister "ruined her life."

The differences between Emma and Clarence couldn't be more stark. The sister has embraced a simple, ambition-free life that is perhaps hard for her driven brother to understand. There is little, except bloodline, that bonds them. They don't talk politics or law or philosophy. It's fair to say she doesn't share many of his views, notably about limited government and the responsibility of individuals to lift themselves out of their circumstances.

She would not agree with the Clarence Thomas who gave a speech in 1994 mocking those who show empathy for the less fortunate in legal cases. Her son, after all, is serving a thirty-year sentence for crack cocaine trafficking, and before then had been struggling to find work. "Once our legal system accepted the general premise that social conditions and upbringing could be excuses for harmful conduct," Thomas said in the speech, "the range of causes that might prevent society from holding anyone accountable for his actions became potentially limitless. Do we punish the drunk driver who has a family history of alcoholism? A bigoted employer reared in the segregationist environment who was taught that blacks are inferior? . . . A thief or drug pusher who was raised in a dysfunctional family and who received a poor education? A violent gang member, rioter, or murderer who attributes his rage, aggression, and lack of respect for authority to a racist society that has oppressed him since birth? Which of these individuals, if any, should be excused for their conduct?"

"He's supposed to be a judge," said Martin, "but you can't judge anybody unless you judge yourself. I've never judged anybody, but people judge me all the time."

In a 1995 speech to the University of Mississippi Law School, Thomas said: "Today, victims of discrimination, racism, poverty, sickness, and societal neglect abound in the popular press. Today, there are few (if any) heroes. Often it seems that those who have succumbed to their circumstances are more likely to be singled out than those who have overcome them."

Her brother may be confident in absolutes, but Martin is not. "That philosophy on people, you know, people can try to help themselves and still fall short," she said. So why shouldn't government help those who can't make it on their own?

She and her brother avoid such debates. Their conversations tend to be about, "well, not much really," Martin said. "Find out how I'm doing, what I'm up to, that's about it." She holds nothing against him, though, not even his wrapping her in that welfare-queen package. "Life has to go on," she said. "I tell my children the same thing. You cannot hold grudges."

For sixteen years, the Thomas chroniclers have been coming down to Pin Point to see her—to sit with the sister who's been notoriously dissed by her famous younger brother, to see what she's all about. What does she really think of Clarence? What is her life like?

Her world is anchored in Pin Point, and she doesn't do much of anything. She doesn't go to movies or plays or restaurants or sporting events. "Too scared to go into the city," she said. An awful time at a nightclub years ago is still fresh in her mind. "One night I went out and lost my shoes and I said no more for me. They was shooting, stabbing, and I said no more for me." Every now and then she goes shopping. She reads books like *Strongman's His Name . . . What's His Game? An Authentic Biblical Approach to Spiritual Warfare*. Sometimes she visits cousins and church members who are sick. "Otherwise, I'm here, doing something in my house."

The house needs work, especially the interior. Martin seems oblivious. During one visit, a couple of skinny dogs on chains were barking ferociously in the yard. A disabled car was parked nearby. The front porch was crowded with junk—a rusted deep freezer, a propane tank, old coolers, a half bag of lime. Martin sometimes sounds overwhelmed. "I cut grass when I can."

She is a heavy smoker; her ashtray is rarely empty. When she smiles and laughs, which she does often, you notice she has two missing front teeth. A fifty-two-inch Phillips color TV, which she won at a charity raffle, is always on. One Sunday night, as we sat talking in the dark for hours, the DVD menu of the movie *Barbershop* was on the screen, and the menu music kept playing over and over again. Martin never stopped it, never turned on a light. She had just returned from a weekend visit to Atlanta and was wearing an orange T-shirt from her cousins' family reunion. On the coffee table was a store-bought pound cake and a bottle of hair spray. A pair of red and white Nike sneakers were on the floor. A Compaq computer rested on a desk in the living room, but she never uses it—except to play Solitaire. "I do not mess around with the Internet."

The computer belongs to her oldest son, Clarence, who is in the navy and served during the Persian Gulf war. When Clarence was in high school, he went to live for a while with his uncle Clarence. But it didn't work out, and he called his mother one night pleading to return home. According to Martin, he told her there were too many gangs and too many fights at his school—someone was even killed right in front of him (a fact that could not be verified by us). At the time, Thomas was living in Hyattsville, Maryland, a Washington suburb, and was chairman of the EEOC. He also was a single parent, having split with his first wife, Kathy. He had custody of his son, Jamal. So he was attempting to raise two boys by himself.

Martin feels her brother was mad at her for a while because she sent for Clarence. "I said, 'Well, I'm sorry. My child said he wants to come home, he's coming home,' " she recalled telling her brother.

It's impossible not to notice Martin's collection of praying hands—ceramic hands, plastic hands, hands in worship on every wall, mantel, and table. She began collecting them during her brother's confirmation process, as an effort to ensure that everything would turn out well for him. In the end it did, though not without considerable anguish for the whole family.

Her little brother made it all the way to the Supreme Court, but she wouldn't trade places with him for a day. "He just got a little bit more money than I do, and I don't have a dime," she said. "I work from paycheck to paycheck, and I don't worry about it." She has everything she needs, she said, and not the stress that's seemingly part of her brother's life. "I can get up every day and come over here and work. I thank God for that. I don't have to worry about all them people, looking over my shoulder to see if somebody is going to try to hurt me."

Emma rises at 5 a.m. most days to begin her shift as a cook at the Bethesda Home for Boys, five minutes from her house. She works in an industrial kitchen making meals for boys who've lived hard-knock lives: kids with temper problems, kids from broken homes, kids with chronic problems in school, delinquents, runaways, kids whose parents can no longer deal with them. Ranging in age from six to fourteen, they get help and another chance at Bethesda, which sits on 650 serene acres. Driving through Bethesda's entrance is like entering a rural college campus. Lining the drive are towering oak trees draped with Spanish moss. In the near distance are horse and cow pastures. The children reside in cottages, and in addition to the standard school curriculum they learn such skills as shrimping, carpentry, and animal husbandry.

On this morning, Emma and her cousin Minnie are fixing lunch for three shifts. Emma's handling the chicken-and-rice stir fry. She pours half of a gallon jug of soy sauce over her concoction and puts the huge pan in the oven. Then, brow furrowed, she goes about cleaning a large, flat industrial griddle she has just used. She pours on the cleaning solution while the griddle's still hot and scrubs with a steel pad, trying to be careful not to burn her hands. Minnie has made the carrot salad with pineapple and raisins. And that's lunch.

Later in the afternoon, after preparing spaghetti for dinner, Emma casts off her green apron and heads outside to the field to watch the boys play flag football. It's a big game, and she's promised them she'll be there. Some teachers have driven their cars right up to the field. Emma just stands off in the distance watching, analyzing plays, rooting on individual kids. She eyes one of the staffers and playfully calls out, "Skinny Legs!"

To her, this is a good time. As for her brother, she can only go on about him for so long before her interest wanes. She runs out of things to say, and she doesn't have it in her to engage in philosophical discussion about their disparate lives. There is no indication that she has ever spent much time chewing over Clarence Thomas in her head. She is content with her own life—living plainly, simply.

She is asked if she admires her brother. "Yeah, I admire him well. He's made his destiny, and I'm in my own world."

5

"Radical" Times

Clarence Thomas returned to the rolling hills of northwest Missouri in 2001 for his thirtieth class reunion at Conception Seminary. He was the event's honored guest, although he never graduated with the class of 1971. Thomas had left Conception after his freshman year in 1968, enraged by the racism of his fellow seminarians, scornful of the empty promise of integration, and disillusioned with his faith.

But thirty-three years later, he apologized for having felt that way. He happily posed for pictures with his former classmates, brimmed with poignant recollections of the school, and confessed a renewed reverence for Catholicism.

"Just like others, I got swept away," he said. "It took me just a few months to go running away from my faith; it took me the bulk of my adult life to crawl back."

Being back on Conception's pastoral campus, with its red brick buildings framing a beautifully appointed nineteenth-century church, stirred in Thomas warm memories of the seminary. "I used to make that walk through the snow and go into the basilica whenever I had a tough decision," he told an audience that included thirty-five of his former classmates. "But for that experience, God only knows where I would be now or how I would do the job that I have done. It's with that feeling that I return. It's a renewal of a connection that I've always thought I had with the institution."

Thomas enrolled at Conception in August 1967. He was one of just four black students in a freshman class of sixty-four, but he was ready for that. At St. John's he had learned to josh, joke, and appear to fit in with his white classmates even when he did not. Little did his classmates at either school know that Thomas was already adept at hiding his anger. Decades later, he complained in speeches and conversations with friends that he was wounded by racism every single day both at St. John's and at Conception. The observation stunned many of his white classmates, who had mistaken Thomas's broad smile, booming laugh, and easy manner for contentment.

He had come to seminary propelled by a stubborn sense of duty. He had endured at St. John's and he was determined to take the next steps toward fulfilling his promise to his grandfather of becoming the first black priest in Savannah. The pledge was a source of pride for the old man, who credited the church with teaching him to read and providing his grandsons with a good education. It also suited Thomas. The voids left in his life by the dysfunction and chaos of his family were filled with the discipline, tradition, and stark morality of the church. A budding priest's responsibility to stay away from girls and any other sinful temptation helped insulate Thomas from the growing calls to revolution, sexual and otherwise, that permeated the times. Conception's physical isolation didn't hurt, either.

The seminary sits on a 960-acre tract that amounts to a self-contained village. Beyond the basilica, academic buildings, and dormitories, there is a post office, a monk-run print shop that sells more than five million greeting cards a year, and a small reservoir stocked with several species of fish. Benedictine monks founded the seminary in 1886 to train priests to serve the burgeoning population of German and Irish immigrant farmers in the area—a mission that continues. The closest town of any note is Maryville, Missouri, population 10,000, which is twenty miles to the west.

The sixties revolution may not have rocked Conception as it did Berkeley or Boston, but Thomas was there at a time when the Catholic Church was undergoing its most fundamental change in a millennium, shifting some of the traditions he had learned to hold dear. The Second Vatican Council, which held its final meeting in 1965, had spurred wide-reaching reforms in Catholicism that Conception quickly embraced. The meeting of Catholic leaders from around the globe produced changes in doctrine intended to bring the church closer in line with modern life. Masses were performed in a congregation's native tongue, not Latin, helping to demystify the act of worship. And the very concept of salvation now emphasized the direct relationship between a believer and God, rather than viewing the clergy as the sole conduit. Dress codes were relaxed, with graduate students no longer required to wear cassocks, the ankle-length vestments worn by priests. Seminarians were encouraged not only to pursue the sober disciplines of work, study, and prayer but also to discuss, and reflect on, contemporary issues in their own lives.

Even before Vatican II, Conception had earned a proudly progressive reputation. Its Benedictine monks earnestly answered the call of the times, leaving campus to take part in civil rights protests. As a seminarian, Thomas himself would march in Kansas City after the assassination of Martin Luther King Jr.

Outwardly, Thomas seemed to thrive here much as he had seemed to thrive at St. John's. He was a fine student, notable for his self-discipline, which was needed to handle the challenging curriculum. He was also a standout athlete. He pumped iron in the seminary's recreation center and his former classmates still marvel at his ability to throw a football more than seventy yards in the air. He played an enthusiastic game of basketball, even if he tended to overdribble and his jumper was a bit erratic. But despite the happy appearances, Thomas was roiling inside. His seminary years presented a welter of contradictions, he would say later. The church was supposed to be about brotherhood and understanding, but instead he found racism and hypocrisy at nearly every turn.

His first roommate greeted him by opening a knife when Thomas entered the room. It was meant as a joke and Thomas seemed to take it that way, but he never forgot the incident. Thomas often tagged along with Tom O'Brien, his best friend at seminary, to O'Brien's hometown of Kansas City for the weekend. During one visit, the two went out to a Shakey's pizzeria for beers. They sat quietly and waited—for about twenty minutes. Finally, an employee came over and asked them to leave, complaining that they were making too much noise. O'Brien protested, but Thomas knew the deal: the place simply did not want to serve a black customer. Seething, he and O'Brien left.

Thomas's turmoil came to a head on April 4, 1968, the day King was felled by a sniper's bullet in Memphis. The news devastated Thomas. He grew more distressed after witnessing a fellow seminarian's reaction when word of the shooting reached Conception.

"While walking into the dormitory, someone watching TV yelled that Dr. Martin Luther King had been shot," Thomas said. "A fellow white seminarian who was walking up the stairs in front of me, upon hearing this, and without knowing that I was behind him, replied, after he heard that Dr. King had been shot, 'That's good; I hope the SOB dies.' "

Thomas was stunned. The episode crystallized all the misgivings he had been feeling both at Conception and earlier at St. John's. "I will never forget that moment," he said years later. He called it an expression of his four years in seminary, when every day his consciousness was "pricked by prejudice."

Before the end of the semester, Thomas approached O'Brien and told him that he was leaving Conception. "I've run into too many rednecks," Thomas explained. Soon Thomas would abandon Catholicism as well. The racism he encountered at Conception was too much. How could people studying for the priesthood harbor such notions? How could the church tolerate them?

The experience provided another occasion for Thomas to question the value of integration, something he continues to challenge. Segregation is immoral and illegal, he says, but government need not go so far as to try to foster integration through measures such as school busing. Black and other minority students can learn just fine outside of integrated environments, he says. Besides, who needs the kind of grief that he encountered at seminary?

Thomas made the wounds he suffered at seminary public knowledge through the years in speeches and comments to friends. Those old insults remain a regular topic of conversation with visitors to his Supreme Court chambers, where he sometimes pulls his high school yearbook off the shelf—his was the only black face among the smiling graduates—to drive home the isolation he silently endured at seminary. His point is not just to make clear how prevalent racism was but also to emphasize his resilience in the face of it. Other times, particularly before black audiences, he recounts the incidents in a way apparently calculated to establish his racial credibility.

"It was this event that shattered my faith in my religion and my country. I had spent the midsixties as a successful student in a virtually white environment," he told the National Bar Association, the black legal group, in a 1998 speech. "I had learned Latin, physics, and chemistry. I had accepted the loneliness that came with being 'the integrator,' the first and only. But this event, this trauma I could not take, especially when one of my fellow seminarians, not knowing that I was standing behind him, declared that he hoped the SOB died. This was a man of God, mortally stricken by an assassin's bullet, and one preparing for the priesthood had wished evil upon him."

Thomas's description of the attitudes that prompted him to abandon seminary strikes some of his former classmates as too broad, the slights more numerous than anything they can recall. Thomas remembers athletic awards being suspended for fear that he would win. But at Conception, his classmates named him "class superjock." All of them remember him as a friendly and engaged classmate—certainly, the easiest black guy among the seminarians to talk to. No one questions that he was the victim of a racist remark after Dr. King's assassination, even if no one witnessed it. But some former Conception students challenge the impression left by Thomas that the seminary was rife with racist attitudes.

Frank Scanlon, a Nashville lawyer who was a senior at Conception during Thomas's freshman year, was skeptical of Thomas's recounting of the incident when he first heard it in 1991 when Thomas was nominated to the high court. He was equally incredulous years later when Thomas came back for the reunion. "The reaction of a lot of people associated with the seminary was to be kind of apologetic to him," he says. "My reaction was that we don't need to be apologetic. I thought the atmosphere there was so far from what he described. I thought, 'Come on, man, that was a good place.' His comment . . . left the impression that the joint was full of a bunch of bigots. But that wasn't true." Scanlon's recollection of the impact of King's assassination at Conception was much different from Thomas's. Scanlon says fellow seminarians were stunned and sickened by the news. "We said, 'Good Lord.' The place was just in shock. There weren't people high-fiving or jumping around by any means. Maybe some idiot made that comment that Thomas remembers, but it sure didn't reflect the attitude of the people there."

In his speech before his former Conception classmates in 2001, Thomas's memories of his seminary years were much softer. There he said he never felt any ill will toward the church even if at one point he had mistaken the bigotry of a few for the values of many. He said he regrets having communicated that the church tolerated open racists. "That has been painful for me to have had that said," Thomas lamented. "I think without Conception, without the nuns who taught me in Savannah, without my years in the seminary, nothing else would have been possible."

In fact, Thomas said, he may have left seminary but he never completely abandoned its rituals. The solitary study required of a Supreme Court justice, he explained, is not unlike the existence of a monk. He always valued the solitude that infused life at Conception. He even said that he had considered returning to the seminary in the 1980s when he was the target of criticism in Congress and among civil rights groups angry about his handling of discrimination complaints while he headed the EEOC. At the time, Thomas was divorced and raising his son, Jamal, as a single father. "I thought very seriously that when he was grown," he said, "one of my options was to come back to Conception and enter monastic life."

Thomas had no such thoughts when he packed his belongings and headed back to Savannah in 1968. The once wide-eyed student, diligent altar boy, and aspiring priest was frustrated and gripped by uncertainty. "It all seemed so pointless," Thomas said later. "My dreams of becoming a priest had been dashed, my faith shattered. I was consumed by an almost uncontrolled anger and frustration. All that religion and education had seemed to promise no longer mattered to me. It seemed irrelevant."

Just four years earlier, everything had seemed so clear. He had promised his grandfather he would be a priest. Now he was breaking that vow. He was anguished when the time came to tell his grandfather, who he knew would not understand.

"He was crying," his mother said of Thomas. "Well, he couldn't get nowhere with Daddy. . . . So Clarence came to me, he didn't want to go back. And he didn't tell anybody but me why he didn't want to go back and I kept his secret all these years until he talked about it. . . . He didn't want to go back because the boys at the seminary was saying that they wish Martin Luther King Jr. would die, that's when he had got shot. And Clarence didn't think that if you're studying to be a minister you should wish people death."

Thomas's decision ruptured his relationship with his grandfather, and it was never fully repaired before the old man died in 1983. Not long after Thomas quit, Anderson put him out of his house. He told his grandson that if he was man enough to drop out of seminary, he was man enough to take care of himself.

Looking back, Thomas compares himself to Bigger Thomas, the tortured protagonist of one of his favorite novels, *Native Son*, to explain what he was going through that summer. "Just as Richard Wright's Bigger Thomas had been consumed by the conflagration of prejudices, stereotypes, and circumstances beyond his control and understanding, I felt myself being similarly consumed," he said. "I stood at the great abyss of anger, frustration, and animosity."

With nowhere else to go, Thomas moved in with his mother and her husband Perry Ling, a Sealtest dairy products salesman. He spent an uneasy summer working in a factory that made paper bags and pondering what to do next. He flirted with the idea of transferring to the University of Missouri and studying journalism. He also thought about going to a historically black college; Savannah State and Tuskegee Institute in Alabama were on his list.

A turn of fate would change those plans. One day Thomas bumped into Sister Mary Carmine Ryan, his high school chemistry teacher. She was upset by his decision to leave Conception and urged him to look into Holy Cross, a highly regarded men's college one hour west of Boston. But after his seminary experience, Thomas was unsure about going to another white Catholic school. Ryan took it upon herself to contact a Holy Cross student from Savannah, who saw to it that an application was sent to Thomas. "I filled it in mainly out of respect for the nun who had made such an effort to help me," Thomas said.

Thomas's application coincided with a stepped-up attempt by Holy Cross to recruit black students. By one count, Holy Cross had graduated fewer than twenty black students in its 125-year history between 1843 and 1968. But in the wake of King's assassination, the school launched a hasty effort to scour predominantly black Catholic high schools along the East Coast and in the South for black students. The school also launched a new scholarship program for black students in honor of the slain civil rights leader.

Thomas's application arrived late in the admissions cycle, but he was accepted. Race did not appear to play a role in Thomas's acceptance to Holy Cross, but the deal was sealed when Holy Cross offered him one of the new scholarships, along with a loan and job that covered much of the school's $2,850-a-year cost. In the years to come, Thomas's critics would point to that financial package in calling him a hypocrite for opposing affirmative action after benefiting from it. School officials have acknowledged that Thomas benefited from its new scholarship program, which by any measure was an affirmative action program. For his part, Thomas doesn't acknowledge race as a factor in Holy Cross's treatment of his application; he says only that he was admitted to the school as a transfer student.

In September 1968, Thomas boarded a train in Savannah to begin his journey to Holy Cross. He had with him a chicken sandwich for lunch and $100 stashed in a sock. He also carried his share of doubt. "When I got to Holy Cross, my greatest fear was that I would flunk out immediately," he said.

Built along one of the seven hills overlooking the dreary city of Worcester, Massachusetts, Holy Cross was a place steeped in tradition and governed by a long list of rules. For years, students were required to attend daily Mass and regular confession. Jackets and ties were recommended for class, chapel, and meals. Students enjoyed their food served on china by student waiters, a class of workers Thomas would join. Priests not only taught theology but also patrolled the residence halls.

"It was a real monastery, a bleak place," recalls Steve Urbanczyk, who entered Holy Cross in 1967. Despite all the rules, he said, the students "weren't highly churched. It was a rabble-rousing, unchurched group of people."

By the time Thomas arrived, the swirling social forces of the late 1960s were altering many Holy Cross traditions. Student resident assistants replaced Jesuits in the dorms. The college permitted students to entertain women in their residence halls. Mandatory daily Mass was ended. Students could bring alcohol to their rooms.

One of the biggest changes to hit Holy Cross was the arrival of a significant number of black students. Thomas was among nineteen new black students in the fall of 1968. Even with the influx, the school was just 1.2 percent black. But for a school long populated largely by Boston-area Irish Catholics, that amounted to a transformation.

It wasn't an easy one. Black students accused the school of making phone calls to the homes of white students, asking whether they objected to having black roommates. Some did object. One white student sought a transfer after discovering that his roommate was black. Once, a carload of white students came close to running down a black student who was walking on campus; there were even reports of death threats against black students. A survey of Holy Cross students taken during Thomas's time there found that 49 percent of the respondents agreed with the statement "Negroes tend to have less ambition." Nearly a third agreed that Negroes "have looser morals than whites," and almost a quarter of those surveyed concurred with the statement that Negroes "smell different."

Despite those attitudes, Thomas said he fit right in with his white schoolmates. His first home was in Hanselman II, where he was warmly received. "My new dormitory was a fabulous place to live," he said. "I made friends quickly, and they made every effort to make my roommate and me feel accepted."

His roommate was John Siraco, a white transfer student from Northeastern University who majored in biology. Thomas said

Siraco was "very good for me. His side of the room was always neat, he had excellent study habits, he never patronized me." As always, Thomas was a dedicated student who would sometimes squeeze in a couple hours of studying before breakfast. An English major, Thomas said he chose the concentration mostly because he always struggled with English. He spent many evenings buried in his work in the library's basement stacks. He once petitioned school administrators to reverse a plan to reduce the library's Saturday night hours.

Among his professors, Thomas stood out for his determination and hard work. "He never talked very much in class," said Tom Lawler, an English professor. "He was the kind of person you really might not notice." Lawler remembers Thomas coming to his office to review a paper he had written in a particularly difficult literature course, Readings in Renaissance Prose. "I was pointing out corrections, mistakes, things like that," Lawler said. Thomas barely said a word. "I can almost see his face now, which was very quiet and a little overawed. That way of being silent, that is part of my memory of him. When I was going over his paper, he was looking at me almost as if he was appraising me or something."

Cut off from his grandfather's financial support, Thomas worked as a waiter and dishwasher at the school's Kimball dining hall to help cover his expenses. He worked as much as 5½ hours a day, earning $1.10 an hour. Wearing a white jacket, he carried a silver tray loaded with a dozen quart-size cartons of milk to the student tables. Next, he would bring out platters of food that were placed at the ends of each table. If he was on cleanup duty, he often wore a black stocking cap as he scraped plates and ran them through the kitchen's huge dishwasher. "Clarence would hand-catch the dishes as they came out of the dishwasher" steaming hot, said Tony Stankus, who grew up a half hour away in Hudson, Massachusetts, and worked alongside Thomas at Kimball. "Most people needed gloves. Another thing about him was that he was very studious. He used to always carry a paperback in his pocket that he would read during down periods."

But if Thomas appeared to be getting along just fine, he wasn't. Years later, he would say he was haunted by familiar feelings of exclusion, which puzzled many of his classmates, white and black, who remember him as approachable—even jovial. "I felt alienated, like you'd be in a foreign country," Thomas said. Holy Cross, he concluded, was "lonely, miserable, and cold."

Just months after coming to Holy Cross, Thomas was among the group of students who helped form the school's first Black Student Union. He was the secretary-treasurer and he personally typed the constitution and bylaws. The group pressed the school to increase the recruitment of black students and faculty. It also secured the use of a van to transport members to parties given by black students at nearby colleges. The BSU helped support a free breakfast program in Worcester, and Thomas and other students would rise before the sun once or twice a week and venture into town to cook and serve meals for poor families. The BSU also sponsored concerts and events such as the 1971 Black Arts Symposium, a weekend of dance, film, and discussion capped by lectures by civil rights activist Bayard Rustin.

In short order, the student group would become a major part of Thomas's campus life, launching what he now refers to as his "radical years." It is a phrase he often utters with regret: I was once a radical, "then I grew up," as he put it during a 2001 lecture at James Madison University. Other times, he invokes it in a way that seems aimed at surprising those likely to be suspicious of his conservative views. Supreme Court clerks, particularly those who work for liberal justices, say that Thomas frequently mentions his college experiences working in the Black Panther–style free breakfast program and marching against the Vietnam war and for minority rights.

The nation was still reeling from the assassinations of King and

Senator Robert F. Kennedy when Thomas arrived at Holy Cross. The expanding war in Vietnam radicalized students, who were taking part in massive peace demonstrations and targeting defense contractors for protests. Students openly smoked marijuana and experimented with psychedelic drugs. Authority was being called into question everywhere.

The Revolutionary Student Union, a self-described organization of "young socialists and communists dedicated to the destruction of the internationalist capitalist system," was formed at Holy Cross in 1969. Among other things, it called for abolition of the Reserve Officers' Training Corps (ROTC) at the school and railed against the military-industrial complex. Black students, meanwhile, complained about the sometimes hostile racial atmosphere on campus, often punctuating their grievances with revolutionary flourishes.

Edward P. Jones, who would go on to win the 2004 Pulitzer Prize for fiction, invoked a series of racial incidents that occurred on campus to explain a growing separatist attitude among black students. It was he who claimed that Holy Cross administrators called white freshmen to ask if they would be willing to room with "a Negro" before the fall semester in 1968. He also said black students were subject to anonymous death threats and racist remarks. A white student leader, he said, openly talked of banning black women from Holy Cross mixers, a proposal that Jones said had broad support at Holy Cross.

"The more Holy Cross people have tried to avoid the reality of racism at Holy Cross, especially the students, the greater evidence of such flows in," Jones wrote at the time in an alternative student publication. He added that "as slight suspicions are increasingly confirmed, a somewhat total interaction among whites is decreased and replaced by the need to survive." A sketch of a black revolutionary spraying gunfire from an automatic weapon accompanied his piece. The caption read: "For every act of aggression waged upon us, we will unleash the ultimate political consequences upon the oppressor."

This kind of rhetoric was in the air as Thomas found himself free in a relatively uncloistered environment for the first time in his life. For him, there was no more seminary and no more of his grandfather's iron rules. He put a poster of Malcolm X on the wall of his dorm room, and he immersed himself in Malcolm's speeches. Just a couple of years earlier, Thomas had donned a black cassock for his trips back to St. Pius in search of recruits for the priesthood. But at Holy Cross, he most often wore army fatigues. He grew his hair out into a nappy Afro, which he sometimes parted down the middle. Often he topped his outfit with a leather jacket and a beret, Pantherstyle. He almost always wore his black combat boots. A Holy Cross friend, James Millet, recalls once asking Thomas, "What's with the boots?"

"In case I get in a fight," Thomas replied.

Still, Thomas studied hard, and he was always encouraging his black colleagues to do the same in order to prove they belonged. "He came across like a philosopher from the South," said Gordon Davis, a classmate. "A lot of things he said made sense. When he talked, people listened." He also was one of the guys—he played touch football and ran one year of varsity track. His nickname, "Cooz," followed him to the basketball courts of Holy Cross, where the real Bob Cousy had played before going on to stardom with the Boston Celtics. Occasionally, Thomas would sit around with his friends guzzling Boone's Farm wine and talking trash. He was notorious among his buddies for having a foul mouth and ribald sense of humor. Usually, though, he was the proper, perfect gentleman, almost chivalrous, they said. He even once penned a poem—"Is You Is or Is You Ain't"—exhorting black men to respect black women.

But then there was the rest of the time—his raunchy moments.

"There were some things that would completely shock me in terms of sexual jokes," said Davis. Such behavior apparently was not uncommon. Al Coleman, a BSU member whom Thomas knew from Savannah, had gotten kicked out of school but still hung around, camping in friends' rooms on extra mattresses. He also had a girlfriend in town and, apparently, he used the mattresses for more than sleeping. Millet, a 1972 Holy Cross graduate, remembers Thomas coming into a room where Coleman had stayed and sitting down on the mattress. Thomas looked around for a moment before announcing: "Excuse me. This smells like somebody has been fucking on this thing."

The discussions among students in Thomas's social circles could go anywhere, but they frequently came back to race. Eddie Jenkins, a football star at Holy Cross, said some of the brothers at the school once held a mock trial for a comrade caught dating a white woman. The tribunal found the accused guilty as charged and imposed its penalty: "We broke his Afro comb and threw it out of the door," Jenkins said with a laugh. After the verdict, Jenkins added, "I think he and his girlfriend took their bicycles and rode to Montreal."

The trial was a joke, but the prevailing sentiment against interracial dating was real. In its eleven-point statement of principles, the BSU included this plank: "The Black Man does not want or need the white woman." Thomas—who years later would engender scorn among some of his black critics for having married a white woman—was among those who helped enforce the sanction.

Looking out of a window at the Hogan Campus Center during one BSU meeting, Thomas spotted a particularly attractive black woman from a nearby school strolling through a parking lot with a white guy. "Do I see a black woman with a white man?" Thomas said, according to Davis. "How could that be?" That edgy race consciousness was something that friends noticed in Thomas for years. Henry Terry, who graduated from Yale Law School a year after Thomas, said he always felt that Thomas resented his white wife. "A lot of black students, including Clarence, didn't like the fact that I was married to a white woman," Terry said. "He never said it, but people don't have to say it."

At Holy Cross football games, black students would stake out the best seats, right on the 50-yard line. White students were not allowed. Before one game, there was a rumor that a group of white guys from one of the dorms was going to try to claim the perch. So some of the black students came to the game with ax handles hidden under their coats and in their bags—just in case. "We figured it was our boy out there, Joe Willie," said Dhafir Jihad, explaining that the black students wanted the good seats to watch Joe Wilson, a star running back who went on to play professionally. But there was no confrontation. "We carried our sticks and went where we always go," said Jihad, whose name was Doug Johnson before he converted to Islam. "For four years, we owned the fifty-yard line." Thomas was part of that, he said. "In school he got down like the rest of us," Jihad said. "He was involved in the climate of the times."

Thomas was particularly outspoken at the BSU's Sunday night meetings, which almost always were lively affairs. To begin with, the intellectual firepower of the group was top-notch. Ted Wells, for example, would go on to become one of the nation's top lawyers. The dapper Wells often lined up opposite Thomas in the debates at BSU meetings. Interestingly, their intense but respectful rivalry would continue later in life as Thomas gravitated toward conservatism and Wells became a board member of the NAACP Legal Defense and Educational Fund, a civil rights group that opposes many of the positions Thomas has taken on the Supreme Court. They would serve together as Holy Cross trustees.

Others in the group also went on to distinguish themselves professionally. Clifford Hardwick became city attorney of Atlanta. Malcolm Joseph became an air force doctor and for a while staffed Air Force Two. Stanley Grayson went on to become a deputy mayor of New York City and later an investment banker. Jones became a bestselling novelist who won a $500,000 MacArthur Foundation "genius award" and a Pulitzer Prize. Jenkins earned a Super Bowl ring with the Miami Dolphins before becoming a lawyer and political figure in Boston.

Thomas may have been a quiet student who rarely talked in class, but frequently he was at the center of the action during BSU meetings. He liked to play devil's advocate, taking boldly contrary positions that seemed calculated mainly to incite debate. "The first thing he'd throw out there, you'd know he wasn't serious," said Jenkins, adding that he could "turn on a dime and reduce you to intellectual rubble."

Thomas asserted his independence when the BSU confronted its first real controversy in 1969, when the group demanded that the administration set up a black corridor in one of the dormitories. Arthur Martin, the BSU president, explained that "a black corridor will make it possible for us to relax in our own environment." As things were, he said, "black students feel like they are constantly on display and find it difficult to be themselves." The BSU passed the measure 24–1. Thomas was the lone holdout. He argued that blacks had not come to Holy Cross to segregate themselves from whites. When the administration granted the request, Thomas struck his own compromise: The following fall, he moved to the black corridor in the school's Healy dormitory, but he brought along Siraco, his white roommate.

Thomas's vote on the black corridor reflected his oft-repeated belief that black students at Holy Cross should mingle with and learn from whites. "His message was: In order to compete in our society, you've got to compete with them, as in white folks," said Bob Tomlinson, a Holy Cross graduate who went on to become an air force colonel.

Through the years, Thomas's belief in integration wavered. He would bitterly recall how integration led to the demise of Pius, the all-black high school in Savannah that launched many black professionals. As a justice, he would write passionately about the effectiveness of historically black colleges and in opposition to school busing for desegregation, warning that integration often comes at a steep cost to black traditions, communities, and achievement.

At Holy Cross, even as he complained that he felt alienated from many whites and as he was drawn toward radicalism, Thomas still forged relationships with mostly white, mainstream organizations on campus. He wrote for the weekly student newspaper, the *Crusader*, chronicling events such as the school's experiment in allowing women from nearby colleges to cross-register for classes at Holy Cross, which preceded the school's going coed in 1972. Steve Urbanczyk, who helped start an alternative paper, *Today*, recalled the *Crusader* as an "establishment newspaper" that "was way too conservative and too much an organ of the college."

In his junior year, Thomas was the only black student in his class selected for Purple Key, a campus service organization that did things such as help students on move-in day and participate in parents' weekend. He also was inducted into Alpha Sigma Nu, the Jesuit honor society. "He was more conservative even then than the others were," observed Father John E. Brooks, then a Holy Cross vice president who was the driving force behind the school's efforts to recruit black students. "I don't think people saw him as a far-off leftist or anything. I didn't see him as a radical."

Thomas kept his feet planted in two worlds at Holy Cross, one white and the other black. It was unclear whether he was comfortable in either. Years later, Thomas said the pressure he felt being a black student at mostly white Holy Cross led him to seriously consider dropping out on several occasions, despite carrying the kind of grade point average that would later allow him to graduate cum laude. Once, he went so far as to pack all his gear in his trunk, determined to leave. But Father Brooks talked him into staying. "I had decided that it was true, what the other blacks had been saying— that Holy Cross was a crusher, that it would break your spirit," Thomas said.

Thomas fell into his first serious romantic relationship early in his junior year when Eddie Jenkins introduced him to a young woman from nearby Anna Maria College. Her name was Kathy Ambush, and a week after meeting her, Thomas told Jenkins he was in love.

Ambush was blessed with a wonderful singing voice and a feisty spirit that sometimes was obscured by a quiet demeanor. Hers was a loving, stable, socially conscious family and it welcomed Thomas with open arms. Nelson Ambush, Kathy's father, who worked as a dental technician and was a longtime NAACP fixture in Worcester, recalls meeting Thomas on the Holy Cross campus. They sat outside one of the campus buildings and chatted about the young man's life and his plans. "That's how we got to know each other," Ambush said.

The Ambush home was always open to the friends of the four children in the family, and before long Thomas was a regular. He would come over for dinner, shoot pool in the basement, help trim the hedges, stop by after jogging to take a shower. As time went by, he accompanied the Ambushes on camping trips around New England and joined them for holiday dinners. In many ways, the Ambushes were the kind of tight-knit, open-minded family Thomas never had. Thomas and his grandfather were on the outs, his mother was occupied with her own life, and his trips home to Savannah were infrequent.

Thomas dated Kathy for the remainder of his Holy Cross years and they were married on June 5, 1971—one day after his graduation. His mother and grandmother made the trip to Worcester for the occasion. Thomas's grandfather stayed behind in Savannah.

The marriage collapsed after just over a decade, but Thomas remained on good terms with the Ambush family. Many years later, he would still write warm letters to his former father-in-law to express appreciation for the time they spent together. In 2002, Thomas wrote: "I have been thinking recently that prior to buying my own motor home the only camping trips I had been on were with you. I can still remember packing and all the fun we had setting camp with you. In case I never said it, thank you so much."

During the middle of his junior year, Thomas played a pivotal role in the school's first major racial crisis. The Revolutionary Student Union, joined by several black students, led a protest in the school's

Hogan Campus Center against job recruiters from General Electric. GE was singled out because of an ongoing strike and its work as a major defense contractor. As nearly forty other students chanted, shouted slogans, and cheered them on, twenty demonstrators formed a human wall, blocking students from interviewing with GE. School administrators were livid about the flagrant violation of its open-campus policy. They were able to identify sixteen of the protesters—twelve whites and four blacks—and targeted them for expulsion.

The BSU was outraged because the punishment fell disproportionately on black students: Four out of the five blacks involved in the protest were brought up for disciplinary action, while only a quarter of the whites who had taken part in the demonstration faced expulsion. When the school's administrators failed to be moved by the BSU's grievances, the group met in a heated session to figure out the next step. Almost immediately, there was near-unanimous support for taking over a building on campus to draw public attention to the injustice. But as the students brainstormed the details of a takeover, Thomas spoke up. "I don't know about you guys, but the way I was raised was that if someone is treating me unfairly, they are demonstrating to me that I am simply not welcome," he said. All the school's black students, he felt, should just leave. "It was his suggestion alone," recalls Clifford Hardwick. "There were a lot of amens around the room and that's what we decided to do."

The school's Judicial Board moved ahead with the expulsions the next day, propelling the black students into action. Just hours after the 3 a.m. board decision, black students agreed to meet at Hogan for the walkout. Thomas may have sounded bold in proposing it, but inside he was sick: "What would I tell my grandparents who had suffered far more indignities than I had? What would I tell my neighbors? What would I say to my friends who had always said that the 'man' wasn't going to let me do anything?"

He was hardly alone in worrying about throwing away a college education. "I think the feeling of wondering whether this was the right thing to do was on everybody's mind," said Leonard Cooper, another student who took part. Still, about sixty black students—virtually the school's entire black population—walked out. Eddie Jenkins remembers looking down the hill from the Hogan Campus Center to see if Thomas would be among them. Soon enough, Thomas appeared in the distance, trudging toward Hogan with his suitcase in hand. "He was the last one up the hill with his bag," Jenkins said.

The Hogan ballroom was full of curious onlookers as the black students filtered in. With hundreds of students and administrators looking on, Arthur Martin and Ted Wells read a brief statement to the press. The black students then tossed their identification cards on a table and filed out to a waiting line of cars that whisked them off campus.

News of the demonstration was picked up by papers around the country. Meanwhile, white students at Holy Cross called for a campuswide strike, increasing the pressure on school administrators to fix the problem. Members of the school's Judicial Board met that afternoon in the president's office to discuss modifying their decision. "I personally felt that the loss of the black students would be a real tragedy for the students involved and for the college," the Reverend Raymond J. Swords, the president of the college, wrote in a special report to parents and alumni about the incident.

Within two days, the school administration backed down, rescinding the expulsions and granting amnesty to all the protesters. The black students, most of whom never left Worcester, returned to campus victorious.

"Whether or not the blacks went home or not does not really matter. They were willing to forget Holy Cross and make new futures," Thomas wrote later that week in the *Crusader*. "The blacks acted as men, and that was all that counted. They did not plan to compromise manhood for a 'good' education, and didn't."

Later that year, Thomas ran for president of the BSU against Wells, a popular figure whom Thomas frequently compared himself with. "Ted was the quintessential smooth, eloquent, tall, light-skinned, good-looking guy," Hardwick said. "Clarence was the antithesis of this."

Most BSU members assumed Wells would walk away with the election. But the vote turned out to be a surprise: Thomas won a narrow victory mostly because of a feeling among BSU members that Wells's ego was getting out of control. "People didn't like Ted's swagger," Jenkins said. But the group also did not really want Thomas as president, either. He was more comfortable challenging convention and laying out his own views than doing the hard work of forging consensus. Within minutes of the vote, there was a motion to reconsider it. Thomas didn't object and this time Wells won handily.

"I wouldn't be surprised if Clarence voted for Ted Wells the second time," Jenkins said. "I think Clarence was relieved. He went back to doing what he does best—being a dart thrower."

Some of Thomas's Holy Cross friends think otherwise. They believe the episode drove a wedge between him and the BSU. "I don't think Clarence ever felt the same about BSU after that," Cooper said. "I don't blame him."

In recent years, Wells has hosted a couple of reunions for black Holy Cross alumni at his palatial New Jersey home. Most of the men come to relive old times and catch up with changes in their lives. But Thomas stays away, ignoring the invitations extended to him. Wells says that Thomas has simply had scheduling conflicts that prevented him from coming. Still, his absence is a subject of speculation among many of his BSU friends, who were almost to a man supportive during his confirmation travails. Some wrote him letters of encouragement and many of them turned out for a big party in his honor at a Washington hotel after his unofficial swearing-in on the White House lawn. Some wonder whether Thomas is still sensitive because he and Wells bumped heads so often as students. Others suspect that he does not want to have to defend the radical shift in his political views that has occurred since his college days.

"He probably feels he'll be cornered and somebody would get in

his face and say, 'You handkerchief head motherfucker,' " said Jenkins, only half joking.

Which would seem incongruous for a man who professes to love
intellectual challenge and arguing ideas. But the fact is, Thomas usually avoids rip-roaring debate. Most of his public appearances are
before safe crowds—students, respectful lawyers and judges, ideological soul mates. On the rare occasion he agrees to a controversial
engagement—for instance, the 1998 convention of an association of
black lawyers and judges—he refuses to submit to questioning.

So the Q & A session that followed Thomas's Hanify-Howland
Memorial lecture at his alma mater in 2002 was especially intriguing. Much of Thomas's talk in the packed Hogan ballroom was about
the drawbacks of taking unpopular stands. As Thomas put it, the
emphasis on civil discourse has triggered the "silence of self-
censorship." His charge: Stand up for your convictions. Don't be in-
timidated.

This was just the opening Gordon Davis needed. He had rarely
seen Thomas since their days together at Holy Cross, so when he
was called on during the Q & A portion of the program, he reintro-
duced himself and Thomas said he remembered him. Davis then
complained about Thomas's views on school desegregation, abortion, and police authority. He called him "a token" on the court who
had benefited from affirmative action but now opposes it. "How can
you do that? How can you do that without being a hypocrite? That's
my question."

"Well, it's not much of a question," Thomas replied. "It's more of
an assertion."

Davis persisted, saying that Thomas's race played a part in his
even coming to Holy Cross. "No, buddy, I was a transfer student,"
Thomas replied. And when Davis maintained that the same had been
true of Thomas's admission to Yale Law School, the justice just rolled
his eyes. In the end, he wound up dismissing Davis's questions as
"based on false premises" and thus unworthy of a response.

Davis, an engineer in Massachusetts, reflected on the encounter later, recalling the days when the black student population of Holy Cross was sparse and he and Thomas and the others were enlisted to recruit more black students with the understanding that those with good grades would be given full rides. "The Clarence Thomas I knew would've been more honest and frank, and not hypocritical about that situation," Davis said. "Every job he got, every admission he got in education, race was a factor. It just sticks in my throat." The Clarence Thomas he knew at Holy Cross was a good man, Davis said, someone who did social work, told a few bawdy jokes, was a big brother to the students from Georgia. Not an outcast. "When I knew him, he was good guy. The person I saw on that stage, I'm not sure who he was."

During his final year and a half at Holy Cross, Thomas took part in a fair share of student protests. But, he would later say, his heart wasn't in it. His rebelliousness was fading and he found himself drawn again to the values that guided him as he was growing up, the values espoused by his grandfather. In April 1970, while attending a large demonstration in Cambridge, Massachusetts, to "free political prisoners," he has repeatedly told audiences, he heard a voice in his head telling him he was traveling on the wrong road.

The epiphany occurred during what was reported at the time to be the worst disorder in Cambridge's history. According to a *Boston Globe* account, the violent disturbance involved three thousand youths and two thousand police from seven jurisdictions, a melee that lasted for more than four hours. Stores were looted and windows smashed in the Harvard Square area. Dozens of fires were set in the streets—a bank was briefly ablaze and two police cars burned. Demonstrators hurled rocks, bricks, and bottles at the police, and the police administered beatings to at least two dozen demonstrators. In all, nearly two hundred people were injured, including seventeen police officers.

What began as a march and rally had been organized by a white radical youth group known as the November Action Coalition. Its purpose was to protest the New Haven trial of Black Panther leader Bobby Seale. He and other Panthers had been charged with conspiracy to kidnap, torture, and murder a fellow Panther. The Panthers maintained that police had killed their cohorts.

The events of that night have never left Thomas's memory. "I finally began to question openly what had happened to me," he recalled. "It should have been obvious. I was becoming drunk with anger. I had become addicted to being a victim of oppression, and I was angry that whites controlled the fate of blacks." His anger, he said, was made worse by living on Holy Cross's black corridor, which he felt limited his opportunity to broaden as a person and fed an irrational sense of victimhood. "I was consumed by animosity even though little had happened to me personally and even though I got along fine with all of the other students with whom I came in contact and even though I was doing just fine academically. I was angry for all oppression and injustice, not mine personally."

Years later, such somber mea culpas would be a standard part of Thomas speeches. Even in private, he openly wonders why he was so willing to demonstrate on behalf of the Angela Davises, Bobby Seales, and Huey Newtons. As he asked one recent visitor to his chambers: Who were they? He did not know them personally and could not vouch for their values.

So he has become Thomas the apologist—except when he uses his participation in protests to credential himself as a former activist. Mostly, though, he looks back on his years of rebellion as foolhardy. He was rude and disrespectful, he says, and wasted time that would have been better spent soaking up more of what Holy Cross had to offer. "I prayed that I would be relieved of the anger and the animosity that ate at my soul," he has said. "I did not want to hate anymore, and I had to stop before it totally consumed me. I had to make a fundamental choice. Do I believe in the principles of this country or not? After such angst, I concluded that I did."

From then on, Thomas gradually narrowed his focus to his class work at Holy Cross. He was always a hardworking student and his discipline paid off with stellar grades. He made up his mind to put his education to use righting the wrongs that he had witnessed growing up in segregated Savannah. He thought he would be a civil rights lawyer—an ambition that many of his detractors now find cruelly ironic.

"The reason I became a lawyer was to make sure that minorities, individuals who did not have access to this society, gained access," Thomas said during his Supreme Court confirmation hearings. "I may differ with others on how best to do that, but the objective has always been to include those who have been excluded."

He aimed for the top in law schools, applying to Harvard, Penn, and Yale. Yale offered the most financial aid and that's where he decided to go. Upon graduation from Holy Cross, he told an interviewer for the school's news service that he planned to go to Yale and then return to the South "to begin helping some people."

Thomas was rethinking his racial views by then, but racial realities constantly confronted him. During the break between the end of his senior year and graduation, he traveled from Worcester to New Haven to interview for a summer job and to look for a place to live with his new wife. When he arrived at one prospective rental unit, the landlady seemed skeptical, asking to see his marriage license. He was annoyed, according to James Millet, who accompanied him on the trip. The two later stopped at a restaurant for lunch. A friendly white waitress came over and began lavishing attention on Thomas. Drawing close to him, she said: "Now, what can I do for you, honey?" Thomas flinched. The waitress noticed, remarking to Millet: "What's the matter with him?" Millet, who grew up in the nation's capital, didn't explain. He knew that Thomas—who had little experience with women of any race and none that his friends knew of with white women—felt he had to be careful around white women. It was something he had learned being raised in the South.

But Thomas's racial concerns would take a back seat to the impending excitement of law school. "He always said he wanted to be the best black lawyer in the world," observed Millet.

Just the best *black* lawyer? It was an odd aspiration for a man who would go on to find himself burdened by racial labels and the expectations that came with them.

6

THE MAKING OF A CONSERVATIVE

onfronted with demands to increase the number of black students, Yale Law School experimented with a couple of affirmative action efforts before settling on a plan that was in effect when
Clarence Thomas was accepted. The program called for about 10
percent of each entering class to be minorities. Those applicants
were admitted to the nation's most exclusive law school if officials
concluded they were smart enough to benefit more by attending
Yale than by going to a less rigorous law school. In short, Yale officials wanted to know not only whether minority students could do
the work but also whether they would thrive at the school. The
practical effect of that standard was that black and other minority
students did not have to be in the very first rank of candidates. But
they could not lag far behind.

"They had to be good," says Abraham Goldstein, who served as
dean of the law school between 1970 and 1975. Yale officials cannot
say whether Thomas would have been admitted to the prestigious
law school without affirmative action, a fact that still galls him more
than three decades later. "This is because admissions among people
of top ability are always highly subjective," another former Yale Law

School dean, Guido Calabresi, testified when the question was raised during Thomas's Supreme Court confirmation hearings.

When Thomas arrived in 1971, he was among only thirteen minority students—twelve blacks and one Hispanic—in a first-year class of 175. That figure marked a steep reduction in the number of minority students from the previous two years, when the school admitted a larger number of minority students—some of whom proved unprepared for Yale's rigors—under more ambitious affirmative action schemes. The decline irritated many black students at Yale.

Thomas initially shared their sentiments—friends remember him speaking up during informal student discussions about the need for Yale to bolster its affirmative action efforts. His view was part of a general race consciousness that he voiced early in his law school career. He was in favor of affirmative action and he distrusted standardized tests, those seemingly objective measures of merit that some say do not reliably predict black success. Early on at Yale, for example, Thomas was close to joining an effort by the NAACP Legal Defense and Educational Fund to challenge bar exams across the South. Blacks were failing the licensing tests disproportionately, and civil rights lawyers suspected the reason was an effort by Southern states to suppress the number of black lawyers. In the end, Thomas did not take part in the challenge. And before long his views shifted, in no small part because of the attitudes and people he came across at Yale.

As a Supreme Court justice, Thomas remains wary of tests that purport to gauge merit. But his suspicion is eclipsed by his feeling that affirmative action only undermines the accomplishments of black students. It was at Yale that Thomas first encountered white classmates who were openly skeptical of his credentials. If Yale could not say whether he would have been admitted had he been white, who could blame white students for questioning his presence there? Even some instructors at the generally liberal law school shared the feeling that black students did not measure up. Lovida Coleman, a classmate of Thomas's, remembered joining a group of black students for lunch with Ralph K. Winter Jr., a member of the admissions committee and one of the few conservatives on the Yale faculty (and now a federal appeals court judge), who said flatly that there were no black students at the law school qualified to be there.

The comment was outrageous on its face, but it left some students flustered. "I was upset," Coleman said in an interview, adding that over the years she became convinced that Winter—who had been Thurgood Marshall's first law clerk when Marshall was an appeals court judge—probably meant the comment as a challenge to Yale's black students. When Thomas heard about it, he took it to heart. He felt he had earned his way into Yale and the only reason someone would think otherwise was because affirmative action blurred the picture. "This thing about how they let me into Yale— that kind of stuff offends me," Thomas once told an interviewer. "All they did was stop stopping us."

Goldstein does not remember much grumbling among the faculty about the separate admissions standards applied to minority students, although he allows that some backlash was inevitable. "We never talked about there being a different criterion," he says. "But maybe it was in the air. . . . I recall edgy situations but not important problems."

As much as Thomas disliked having his credentials questioned, he also hated the idea that affirmative action at Yale seemed to help black people who least needed it—the mostly light-skinned children of the black professional class. As Thomas saw it, they were the same caste of people—the self-important sons and daughters of doctors, dentists, lawyers, and educators—who he felt excluded his family from the upper social reaches of black Savannah. Thomas resented them, and his years at Yale only heightened his feeling.

Jeffrey Zuckerman, a fellow Yalie who served as chief of staff for Thomas when he headed the Equal Employment Opportunity Commission, says Thomas mentioned that one of his black Yale classmates hailed from Scarsdale, a wealthy suburb of New York City. Why did that person qualify for affirmative action? Thomas wondered. To him, affirmative action had the insidious effect of diminishing the achievements of hardworking minority students who would have made it without any outside help, while too frequently awarding its benefits to privileged black folks from places like Scarsdale. Worse, he concluded, affirmative action turned the reality of race on its head. At places like Yale, he felt, the assumption was that black students had it made—which certainly wasn't the case in most of the rest of the world, including back in Savannah. "Thomas, as he told it, was struck that at law school everyone was saying how far he got because of his race," recalled Zuckerman, "while at home, everyone was saying how far he had gotten despite his race."

Two of Thomas's best friends at Yale were Frank Washington and Harry M. Singleton, fellow black students who, like Thomas, were the first in their families to go to college. The three called themselves "the triumvirate," and they would spend hours debating the issues of the day, sometimes over a few beers or some cheap wine. In many ways, they saw themselves as distinct from their other black classmates. "We had to sort of pull ourselves up by our own bootstraps in a way that made us a self-defining fraternity," Washington says.

While black classmates say Thomas mingled easily among them, he was nonetheless acutely aware of their backgrounds—and he sorted them accordingly. Clarence Martin, a fellow summer associate at a Savannah law firm Thomas worked at following his second year at Yale, remembered his confiding that William T. Coleman IV—whose father was a prosperous lawyer and went on to be the first black secretary of transportation—was not an up-by-his-bootstraps guy. Coleman, who also worked that summer at the Savannah firm, was all right, Thomas would say, but "he was not like us"—meaning he was more privileged.

Such class distinctions did not fade in his mind even as he climbed to the pinnacle of his profession. Years later as a Supreme Court justice, Thomas would mock his black law school classmates for being part of what he saw as a privileged, out-of-touch elite. Affirmative action may be best justified as a policy to remedy the effects of past and present racial discrimination, but in Thomas's view it does almost nothing to uplift the masses of disadvantaged black people—his people, as he sees it—while doling out coveted university slots, jobs, and government contracts to those who were already well off. For him, his fellow black students at Yale were Exhibit A.

Some of that disdain no doubt helped Thomas mask his insecurity. Two years before Thomas came to Yale, the law school abandoned traditional letter grades and formal class rankings for a modified pass-fail system that allowed students to earn one of four marks: honors, pass, low pass, and fail. The laid-back grading mechanism was just one sign of the intellectual assurance and academic freedom that permeated Yale. The students were assumed to be the nation's best and brightest—and they did not need grades or formal class rankings to prove it. Yet, if Yale was a comfortable place for those who knew they were top students, it was daunting for those like Thomas who were unsure of where they stood. Certainly, Thomas had done very well at Holy Cross, but Yale was a new, more difficult world. And for him, being black only made that world harder to negotiate.

"You had to prove yourself every day because the presumption was that you were dumb and didn't deserve to be there on merit," Thomas told an interviewer during a meeting of black conservatives in 1980. "Every time you walked into a law class at Yale, it was like having a monkey jump down on your back from the Gothic arches."

Thomas set out to conquer Yale in much the same way he had engaged every other academic challenge he ever faced: by outworking everyone else. He and his wife Kathy took a tiny apartment off campus, but Thomas spent precious little time there. Usually he arrived on campus in time to meet other students for breakfast at 7 a.m. After that, it was on to class and then to study, often in a carrel on the library's third floor. Thomas also worked part time at the New Haven Legal Assistance Association, screening poor people seeking free legal services. Many days, he did not return home until close to midnight. The schedule had to be hell on his new marriage—one friend described Kathy, who at one point took a job as a bank teller, as subdued. But the rigorous routine was necessary for Thomas to make it at Yale.

Fellow students and professors remember Thomas typically sitting in the back of his classes, making contributions only when called on. He was more distinctive in his dress. He discarded the revolutionary garb he favored at Holy Cross for a country aesthetic. Instead of fatigues, he wore bib overalls or work pants held up by suspenders. He kept his black combat boots, but a floppy denim hat replaced his beret. Once he rose to prominence, some teachers and classmates interpreted Thomas's clothing choices as defiant affirmation of his unpretentious, rural roots, even if others saw them as more reflective of the sorry state of his finances.

"He dressed like a Georgia farm boy," says Quintin Johnstone, one of Thomas's favorite professors at Yale. "He looked like he came right out of a cornfield. There was no pretense by the man at all."

Ever race conscious, Thomas did his best to stay away from classes that he feared would mark him as black. He once told an interviewer that he avoided most civil rights courses, even if he ended up taking the summer job at the law firm in Savannah, which was known for its civil rights work, before his final year in law school. At school, he focused on property, antitrust, and other business law courses.

In the cafeteria, he always sat at the unofficial "black table," where one of the few whites known to integrate the mealtime conversations was future president Bill Clinton, who moved easily among his law school classmates. Thomas's black friends remember Thomas as outspoken, thoughtful, and animated. The whites at Yale knew a different Thomas, a quiet, earnest colleague who worked hard to both get by and fit in. That pattern of perception would follow him throughout his career as Thomas showed different parts of his personality to blacks and whites.

Although Thomas worked hard to be accepted as an equal by whites at Yale, he often felt he wasn't. He complained to friends about being underestimated because he was black. He was convinced that white professors took white male students more seriously than black students. "It's nothing but politics," Thomas would say to one of his black classmates, to explain what he saw as the unspoken advantage accorded the white guys at Yale.

In the spring of his first year, Thomas took a property law class from Johnstone, a notoriously tough professor, and managed only a "low pass." Thomas flirted with dropping out of Yale not long after that. The doubts raised by the poor grade were just part of the problem "I didn't belong there. I didn't fit in. I was unhappy," Thomas told one interviewer. "I was twenty-something years old. I was married. . . . I was working. I had no money. I had no clothes. How was I supposed to feel? I'm working every hour I can at New Haven Legal Assistance. I live in a little, dumpy one-room apartment. It wasn't dumpy, but it was one room. I see all sorts of injustices in society. How are you supposed to feel?"

Johnstone, who was white, helped persuade Thomas to stick it out. And rather than shy away from the tough professor, Thomas not only took a second property law course with him but also chose to complete his senior dissertation under Johnstone's tutelage. On that final paper, he earned an "honors," the school's highest grade.

Thomas worked hard at Yale, but he also found time to play. He was a star in the law school's intramural football league and one year he was brought in as a ringer to quarterback the *Yale Law Journal*'s team in its annual game against its archrival, the *Harvard Law Review*.

Classmates also remember Thomas as a regular at a downtown New Haven movie theater that featured hard-core pornographic films. "He was into going to these porn flicks and coming back laughing about them," says Henry Terry, a Boston lawyer who graduated from Yale a year behind Thomas. On several occasions, classmates remember Thomas returning from the movies brimming with hilarious descriptions of orgies, bestiality, and other wild sex scenes.

"He did porn, he liked it," says another Yale classmate, Dan Johnson, adding that X-rated movies were widely popular among students. The law school itself would regularly show movies featuring explicit sex acts, and the screenings drew a large coed crowd of students, who treated the films mainly as comic relief from their daily grind. Johnson, now a lawyer in the San Francisco area, remembers waiting outside the law school auditorium with Thomas one evening for a showing of *Deep Throat*, a porn classic about a sexually frustrated woman who finds satisfaction once she discovers that her clitoris is located in the back of her throat. He remembers Thomas being all fired up about seeing the film. "My favorite movie of all time is *Deep Throat*," Thomas told Johnson. "I've seen that motherfucker six times."

Thomas's interest in pornography at Yale would surface during his Supreme Court confirmation hearings. But the full extent of it would not become known until after he had ascended to the Supreme Court. When it became known, some of Thomas's opponents thought it lent weight to Anita Hill's allegation that Thomas had sexually harassed her while he was her boss at two federal agencies. Among other things, Hill testified that Thomas would regale her with tales of bizarre sex acts he had seen in the movies. Although Thomas flatly denied her claim, his past activities made clear that he would have been familiar with such material.

In those days, such recreation hardly raised an eyebrow, as pornography bordered on the chic. In the early 1970s, the New York intelligentsia would queue up in Times Square to see movies such as *Deep Throat* and *The Devil in Miss Jones*. Lovida Coleman, who supported Thomas's Supreme Court nomination, said that she found Thomas's interest in porn at Yale neither offensive nor unusual. "Indeed, we would have been hypocrites to have been offended since very few of us failed to attend one or more similar films that were shown on the Yale University campus while we were in school," she said.

In an interview, Coleman said Thomas had a tight law school routine. On campus at 6 in the morning for an hour of study. Breakfast in the cafeteria at 7. More study. Classes. Work. Then late in the evening, he'd relax by going to see some porn with one of his buddies. "It was part of his disciplined routine," she said of the movies. Beyond his interest in blue movies, Thomas also had "the greatest collection of dirty jokes I've ever heard in my life," Johnson says. Once he told Johnson: "You're so lame that if you fell into a pit of titties you'd come up sucking your thumb."

Porno flicks, crude language, bad jokes—they were all part of the fabric of student life during Thomas's law school days. None of it stood out as odd to Johnson, who says Thomas's activities made him just a regular guy at Yale. "They can't accuse Thomas of being a womanizer, so they accuse him of making some lewd remarks to a woman when he was probably joking—because Clarence joked like that," Johnson says.

Thomas was a new father when he went to work the summer after his second year of law school at the Savannah firm of Hill, Jones and Farrington, one of the most prominent civil rights law firms in the South. The new addition in his and Kathy's lives no doubt lent urgency to his efforts to get a better fix on his future as a lawyer.

The firm had been founded by Bobby Hill, a celebrated lawyer who went on to prominence in the Georgia legislature before personal demons ruined his career prior to his death in 2000. Thomas deeply admired Hill and he arrived at the firm committed to its mission. Camped out in the second-floor library in the firm's office on the edge of Savannah's historic district, Thomas spent much of the summer working on a case involving black property owners on nearby Hilton Head island. Developers were trying to secure the land to add to the island's expanse of golf and tennis resorts, and Thomas's task was to help ensure that the owners got fair prices for their property. "He was a hard worker, serious-minded," says Fletcher Farrington, a former partner at the firm. Thomas had to search land titles and identify the owners of properties that had been handed down to as many as fifty heirs. Once he figured out who the owners were, he had to get their signatures on legal papers. "That required a lot of shoe leather," Farrington says, adding that Thomas did not seem to mind.

But if Thomas embraced the hard work that awaited him at the firm, he was surprised by the loose, raucous ways of his colleagues. Farrington says some of the lawyers partied almost as hard as they worked. After hours, they would drink and chase women and some of them would smoke a little pot, Farrington says. To his knowledge, Thomas never participated. After being nominated to the Supreme Court, Thomas would tell the White House that he indeed had smoked a little marijuana while in college, but that was not obvious to Farrington. "Clarence always struck me as a person that pays his bills, goes to church, goes home. He may have drank a beer here or there, but I didn't see it."

After work, Thomas would sometimes stop by to visit his friend Lester Johnson, and the conversation would inevitably turn to Thomas's job. "I think that Clarence was very disappointed in what he experienced when he was with Bobby's firm," Johnson says. "Bobby was a brilliant lawyer but Bobby did not have the kind of professionalism that one should have. Bobby, unfortunately, liked to drink, a lot, had numerous girlfriends even though he was married. You know, the classic situation."

By the end of the summer, Thomas had proven himself to be more than able and the partners let him know a full-time job awaited him when he graduated from Yale, the salary a not-too-shabby $12,000 a year. Thomas turned them down. He put the weight on his wife, saying she did not like Savannah, Farrington says. But his real reason, according to Johnson, was that he was disillusioned with the firm's freewheeling ways. "I just can't see working in that kind of environment," Thomas told Johnson. "In the office, the man is about the office, professionalism, get the job done," Johnson explains. "And that's one of the reasons why he didn't want to stay down here and work with Bobby."

Thomas entered his final year of law school focused mainly on the task of finding a job. His dreams had changed since he arrived at law school. If he came to Yale determined to be the best black lawyer in the world, who would right the wrongs of his hometown, now he was at least as interested in being well paid. Gone were the idealistic notions of returning home to "begin helping some people," as he put it upon graduating from Holy Cross. Once his grandfather had recovered from the hurt of Thomas's abandoning the seminary, the old man had embraced a new hope: that his grandson would put his legal education to use as a civil rights attorney in Savannah. But Thomas's experience at Hill's law firm squelched that. And he wanted no part of a full-time job being offered him by the New Haven Legal Assistance Association's law clinic.

Instead, Thomas set his sights on a good-paying post in a major law firm, the kind of job the white boys would respect. Thomas applied to and interviewed mostly with firms in the South, but to no avail. Thomas told journalist Juan Williams that he stalked out of several interviews when it was suggested he would be allowed to do pro bono work. Thomas was indignant because, from what he was told, that did not come up in his white classmates' interviews. "I went to law school to be a lawyer, not a social worker," Thomas fumed. "If I want to be a social worker, I'll do it on my own time."

Thomas's resentment mounted with the job rejections. All around him, classmates were nailing down promising positions, work befitting Yale graduates. "Most of the people got pretty good offers," says one black Yale classmate. Thomas, meanwhile, was collecting rejection letters. To this day, the Supreme Court justice keeps those letters in a neat pile in the basement of his Virginia home—a fact he frequently mentions when he delivers speeches touching on the disenchantment he felt as he finished law school.

Thomas was still looking for work when John C. "Jack" Danforth, the Republican attorney general of Missouri and a Yale graduate, returned to his alma mater in search of promising recruits. He contacted Guido Calabresi, one of his former law professors, for recommendations. "Danforth wanted somebody who was bright, preferably an African American," Calabresi says. Calabresi thought first of Rufus Cormier, who had graduated the previous spring. But Cormier, who went on to become the first black partner at a major firm in Texas, wanted no part of a low-paying government job in Jefferson City, Missouri. Instead, Cormier recommended Thomas. Cormier's only hesitation, Calabresi recalls, was that Thomas's politics might be "too far left" for him to be interested in working for a Republican attorney general—or any attorney general, for that matter. Although Thomas questioned affirmative action, he also was intrigued by the economic separatism championed by the Nation of Islam. His theory was that blacks would never get any respect from whites until they developed their own economic base. But as it turned out, Thomas, still in need of a job, was interested in talking and his name was given to Danforth.

Danforth, who later spent eighteen years in the Senate, where his reputation for integrity and his standing as an Episcopal minister earned him the nickname "Saint Jack," gave Thomas his first job out of Yale. He also became the political mentor who led Thomas to the Republican Party, and he eventually sponsored him all the way to the Supreme Court, standing by him through the storm of his confirmation hearings.

Danforth, an heir to the Ralston Purina fortune, and Thomas, the struggling kid from Pin Point, hit it off when they met at Yale to talk about the job. Later, when Thomas traveled to Jefferson City for a second round of interviews, his main concern was that he be treated like everyone else and not be given race-oriented work. Danforth agreed and offered Thomas a position that would make him the only black in the forty-five-lawyer office. Thomas took it but was ambivalent. The post paid under $11,000 a year, which was not the kind of salary he had in mind and much less than most of his classmates were commanding. When they heard about his job, "some of my classmates warned that I had wasted a Yale law degree," Thomas said years later. "Others laughed and some seemed to look at me with pity." Johnson, Thomas's friend from Savannah, remembers asking Thomas, "Why in the world would you want to go to Missouri?" Thomas replied: "Well, hey, man, it's the attorney general's office. They represent the state and it will be good experience."

Still, Thomas's disappointment was clear. Through the years, Thomas has noted in numerous speeches that his Yale law degree did not help him get the type of job he most wanted. That failure contributed to a rift between Thomas and Yale, and the damage remains. "I couldn't get a job out of Yale Law School," he told a group of black conservatives in 1998. "That's how much it did me. I ought to send them that degree back, too, while I'm at it."

Proudly displayed on the walls of Yale Law School are portraits of five former students and faculty members who went on to serve on the Supreme Court: William H. Taft, William O. Douglas, Potter Stewart, Abe Fortas, and Byron R. White. Thomas's picture is conspicuously absent and it is because of his lingering bitterness toward Yale.

Thomas supporters approached Dean Anthony T. Kronman in 1994, saying they were willing to raise money to have a portrait of Thomas commissioned for the school. Kronman twice traveled from New Haven to Washington to speak with Thomas about the prospect. On one occasion, the *Washington Post* reported, Kronman brought a judicial robe embroidered with the Yale Law coat of arms as a gift. Thomas was tickled to receive the robe and proved to be a warm host, spending nearly two hours with the Yale delegation. "He was totally engaging," says Michael Doyle, who was then head of Yale's alumni association. "All in all it was a grand occasion." Still, Thomas declined to have a portrait hung at the law school and the matter was eventually dropped.

"I think Clarence's feelings about the law school all come from the confirmation," Calabresi says. "I think he expected the school to rush to support him as a distinguished graduate being nominated to the Supreme Court. But that didn't happen. The idea that he would have full support from Yale was a rather lovely and romantic notion. The Yale Law School is anarchy. The idea that it would unanimously support anything is not in the nature of the place."

That reality has done little to assuage Thomas's hard feelings. Many conservatives who have gone to Yale, long known for its liberalism, have complained about what they see as the school's hostility to their views. Steven G. Calabresi, a Northwestern University law professor and nephew of the former Yale dean, felt strongly enough to help found the Federalist Society. Since its inception in 1982, the legal organization has become a bulwark of conservative jurisprudence, offering intellectual support for right-leaning legal theories and even helping to vet potential Supreme Court nominees for President George W. Bush.

As a justice, Thomas has occasionally laid out his bill of particulars against Yale to his law clerks. He was upset, he has said, that some professors testified against him. He also was rankled when Calabresi, who initially supported his confirmation, later declared that he thought both Thomas and fellow Yale graduate Hill were telling the truth, as each saw it, when it came to Hill's sexual harassment allegations against Thomas.

Drew S. Days III, who served as U.S. solicitor general from 1993 to 1996, was among the Yale faculty members who opposed Thomas's appointment to the high court. Days went before the Senate and testified that Thomas gave short shrift to the nation's history of racial discrimination. "I was concerned about how he would function as a Supreme Court justice," Days explains today. But, to Thomas, the slight was personal. And it was not forgotten. A visitor to Thomas's chambers says the justice still retains a special animus for Days. The visitor, who is white, was surprised to hear Thomas characterize Days as another of those light-skinned blacks who look down on blacks like him and can never accept them as equals.

Members of the Supreme Court regularly visit their old law schools for teaching and speaking engagements and are welcomed as returning heroes at class reunions. Not Thomas. He has not visited Yale in all his years on the high court. "People notice that he doesn't come to reunions," says Marvin Krakow, a Los Angeles lawyer who graduated from Yale with Thomas in 1974. "He's the most famous person in our class and he doesn't show up."

7

METEORIC RISE

Clarence Thomas's decision to begin his legal career working for Danforth put him in position to be catapulted to the upper reaches of the federal government and, in an amazingly short period of time, onto the Supreme Court. But none of that was obvious when Thomas arrived in St. Louis after graduating from law school in May 1974, still stewing about being rejected for the jobs he wanted most. He did draw the interest of a big Atlanta law firm before leaving Yale. But it was too late; he had already accepted Danforth's offer.

Thomas's first stop in Missouri, as he prepared to study for the bar exam, was an extra bedroom in the St. Louis home of Margaret Bush Wilson, a civil rights stalwart who later served nine years as national chairwoman of the NAACP. Wilson, the second black woman to practice law in Missouri, was on one level the type of person Thomas had always resented—light-skinned, a scion of the middle class, and active in a leading black sorority. Her mother had served on the executive committee of the St. Louis NAACP. Her father was a pioneering real estate broker whose advocacy contributed to a lawsuit resulting in a landmark Supreme Court decision outlawing racially restrictive housing covenants.

But despite their divergent pedigrees, Wilson and Thomas hit it off well and she stood by him years later when much of the nation's civil rights establishment opposed his nomination to the Supreme Court. Wilson admired what she saw as Thomas's intellectual independence, open-mindedness, and self-discipline, and she came to regard her summer boarder as a surrogate son. "He was an impressive young man; still is," Wilson says. "I have no quarrel with people who have a difference of opinion with me."

Thomas had come to Wilson's attention through Danforth. While sitting next to her at a dinner, Danforth told Wilson that he had hired a bright Yale graduate who needed somewhere to live while studying for the bar. St. Louis, he thought, would make for a much better summer experience than the sleepy state capital, Jefferson City. "Do you know of any place he might stay?" Danforth asked. Wilson did not hesitate. "He can stay in my home."

Before long, Thomas came to St. Louis, leaving his wife and young son behind at his in-laws' in Worcester, Massachusetts. Once there, he followed a strict daily regimen. First thing in the morning, Thomas would do push-ups or go down in the basement to work out with a set of weights left behind by Wilson's son, who was away at law school. After that, he would leave for his bar review class and to study, before reporting back to the house for supper.

Wilson, the veteran civil rights leader, and Thomas, the brooding iconoclast, would often discuss the issues of the day—welfare, school busing, affirmative action. The conversations left Wilson with the clear impression that Thomas—who had voted for liberal George McGovern for president in 1972—was on his way to becoming a full-blown conservative.

"We had great debates and discussions," she recalls. "I don't agree with all of his views and perspectives, but that's what this country is about, isn't it?"

Staying at Wilson's home was a godsend for Thomas, who was

pressed for money. "She provided me not only with room and board but advice, counsel, and guidance," Thomas said during his Supreme Court confirmation hearings. "As I left her house that summer, I asked her, 'How much do I owe you?' Her response was, 'Just along the way, help someone who is in your position.' "

After taking the bar examination in August 1974, Thomas retrieved his family and moved to Jefferson City to begin his legal career. Thomas was the only black attorney on Danforth's staff and he arrived determined to defeat any assumptions that might flow from that fact. He had no interest in practicing civil rights law, a point he had made emphatically when Danforth interviewed him for the job. He worried that such work would pigeonhole him as a "black lawyer," a fate that he felt would never allow him to be viewed as an equal by his white colleagues. It was an intriguing worry, given what he had told Holy Cross classmate James Millet about wanting to become the best "black lawyer" in the world. In conversations with coworkers, he made it clear that he was out to prove that he could make it without race being a factor.

Rhetorically, Thomas has advanced that position his entire professional life. He repeated it to coworkers and it is a regular theme of the advice he offers his numerous protégés. Don't take traditionally black jobs, he cautions, those posts will only mark you as suspect.

As it happened, Thomas violated his own advice at almost every turn. A lawyer who worked closely with Thomas, at both the Department of Education and the Equal Employment Opportunity Commission, remembers Thomas talking openly about being the senior black lawyer in the Reagan administration. Thomas thought—improbably but correctly—that such a distinction could one day land him on the Supreme Court.

Thomas often portrays himself as a reluctant but duty-bound public servant lifted to the nation's highest court purely by serendipity. He sometimes jokes that if his goal was to be on the Supreme Court, his route—from Jefferson City, to Senate aide, to Education Department official, to the helm of the EEOC, to the U.S. Court of Appeals—was most unusual. "The problem I have with that is there is a lack of precedence," Thomas once quipped.

But some of the people who knew Thomas during his sprint up the career ladder say he was seriously ambitious. "His feeling was, 'I am the highest ranking African American lawyer in the government and Thurgood Marshall is getting up in age. When they start looking around for a replacement, I want to be in position for that,' " recalls Michael Middleton, deputy chancellor at the University of Missouri, who worked closely with Thomas at the Department of Education and later at the Equal Employment Opportunity Commission. Added Middleton: "He was the HNIC [Head Negro In Charge], as we say, of the government."

Every Thomas employer, from Danforth, who gave him his first job, to President George H. W. Bush, who nominated him to the Supreme Court, chose Thomas at least partly because he is black. Race is a central fact of his meteoric rise, and Thomas has alternately denied it and resented it—all the way to the top. "He was very strong on the notion that he wanted to make his mark as a business lawyer and not have anything to do with civil rights," says Neil Bernstein, now a law professor at Washington University in St. Louis, who worked alongside Thomas in Danforth's office. "But he wound up going down the path he swore he would never go down. He was always conflicted. He was opposed to affirmative action and that got him into Yale." (Yale officials say that assertion is impossible to prove.) "He was opposed to getting jobs based on race when that turned out to get him everything he got," Bernstein continues. "That's Clarence Thomas, and that experience drives him to do and say some of the things he does."

During his two and a half years in the Missouri attorney general's office, Thomas did work that mostly defied racial stereotype. His first job was handling criminal appeals; later, he moved to the civil division, where he focused on tax issues. Those two assignments provided the only real litigation experience of his career. Thomas also served as legal counsel to Lincoln University, a historically black state school located in Jefferson City. Coworkers in Danforth's office remember him as an able, conscientious lawyer who arrived in the office early, worked hard, and always seemed to fit in socially. "He was one of the gang all the way," Bernstein recalls. "He was a delightful guy, very outgoing. He liked to argue."

In office conversations, Thomas would debate school busing, welfare, and affirmative action—policies that he opposed as harmful to black progress, a decided change from his views while he was a student at Holy Cross. Coworkers identify him as the most conservative lawyer on a staff that included John Ashcroft, who went on to become a hero of the Christian right as a U.S. senator and, later, as the nation's attorney general.

Then as now, Thomas enjoyed confounding expectations. Some coworkers recall his displaying over his desk a large Georgia state flag, which in those days was dominated by the stars and bars of the Confederacy. Some coworkers remember the banner as the Confederate flag. No matter. Either way, it was an eye-catcher and a conversation starter. "People would stop by and say, 'Clarence, what are you doing with a Confederate flag over your desk?'" Bernstein says. "He would say, 'Well, they discriminated but they were honest about it. You knew exactly where you stood with the Confederacy. Today people discriminate but they are sneaky. But I just as soon that people be honest.'"

Thomas says he cast his first vote for a Republican when he backed Gerald Ford in the 1976 presidential election. About then, he also began to link his own evolving views to those of some of the nation's most combative black conservatives. One of his first ideological mentors was Thomas Sowell, a prickly free-market economist who studied under Milton Friedman and went on to become a senior fellow at Stanford University's Hoover Institution, where he remains one of the nation's best-known and most provocative intellectuals. Born in North Carolina and raised in Harlem, Sowell was a high school dropout who attended Howard University as a night student before graduating from Harvard and the University of Chicago. Over the past three decades, Sowell has made a name for himself writing books and newspaper columns questioning many of the assumptions underpinning what many conservatives disdainfully call civil rights orthodoxy.

In its place, Sowell offers up some orthodoxy of his own. Sowell says racial disparities have existed throughout recorded history. Many people point to them as indisputable evidence of racial discrimination. But the question, Sowell says, is not so much why there are disparities between groups but rather why anyone expects equality in the first place.

When it comes to the myriad struggles of African Americans, racism has been a factor, Sowell says. Far more important, he says, has been a self-destructive, rough, rural culture—he calls it "redneck culture"—first evidenced among Southern whites that has prevented some blacks from rising above the bias. By contrast, Sowell says, other groups of people—Chinese in Singapore, Germans in Brazil, and Jews just about everywhere—exhibit cultural habits that leave them well equipped for success, whatever the odds. By working hard, stressing education, saving for the future, and cultivating an entrepreneurial spirit, Sowell maintains, people almost always triumph over discrimination.

Thomas loves that kind of tough-love analysis. As Thomas sees it, Sowell confronts uncomfortable truths and possesses a unique ability to flip conventional wisdom on its head. Sowell also enjoys toying with taboos. He writes about mental ability and the varying performance of racial and ethnic groups on IQ tests, concluding that real differences exist among groups. But, he adds, those differences can change with time. When IQ tests were developed in the early twentieth century, he says unflinchingly, immigrants from northern Europe scored higher than their counterparts from southern Europe, many of whom had IQs similar to those of American blacks.

Sowell argues that society should not shrink from the uncomfortable reality that there are group differences in intelligence, but he also says those differences are neither static nor innate. It is controversial stuff that makes many people cringe. But Thomas sees it as courageous.

When Thomas was at Yale, someone had given him a copy of one of Sowell's early books, which he says he only flipped through before deciding it was heresy and tossing it into the garbage. In Jefferson City, though, when a friend mentioned to Thomas a book he saw reviewed in the *Wall Street Journal* by a guy "who has the same ideas that you have," Thomas was curious. He read the book, Sowell's *Race and Economics*, and felt transformed. The book criticizes the wrongheadedness of government social reforms and trumpets the importance of individual initiative in overcoming circumstance. Suddenly, Thomas had an intellectual foundation for a worldview that was compatible with his grandfather's. Practically speaking, reading Sowell was the beginning of Thomas's shift to the right. The experience was like "pouring half a glass of water on the desert. I just soaked it up," Thomas told an interviewer years later.

Thomas went to great lengths to seek out Sowell, who even then was a reclusive and difficult figure. (His mystique would grow over the years at the Hoover Institution, where he has developed a reputation for coming to his campus office late at night and for stalking out of interviews he feels stray off course.) After trying unsuccessfully to reach Sowell by phone, Thomas learned that he was going to debate Ruth Bader Ginsburg at Washington University in St. Louis. Ginsburg, then a Columbia University law professor active in the American Civil Liberties Union, would become Thomas's colleague on the Supreme Court. Thomas made the two-hour drive to St. Louis for the debate and, afterward, approached Sowell to autograph his book. Thomas then pursued Sowell with letters and phone calls, kindling a relationship that continues three decades later. "He has predicted much of what has happened in so many areas, particularly in education, about members of our race," Thomas once told a meeting of black conservatives.

Sowell's work deepened many of the arguments that Thomas made around the office: School integration is not needed to improve school achievement. Affirmative action breeds contempt among whites. Sowell also talks about another issue close to Thomas's heart: the differences that have divided dark-skinned and light-skinned African Americans. Sowell, who is dark-skinned, delights in skewering light-skinned black "elites" who, in his view, talk black but live white. He says that many of them could not find their way to Harlem, the fabled capital of black America. Sowell, by contrast, once lived there—just as Thomas lived in Pin Point and black Savannah. For both men, that personal history became the answer to those who questioned their blackness because of their conservative philosophies.

Sowell could also be as combative as Thomas would eventually become with the nation's civil rights establishment. The late Carl T. Rowan, then one of the nation's few black syndicated columnists, challenged Sowell in a 1981 commentary. The column quoted Patricia Roberts Harris, a doyenne of Washington's black middle class who served as secretary of health, education, and welfare under President Jimmy Carter. Harris said that Sowell and fellow black conservative economist Walter Williams, who also would become a close Thomas friend, "don't know what poverty is."

Sowell fired back in his own column, saying that he knew more about being poor than Harris ever did. "Patricia Roberts Harris and I were students at the same college [Howard University], but under entirely different conditions. I worked full time and went to school at night. Patricia Harris was a campus social leader in an 'exclusive' sorority—meaning it was for middle-class, light-skinned women. That was before it became fashionable to be blacker-than-thou," Sowell wrote.

In time, Thomas would adopt the same posture and Harris would become one of Thomas's targets, at least in office conversation, Middleton recalls. Nothing personal. It was just that Thomas saw Harris as the type of light-skinned, privileged black person who he suspected always held him in contempt. So he returned the favor. The resentment was already there, planted early in the humidity of coastal Georgia. At Yale, it really began to grow. It would become part of the baggage that Thomas would carry with him to the Supreme Court.

In November 1976, Danforth won election to the U.S. Senate, providing an opening for Thomas to address an increasing concern: the need for more money. Who could blame him? He was a young father struggling to keep pace with mounting expenses. His wife, Kathy, had enrolled at Lincoln University in Missouri to finish her undergraduate degree. His student loans were a financial burden, as were the demands of fatherhood.

He also was struggling to keep his family together. Thomas did not talk about his wife much at work, some coworkers recall, and perhaps his reticence portended the problems that several years later would cause the marriage to collapse. Looking back, friends say they knew little of the problems between the two, other than that Thomas proved to be far more ambitious than his wife. "I thought he was single," Bernstein says.

Thomas took the opportunity of Danforth's leaving to apply for jobs at law firms and corporations around Missouri. With Danforth's recommendation, he landed a job on the legal staff of Monsanto, the St. Louis–area chemical giant. Thomas was hired at least partly because Monsanto general counsel Ned J. Putzell Jr. was looking to hire an African American lawyer. "I set about looking for a female lawyer and black lawyer, and I ended up hiring both," Putzell told Thomas biographer Andrew Peyton Thomas.

When he started at Monsanto in early 1977, Thomas was one of two black lawyers in the firm's legal department. He worked on environmental and regulatory issues. His former boss remembers him being a solid addition to a sharp group of lawyers. Other coworkers say Thomas was friendly and had a pleasant sense of humor. "He was one of those guys who kept you laughing a lot," says Angelyn Blanchard, who worked for fifteen years as a secretary and receptionist at Monsanto.

Thomas's jokes were not the stuff of *Saturday Night Live*, but they did lend him an endearing quality. Once, Blanchard and a female coworker were chatting in a corridor at Monsanto when, from up the hall, Thomas's booming voice overwhelmed their conversation. "Clarence, you're going to have to lower your voice," Blanchard said. "OK," Thomas replied, as he squatted down and continued to talk just as loudly as before. "We fell out laughing," Blanchard recalls.

The men—the black men, at least—called Blanchard "Queen Bee," testament to an appeal that kept them buzzing around her. After work, she and a group of employees—typically Thomas and four or five other guys—would occasionally hang out for happy hour. They'd sip margaritas at a Mexican restaurant or hit one of the other local spots for drinks and appetizers. Afterward, they would sometimes retreat to Blanchard's townhome in Bridgeton, not far from the St. Louis airport, for a few more drinks and maybe a card game.

"It was just clean fun," she recalls. Things never got wild. Some of the guys would hit on Blanchard, but not Thomas. He would toss her nice compliments, but he never crossed the line. "He didn't seem to be the runabout, street kind of guy," Blanchard says. Years later, she would be surprised by Anita Hill's sexual harassment allegations, which certainly did not sound like the Clarence Thomas she knew.

Thomas was introduced to Larry Thompson, Monsanto's other black lawyer, while attending a company law department luncheon. The two had met previously back in 1974, during a bar review class they both attended when Thomas first arrived in Missouri. Reacquainted, they forged a relationship that proved lasting as they pursued separate paths to the pinnacle of the legal profession.

Thompson went on to be a U.S. attorney in Atlanta and deputy U.S. attorney general, a role that made him the Justice Department's point man for the war on terrorism. He later was hired as general counsel for the snack food giant PepsiCo, and he would even be mentioned as a possible Supreme Court nominee after Justice Sandra Day O'Connor announced plans to retire and Chief Justice William H. Rehnquist died in 2005. Back when Thomas and Thompson were young lawyers, they could only dream of such success.

The two highest-ranking black employees at Monsanto both had working-class backgrounds. Thompson's father was a railroad worker, his mother a cook. They also shared conservative political views— "weird ideas," Thompson jokes—that caused them to question the tactics and rhetoric of the nation's civil rights leadership. The two friends lived in nearby town houses in University City. They would get together on weekends to watch sports on television, and they met for lunch regularly at a Chinese restaurant just outside St. Louis. They would talk about being young black lawyers and about where their futures might take them.

Thompson wanted to be a big-time litigator, making a bunch of money. Whenever, in the course of his career, he took a job in the public sector, he says, it was with Thomas's encouragement. "I always took a pay cut," he jokes, about following his friend's advice. Thomas was different. "I could never totally understand where he wanted to go," Thompson says. Thomas was interested in policy and he was outspoken about it. Although Thompson does not recall Thomas saying he wanted to be a judge, he knew that his friend would somehow get involved in public life. "I always felt he was reading more than me," Thompson says. "I was fairly narrow. I was focused on cases."

Thompson's intuition was correct. Thomas grew restless at Monsanto and was eager to jump back into the public policy mix. Eventually, he contacted his old boss about a job. In August 1979, Thomas was on his way to Washington for a spot as a legislative assistant on Danforth's Senate staff. Once again he saw to it that his portfolio was color-blind: energy, public works, and environmental issues.

Still, Thomas could not escape the burden and the assumptions that often accompany race. He had his degrees from Holy Cross and Yale. He had experience working in the legal trenches for the state of Missouri and for Monsanto, one of the nation's corporate titans. But on Capitol Hill—where in 1979 he was among just a half dozen Senate staffers who were not white—he faced questions about whether he was qualified for his job or whether he was there only because of his race.

J. C. Alvarez says she, too, was regularly subjected to similar insults. A Hispanic graduate of Princeton and Columbia, Alvarez became a close friend of Thomas's, working with him at Danforth's office and later at the EEOC. At times, she found herself questioning her own credentials. "I was almost apologetic that I wasn't a white, Anglo-Saxon Protestant male or my daddy had not made some enormous financial contribution to some campaign," she says. That feeling changed after she saw Thomas dispense with a white staffer for Danforth who directly questioned his success. "Let's face it," the staffer told Thomas. "The only reason you are here is because you went to Yale, and the only reason you got into Yale was not because of your ability but because of affirmative action." Momentarily taken aback, Thomas took a deep breath. "You know, I may have been lucky enough to get in," he said, looking his questioner straight in the eye. "But I was smart enough to get out."

In recounting the story during Thomas's Supreme Court confirmation hearings, Alvarez said the incident transformed her, giving her self-esteem where there was once doubt. "Clarence that day gave me a confidence that I had never felt before," she said. "I realized that affirmative action was perhaps just a minority's version of the same nepotism that had gotten that staffer his job."

Alvarez was impressed, but little did she know that Thomas had displayed more confidence than he actually felt in fending off his colleague's barb. Just as it had since Yale, the issue of affirmative action gnawed at him. He was convinced it shaped how others—mainly whites—saw him and other African Americans. And he couldn't just shrug that off. He worried then, as he worries now, that it leaves whites to assume that black people are second-rate.

During his rapid ascent through the federal government, Thomas would align himself with mentors who felt much the same way. One of the most influential was J. A. "Jay" Parker, an archconservative who became an invaluable friend and supporter of Thomas through the years.

The son of a maid and a short-order cook, Parker was another admired friend who shared Thomas's working-class roots. A dozen years older than Thomas, Parker had a long history of backing right-wing causes. As early as 1959, Parker supported efforts to draft conservative Senator Barry Goldwater of Arizona to run for president. In 1965, he became the first black board member of Young Americans for Freedom, a group that fervently supported the Vietnam War. And he was a member of the World Anti-Communist League, an organization that aggressively supported repressive right-wing governments and movements such as South Africa's apartheid regime and the Nicaraguan Contras because of their staunch anti-Communist stances. For several years, Parker represented South Africa as a well-paid Washington lobbyist.

When it came to domestic issues, Parker was no less conservative. He opposed government antipoverty programs, whose work, he said, should be handled solely by private charities. Parker trumpeted his views in the *Lincoln Review*, a newsletter he still edits. The publication is as controversial as Parker himself. At various points, it has questioned the existence of racial discrimination and opined that abortion is an attempt to exterminate blacks.

A coworker in Danforth's office shared a copy of the journal with Thomas, who called Parker within minutes: "I'm Clarence Thomas . . . and I like what you've got to say." Before long, the two went to lunch, sparking a long friendship that would prove pivotal to Thomas's career in Washington. Thomas went on to serve on the editorial advisory board of the *Lincoln Review* from 1981 through 1990. While his byline would appear in the journal on occasion, Thomas said that his role on the board was otherwise honorary. "A few dissidents like Thomas Sowell and J. A. Parker stand steadfast, refusing to give in to the cult mentality and childish obedience that hypnotize black Americans into a mindless political trance," Thomas told the Heritage Foundation, when his ideological transformation was all but complete in 1987. "I admire them, and wish I had a fraction of their courage and strength."

One month after Ronald Reagan was elected president in 1980, Thomas was asked to take part in a conference at San Francisco's Fairmont Hotel aimed at airing new approaches to the problems of black and other minority communities. It was dubbed the Black Alternatives Conference, and Sowell assembled much of the program, inviting an eclectic mix of black conservatives and others to weigh in. Thomas traveled on his own dime to the conference, where Sowell asked him to talk about education for African Americans. In his remarks, Thomas made clear that he was no fan of forced school integration—a point he would make continuously throughout his career. He fondly recalled St. Pius X, the all-black Catholic high school he attended for two years back in Savannah. The diocese made a mistake in closing the school during desegregation, he said, because it left black students with the unhappy choice of going to more expensive white schools or inferior public schools. He wryly noted that whites did not integrate black schools. "We did have the bad physical plant; we did have the constant problems with paying bills, and so forth, and we did have the poor books," Thomas said of St. Pius. "We also had an excellent education."

Thomas's candor was compelling, and it only began with the ideas presented in his formal paper for the conference. Juan Williams, then an editorial writer at the *Washington Post*, covered the conference and found himself intrigued by Thomas's unvarnished honesty. In conversations with Williams at the conference, Thomas explained his opposition to welfare, saying it saps recipients of the motivation to do better. He underscored his point by invoking the experience of his sister, Emma, saying she "gets mad when the mailman is late with her welfare check." In talking about his own career options, Thomas told Williams, "If I ever went to work for the EEOC or did anything directly connected with blacks, my career would be irreparably ruined. The monkey would be on my back to prove that I didn't have the job because I was black."

Williams wrote a column about Thomas that ran on the paper's op-ed page. Williams later said he chose to focus on Thomas because he saw him as the best representative of the new ideas presented at the conference: He was young, fresh, and outspoken. But the exposure in one of the nation's best-read newspapers produced a backlash that stunned Thomas. A steady stream of letters to the editor scolded him for his views and for what was seen as his callous treatment of his sister. Senior black leaders publicly castigated him, and he has said that former friends on Capitol Hill shied away from him.

Caught off guard by the criticism, Thomas was peeved with Williams and initially refused to meet with him again. Sometime later, the two met for lunch in Washington to discuss the episode. Thomas told Williams that he felt his critics misunderstood him and maliciously impugned his motives. The column was the first of many encounters that would sour Thomas's view of the press and civil rights leaders, leaving him wounded and isolated. "It was clear from lunch with him that he had been beat up," says Williams, who subsequently developed a close relationship with Thomas that endures today.

Whatever the pitfalls of his new visibility, the story had the virtue of bringing the young congressional aide to the attention of the incoming Reagan administration, which was looking to fill thousands of high-level jobs. Edwin Meese III, who went on to become attorney general, headed Reagan's transition team. He had addressed the conference in San Francisco, memorably vowing that the administration would hire blacks in their areas of expertise, not just in civil rights or other "black" jobs.

It seemed to be a promise right up Thomas's alley. Thomas's friend Parker headed the transition team's efforts to review the EEOC, and he asked Thomas to join his committee. Thomas produced a memo saying that the EEOC should focus its resources on being a true law enforcement agency that held employers accountable for demonstrable acts of discrimination against individuals, rather than pushing for affirmative action plans and other remedies for firms that employed disproportionately small numbers of minority or female workers. It was a policy that he would soon have a chance to implement personally.

After working on the transition team, Thomas was poised to move up and he was not to be disappointed. He was offered a job at the White House handling energy and environmental policies, his specialties on Danforth's staff. But he turned it down, apparently because he considered the position too junior—or not high-profile enough. Subsequently, Thomas was offered a post as head of the Education Department's Office for Civil Rights—precisely the kind of job he said he would never take. He had never worked as a civil rights lawyer, so what qualified him for the job? He was insulted by the offer. "What other reason besides the fact that I was black?" Thomas said. Thomas talked the offer over with friends, who urged him to accept it. As a result of those conversations, he began to think more about the good he could do in the job. Who better to work on issues involving topics he cared deeply about, such as race and education?

His mentor, Parker, put it most succinctly: "Clarence, put up or shut up."

Thomas started work as assistant secretary for civil rights at the U.S. Department of Education in May 1981. He was not quite thirty-three years old and his aspirations were expanding with his résumé. Displayed on his desk was a framed photograph of a private jet on an airport tarmac, with a stretch limo parked nearby. Standing in front of the car was a white man dressed in a black tuxedo. Colleagues took it to mean that Thomas wanted to be rich. "He said that is what he aspired to," says Michael Middleton, who worked closely with Thomas and knew that, at that time, Thomas talked about one day having a lot of money.

On policy issues, Thomas mostly played it cautiously, sometimes restraining his conservative instincts for fear of doing harm. For one thing, he was new to civil rights work and was worried that he would overreach. That fear would evaporate with time. "As a black man, he was concerned not to damage the progress that had been made through the years on civil rights," Middleton says. "He understood that his more conservative positions were thought by many in the movement to be detrimental."

Despite his caution, Thomas stirred the ire of civil rights leaders when he moved to reverse the federal government's policy of pressuring Southern states to unify their separate white and black systems of higher education. In Thomas's view, the government's efforts to attract whites to black colleges were failing. And if large numbers of black students abandoned historically black colleges and universities, those institutions would eventually collapse. Better to bolster black schools with new buildings and beefed-up programs than to focus so much on desegregation, he concluded.

"The media pounced on the fact that we were not implementing a policy that would require some white kids to go to the black colleges and said we were cutting back," Thomas later explained to the *Crisis*, the NAACP's magazine. "How in the hell is that cutting back if your ultimate goal is to educate these black kids? Are you saying that black kids cannot learn without white kids if they have these facilities?"

Many civil rights activists, wary of the Reagan administration's efforts to roll back school busing and affirmative action, did not buy that argument. Their suspicion only deepened when in early 1982 the administration announced its support of tax-exempt status for South Carolina's Bob Jones University, despite the school's rules banning interracial dating. Thomas staunchly opposed that decision in internal administration discussions, even while activists bitterly accused him of doing the dirty work of those eager to erode civil rights protections—a perception he battled throughout his years working for the Reagan administration.

"I don't fit in with whites, and I don't fit in with blacks," Thomas told an interviewer years later. "We're in a mixed-up generation—those of us who were sent out to integrate society. . . . If it were not for the few friends I have who do not give a damn about this stuff, this place could drive me insane."

Despite the pressures, Thomas was now a major player in decisions affecting educational institutions across the country. But at home, things were falling apart. A close friend remembers running into Thomas on a bus after work. He was complaining bitterly about his young son's poor school performance. When she gently suggested that the boy could be struggling with a learning disability, Thomas bristled. Jamal, he snapped, just needs to buckle down.

Meanwhile, as Thomas was making his way into the upper reaches of the federal government, his wife, Kathy, did not keep pace. She worked, including for a while as an advance person for the Republican Party, her father says. To some of Thomas's friends, the growing divide reflected the early differences they saw between the couple. "The first time we met her, you know, we kind of said, man, you know, Kathy, she ain't the down sister that we would have expected Clarence to bring around," says Lester Johnson, who followed Thomas from Savannah to Holy Cross. "But after we got to know her, we found out she's a fine individual and we enjoyed her tremendously. But at first look . . . we didn't think this was a match made in heaven." By the end of their marriage, Kathy seemed to recede into her husband's shadow. A friend of Thomas's remarked that she seemed very deferential, almost like a woman from the Nation of Islam, who seemed to speak to her man only when spoken to.

The couple separated in early 1981, only to briefly reconcile before parting for good that summer. In 1984, they divorced, legally ending their thirteen-year marriage with Thomas taking custody of Jamal, as his wife had insisted. "That was Kathy's idea," her father says. "She wanted Clarence to raise him, she thought Clarence could raise him better than she could." Years later, Thomas would sometimes grumble that his son had been dumped on him.

"Kathy was quiet, very intelligent, and a very giving person," says Alphonso Jackson, a longtime Thomas friend who went on to become secretary of housing and urban development under President George W. Bush. "Clarence has always been outgoing, and the juice just didn't mix. Some people just grow apart." Nelson Ambush says he knew nothing about the depth of his daughter's marital problems until Thomas had already moved out. "I went to visit her and everything, and he wasn't at home, you know, and that's when she said, 'He's not here anymore.' And that was it. I didn't question her. If it didn't work out, just go on with your life." Ambush says he wasn't surprised that his daughter had not alerted him to her marital problems. That just is not Kathy's style. "She wasn't one to talk about her life like that because she would never say anything to hurt him. She wouldn't do that and he's not about to do anything otherwise—too much respect."

Through the years, Kathy has remained mum about the reasons for the breakup. After his nomination to the Supreme Court, she said only that her former husband had remained a good friend. Their divorce papers offer no clues. Reached at her job as development director for a nonprofit organization in Massachusetts that teaches

English to immigrants, she stuck to her silence. "I don't give any interviews," she said pleasantly. "I never have." Asked why, she explained, "It's a matter of privacy, and some other things." Thomas's family has had only nice things to say about Kathy. "Love her, love her, I love her," says Leola Williams, Thomas's mother. "She's a sweetie pie."

As his marriage was collapsing, Thomas moved into the Washington apartment of his best friend, Gil Hardy. Friends with Thomas since their days at Holy Cross, Hardy was working at a Washington law firm, where he had befriended a struggling twenty-five-year-old associate who was casting about for a new job. Her name was Anita Hill.

Hill was a Yale Law graduate whom Hardy had helped recruit to the firm where he worked, Wald, Harkrader & Ross. Hill's performance during her eleven months at the firm would become a matter of contention during Thomas's Supreme Court confirmation hearings. Thomas's supporters said she had been asked to leave because her work was not up to snuff. But during her Senate testimony, Hill refuted that characterization, saying she was never asked to leave the firm. Later, she wrote in her memoir that she rarely received meaningful assignments at the firm, something she blamed on failing to stake out a valuable specialty at the firm and the feeling that she was overlooked because she was young, black, and female.

Hill shared her struggles with Hardy, who suggested that Thomas talk to her about joining his staff at the Department of Education. Hill and Thomas met during a small gathering at Hardy's place, where Hill recalls the two sparred over some of Ronald Reagan's policy proposals. Still, Thomas agreed to interview her, eventually hiring Hill as his special assistant in August 1981. In her memoir, Hill said she was reluctant to join the Reagan administration, but Thomas allayed her fears by assuring her that day to day she really would be working for him, not the president. "He encouraged me to think of myself as his 'personal assistant,' " Hill wrote. "The position was one that was directly supervised by, maintained by, and related to him, not to Ronald Reagan. President Reagan, he claimed, was uninterested in what was to occur in 'his shop.' "

Perhaps because they had met through a mutual friend, Hill and Thomas initially had an easy professional relationship. They would amiably debate policy, and it wasn't long before Thomas and the low-key Hill had become not just coworkers but friends. Thomas began sharing with Hill his most intimate problems and desires, she said. He would confide in her about his failing marriage, issues with his son, slights he incurred during his childhood in Georgia. Soon, he began pressing her for dates. When she refused, Hill said, he began regaling her with vivid descriptions of sexual acts he had seen in pornographic movies. Thomas vigorously disputes Hill's account, which wouldn't become public until many years later. But even today, according to people who have spoken with him about Hill, he continues to wonder aloud: Why would someone I trusted so much do this to me?

Thomas's behavior, Hill said, made her uncomfortable, and at times she dreaded going to work. But it ebbed and flowed, Hill said, and Thomas's crassness sometimes disappeared for weeks or months. His unwanted overtures were just irregular enough, Hill explained, that she decided not only to keep her job but to follow her boss as he made another big move up the federal ladder.

A Reagan aide told Thomas of the president's intention to nominate him as head of the Equal Employment Opportunity Commission in February 1982. With thirty-one hundred employees, forty-eight field offices, and a mandate to police racial, gender, religious, and other forms of discrimination among the nation's employers, the post marked a significant promotion.

Thomas got his first glimpse of the immense challenge he would face when he started his new job three months later. First, his cab driver had a hard time finding the agency, then located in a crummy building in a far corner of northwest Washington. When they finally found the place, Thomas had difficulty getting past a skeptical security guard. When he got to his office, he found that it had been plundered: There were no pencils or pads or even a chair to sit on.

The building was a dump. The roof leaked. There were two aging computers in overheated rooms, where the temperature was controlled by opening and closing doors and turning on fans. Mold grew in the halls and fleas resided in the dirty carpet.

Operationally, things were no better. Not long after Thomas assumed command of the EEOC, the General Accounting Office issued a report that called the agency a management disaster. Case files were found hidden behind ceiling tiles and the agency had accumulated more than $1 million in outstanding employee travel advances. "We did not know from one day to the next how much money we had on hand," Thomas said. "We had an automated payroll system and a manual personnel system, which meant that we often paid dead people and former employees."

In time, Thomas got a handle on those problems through his single-minded focus and a sometimes cold-blooded administrative style. Thomas interviewed his financial staff, one by one, clearly laying out his expectations and offering his firm support in straightening out the agency's books. He was known to walk the halls, chatting up everyone from custodians to union officials to build camaraderie. He would stand by the building's entrance in the mornings, Diet Coke in hand, noting who arrived late. Then there was the Frank Quinn case. Quinn, a seventeen-year chief of the EEOC's San Francisco office, complained to *Newsweek* that Thomas had refused to approve lawsuits against employers that field officers had determined were guilty of discrimination. As punishment, Thomas tried to transfer Quinn to Birmingham, Alabama. Just months from retirement, Quinn sued and a federal judge blocked the move.

When Thomas dismissed Angela Wright, the agency's public affairs director, he did so by taping a note to her chair. "You're fired," it read.

Within a year, auditors had given the EEOC a clean bill of financial health, although Thomas hardly resolved all of the agency's problems. Throughout his tenure, Thomas was frequently hauled before Democratic congressional overseers who thought he was not vigilant enough in enforcing equal employment law. And as he was moving on to a federal judgeship in 1989, he was forced to acknowledge that nine thousand age discrimination cases had lapsed under his watch because of EEOC inaction. Also, his approach to EEOC enforcement—conducting lengthy investigations of claims—led to fewer settlements and a growing backlog of EEOC cases.

Such administrative challenges were minor compared with the conflicting pressures Thomas felt to reshape the EEOC's mission. Empowered to conduct investigations and file lawsuits against employers thought to be discriminating, the agency was a prime target of zealous conservatives in the Reagan administration who believed it had gone too far. The EEOC's weapon of choice was the class action lawsuit, which often resulted in employers agreeing to pay large settlements for back pay and implement affirmative action plans that included numerical goals for the hiring and promotion of minorities or women. The agency regarded disparities between the percentage of minorities or women in a job and the number in a region's workforce as evidence of possible discrimination. Many in the administration were against that tactic and they looked to Thomas to do away with it.

But the same affirmative action plans targeted by the Reaganites were the catalyst for integrating police and fire departments and private companies around the country that were once all but lily white. And civil rights advocates saw statistical analysis and class action suits as among the few viable ways to smoke out and punish discrimination that would otherwise go undetected.

Mostly Thomas agreed with what Reagan's people wanted. But he wavered for years. His misgivings about affirmative action extended all the way back to law school. He also believed that the EEOC should work like other law enforcement agencies, imposing tough penalties on employers but only when discrimination against individuals could be proven. Numerical disparities, he argued, could be the result of different levels of training or interest in a particular field and were not necessarily a sign of discrimination.

Testifying before a congressional panel in 1984, Thomas invoked Georgetown University's No. 1–ranked basketball team to make his point. Although Georgetown was predominantly white, the team was all black and had a black head coach—a situation that Thomas said could be falsely attributed to racism if one were to examine only the numbers. "You could conclude from the results of a study of the Georgetown basketball team that statistically you have to be black," Thomas said, "or you could also conclude, if you did not use race conscious statistics, that you have to know how to play basketball."

Hearing this, Representative Augustus F. Hawkins, the Democratic chairman of the panel quizzing Thomas, reacted the same way many civil rights activists have through the years. "Well, if your views ever become universal in this country, God help us because . . . you simply want to emasculate all the progress we've made in the last fifty years."

In reality, Thomas was at war with himself, torn about which way he wanted to go on civil rights, particularly on the issue of affirmative action. Over the next twelve years he would spin this subject around in his head and at times even contradict himself. "I am tired of rhetoric—the rhetoric about quotas and about affirmative action," he said in a 1985 speech in Tampa, Florida. "It is a supreme waste of time. It precludes more positive and enlightened discussion, and it is no longer relevant." In a 1988 speech, he said this: "I think affirmative action is good. I've said that time and time again. I think the debate has been over quotas, not affirmative action." In a 1996 speech, he said this: "Not much has come from affirmative action. Discrimination is discrimination. We don't allow racial classification and it's stated very clearly in the Declaration of Independence."

One prominent civil rights attorney witnessed some of Thomas's early struggles with affirmative action when she was teaching a course at Harvard in 1982. Thomas had come as a guest speaker. Driving him back to Boston's Logan Airport, she got into an extended conversation with him on the subject. "We sat in the car for an hour," she remembers, "talking about how affirmative action could coexist with the Fourteenth Amendment," which requires people to receive equal treatment under the law. As she recalls, Thomas was sympathetic to the goals of affirmative action but dubious about its legality. Overall, though, she left with the feeling that he was at least willing to wrestle with alternative viewpoints.

Unbeknownst to many outsiders at the time, Thomas was battling other members of the Reagan administration. He worried that the Reaganites took too harsh a tone in articulating their desire to change how the nation's civil rights laws were enforced. A year after Thomas took over at the EEOC, the administration was working on a statement to clarify its equal employment opportunity policies. The document equated many affirmative action programs with quotas and sharply criticized the federal bureaucracy.

"I must confess that an uninformed person who reads this memorandum would quickly arrive at an incomplete understanding of our views," Thomas wrote in a memo to Edwin Harper, an assistant to the president, criticizing the document's tone, if not its substance. "Such a person may even read the statement as merely defining what we are against as opposed to the principles we are for."

Thomas understood that *quota* was an explosive term with the public. Quotas had been largely outlawed by the Supreme Court in 1978, although they were allowed, in some specific instances, to make up for past discrimination. Affirmative action programs, meanwhile, could also include outreach efforts to minority groups and women. Under affirmative action, it was possible to use race and gender as factors among many in choosing students or hiring employees.

Thomas frequently butted heads with the two chief architects of Reagan's civil rights policy, Michael Horowitz, general counsel of the Office of Management and Budget, and William Bradford Reynolds, the Justice Department's assistant attorney general for civil rights. In 1983, the Justice Department moved to invalidate a legal settlement between the New Orleans police department and its black officers that required the department to promote equal numbers of black and white officers in an effort to ameliorate past discrimination. Although Justice Department lawyers argued that the agreement was unconstitutional in a case pending before a federal appeals court, Thomas had the EEOC prepare a competing legal brief backing the plan. The EEOC brief was sharply critical of the administration's stand on affirmative action. In the end, the Justice Department, concerned that the administration speak with one voice, ordered Thomas not to file the document and he reluctantly backed off.

It was the type of episode that perturbed those in the Reagan administration who wanted Thomas—one of the highest-ranking black officials in the administration—to assume a more prominent public profile in favor of their policies. Once, during lunch at the White House, Reynolds made it plain that Thomas should be more aggressive in promoting Reagan's civil rights vision. His injunction pricked Thomas's strong sense of independence. "Don't tell me what to do, Brad," Thomas responded. "All I have to do is die and stay black."

At times, Thomas was haunted by the feeling that he was taken for granted and seen as a mere token. On one occasion, Reynolds raised a glass to toast Thomas's confirmation to a second term as EEOC chairman and lauded him as "the epitome of the right kind of affirmative action working the right way." Thomas was mortified, something Reynolds didn't realize until a mutual acquaintance told him later. Reynolds called and apologized. Reflecting on the episode recently, Reynolds said: "I understand—Clarence feels very strongly that it is an insult to suggest that he got where he got because he took some handout or because he didn't earn it. . . . The thing that was most disturbing to him, he didn't want to have people who were close to him seemingly reaffirm what the left was trying to say, which was, 'You're a product of affirmative action. How can you be against affirmative action?' "

But as time wore on, Thomas fell into line. Part of it was the culmination of his own ideological journey, which ended with his growing more comfortable with his conservative instincts. Another part may have been ambition and a growing sense of power. "Think about this. I can pick up the phone and get an appointment with the president any time I need that," Thomas once told Jaffe Dickerson, a friend from Holy Cross. "Coretta Scott King can't get that. Jesse Jackson can't get that."

Some maintain that Thomas was never really bothered by the Reagan administration's course of action. "I never felt that he was uncomfortable with those policy positions," says Reynolds. Nor, according to Reynolds, did Thomas in any way believe the president's "overall policy was too shrill or too antagonistic." Rather, Thomas worried about public perception, especially about how minority communities were reacting to Reagan's initiatives. "Clarence is, in many ways, a pragmatist," Reynolds says.

Ken Masugi, one of Thomas's EEOC aides, spent many hours discussing ideas and ideology with Thomas. He recalls one conversation in which Thomas posed this question: "Is there some way to be a conservative without being a Confederate?"

"He liked some things conservatives were saying," says Masugi, "but he didn't like the implications—the race baiting. . . . He was rather dissatisfied with the conservatives. He was probably more inclined toward the Libertarians back then than he is now." Evidence of those leanings can be seen in the influence of Libertarian icon Ayn Rand on Thomas. In Rand's work, Thomas saw a model for independence and self-sufficiency, which he undoubtedly related to his own experience. He required EEOC staffers to watch the 1949 film version of Rand's best-selling book *The Fountainhead*—a practice he continued with his Supreme Court clerks. The plot centers on an architect's struggle to preserve his integrity against the voices of conformity.

Thomas also found himself sniping back and forth with leading black leaders, which ultimately had the effect of alienating him from broad sectors of his own race. "What offends me is the civil rights community saying I'm not black," Thomas told an interviewer in 1984. "I may disagree with Brad and the Justice Department, but they don't offend me."

Soon, such skirmishes would take on less importance. He would finally find his soul mate.

They met by chance in June 1986 at an Anti-Defamation League conference in New York. Thomas appeared on a panel as a last-minute substitute for his chief of staff, Jeffrey Zuckerman. Virginia Lamp was also on the panel.

A labor relations attorney and spokeswoman for the U.S. Chamber of Commerce, Lamp was tall and attractive and single. *Good Housekeeping* had once named her one of "28 Young Women of Promise." The daughter of a well-connected Republican family from Omaha, she hoped to one day run for Congress, an ambition Thomas would later discourage. In Washington, she already had a reputation for effectively representing the business community on Capitol Hill. Long before meeting Thomas, she found herself aligned with him in a huge battle over the labor issue known as "comparable worth."

Like Thomas, she felt that just because women don't receive the same pay for dissimilar jobs that require equal training and responsibility doesn't mean they are being discriminated against. "Rather than using our civil rights laws to identify and address discrimination as it exists in the workplace," she said, "comparable-worth advocates want to label a social phenomenon—the fact that women on average make less than men on average—as 'discrimination' and then use our civil rights laws for purposes for which they were never intended."

Thomas and Lamp left the ADL conference together and shared

a cab to the airport. A movie date followed, then a walk around Baltimore's Inner Harbor. Thomas found it easy to talk to her. He loved her mind. Her ambition matched his. It didn't take them long to fall in love. On May 30, 1987, not quite a year after they'd met, Virginia Lamp and Clarence Thomas were married in a largely white Methodist church in Omaha.

That Thomas was black took some of Ginni's family members by surprise. "But he was so nice, we forgot he was black," said Ginni's aunt Opal from Iowa, "and he treated her so well, all of his other qualities made up for his being black."

Having grown up in the segregated South, Thomas was conscious of the social barriers delineated by race. In fact, when he realized he was serious about Ginni he apologized for dragging her into the "race thing." He knew there would be criticism of their union—from blacks and whites—and he was right. Ginni, who had grown up in an all-white suburb, seemed unfazed.

The irony is that a much younger Thomas had been down on interracial relationships, according to classmates at Holy Cross and Yale Law School. He thought nothing good could come from dating a white woman. Back then his prototypes of a fine woman were Angela Davis and Kathleen Cleaver, two black militants with big Afros. But by the time he met Ginni, he had expanded his worldview. "The initial attraction apparently was a real intellectual click," recalls Zuckerman. "Except for Ginni, I don't ever remember him discussing with me any particular woman he dated."

And then Zuckerman offers a curious addendum about his former boss: "If you told me he went out on two hundred dates, I'd say OK. If you told me he dated two dates, I'd say OK." Thomas didn't talk much about women; he kept his romantic interests a mystery.

The only public girlfriend Thomas had pre-Ginni was Capitol Hill aide Lillian McKewen, now an administrative law judge in the District. Thomas's friends would cite her during the confirmation period to counter the allegation that he had crude designs on Anita

Hill. The suggestion: Why would he be so obsessed with Hill when he already was dating a striking woman?

Thomas himself would refer obliquely to McKewen during the hearings. In an exchange with Senator Arlen Specter of Pennsylvania, he said there seemed to be some tension between Hill and him "as a result of the complexion of the woman I dated and the woman I chose to be my chief of staff." Both are light-skinned, and Hill and Thomas are dark-skinned.

The truth is, Thomas didn't have much experience courting women of any complexion—and it showed. Even his best friend, the late Gil Hardy, considered him socially awkward. Growing up, he didn't get much practice. "He never talked about no girls," says his mother. After all, he spent three years at a high school that prepared boys for the priesthood, and from there he went to seminary for a year before transferring to the all-men's Holy Cross College. It was in Worcester, Massachusetts, that he met his first true girlfriend, Kathy Ambush.

Thomas guarded Kathy like she was the Hope Diamond. "Nobody better not graze in my grass," he'd tell classmates. In fact, Kathy was the first young woman Thomas ever introduced to his mother. And as we've seen, they got married the day after Thomas graduated. "I think he wanted to get married fast," recalls classmate James Millet, who noted how clumsy Thomas could be just asking girls to dance at parties. "He started getting mad when he was turned down," Millet adds. "So everybody knew Cooz"—as he was nicknamed— "wanted a girl real bad."

Before meeting Ginni, Thomas would sometimes muse with buddies about why black women in D.C. were so difficult. As Thomas saw it, the city known for having an abundance of highly educated "sisters" was not kind to black Republicans. It didn't matter that *Jet* magazine would name him one of Washington's most eligible bachelors or that he was one of the most prominent black men in the federal government. He still worked for Ronald Reagan, and that was like a scarlet letter.

"This is a rough town," he told a black conservative friend. "Can't get no pussy out here from these women."

Apparently over his ambivalence, Thomas became an outspoken advocate of Reagan's policies during his final years at the EEOC. He also traveled the country giving speeches denouncing Supreme Court decisions on school busing, affirmative action, the drawing of voting districts, and the constitutional guarantee of privacy underlying abortion rights. The interior debate that took place earlier in his tenure was over. And it was clear Thomas the doctrinaire conservative had won.

That did not go unnoticed by superiors in the administration, who were on the lookout for like-minded African Americans to appoint to the federal appellate bench, which is seen as a training ground for the Supreme Court. They identified Thomas as someone who could be groomed to replace the aging Thurgood Marshall, the high court's first black justice.

"Clarence was first discussed as a circuit court candidate when he was over at EEOC," Reynolds said. "And at that time, certainly a number of us who were involved identified him as a wonderful candidate for the Supreme Court." In the event Marshall retired, Reynolds added, "I think everybody recognized that it would be next to impossible to name a nominee to that seat who wasn't black."

Not long after George H. W. Bush was elected president in 1988, Thomas was put on a short list of judicial candidates. On July 7, 1989, Bush nominated him for a seat on the U.S. Court of Appeals for the District of Columbia Circuit, sometimes called the second-highest court in the land because of a caseload heavy on federal administrative appeals and the fact that four of its alumni now sit on the Supreme Court. During his confirmation hearings, Thomas was asked about some of the controversial positions he had staked out as an administrative official: his support of school prayer, his tiffs with civil rights leaders, his opposition to affirmative action all came up.

And he essentially had the same answer to every challenge. His personal views were his personal views, and they would not come into play on the bench. There he would be guided by two things, he said, the laws before him and Supreme Court precedents. "Any personal views are inconsequential in that process," Thomas said of being a judge.

After a quiet lobbying campaign, in which Thomas convinced civil rights groups not to oppose his nomination, he was confirmed to the bench the following March. He served for nineteen months, earning a reputation as a quiet, hardworking jurist who one former colleague said was extraordinarily slow in turning out his work. He often worked out with the guards at lunchtime, and when he dined with his fellow judges, it was frequently at a low-brow café nearby.

In all, he wrote nineteen opinions—some of which were published after he had left the court. Most of them dealt with regulatory issues and criminal appeals. None of them concerned important constitutional issues. His work offered little evidence that he would become regarded as the Supreme Court's most conservative justice. The only case that stirred controversy while he served on the court was one in which he threw out a $10.4 million damage award against Ralston Purina, the firm owned in large part by the family of Danforth, his political patron.

"He's not considered a heavyweight," one law clerk told *Newsweek*. "It's too early to tell if that's due to inexperience or lack of candle-power."

The cloistered and independent life of a judge seemed to suit Thomas, as he would invite protégés up to his office for hours-long counseling sessions. He lifted weights in the court's basement gym and would sit in his chambers reading briefs while puffing big cigars, the smoke filling his office and seeping over to the adjoining chambers of colleagues. "I don't know what I'm going to do," a clerk for another judge complained. "This stuff is just coming through the walls." Eventually, the clerk bought a dehumidifier to help clear the air.

The life of contentment did not last for long. Marshall announced his plans to retire from the Supreme Court in June 1991. With the retirement of Marshall, a civil rights hero and the only nonwhite on the court, the stakes were high both for the Republicans who controlled the White House and for the Democrats who ran Congress. President George H. W. Bush, who earlier had come under harsh criticism from conservatives for his nomination of the relatively unknown David H. Souter, who would prove to be a centrist justice, was trying to steer a course between the wishes of the GOP base and those of Democrats, with whom he did not want to pick a fight that would reverberate into the 1992 elections.

The biggest issue for conservatives was that Bush pick someone who would vote to overturn the 1973 ruling guaranteeing the right to an abortion. But abortion was far from the only issue in play: The role of religion in public life, affirmative action, and other civil rights issues also were being hashed out at the high court.

Race, of course, was the elephant in the room, even if Bush himself would not acknowledge it. Speaking to reporters as he flew to his Maine home for a long weekend after Marshall's retirement, Bush said he felt no pressure to choose a black candidate and instead would "like to weigh all the options and go for the best-qualified candidate." Bush said he was looking for someone who would be open-minded on the issues and who would interpret law and not make it with sweeping court rulings. White House officials told reporters that Bush's short list included about nine people, including several Hispanic judges, two women, at least two white men, and at least one black man, Thomas. "Until we're told otherwise, we'll continue looking at white men. But it seems to be focusing on nonwhite men, on a couple or three Hispanics," a senior administration official told the *New York Times*.

Judge Ricardo H. Hinojosa, a federal trial court judge for the Fifth Circuit, in southern Texas, and Judge Emilio M. Garza, of the United States Court of Appeals for the Fifth Circuit, in San Antonio, were two of the Hispanics on the list. Edith H. Jones, also of the United States Court of Appeals for the Fifth Circuit, was one of the two women on the list. Also considered was Kenneth J. Starr, then solicitor general of the United States, who would go on to fame—or infamy, depending on one's politics—as the special prosecutor whose work led to the impeachment of President Bill Clinton. And then there was Clarence Thomas.

"The politics of the situation suggested that if Thurgood Marshall's seat comes open we better get the best-qualified person who is black whom we can put in that seat," said Brad Reynolds, who was involved in the judicial selection process. And Thomas, he added, was "eminently qualified, and probably better than most."

For the greater part of the twentieth century, presidents didn't have to worry about Senate opposition to their judicial nominees. Up until 1968, only one Supreme Court nominee—Herbert Hoover's pick, John J. Parker—failed to win Senate confirmation. But things started to change when Republicans and Southern Democrats joined in 1968 to block President Lyndon Johnson's attempt to promote Justice Abe Fortas to chief justice. Democrats then led the Senate to topple two Nixon nominees, Clement Haynsworth and G. Harrold Carswell, in 1970. And in 1987, President Reagan's nominee, Robert H. Bork, was defeated in a battle royal that would not be forgotten by either side.

A nervous Clarence Thomas was about to enter this arena, not yet realizing that he would wind up in the fight of his life.

8

WHO LIED?

J. Michael Luttig detected apprehension in Clarence Thomas. As a deputy assistant attorney general, Luttig had participated in the screening of prospective nominees to replace the retiring Thurgood Marshall. Like others on the short list, Thomas had taken the elevator to the Justice Department's sixth-floor command center to be sounded out by senior Bush administration officials. A key line of questioning centered on the enormous pressure a nominee would face. Could Thomas handle the intense scrutiny—from the public, from opposition groups, from the media? "He was ambivalent about the process," recalled Luttig, who added sympathetically: "There is a surreal dimension to it. You are just a regular guy out there and in a moment the whole world is riveted."

Thomas would find out soon enough just how intense the scrutiny would be. On July 1, 1991, President George H. W. Bush announced that Thomas was his choice to succeed Marshall, who was about to turn eighty-three and had served the court for twenty-four years. Thomas had no idea how vigorous the debate over his nomination had been among Bush's advisers. White House Chief of Staff John Sununu strongly favored naming the first Hispanic justice for the political benefit it would bring to the Republican Party. Attorney General Richard Thornburgh, though he liked Thomas, had warned that selecting him could trigger a bruising confirmation battle. For starters, Thornburgh cautioned, any nominee who was seen as suspect on civil rights—given that Marshall was revered as a civil rights champion—would face an all-out war by the civil rights establishment. Thornburgh also worried that Thomas would get a lackluster evaluation from the influential American Bar Association screening committee. (His fear would prove prescient, as the panel would give Thomas the lowest rating of any high court nominee since 1955.)

The president, though, seemed utterly pleased with his choice that Monday as he stood with Thomas in front of a wood-shingled cottage at the Bush family's oceanfront compound in Kennebunkport, Maine. Taking questions from reporters, Bush suddenly became defensive when the questioning turned to race. "The fact that he is black and a minority had nothing to do with this in the sense that he is the best qualified at this time," the president said. Reporters hammered at what seemed like a contradiction. On the one hand, Bush was adamantly opposed to racial preferences. On the other hand, he was seeking to replace a legendary black Supreme Court justice with another African American judge who seemed relatively junior for the job: Thomas had been on the appeals court bench, his only judicial appointment, for just fifteen months. Race was no factor in the choice of Thomas?

"I don't see it at all," Bush said. "I don't feel he's a quota."

In an e-mail to us Bush did not back away from his assessment of Thomas sixteen years ago. While admitting he had "some qualms about the 'black seat' question," Bush wrote in reference to replacing one black justice with another, he was reassured by advisers that Thomas had amassed a record of public service that warranted his nomination. As for calling him the "best qualified" candidate available, a statement that would be widely ridiculed and would follow Bush into retirement, the former president added: "In hindsight, my choice of words was fine by me. Others, of course, disagreed but I have no regrets—none at all."

Thurgood Marshall had held on to his seat for as long as he could. He was tired and overweight, and his health was worsening. He had a weak heart that his doctors worried about. Circulatory problems slowed his movements, and he walked with a cane. Glaucoma caused his eyes to tear steadily, making it difficult for him to read. He had become even more isolated on the court with the 1990 retirement of fellow liberal stalwart William Brennan. And now, Marshall conceded, it was finally time for him to say good-bye too. Watching Bush nominate Thomas, though, was painful. It angered the feisty justice that his successor would be someone with Thomas's thin legal credentials and conservative philosophy.

Marshall hinted at his feelings during a packed news conference on the day he submitted his resignation, just four days before Bush tapped Thomas to replace him. Asked whether the president should name an African American to succeed the court's lone other one, Marshall advised that Bush shouldn't use race as cover to put the "wrong Negro" on the court. "My dad told me way back that there is no difference between a white snake" and "a black snake," Marshall said. "They'll both bite." Several former Marshall law clerks regarded the comment as an unmistakable reference to Thomas, who at that point had already been touted as a leading candidate to fill the vacancy.

It was hard to find a living civil rights figure more admired than Marshall. As lead attorney for the NAACP, he had been the architect of a series of legal challenges that broke Jim Crow's back. President John F. Kennedy nominated him to the federal appeals bench in 1961, and four years later President Lyndon B. Johnson appointed him the nation's first black solicitor general, the federal government's representative before the high court. When Johnson nominated Marshall to replace retiring Supreme Court Justice Tom Clark in 1967, few lawyers in history had argued more cases before the high court. Marshall's record: thirty-two cases argued, twenty-nine victories, including *Brown v. Board of Education*, the 1954 landmark decision that forced public schools to desegregate.

The inevitable comparisons between Marshall and Thomas would hound Thomas throughout his confirmation fight. It's a burden that remains difficult for him to bear. The Alliance for Justice, which led the opposition to his confirmation, was quick to produce a short tract comparing the two. Entitled "Marshall and Thomas: The Starkest of Contrasts," it listed nearly a dozen issues on which Thomas and Marshall disagreed. Whereas the *Brown* decision marked Marshall's biggest legal triumph, Thomas had questioned the legal basis for the decision, believing it relied too heavily on squishy psychological evidence rather than rock-solid constitutional principles. Marshall was for school busing; Thomas was against it. Marshall supported affirmative action, abortion rights, and, more broadly, an expansive reading of the Constitution. Thomas opposed all of that. In repeatedly measuring him against Marshall, Thomas felt, his critics were only trying to make him look small and minimize his own remarkable story of achievement. Though this open disrespect by liberal activists was eating away at him inside, he was determined to win confirmation.

The White House wasted no time mounting a vigorous campaign on his behalf. Kenneth Duberstein, the veteran GOP political consultant who had managed David Souter's confirmation, was put in charge of overseeing strategy again. At his disposal was a reenergized army of conservative activists itching for a fight. Still smarting from the 1987 defeat of Supreme Court nominee Robert H. Bork and feeling duped by the White House over Souter (it was clear he was not one of their own), the conservative movement now had a nominee their troops truly believed in.

At the centerpiece of the Thomas confirmation blueprint—the so-called Pin Point Strategy—was an emphasis on his humble upbringing and rural Southern roots. White House advisers realized they would need to neutralize black opposition. Splintering the broader black community was considered essential if Thomas was to have a chance, especially at winning the crucial votes of Southern Democratic senators with large black constituencies. A series of carefully orchestrated lunches and dinners with black lawyers, judges, and others of prominence was arranged. White House strategists even culled the government's personnel rolls and developed a list of black Bush appointees with law degrees in an effort to find people who could help influence the National Bar Association on behalf of Thomas, according to an internal White House memorandum.

Thomas could be very effective in small gatherings, and none was more important than a private session with selected leaders of the NAACP. The meeting, considered so sensitive that participants on both sides agreed not even to confirm its existence, was held on July 19 in the Washington home of Constance Newman, a senior Bush administration official and close Thomas friend. Newman, an NAACP member herself, knew many of the organization's leaders well.

Thomas came prepared to surprise the group. According to the confidential draft minutes of the two-hour meeting, Thomas told the NAACP officials that he supported affirmative action (and only opposed quotas, like most other Americans). He also said he had supported class action lawsuits to fight discrimination while at the helm of the EEOC, implying that any views to the contrary attributed to him had been mischaracterized. He pointed out that he had been especially helpful to minorities at the EEOC (67 percent of his hires were minorities). As for his criticisms of LBJ's Great Society poverty programs, Thomas conceded he may have been too sweeping in pronouncing their failure—some of the programs had indeed benefited the poor, he acknowledged. On a personal note, Thomas said the disparaging comments he had made about his impoverished sister some years back also had been misunderstood. He and his sister were actually very close, he told the civil rights delegation—in fact, he had helped raise her oldest son. Against virtually every challenge, Thomas tried to soften the sharp edges of his conservative philosophy and present himself as a sensitive man who had been misjudged, someone who shared the NAACP's goals of equal opportunity and justice for African Americans. It was an extraordinary performance.

Returning to their hotel to discuss the session, the members of the NAACP delegation acknowledged Thomas had been impressive. Hazel Dukes, an influential board member who had initiated the meeting, said Thomas had confirmed his "blackness" and seemed to remember "where he came from."

It would take the NAACP another twelve days to take a stand on the Thomas nomination—a full thirty days after Bush had announced his choice. Some within the liberal activist community were frustrated by the struggle inside the NAACP. They knew that a war loomed ahead, and it would require a quick mobilization of opposition forces. Without the nation's oldest and largest civil rights organization leading the way, efforts to galvanize a coalition against Thomas were slowed.

On July 31, the NAACP finally announced it would oppose Thomas's confirmation. The following day it released a lengthy, footnoted report based on a review of Thomas's performance in government, including an analysis of his speeches, writings, and interviews. The conclusion: Thomas "fails to demonstrate a respect for or commitment to the enforcement of federal laws protecting civil rights and individual liberties."

But by that time, Thomas was having a pretty good summer—at least image-wise. Not only had he made it difficult for the leading civil rights group to reach a decision, he was causing many other African Americans to take a second look at him as well. On the day the NAACP announced its opposition, a busload of thirty-five Georgians descended on Capitol Hill in support of him. The trip, led by

State Senator Roy Allen III, a Democrat, drew widespread media attention. Some of the Georgians were from Pin Point, some from Savannah, others from Liberty County, where Thomas still had relatives and his grandfather had owned a farm. The White House loved this imagery—salt-of-the-earth black folks seen on television walking the halls of Congress, having breakfast with Thomas, sharing childhood memories.

The trip was not all that it seemed to be. Thomas's own mother, for one, considered it just a PR gimmick designed to further Allen's political ambitions. "Oh, yeah, he wanted to be in the limelight then," Leola Williams said. To Williams, Allen was a shady character—he would later serve more than three years in prison for swindling law clients and be disbarred. The trip from Georgia to D.C. was financed largely by a conservative legal foundation. And the bus, she noted, was filled primarily with people who had no connection to her son. "Just a few people that he took . . . knew Clarence." Adding to her gall, Allen didn't even inform her of the trip, Williams said, until the night before the bus was to leave. She refused to go.

Relations between Allen and Thomas's family already had been strained. In the aftermath of Myers Anderson's death in 1983, the family had retained Allen to do some legal work related to Anderson's estate. In an interview, Williams told us the incredible tale of retrieving a hatchet from her kitchen to shoo Allen away when he came to collect money she didn't believe he was entitled to collect, "and he had one second to get out of my door."

Before the C-SPAN cameras, Thomas had thanked Allen warmly for spearheading the bus excursion. But according to Thomas's mother, privately her son was surprised that Allen had been in charge of the trip and disappointed that there were not more people aboard who "really knew him and how he was raised." The truth was Allen and Thomas weren't particularly close. Though they had been altar boys together and had attended one Savannah Catholic school together, Allen was much younger. Thus, he was never a

Thomas classmate, as he had suggested he was to reporters and confirmation handlers.

Another truth: Thomas's good summer was about to be ruined.

George Kassouf had been investigating Thomas for two years—
dating back to when the White House was rumored to be considering him for a federal appeals court vacancy on the D.C. Circuit. As a
senior staffer with the Alliance for Justice, the liberal watchdog group
that lobbied Congress on judicial matters, Kassouf was dogged and
thorough. His Thomas file included more than a hundred interviews
with friends, coworkers, congressional staffers, and others who had
interacted with Thomas. In a town consumed by politics, there were
always people with reason to talk. Kassouf also had reviewed more
than one million pages of documents related to Thomas's government service, most of them dealing with his long tenure at the
EEOC. His conclusion: "To be brutally honest, this was a man oper-
ating by the seat of his pants at the EEOC. He was too young to be
heading an agency and too mediocre of a lawyer."

Kassouf thought Thomas's public record was egregious enough to
block his elevation to the high court—things like the mishandling of
age discrimination complaints, examples of retaliation against employees, indications of an extremist legal philosophy, and so on. In
mid-July 1991, as Kassouf was preparing to turn his research into a
series of reports, he got a telephone call at home from a friend. The
friend had been at a party and someone had mentioned that Thomas
had sexually harassed an employee at the EEOC, a woman who now
taught law in Oklahoma.

"Oh, that's important," Kassouf told his friend.

The following day, Kassouf shared the information with his executive director, Nan Aron. Looking through a law directory, it was
easy to determine that the woman was Anita Hill, a former EEOC
employee, Yale Law School graduate, and now University of Oklahoma law professor. Kassouf gathered every piece of information he

could to flesh out her biography, searched his files to see if her name had ever surfaced before—it hadn't—and wrote down her office number. Aron did not think it was appropriate to call Hill directly. So Kassouf passed on the tip and what he had compiled about Hill to Bill Corr, a counsel for Senator Howard Metzenbaum, Democrat of Ohio, a Judiciary Committee liberal who had been tough on Thomas in past congressional hearings.

Kassouf continued to do his own research on Hill, tracking down people who had worked with her in the 1980s. What was her story? Was she credible? A crackpot? But Kassouf could find no one who had a strong recollection of her. Meanwhile, Aron would periodically check in with her investigator: "Have you heard anything?"

Nothing. The Hill allegation was getting no traction on Capitol Hill. Not only did Metzenbaum's staff not pursue it aggressively, they were reluctant to even bring it to the senator's attention. They knew how uncomfortable he was with personal matters like sexual harassment.

Thus, the summer ended and the Hill allegation had gone nowhere. With the confirmation hearings about to begin, Thomas's handlers were reasonably confident. But not overly so.

The Senate can be a frustrating institution for those who must deal with it. Members are sometimes hard to read, but they all—to a greater or lesser degree—want to be courted. Each lawmaker has the comfort of a six-year term and an outsize influence the body's rules confer on the individual member. Thus, no senator, regardless of whether he or she holds a committee chairmanship or party leadership title, regardless of whether he or she is famous or obscure, can be taken for granted. The ritual dance a judicial nominee must do to get confirmed—the courtesy visits to lawmakers' offices, making oneself available to answer every mundane question—can't be avoided.

The instructions to Thomas were to play the inside game: remain as stealthy as possible, evade when evasion is called for, and otherwise say whatever the senators want to hear. Bork had not bothered listening to this advice, and he went down in flames. Thomas, too, was uneasy following this script. "He was coached to answer in certain ways that might have made him feel uncomfortable," acknowledged C. Boyden Gray, the White House counsel at the time. But as Gray put it, "it's how you handle yourself that's far more important than what is actually said. And Thomas handled himself fine."

The Bush White House had employed this strategy with Souter, its last Supreme Court nominee, and he breezed through. Souter was the perfect portrait of dull and nonthreatening. But it also helped that he was from the tiny state of New Hampshire and came without Thomas's burdensome record of national service that included running a controversial federal agency and delivering well over a hundred speeches that could be picked through.

Appearing before the Judiciary Committee, a visibly uncomfortable Thomas managed to tiptoe through the minefields of abortion, civil rights, equal employment enforcement, natural law, and other topics that could have detonated his nomination. He was vague and a bit coy, and not especially inspiring. Overcoached, some supporters thought. All in all, not a terrific performance—but good enough.

On September 27, after seventeen days of questioning and contemplation, the committee deadlocked—7–7—but sent Thomas's nomination to the full Senate for a vote on October 8. The White House felt it could muster enough votes to send him to the high court. Though Democrats controlled the Senate by a 57–43 margin, the defection of Senator Dennis DeConcini, Democrat of Arizona, in the Judiciary Committee was a good sign. (Without DeConcini, who had opposed Bork, the Thomas nomination would have been voted down in committee.) The White House scenario called for locking down the votes of virtually the entire Republican caucus, inasmuch as there were a couple of moderates who couldn't be counted on. That would mean approximately ten Democratic votes would be needed to secure confirmation, and by some estimates anywhere from thirteen to nineteen Senate Democrats were likely to support Thomas. Unknown to all but a few in the inner circle, however, a crisis was looming behind the scenes that would threaten those calculations.

Ricki Seidman, an influential staffer for Senator Edward M. Kennedy, Democrat of Massachusetts, had been made aware of Anita Hill's allegations and had started asking questions. Hill had been contacted. Though reluctant, she agreed to be interviewed by James Brudney, a Metzenbaum staffer who had been a Yale Law classmate.

On September 23, Hill faxed to the committee a four-page statement outlining her allegations of sexual harassment. In 1981, soon after she was hired by Thomas as a special assistant at the Department of Education, she said, he began asking her out socially. She did not think it was appropriate to date her boss and refused. Thomas then would call her into his office repeatedly or ask her to go to lunch in the government cafeteria under the guise of discussing work. Quickly, he turned the conversations to sex. He spoke vividly of the pornographic movies he had watched, scenes involving group sex, rape, women having sex with animals. He spoke of pornographic materials depicting women with large breasts and men with big penises. After some months, the conversations ended—Hill thought it was perhaps because Thomas had a girlfriend. Believing his behavior had ceased, she accepted a job offer from Thomas when he left to become chairman of the EEOC in May 1982. But at the EEOC, his advances resumed. In 1983, following a hospitalization for stomach pains she attributed to stress, Hill resigned.

The allegations were explosive. Fred McClure, the White House point man on the nomination, was tracked down as he headed for the airport in San Francisco, where he had just delivered a speech. Given the grim news by an aide—they weren't on a secure phone line so not many details were shared—McClure had a sick feeling. After his plane landed, he headed straight for the White House. Sitting in his office at 1 a.m., he kept staring at Hill's statement. "Oh, my God," he thought to himself. "We're going to have to go through this all over again."

Instinctively, McClure knew there would be another investigation of the nominee and probably a reopening of the hearings—in short, a separate, tougher battle to get Thomas confirmed.

And how would Thomas handle that? On the morning of September 25, the White House informed him that a new allegation had been raised against him and the FBI would need to investigate. No specifics were mentioned, and a nervous Thomas scheduled an interview with the FBI that afternoon. When the agents arrived at his suburban Virginia home and detailed Hill's allegations, Thomas was stunned. "Anita? You can't—you've got to be kidding. This can't be true."

The accusations sapped the life out of Thomas and made him morose. A friend from Yale Law School remembers speaking to him during this period, before the allegations surfaced publicly. Based on what he had been hearing and reading, the friend told Thomas, things were looking good for confirmation. No, Thomas responded. "She's lying about me. I'm going to have some problems." Thomas had assumed Hill's allegations were a hot item on Washington's social circuit. "But I didn't know what he was talking about," recalled the friend, a well-connected Washington attorney, and he didn't ask.

Soon, the whole world would know. On October 6, Hill's allegations were disclosed by Timothy Phelps in *Newsday* and by Nina Totenberg on National Public Radio. The ensuing uproar forced the Senate to delay its October 8 vote on the nomination. The Judiciary Committee, amid charges that it had failed to properly investigate Hill's claims, was pressured to reconvene for a special three-day hearing.

Washington, for all its concentrated power, often seems like a podunk town. Secrets are difficult to keep, especially political secrets. As it turned out, Anita Hill had set the chain of events in motion herself by confiding in an old law school chum, Gary Phillips, early in the summer. Without providing details, she told him why she had left the EEOC. Phillips, then a lawyer at the Federal Communications Commission, shared her story of sexual harassment with a few close friends, without naming Hill. The story circulated further until it became the topic of a dinner party, which is how George Kassouf found out about it—from a friend at that dinner party.

Now a personal trainer with the compact build of a gymnast, Kassouf no longer investigates judicial nominees. He spends his days working out, traveling around town by bicycle. "I spent all of this time building this big case [against Thomas], and the Anita Hill thing probably took two hours of my time," Kassouf says with amazement.

The Anita Hill thing would destroy Clarence Thomas.

There was no other way to describe Thomas during this period: He was a mess. Hill's allegations had become the nation's top news story, and Thomas felt powerless and broken. He could not even summon his trademark defiance as a strength. His wife, Ginni, was a fighter and the rock behind her husband. But she was struggling to find ways to help Clarence now. "His anger is gone," she told a friend of her husband's one evening.

His friends were worried. On October 9, two days before the Hill-Thomas hearings were to begin, several made a pilgrimage to his home and brought dinner. They found him in a state of dishevelment. He was wearing beat-up pants and a polo shirt, thick socks but no shoes. His eyes were red—lots of crying and too little sleep—and he needed a haircut. "I feel like someone has reached up inside me and ripped out my insides," Thomas told one of the friends later in the evening.

They had hoped to lift his spirits, but the evening didn't go well. All had worked with Thomas in Senator John Danforth's office and had grown close to him. Discovering him more despairing than they had even imagined, they were determined to help him find a way out of his predicament.

Allen Moore thought there must have been something Thomas had said that Hill simply misinterpreted. Moore, Danforth's legislative director when Thomas was on the staff, had been the one arguing that in order for Thomas to clear his name a delay in the confirmation vote and hearings on Hill's allegations were essential. Now, he needed some answers. Was Thomas sure there was nothing between him and Hill? Mistaken intentions, perhaps? "I don't want to talk about it," Thomas said, his head buried in his hands.

The friends quizzed Thomas because they hoped to land on a strategy to win a confirmation that was now imperiled. But to Thomas, the quizzing seemed like a grilling. Instead of relaxing him, he later said, the evening just further wore him down. Already wary of handlers, Thomas did not want to be surrounded by friends whose focus was strategy. By contrast, that morning the Thomases' prayer partners—Charles and Kay James, Steven and Elizabeth Law—had come by the house. For three hours, the couples prayed and read the Bible. How uplifting these friends were, Ginni later recounted, "versus people strategizing and not thinking about God and that element of it."

That night was awful for Thomas. Unable to sleep, he tossed and turned until finally he crawled out of bed and onto the floor, where he squirmed in agony "like something was inside of him, physically," Ginni recalled, "like there was this battle going on inside of him. . . . What it felt like was that Clarence still had some sin in his life and he had to get that out in order to be open to the Holy Spirit." The contortions on the floor, the emotional distress, continued until 5:30 or 6:00 a.m.

To his family and friends from Georgia, Thomas had become almost unrecognizable. "He had one foot in the grave and one on earth," recalled childhood friend Abe Famble. Thomas's sister, Emma, wondered why her brother had relied so heavily on the advice of Washington insiders in the first place. That was part of the problem, she thought. She had sat through the initial phase of the hearings thinking Clarence had been transformed into a neutered shell of himself, stripped of his robust confidence and humor. "Just like an alley cat or a leopard," she said, "he changed his spots."

All the hotshot strategists and advisers hadn't been able to get the job done. The way Emma Martin figured it, What had all this smart advice gotten her brother? He was now looking at three days of televised hearings over a leaked allegation of harassment that had crushed his spirit and embarrassed his family. Emma could hardly stomach it.

Family members had more confidence in the Reverend Henry Delaney than they did in Ken Duberstein and his ilk. Delaney, pastor of the St. Paul C. M. E. Church in Savannah, had foreseen Thomas's nomination two months before it happened and would later prophesy the trouble that was threatening to derail confirmation. "I'm not a psychic," Delaney made clear. "It's kind of like I'm charismatic," he said. "I guess that's the term they'd use now."

Whatever the term, on the day Thomas was nominated to the high court Leola Williams was at St. Paul's evening Bible study. Delaney told her to have her son read Psalm 109, verses 26–28:

Help me, O Lord my God!
   Save me because of your unfailing love.
Let them see that this is your doing,
   that you yourself have done it, Lord.
Then let them curse me if they like,
   but you will bless me!
When they attack me, they will be disgraced!
   But I, your servant, will go right on rejoicing!

If he reads those passages each day, Delaney told Leola Williams, he will be protected. Thomas followed that advice and later drew closer to Delaney. After he was confirmed, he spoke at Delaney's church. And when Thomas came back home, he often made a point of stopping by Delaney's office for a visit. In 1993, when Delaney was starting an all-boys' religious academy, Thomas assisted him in getting funding. Thomas turned to Clint Bolick, a conservative legal activist who had been a key figure in his confirmation campaign and asked him to give Delaney a call. Bolick put Delaney in touch with the Randolph Foundation, which donated $15,000. This is the way

Thomas operates. He is fiercely loyal to those who have helped him and holds long grudges against those who haven't.

Delaney was someone Thomas's mother trusted. She couldn't say the same about everyone.

Among Thomas's advisers, there was greater unease about the nominee than anyone had publicly conveyed. Danforth, for one, was concerned about "the danger of perjury" if Thomas went too far with his categorical denials of Hill's allegations, according to his remarkably candid book, *Resurrection: The Confirmation of Clarence Thomas*. "My worry," he wrote, "was that Clarence, in his insistence that he had said nothing intentionally offensive, would wrongly state that he had said nothing at all." Danforth asked Mike Luttig, the Justice Department lawyer who was coaching Thomas, to "warn Clarence of this and to tell him that there was one thing far worse than failure to be confirmed for the Supreme Court: impeachment from the circuit court."

Luttig, who would go on to become a Fourth Circuit Court of Appeals judge, did just that at a preparation session on the morning of October 10, the day before the hearings were to begin. "Clarence," he instructed, "you cannot lie to the nation for the next two days." And then Luttig grilled Thomas—not only about his relationship with Hill but about sensitive aspects of his personal life, including dealings with other women. Thomas convinced Luttig he was being truthful, in part because of his willingness to reveal embarrassing details about his past, details Luttig would not divulge to us. Still, Danforth wanted some insurance against perjury, and he and Duberstein pushed Thomas to include some equivocating language in his opening statement. Thus, Thomas would end up telling the Judiciary Committee that "if there is anything that I have said that has been misconstrued by Anita Hill or anyone else, to be sexual harassment, then I can say that I am so very sorry and I wish I had known."

This concession to Danforth ran counter to the thrust of Thomas's statement of categorical denial. And it certainly didn't reflect his disposition about the proceedings, which he considered a gross injustice to him. But it would not be the last time that Thomas's confidants would try to protect him against the possibility that he might not be telling the truth.

Within the Bush administration, there were senior officials who wanted to ditch Thomas. "Oh, yes, sure," acknowledged the former White House counsel, C. Boyden Gray, adding that there are always people who sweat when the heat is turned up high. Gray wanted to stick with Thomas, and so did the president. "I knew he was being put through hell," Bush told us. "He once came to the White House and offered to step down if I felt he was hurting me or my administration. I walked with him around the South Lawn, put my arm on his shoulder, and told [him] he must stay in the fray."

OK, Thomas relented, he would hang in there. But truthfully, he wasn't sure he really wanted the job anymore.

"Mr. Chairman and Senators, my name is Charles A. Kothe."

The founding dean of Oral Roberts University's law school knew both Anita Hill and Clarence Thomas. In fact, he met them at the same time, at a 1983 seminar on civil rights he organized. Kothe had invited Thomas to participate, and the EEOC chairman asked if he could bring staff. During a luncheon at which Thomas was the featured speaker, Kothe discovered that one of the two aides accompanying the chairman, Anita Hill, was a native Oklahoman. Impressed with her, he asked on a whim: "How would you like to come home and teach?" Two months later Hill was offered a faculty position, and she started work in Tulsa that summer. A year later Kothe resigned as dean, and in 1985 he ended up working as a special assistant to Thomas. He stayed in contact with Hill and became friends with Thomas, and on a couple of occasions they all shared meals together.

And that is how Charles A. Kothe wound up testifying at a special session of the Senate Judiciary Committee on October 13, 1991. He was the rare witness who had befriended both of these engaging human beings whose reputations were now being simultaneously bolstered and bludgeoned on national television. The committee, with a process that teetered between clumsy and excruciating, was trying to get at a truth that ultimately proved unknowable: Did Clarence Thomas sexually harass Hill, as she alleged, when he was her boss at the Department of Education and then at the EEOC?

Stumbling into territory that was both racially and sexually charged, the all-white, all-male committee hosted an unprecedented discussion of penis and breast sizes, pubic hair, and a certain adult film star named Long Dong Silver. The proceedings often seemed surreal, the questions frequently embarrassing—and yet the nation followed this televised entanglement as though it were a riveting new miniseries. Michael Crichton, the novelist who would go on to create the TV drama *ER*, was among those who were fixated. He phoned his college classmate Boyden Gray to offer Thomas his support and to admit it was television he couldn't turn away from. This was not your standard C-SPAN programming.

"In the mail that you might have opened," Senator Howell Heflin, Democrat of Alabama, drawled to Thomas's former secretary Diane Holt, "did you ever open any mail that contained pornographic materials?"

"I did not," Holt replied.

Allegiances quickly formed at health clubs, on college campuses, around employee lunch tables—anywhere spirited debate could be had. This was especially true in black communities.

Hill or Thomas?

Thomas addressed the committee first, his choice, on the morning of October 11. He had not had much sleep. He had been working on his statement, alone, through much of the night and into the morning. Only Ginni had seen it. At 6:30 a.m., he had read it to Danforth.

"I have been wracking my brains and eating my insides out trying to think of what I could have said or done to Anita Hill to lead her to allege that I was interested in her in more than a professional way, and that I talked with her about pornographic or X-rated films," he testified. "Contrary to some press reports, I categorically denied all of the allegations and denied that I ever attempted to date Anita Hill, when first interviewed by the FBI. I strongly reaffirm that denial." Thomas went on to outline his relationship with Hill, a professional relationship that never strayed beyond that, he said. "I have never in all my life felt such hurt, such pain, such agony. My family and I have been done a grave and irreparable injustice. During the past two weeks, I lost the belief that if I did my best all would work out. . . . Perhaps I could have better weathered this if it were from someone else, but here was someone I truly felt I had done my best with. Though I am by no means a perfect person, I have not done what she has alleged, and I still do not know what I could possibly have done to cause her to make these allegations."

Hill testified next. Calm and persuasive, she accused Thomas of crudely pursuing her with explicit, unwanted, "ugly" sexual overtures. The youngest of thirteen children, she was raised by devoutly religious parents on a farm in rural Oklahoma. Albert and Erma Hill, both nearing eighty, had come to Washington to be with her. And at one point, as she hugged her mother, the emotional weight of the ordeal made her want to cry. She would later recount how she fought that desire, determined to show strength, not tears. Her background was not unlike Thomas's. Like her former boss, she had defied expectations and graduated from Yale Law School. Before heading off to Yale, she had never spent more than two weeks outside of Oklahoma. Now she had a sophisticated bearing. Some saw her as prim, others as cool and detached. But no one thought she was unimpressive.

Thomas repeatedly asked her out, she testified, but wouldn't accept no for an answer. Work discussions, she said, quickly turned to the subject of sex. "On several occasions," Hill testified, "Thomas told me graphically of his own sexual prowess. . . . My efforts to change the subject were rarely successful." She remembered Thomas telling her that some day she would have to explain the "real reason" she wouldn't go out with him. "He began to show displeasure in his tone and voice and his demeanor in his continued pressure for an explanation. He commented on what I was wearing in terms of whether it made me more or less sexually attractive. . . . On other occasions he referred to the size of his own penis as being larger than normal and he also spoke on some occasions of the pleasures he had given to women with oral sex. At this point, late 1982, I began to feel severe stress on the job. I began to be concerned that Clarence Thomas might take out his anger with me by degrading me or not giving me important assignments. I also thought that he might find an excuse for dismissing me."

Hill decided to leave. On the final day of her EEOC employment in the summer of 1983, Thomas took her to dinner, she said. They went directly from the office to a nearby restaurant. Thomas discussed the work she had done at both the Department of Education and the EEOC, work he had been pleased with, she testified, except for one article and a speech he didn't like. "Finally he made a comment that I will vividly remember," she said. "He said that if I ever told anyone of his behavior that it would ruin his career. This was not an apology, nor was it an explanation. That was his last remark about the possibility of our going out, or reference to his behavior."

Under the rules worked out in the committee, Hill would undergo questioning after her statement. Thomas would return afterward to answer questions from the committee. So angry was Thomas that he refused to watch Hill's testimony on television. "I've heard enough lies," he said later. It was a decision even some Thomas loyalists thought was a mistake.

When he did return to the hearing room after Hill's testimony, at 9 p.m. that Friday night, he seemed even more resolute. "Senators, I would like to start out," he testified, "by saying unequivocally . . . that I deny each and every single allegation against me today that suggested in any way that I had conversations of a sexual nature or about pornographic material with Anita Hill, that I ever attempted to date her, that I ever had any personal sexual interest in her, or that

I in any way ever harassed her. Second, and I think a more important point, I think that this today is a travesty. I think that it is disgusting. I think that this hearing should never occur in America. This is a case in which this sleaze, this dirt, was searched for by staffers of members of this committee, was then leaked to the media, and this committee and this body validated it and displayed it in prime time over our entire nation."

Ginni was sitting behind him, looking pained in a black-and-white checkered suit. It had been a long, difficult day and Thomas's face seemed the worse for it. His jaw was tight, like that of a man seething inside. The Supreme Court was not worth it, he said. No job was worth it. Reporters braced, preparing to write stories that he was withdrawing from consideration. And then the bristling Thomas dropped his bomb.

"And from my standpoint, as a black American, as far as I'm concerned it is a high-tech lynching for uppity blacks who in any way deign to think for themselves, to do for themselves, to have different ideas, and it is a message that, unless you kow-tow to an old order, this is what will happen to you—you will be lynched, destroyed, caricatured by a committee of the U.S. Senate, rather than hung from a tree."

Thomas's words froze the committee, Democrats and Republicans alike. By invoking the starkest reminder of a racially gruesome past, Thomas raised questions not just about his level of bitterness and hurt but about his shrewdness. What could have been more divisive and more galvanizing all at once? He had managed simultaneously to exploit white guilt and black rage, not to mention unnerve his inquisitors. Thomas intimates say he spoke from a heavy heart filled with anger. But whatever anger resided in his heart, what came tumbling out of his mouth was not unscripted.

According to Senator Arlen Specter, Republican of Pennsylvania, Thomas later told him the high-tech lynching remark was "not a spur-of-the-moment comment" but something he had written down earlier, having studied the real lynchings of blacks in the South. The week before the hearings, Thomas's close friend Cliff Faddis, a St. Louis attorney who happens to be white, had come up with an idea that was "remarkably parallel," noted John Danforth, to the lynching comment Thomas made before the committee. Faddis's thought was to stand on the federal courthouse steps in St. Louis with a noose around his neck to dramatize, as he told another Thomas friend, that "they're hanging this guy. Let's go do something like they're doing to him." Faddis didn't go through with his plan, and it's unclear whether Thomas learned of it firsthand, but the notion of Thomas as a lynching victim had certainly been planted before the hearings ever began.

The White House was not happy that Thomas had injected race into the hearings, thinking it unhelpful politically. White House congressional liaison Fred McClure, the most senior African American involved in steering the nomination, was personally uncomfortable with the lynching metaphor. "Could he have used other words? Yeah."

As a rule, senators don't like to be dressed down publicly. Senator Herbert Kohl, Democrat of Wisconsin, who as owner of the Milwaukee Bucks was experienced in dealing with the flare-ups of professional athletes, was startled—and upset—by Thomas's characterization of the committee as a lynch mob. "It wasn't true, you know. I thought he was playing the [race] card," Kohl says. Cynically speaking, maybe Thomas knew it was the only card he had left to play. Maybe he knew it would make just enough senators feel guilty to put him over the top.

Looking back on that time, Kohl says he remains most struck by Thomas's performance during his personal interview with him in the senator's office. In Kohl's eyes, Thomas was a fraud, pretending he would not be the kind of conservative jurist some had feared. "So what I think has become clear, as life has played itself out with him over the last [sixteen] years, is that the man that he tried to tell us he was is not the person who has been sitting there for [sixteen] years and voting." Kohl didn't support Thomas's confirmation, after initially being inclined to do so. But what he believes most strongly now is that the nominee deliberately misled senators. "He led me to believe, and I think he led others to believe, that he would be a worthy successor to Thurgood Marshall," Kohl says. "And nobody would suggest that he's been that. I mean, not anybody."

The starkly different testimonies of Hill and Thomas left no possibility for misunderstanding. Wiggle room? There was none. Neither Hill nor Thomas offered a backstory about their involvement with each other that might have led the Senate—indeed, the nation—to conclude something beyond the obvious: One of them was lying, period. Was lying to the committee, to the country, perhaps even to him or herself.

In sixteen years, no new evidence—diaries, bedside death confessions, recantations by witnesses on either side—has emerged to clear up the mystery. All that's left is conjecture. Did Thomas, his reputation sullied, his nomination about to go down in a blaze of humiliation, see perjury as his only out, a last desperate act of self-preservation? Could Hill have been a spurned woman, rejected by Thomas romantically, devalued by him as a staffer, and ultimately prodded by zealous opponents of the man into sabotaging his nomination?

One of the most intriguing unknowables is: What would have happened if Angela Wright had testified? Judiciary Committee chairman Joseph Biden, Democrat of Delaware, said almost a year after the hearings that he was convinced her testimony would have derailed Thomas's nomination. And yet he didn't insist on Wright's testimony—no member of the committee did. Wright, attractive and outspoken, was a *Charlotte Observer* editor. She watched the television coverage sympathizing with Hill, "remembering that Thomas" had treated her much the same way when she was his EEOC public affairs director in 1984. Committee staff members were led to Wright by someone inside the newspaper, and she agreed to be interviewed by Senate staffers via conference call. The transcript runs to thirty-seven pages.

In the interview, Wright recounts how Thomas persistently pressured her to date him even though she told him she had no interest. He showed up uninvited at her apartment one night, once asked her the size of her breasts at an EEOC seminar, and commented about other women's anatomies in her presence. Thomas noted, for instance, that one of his staffers had "a big ass," Wright recalls.

Though Wright was subpoenaed, flew to Washington, and sat in a hotel room expecting to testify, she never did. Republicans were desperate not to have a "second woman" follow Hill on national television with allegations of lewd behavior by Thomas, and Democrats feared that Wright's credibility would be undermined because of her work history. She had been fired by Thomas, who told the committee it was because Wright was ineffective and because he had been told that she had called an EEOC employee a "faggot," a charge she denies. Wright was also fired by a member of Congress and had quit a third job in government, accusing her boss of incompetence and racism.

Wright, however, had much in her favor on the credibility front. She had not hyped her allegations—in fact, she had made a point of saying she did not believe she was sexually harassed. Thomas had given a reference checker at the *Charlotte Observer* a glowing recommendation of Wright. And most significantly, Wright had someone who would corroborate her account. Rose Jourdain, a former EEOC speechwriter, told Senate staffers that Wright had become increasingly uneasy around Thomas during Wright's year at the agency because of comments he made "concerning her figure, her body, her breasts, her legs, how she looked in certain suits and dresses." Once, Jourdain recalled, Wright came to her office in tears.

Biden finally negotiated an out for his nervous committee. He lifted Wright's subpoena, and the transcripts of the interviews with Wright and Jourdain were entered into the record without rebuttal. The practical effect of that decision was to blunt the potential force of Wright's account. Her story gained only modest national prominence.

With no second woman occupying the main stage, Hill's allegations were treated as a perplexing she-said, he-said saga. Because the accusations involved private interactions, only Hill and Thomas know for sure what transpired between them. But loyalists on both sides strongly suspect there is more to Hill and Thomas's shared history than either of them has owned up to.

According to a close relative of Hill's, even some of her immediate family question whether she was completely candid during the hearings. "No one that I know of in the family doubts that she told the truth [about the harassment]," the relative told us. "But many of us were unsure if she was totally open about the details of her overall feelings for and relationship with Thomas." Meanwhile, Fred McClure, the White House aide who was deeply involved in shepherding the nomination, acknowledged to us something Thomas has never publicly admitted: He suspects Hill and Thomas may indeed have had a social relationship but "it just didn't go anywhere for one reason or another." McClure can't pinpoint where he got "this impression," as he put it, and whether Thomas had privately owned up to it or not. But he believes that there was, or could have been, some sort of romantic involvement. "Yes, I do."

The nagging sense that there was a side to the Hill-Thomas relationship that neither of them wished to divulge is something that also has lingered in the mind of Hank Brown, the former Republican senator of Colorado. A Thomas supporter on the Judiciary Committee, Brown had wanted to extend the second phase of the hearings beyond three days to learn more about the Hill-Thomas association. But there was no appetite among his colleagues for more investigation or more calling of witnesses. A motion to extend the hearings was voted down 12–2 in committee. Brown remains puzzled by the "dramatically different stories" told by two "exceptionally credible witnesses," as he puts it. "I personally found that strange, that both of them said they had no interest in each other. That always remained a mystery to me."

Charles A. Kothe, now deceased, was of no help solving the mystery when he was sworn in on the final day of the hearings. Though he was on good terms with both Hill and Thomas, neutrality didn't seem to be an option in this process. Everyone connected with Hill and Thomas was choosing sides, and Kothe chose Thomas. He concluded, without evidence, that Hill's allegations must have been "fantasy," a word choice he later regretted, he said. But what Kothe ended up saying about Thomas seems more insightful today than anyone realized at the time.

As if to establish himself as an expert on Thomas's character, Kothe spoke of their long drives "through the swamps of Georgia together, where he showed me where he was reared." He testified that they had spent considerable time together on planes, at business meetings, at banquets, and, on at least four occasions, at dinners in Kothe's home. Often they had ended up in discussions that lasted until the end of the night. "Never, ever," Kothe told the senators, "in all that time did I ever hear that man utter a profane word, never engage in any coarse conduct or loose talk." And then Kothe put an exclamation point on his certainty that Thomas could not possibly have said the things Hill alleged he said. "If it were true," Kothe testified, "it is the greatest Jekyll and Hyde story in the history of mankind."

What Kothe didn't know—and neither did most of the Senate—is that Thomas had a history of using coarse language, telling raunchy jokes, engaging in sexual banter, watching graphic adult videos. That history got buried during the hearings, and the committee wasn't interested in excavating it. As for Kothe, Thomas simply never shared that part of his persona with the dean. Kothe was like most others in Thomas's orbit—cut in on some things, clueless about others. Thus, the procession of witnesses who cited personal experiences to make a larger point about Thomas's virtue and veracity were reflecting a limited reality. There was much many of them just didn't know about this man whose pattern was to present different sides of himself to different people, even to the point of telling different stories about the same subject. For example, Thomas told some intimates he never aspired to the Supreme Court, and yet others remember him specifically naming the high court as an aspiration. Same with Yale Law School. To some, he constantly disparaged the school; to others, he spoke of his Yale years longingly.

Thomas's shifting opinions on many topics greatly troubled some committee members and raised for Senator Heflin "thoughts of inconsistencies, ambiguities, contradictions, lack of scholarship, lack of conviction, and instability." Especially disturbing to Heflin, a former judge, was Thomas's describing Oliver Wendell Holmes to the Judiciary Committee as a "great judge." In a 1988 speech, Thomas had denigrated Holmes by quoting a Walter Berns essay that said "no man who ever sat on the Supreme Court was less inclined and so poorly equipped to be a statesman or to teach . . . what a people needs in order to govern itself well."

In truth, Thomas had exhibited exactly the kind of Jekyll and Hyde persona that Kothe alluded to. So when EEOC aide Pam Talkin testified that Thomas "has a feminist's understanding of sexual politics" and "loathes locker room talk," she was right—as far as she knew. She just didn't know what James Millet, Thomas's Holy Cross classmate, knew. Millet is a Census Bureau statistician who likes to dance the night away at trendy nightclubs; he lives in suburban Washington but has only seen Thomas once since they graduated, back in the 1980s. As Millet remembers the occasion, they both were at a stoplight in northeast Washington. Thomas, then the EEOC chairman, honked, got out, and told Millet to give him a call. Millet never did. But watching Anita Hill's testimony got him to thinking about Thomas in ways he had not done since they left college.

What especially caught Millet's attention was a particular Hill recollection. "One of the oddest episodes I remember was an occasion in which Thomas was drinking a Coke in his office," Hill testified. "He got up from the table at which we were working, went over to his desk to get the Coke, looked at the can, and asked, 'Who has put pubic hair on my Coke?' "

Millet, who doesn't know Hill and has never been interviewed until now, recalled an almost identical episode at Holy Cross. He was in Thomas's room one evening with several other guys. A Coke can was on Thomas's desk. Thomas walked up to it, as Millet recalls, looked inside and said: "Somebody put a pubic hair in my Coca-Cola." Millet, known for his deadpan humor, quickly shot back: "I didn't do it!" And everybody cracked up. Listening to Hill's testimony, Millet figured this must be one of Thomas's standard jokes, "because it keeps coming up. He must have told it to other people."

Interviewed independently, Gordon Davis, another Holy Cross classmate, recalls Thomas using similar language. "Pubic hair was one of the things he talked about," says Davis. When it came to sex, Thomas was known for telling the craziest stories. For instance, Davis recalls, Thomas said he knew a guy from Savannah who claimed that eating lots of ham enhanced his sexual prowess. According to Davis, Thomas told him the guy "had a penis so long he had to strap it to his knee."

Thomas's pattern of using crude language and telling dirty jokes continued at Yale Law School. Henry Terry, who was a year behind Thomas, said Hill's testimony resonated as soon as he heard it. "Anita Hill could not have made up that stuff," he said. "It was too close to the guy I knew. Listening to her, it was as if I was listening to the guy I knew speak."

Thomas's fascination with pornography has now been well reported. But during the hearings there was only limited knowledge of his enthrallment. Those with details of Thomas's fetish didn't talk, and Thomas himself artfully steered clear of the subject. As we recounted earlier, some of Thomas's Yale Law classmates portrayed blue movies as a fairly common form of entertainment during their time there—no big deal. But Thomas was hardly satisfied with the mainstream erotica shown on campus, and his porn proclivities didn't wane after he left Yale.

As a young federal bureaucrat in Washington, Thomas rented adult videos from Graffiti, a store off Dupont Circle. It was there that

Fred Cooke, the former D.C. corporation counsel, saw him at the checkout line during the late 1980s with a copy of *The Adventures of Bad Mama Jama*, a triple-X-rated flick featuring the sexual exploits of a hugely overweight black woman with abnormally large breasts. Cooke was both struck and amused that the chairman of the EEOC was a consumer of such smut. Cooke shared the tale with friends, and not surprisingly the story wound up on the Washington grapevine during the Hill-Thomas hearings.

Cooke's anecdote was potentially damaging, for it would have helped establish a pattern of behavior by Thomas that he and his supporters had depicted as far-fetched. Though Cooke received some pressure from friends—mainly Hill supporters—to come forward with his information, Cooke was a serious man and considered Thomas's video rentals a circus sideshow. He believed strongly that Thomas was a mediocre judge, and certainly unqualified for the high court. But he didn't want Thomas's nomination to get derailed by *The Adventures of Bad Mama Jama*. So, like others with critical information, he remained silent.

On Sunday, October 13, the final day of the Hill-Thomas hearings, Hill's attorney Charles Ogletree made a surprising announcement at a news conference: Hill had passed a lie detector test. Publicly, the Thomas camp tried to discredit lie detector tests in general and hers in particular. Had she really passed? How was the machine calibrated? The tests are unreliable, not even admissible in court, Thomas's strategists said. And if Hill was delusional, which they alleged she was, then it was not surprising she could pass such a test, they said. Privately, however, there was considerable consternation in Thomas's inner circle about the lie detector results.

Danforth's wife, Sally, believed Thomas should take a polygraph himself to counter Hill's. Thomas's good friend Larry Thompson, who would later become deputy attorney general in George W. Bush's administration, also thought taking a lie detector test might help. Thompson, a former U.S. attorney in Atlanta who had experience with polygraphs, understood the stakes: "We were battling for the court of public opinion." And so it was sort of "like a chess game," he said. Thomas needed to trump Hill's dramatic move.

Thompson went so far as to call a polygraph expert he knew in North Carolina and arrange for him to fly to Washington the next morning. The test would be administered in the Danforths' home. But no one had the heart to broach this plan with Thomas. The task was finally left to Sally Danforth—her husband was against the idea—and when she reached Thomas by phone, sounding awfully nervous and unsure, Thomas figured out what was up. "Is it about a polygraph?" he asked. Sally didn't have a chance to make a pitch for taking the test, not that she could quite summon the courage anyway. "No, I will not take a polygraph test," Thomas said emphatically.

Thomas's close friend Laurence Silberman, a colleague on the D.C. Circuit of the Court of Appeals, was more than a little concerned. He had heard from women who supported Thomas, and they were despondent that Hill had passed a polygraph. Silberman laid out the risks for Thomas. While he thought it was wrong for a federal judge to submit to a lie detector test, he told his friend that if he didn't offer to take one "you might go down because of this."

The way Sally Danforth figured it, Thomas could take a test and if he didn't pass, no one would ever have to know. Said Thompson: "That was never anything I was worried about." But when he called to measure Thomas's temperature about a polygraph, nothing had changed. Thomas refused to do it. In characteristic defiance, he told Thompson that as soon as the senators took *their* polygraphs and answered questions about who leaked Hill's allegations, he would be right behind them.

On October 15, the Senate confirmed Clarence Thomas by a vote of 52–48, the smallest margin of victory for a Supreme Court nominee in more than a century. Thomas earned another distinction in victory—the most negative votes for a successful nominee in history. But, the 107-day battle was finally over. The public also weighed in, with several national polls showing that more people were willing to trust Thomas's word over Hill's. According to a *Washington Post*–ABC News poll, 55 percent of those surveyed said they were not inclined to believe Hill's allegations, while 34 percent said they thought the accusations were true; 11 percent said they were undecided.

As time passed, sentiment on Capitol Hill and in the public at large shifted. More people came to believe Hill than Thomas, and some senators came to regret their vote—enough regretters to change the outcome if the vote had been held even a year or two later with the same cast of senators. After all, it wouldn't have taken much to defeat Thomas—just a change of mind by three senators.

One of the first to express misgivings about his vote was David Boren, Democrat of Oklahoma, who left the Senate and became president of the University of Oklahoma in 1994. "I think that was a mistake I made," Boren told a radio talk show less than a year after being one of eleven Democrats to back Thomas. "If I had thought I was giving Justice Scalia another vote on the court, I would not have voted for him."

Thomas had been persuasive during his confirmation proceedings, convincing key senators that he would not be a rigid ideologue on the court. But like Boren, other Democrats who went out on a limb for Thomas ended up feeling bamboozled. John Breaux, Democrat of Louisiana, now retired from the Senate, said of the justice years later, "I didn't think he would be like he is." The impression Breaux got from Thomas's testimony before the committee was that Thomas would be "looking at the issues and applying the law, instead of being more ideologically driven." A factor in Breaux's vote, and in the votes of other Southern Democrats, was the considerable black support in the South that Thomas and his allies had quietly cultivated. Former senator Ernest "Fritz" Hollings of South Carolina, in fact, disclosed to us that he voted for Thomas primarily on the word of Representative James Clyburn, also of South Carolina, an influential black Democrat who would go on to become chairman of the Congressional Black Caucus. "I got the highest, highest regard for James Clyburn," Hollings said. "And so when he says this is a good fella and vote for him, that made it. I didn't have to listen to any more of that wrangle going on, about the [pubic] hairs on the [Coke] cans and all that crap."

Clyburn not only vouched for Thomas to Hollings, he testified before the committee. Describing Thomas as "my good friend," Clyburn said he had come to know Thomas while a commissioner on the South Carolina Human Affairs Commission. He had found Thomas, as EEOC chairman, to be "highly compassionate, sensitive, judicious," and "of the intellectual honesty that is required in this field." Clyburn mentioned that although Thomas was a conservative Republican and he a moderate-to-liberal Democrat, their differences did not hinder the relationship. They debated vigorously, agreeing on some issues and disagreeing on others. In an effort to counter the skepticism of civil rights leaders, Clyburn testified that he did not believe Thomas was anti–affirmative action. In fact, Clyburn noted, when Thomas was EEOC chairman he required state and local agencies to submit affirmative action plans before they were eligible to obtain contracts with the EEOC.

Today, Clyburn says he deeply regrets his decision to vouch for Thomas. He had thought that Thomas's experiences growing up in the South under Jim Crow, struggling to get as far as he had against considerable odds, would have shaped him differently as a justice. "But we're far enough down the road with Clarence and his record on the Supreme Court for me to know that his life experiences seem to be something that he spends as much time as he possibly can rejecting." That said, Clyburn, who plays golf with former conservative House majority leader Tom DeLay of Texas—anathema to many Democrats—is known as someone gifted in bridging political divides. A personal grudge is not something he would keep. Some years back, he ran into Thomas on a plane, and the justice suggested they get together for breakfast and asked Clyburn to call him. "And I gave him a call, and then I gave him another call, and then I gave him another call," Clyburn recalled. "And he never returned any of the three phone calls."

Of all those who felt they made a mistake supporting Thomas, perhaps none felt as badly about it as Warren Rudman. "It's a vote I'm not proud of," the former Republican senator from New Hampshire told us. At the time, though, Rudman made a practical political calculation: Three federal judicial nominees from New Hampshire were in limbo, and he didn't want to jeopardize their chances. Nobody from the White House threatened him; Rudman just made a logical assumption: If he went against his party's president in a Supreme Court battle, there would be consequences. Rudman also felt pulled by Jack Danforth, for whom he had great respect. Danforth had pleaded both with him and with Senator William Cohen of Maine, the body's other wavering GOP moderate, not to abandon Thomas. Without the votes of Rudman and Cohen, Danforth told his colleagues, Thomas likely would not survive. Sixteen years later none of these rationales make Rudman feel any better. He still thinks Thomas "did not have the depth of knowledge" to sit on the court. "When George Bush made the statement that he was the best qualified in America," Rudman said, "I thought it a bit of hyperbole."

Bush's explanation for his pick was hard to swallow, even for supporters. It still is. Senator Arlen Specter of Pennsylvania, a former prosecutor designated by his Republican colleagues to question Anita Hill during the hearings, voted for Thomas but never bought Bush's argument that he was the most qualified candidate. "And when he said race was not a factor," Specter added, "I disagreed with him there, too."

Specter was a fascinating figure in this drama. He never wanted the role of Hill's inquisitor. He didn't think he had enough time to prepare, for one. He was also keenly aware of the politics involved—the other Republican Senators expected him to be tough on Hill. He was not comfortable playing the partisan. He also realized how closely his performance would be watched, especially in Pennsylvania, where he was up for reelection the following year and was known as a moderate who could draw votes across party lines. His image as a nonideological lawmaker was important to him.

But in the end, he came across as a persistent trial interrogator, a bully in the eyes of many women. Some saw his performance as pandering to his party's base. Citing Hill's testimony that she worried about being demoted or even fired for not submitting to Thomas's advances, Specter sharply challenged her for not having any tangible evidence.

Specter: "As an experienced attorney and as someone who was in the field of handling sexual harassment cases, didn't it cross your mind that if you needed to defend yourself from what you anticipated he might do, that your evidentiary position would be much stronger if you had made some notes?"

Hill: "No, it did not."

Specter: "Well, why not?"

Hill: "I don't know why it didn't cross my mind."

Specter: "Well, the law of evidence is that notes are very important."

Nan Aron, executive director of the Alliance for Justice, the advocacy group that led the opposition to Thomas, recalled paying a visit to Specter right before the confirmation vote. Accompanying her was Joe Rauh, a longtime civil rights leader who had a relationship with Specter. "Arlen, you're not really going to vote for Clarence Thomas, are you?" Rauh asked, according to Aron. "You know he's not qualified. Why are you doing this?" To which Specter replied: "They have not allowed me to live down my vote on Bork. I've got to do this."

As Aron saw it, the exchange reflected just how tortured Specter was over the confirmation. Conservative Republicans had long been suspicious of him; Specter had failed to back Bork, an icon of the right. When Specter was finally in line to become chairman of the

Judiciary Committee after the 2004 elections, conservative groups mounted an organized campaign to block his ascension. They didn't believe Specter could be trusted to push for conservative judicial candidates. Ultimately, the effort failed, but conservative activists got the attention of Senate GOP leaders—and of Specter.

Interestingly, Thomas does not share his fellow conservatives' disdain for Specter, who almost lost his seat in 1992, in part because he was perceived as treating Hill badly. (He accused her at one point of committing perjury.) When Specter encountered Thomas in the Senate dining room in June 1999, he was greeted warmly by the justice, who was having breakfast with Charles Grassley, the Republican senator from Iowa. This in itself seemed odd—Thomas was back in the private eating den of an institution he loathed, dining among those who had caused him more pain, he had stated, than he had ever suffered in his life. Just twenty feet away was Senator Barbara Boxer of California, a vocal Thomas opponent who was presiding over a meeting of Democratic congresswomen. In 1991, Boxer had been among seven female House members who dramatically marched to the Senate to demand that Anita Hill's allegations get a public airing.

Specter asked Thomas if he would grant an interview for a book the senator was doing that would deal with the Hill-Thomas hearings; three days later Thomas was in Specter's office. "You stood in the breech," Thomas repeatedly told Specter, expressing both gratitude and surprise. Thomas explained that he had not anticipated Specter's prosecutorial demeanor toward Hill, given where the senator resided on the ideological spectrum. He had interpreted Specter's performance as a sign of courage and of loyalty. But Specter corrected him: No, it was just a matter of basic fairness to question Hill closely, nothing more.

Specter was not in anybody's camp. He and Hank Brown had cast the sole votes for extending the hearings. He also thought, in retrospect, that Angela Wright should have testified. In fact, three years after the hearings, still believing the committee had "rushed to judgment," Specter said in the *Washington Post,* he "wouldn't object" if someone wanted to reopen an investigation into the Hill-Thomas matter. He had declined to attend a victory party for Thomas after the confirmation vote. And he had not spoken to Thomas, substantively, since the hearings. This had not been deliberate; they just didn't travel in the same circles.

Whatever good feelings Thomas had about Specter's role in his ascension to the court, it was clear the senator was not a Thomas partisan.

In a subsequent interview with one of the authors, Specter had only faint praise for Thomas. "His opinions in the course of the last two or three years have had a ring of scholarship," he said. "He is less a follower of Scalia than he had been. I think he is doing better."

After retiring from the Senate, Alan Simpson served as director of Harvard's Institute of Politics from 1998 to 2000. Unknown to Simpson, some of his students invited Anita Hill to campus. Her first question in pondering the invitation: "Is Simpson still there?"

Hill had good reason not to want to see Simpson again. Ever. He had been a tenacious, anything-goes protector of Thomas on the Judiciary Committee. Taking the Senate floor before the Hill-Thomas hearings even began, the lanky Republican from Wyoming warned of what the process would do to the accuser: "She will be injured and destroyed and belittled and hounded and harassed—real harassment—different than the sexual kind." And once the hearings began, Simpson demonstrated that neither innuendo nor rumor was out of bounds in defense of Thomas. Simpson's staff had worked overtime to help nail down a particularly salacious piece of gossip out of Oklahoma, the bizarre allegation that law students had once found pubic hairs on term papers they got back from Hill. For Simpson, it didn't matter that the story itself was preposterous—he understood it was damaging just to imply there were secrets in Hill's closet. At one point, theatrically tugging at his suit jacket before the cameras in the hearing room, Simpson stated: "And now, I really am getting stuff over the transom about Professor Hill. I have got letters hanging out of my pockets. I have got faxes. I have got statements from her former law professors, statements from people that know her, statements from Tulsa, Oklahoma, saying, watch out for this woman. But nobody has the guts to say that because it gets all tangled up in this sexual harassment crap."

Asked recently if he regretted anything he said or did during the hearings, Simpson responded: "No, why would I?"

This is the same Alan Simpson who left a message on Hill's answering machine years after the hearings saying he hoped she would accept the invitation to come to Harvard. And if she did, he continued, he promised to stay out of her way. "I'll be in Gloucester [Massachusetts] fixing fishing nets that day," he quipped. Hill returned his call and they had, he says, "a very fascinating" and "very cordial conversation." According to Simpson, she asked a lot of questions about the hearings, questions he assumed she would have answered for herself by now. She was curious, for instance, about Danforth's intensity in advocating for Thomas. She asked why Angela Wright hadn't testified. And, still according to Simpson, Hill said both she and the committee had been "manipulated"—she by pro-choice feminists and the committee by the media.

In her 1997 book, *Speaking Truth to Power*, Hill had made clear what she thought of some of Simpson's tactics during the hearings. His "jacket-flapping display," she wrote, "was not to prove any of the contents of the documents which he purported to have, so much as to put the idea in the mind of the public that it could not trust me to be truthful." And she criticized him for dismissing the behavior she attributed to Thomas as not real harassment. "Although Simpson apologized after the hearing for his choice of words," she wrote, "he could not take back the twin message they sent: that sexual harassment is not real and that complaints about sexual harassment should be met with 'real harassment.' "

But somehow Hill and Simpson, long separated from that defining battle, had come together. "I thought it was good for me to talk to him," she told *O, The Oprah Magazine*, adding that it "helped me get through the anger to realize that I had actually been dealing with human beings, even though they didn't always act like it."

Toward the end of their phone conversation, Simpson mentioned that he had spoken to Robert Reich, labor secretary under President Clinton and a teaching colleague of Hill's at Brandeis University at the time. Reich, whom Simpson had known for many years, had volunteered to arrange a get-together with the former senator and Hill. Simpson told Hill he hoped they could have dinner with the Reichs sometime, and she said she'd like to do that. The dinner never happened.

As the years passed and the Hill-Thomas hearings became a fading memory for its participants, some of Thomas's most passionate defenders began a subtle but significant shift in their view of the episode. No longer was the emphasis on his innocence. It was on whether Hill's allegations really even amounted to much. According to Senator Orrin Hatch, Republican of Utah, "If you go back and put the worst slant, let's say you conclude that Anita Hill was right, was telling the truth . . . the most you could say is he talked dirty to her. . . . He didn't try to seduce her. He didn't touch her. He didn't indicate impropriety." Hatch was not so cavalier about Thomas's alleged behavior sixteen years ago. Back then, he found it outrageous and "unbelievable, that anybody could be that perverted. I'm sure there are people like that, but they're generally in insane asylums." For all the commentary about the hearings sensitizing the male-driven Senate and fostering a new national consciousness about sexual harassment in the workplace, Hatch, a former Judiciary Committee chairman, still reduces Hill's accusations to no more than dirty talk.

C. Boyden Gray, the White House counsel who played a pivotal role in Thomas's selection and confirmation, has much the same opinion of the hearings today: "When it's all said and done, what she alleged he did does not constitute . . . violation of anything. Even if you accepted everything she said, it had no legal meaning, no legal consequence. It only becomes important because it sounds bad, you know, in the context of a high-profile nomination and leaks and all the drama of revelation and hiding something and all of that."

Seven years after the Hill-Thomas hearings, the nation was riveted by another sex-related drama—this one involving the president of the United States. Bill Clinton, who attended Yale Law School while Thomas was there, at first denied having sexual relations with an intern in the White House. But irrefutable evidence emerged of his relationship with Monica Lewinsky and he was forced to own up to it. Impeachment followed, and his presidency sank in public esteem. Conservative groups questioned the silence of liberal women's organizations. Why had they not rallied to Lewinsky's side as they had to Anita Hill's?

While most conservatives reveled in Clinton's troubles, Thomas did not. Alan Simpson, curious about Thomas's views on the Clinton impeachment imbroglio, phoned the justice. "Clarence, what do you think of all this?"

"Isn't it something," Thomas replied, "how it happens in this city. They just cut people to bits. And now they're doing it to him."

9

THE AFTERMATH
Thomas's Love Affair with the Right

Thomas arrived at the Supreme Court badly bruised and unsure of himself. He was exhausted, he told his clerks, unable to focus. "Getting the heck beaten out of you," he later recounted, "is quite distracting." Instead of having a chance to "dust yourself off," as Thomas clerk Chris Landau put it, "you're facing one of the toughest jobs in the country as your prize."

The awkward ceremonies that surrounded his confirmation only heightened the unease. First, there had been the lavish White House celebration of Thomas to which three hundred guests were invited, including Thomas's family and friends from Georgia and celebrities such as Sylvester Stallone and baseball great Reggie Jackson. The day before the South Lawn event was to take place, Chief Justice William Rehnquist's wife, Nan, died. The death not only hit the chief hard but deeply affected the close-knit court family. That the Thomas party wasn't postponed struck many at the court as in poor taste.

The White House had been in a difficult spot. It didn't want to offend Rehnquist and his colleagues, but most of the people closest to Thomas were already in town and poised to celebrate after such a difficult battle. For Thomas himself, the situation was agonizing. There also was a political reason to proceed quickly: Who knew how many journalists and activists on the left were still pursuing tips and rumors about the justice-in-waiting? White House advisers didn't want to take any chances that the confirmation might unravel with new revelations before Thomas could actually take his seat on the bench.

On October 18, 1991, the White House "swearing in," as the South Lawn gala was billed, had all the trappings of an official court induction. Thomas placed his hand on a Bible as the president looked on and Justice Byron White presided. Most of the guests did not know that this so-called swearing in would not be the one that counted. It was left to White, filling in for Rehnquist, to set the record straight with a pointed reference to the fact that Thomas would become the 106th justice only when he took the *judicial* oath.

The court's term already had begun, and Thomas recognized he was behind. He was eager to get sworn in. Hastily arranged at Thomas's request, the judicial oath was administered privately at 12:05 p.m. on October 23, 1991, in Rehnquist's office. Only Thomas's wife, Virginia, and Senator Danforth attended. The other justices didn't learn they officially had a new colleague until later that afternoon when Rehnquist sent them a terse one-paragraph memo. "I administered the oath at this time so that Justice Thomas could begin his duties and get his clerks and staff on board," the chief wrote. "A public investiture will still take place on November 1, as previously planned."

Rehnquist, a Wisconsin native known for his devotion to the Green Bay Packers and his enjoyment of the game charades, was not in a festive mood. He was still mourning his wife of thirty-eight years and not keeping regular office hours. Administering the oath ahead of schedule had been a favor to Thomas, and he made that clear.

This was not a comfortable time for Thomas, whose insecurities now included how he would be viewed by his fellow justices. "You are here now," one of them assured him, "and what you do here is all that matters." But convincing himself was more difficult. He paid the requisite courtesy visits to his colleagues' chambers, happy to accept whatever advice was offered. Lewis F. Powell Jr., who had retired, noted that he and Thomas were two of the few Southerners to make it onto the high court this century. "You will not be surprised to find that the work of a justice is demanding," Powell wrote to Thomas in a follow-up letter, "and probably will require a good deal of 'homework' as well as on weekends."

Thomas, who had gotten a late start on the bench, worked tirelessly trying to prove himself, to the point that he was sick for two months at the end of his first term. "When I arrived, I had no staff and no experience with the court processes," he later explained. "It was an uphill battle." On his first day at work, he was staked out by camera crews. But because he was driving a 1985 Chevy Celebrity with a missing hubcap, he managed not to draw attention to himself. One cameraman, however, spotted Thomas pulling away from the court's parking garage and chased his car down the street. "On your first day, you show up and you know nothing," Thomas observed. "Where do you get coffee? Where are the pencils? How do I get along with the other judges?"

There was no way to know what the justices were really thinking about him. They had watched the hearings like the rest of America. And while very little discussion of Hill's allegations had occurred around the conference table where the justices gather among themselves to review cases, that didn't mean his colleagues weren't privately fascinated by the debate over his nomination.

What caught Harry A. Blackmun's eye was Thomas's responses to questions about *Roe v. Wade*, the 1973 landmark ruling legalizing abortion. Thomas had said he could not "remember personally engaging" in discussions of the case and stated flatly to Senator Patrick J. Leahy, Democrat of Vermont: "If you are asking me whether or not I have ever debated the contents of it, the answer to that is no, Senator." Blackmun had written the *Roe* opinion and was puzzled by

Thomas's answers. Wasn't Thomas a Yale Law School student when *Roe* was handed down? "Surely they must have been aware of Roe against Wade up there," Blackmun told an interviewer preparing an oral history, adding that "it seemed a little strange to us."

Whether Thomas just used cleverly crafted language to evade his inquisitors or deliberately lied about his views of the case remains a matter of contention among court observers, legal scholars, and advocacy groups. Blackmun's interest in Thomas's confirmation process, however, wasn't confined to *Roe v. Wade*, as his papers housed at the Library of Congress indicate. He had a habit of collecting all manner of minutiae related to his colleagues—cards, notes, newspaper and magazine clippings. It's instructive that the articles and cartoons Blackmun chose to keep on Thomas mostly relate to the confirmation ordeal, and hardly any of them are flattering. An editorial cartoon from the *Orlando Sentinel*, for example, pictures the nine justices with the script: "Next on the agenda is the issue of sexual harassment. Lucky for us, we have a resident expert."

Combating this notion that Thomas was a sexual harasser who had beaten the rap became a priority of Thomas's friends. No one was more dedicated to rebuilding Thomas's image than his wife. Thomas had barely unpacked his boxes at the court when the November 11 issue of *People* hit the stands, the cover featuring a smiling couple embracing. "Exclusive," the cover screamed. "Virginia Thomas Tells Her Story. 'How We Survived.'" The entire article, based on a three-hour interview by correspondent Jane Sims Podesta, was written in the first-person voice of Ginni Thomas. In it, she divulged her own episode of workplace harassment before she met Clarence—"it was physical"—and how Clarence, upon finding out later, implored her to use "the workplace system to alert management to the problem." This was meant to underscore that Thomas was not the type to tolerate sexual harassment. "He gave me the courage to go forward." As for Anita Hill, Ginni likened her to the character in the movie *Fatal Attraction*, "or in her case, what I call the fatal assistant. In my heart, I always believed she was probably someone in love with my husband and never got what she wanted." It was an extraordinary piece that revealed intimate details of the "hell" the couple went through, as Ginni described the confirmation process, augmented by photos of them drinking coffee in their kitchen and snuggling on a sofa reading the Bible.

This was not the kind of publicity Supreme Court justices normally sought, and it seemed an odd way for a new justice to begin his tenure. But the *People* cover story may have said as much about Ginni as it did about Thomas. Asked by Thomas's handlers to remain silent during the hearings, she would now become his chief protector, seemingly even more deeply mistrustful of the media and those who differed ideologically than even Thomas himself. She dialed in to radio talk shows to defend her husband. And not even the passage of time seemed to ease the impact of the confirmation process on her psyche.

Washington Post reporter Tom Jackman was surprised by a phone call he got on November 8, 1999, the day an article he wrote about a Virginia man falsely accused of being a sex pervert appeared on the front page. The story recounted a Kafkaesque drama in which the chief financial officer of a major defense firm—a fifty-four-year-old grandfather with a good reputation—was charged with indecent exposure for allegedly flashing a nude photo of himself to a sixteen-year-old male lifeguard at his health club. Seven police officers searched the man's home, confiscating his computer and some family photos. The episode made the local community papers and the man was humiliated before his friends and colleagues. Turned out they had the wrong guy, and the charges were dropped. In the *Post* article, the accused man described the lonely feeling of waiting for his public degradation: "You're the only person in the world, other than the actual perpetrator, who knows you didn't do this."

Jackman remembers picking up the phone that November day and hearing a woman on the line weeping. The article, she said, reminded her of the ordeal she and her husband had been through.

She was obviously distraught. "My husband's name is Clarence Thomas," she said.

The notion that Thomas had been set up—*Fatal Attraction*–style—became the prevailing theory advanced by Ginni and other Thomas intimates. For those not emotionally invested, however, what had happened between Thomas and Hill remained an irreconcilable mystery.

Some who encountered Thomas in the aftermath of his ordeal thought they might have detected in his behavior clues to the truth. One of them was Malena Cunningham, a smart local television anchor who also happened to be beautiful. Thomas met her in Savannah when he was an appeals court judge in town to give a speech. Whatever blanket disdain he had for the media—expressed publicly and privately—it did not seem to extend to Cunningham.

She had first interviewed Thomas when he was on the short list for the Supreme Court vacancy ultimately filled by David Souter. She then interviewed him twice during his confirmation process, including at a private church service just hours before he was confirmed. Each time Thomas saw Cunningham he grew more comfortable in her presence. Their interactions, she says, were always professional. After he reached the Supreme Court, Thomas told her she could have an interview anytime she wanted one.

Cunningham, who was well known and popular in Savannah, had grown close to Thomas's mother. When Cunningham took her TV career to Birmingham in 1992, she met Thomas's brother, Myers, who was an executive at the downtown Sheraton Hotel. She'll never forget a dinner for Thomas at his brother's Birmingham home in November 1994. Thomas was in town to give a speech at Samford University's Cumberland Law School. There, he had chided "the elite law schools" for getting away from teaching the basics of legal method and reasoning and instead creating boutique courses such as Thinking About Thinking. "These classes have no relationship to being a lawyer," he told a full auditorium of 2,600. "It produces disillusionment and disgust."

Now, he was at his brother's house relaxing. Seated at the dining room table were Cunningham, Myers and his wife, Dora, their two children, and Thomas. After the meal was over and the two kids had been excused, Thomas at one point "brought up Anita Hill and the Coke can," Cunningham recalls. "He had a look in his eyes as if he were replaying the scenario. And then he laughed. This loud, boisterous laugh . . . I didn't know how to take it. You could tell it caught everybody off guard."

Cunningham's instinct as a journalist was to question Thomas, especially since he had opened the door himself. Was Hill's testimony true? Did he tell her somebody had put a pubic hair on his Coke can? But Cunningham decided that was inappropriate; she had been invited to an intimate family dinner and didn't want to embarrass her host.

It was impossible to know what was on Thomas's mind when he brought up Hill's most provocative allegation. The encounter certainly didn't prove anything. Still, the moment has stayed with Cunningham all these years. "He didn't have this righteous indignation," she remembers. "It was almost as if he were laughing because he got away with something."

Thomas's mail piled up his first year on the court. He just couldn't get through most of it, so overwhelming was the workload. It took him ten months after he was sworn in to reply to Holy Cross classmate Dhafir Jihad's letter. "The past year has been, to say the least, a challenge for me and for my family," Thomas wrote, "but the warmth and support of friends like you have seen us through. Thank you!"

The gregarious side of Thomas often seemed to have gone AWOL. He preferred eating lunch at his desk. He sometimes felt apprehensive in public. It was as if he had a bull's-eye on his back, he told his law clerks. Meanwhile, the amount of news coverage he was receiving was phenomenal for a Supreme Court justice. According to legal scholar Scott Douglas Gerber, Thomas was mentioned in 32,377 newspaper stories during the six-year period from his nomination to December 1997. By comparison, the next highest number of newspaper citations was for the chief justice himself—19,487 mentions over a twenty-five-year period (July 1972 to December 1997).

The outsize coverage did not make Thomas happy; it made him uneasy. The work itself was difficult enough. Thomas faced a bunch of tough cases that first term. There was *Lee v. Weisman*, in which the court ruled 5–4 (Thomas in the minority) that a clergy-led nondenominational prayer at a Rhode Island public high school graduation was unconstitutional. It was the first major school prayer case of the Rehnquist Court, and Thomas joined a biting dissent. There was *Riggins v. Nevada*, in which the court overturned the murder conviction of a man forcibly given antipsychotic drugs during trial. The defendant, Thomas wrote in a dissent, had a "full and fair trial." And even if the man had the right to turn down the medication, Thomas argued, that did not warrant overturning his conviction. There was also *Foucha v. Louisiana*, in which the court ruled that criminal defendants who are found not guilty by reason of insanity and confined to an institution cannot be held indefinitely after a determination that they are sane. Again, Thomas found himself in the minority and wrote a dissent. "While a state may renounce a punitive interest by offering an insanity defense," Thomas argued, "it does not follow that, once the acquittee's sanity is 'restored,' the state is required to ignore his criminal act, and to renounce all interest in protecting society from him."

The most controversial case on the docket during Thomas's first year on the court, *Planned Parenthood of Southeastern Pennsylvania v. Casey*, involved the volatile issue of abortion. The case challenged four provisions of a Pennsylvania law limiting a woman's access to an abortion. One part of the law required doctors to provide women with information about the health risks and possible complications of having an abortion before one could be performed. Another part required women to give notice to their husbands before an abortion was performed. A third provision required minors to receive permission from a parent or guardian prior to an abortion. And the fourth provision imposed a twenty-four-hour waiting period before obtaining an abortion.

Beyond weighing the constitutionality of the restrictions, the case presented a direct challenge to *Roe v. Wade*, which had established a constitutional right to an abortion nineteen years earlier. With the additions to the court of both Souter and Thomas to replace liberal justices Brennan and Marshall, the right to an abortion was very much up in the air. It had become the subject of the 1992 presidential campaign, with Republican strategists seeking to fire up their base of religious conservatives, who were considered essential to President Bush's reelection. Meanwhile, presumptive Democratic nominee Bill Clinton was trying to energize women worried about losing the freedom to make decisions about their own bodies. With only two certain pro-choice justices on the bench—eight of the nine justices had been nominated by Republican presidents—many abortion rights advocates worried that *Roe* would be overturned.

When the Supreme Court issued its ruling in *Casey*, their worries were left for another day. The court upheld a woman's right to terminate her pregnancy, and that basic holding was backed by Justices David Souter, Anthony Kennedy, Sandra Day O'Connor, Harry Blackmun, and John Paul Stevens. But the court's ruling had been so carefully negotiated—and was so fragile—that there was not a single opinion that a majority of the justices signed. The plurality opinion that carried the day was jointly written by Souter, O'Connor, and Kennedy. While the court upheld the right to an abortion, it also approved the restrictions in the Pennsylvania law, except for the one requiring women to notify their husbands before getting an abortion.

Thomas joined a dissent authored by Justice Antonin Scalia that concluded "that a woman's decision to abort her unborn child is not a constitutionally protected 'liberty' because . . . the Constitution

says absolutely nothing about it." Scalia's opinion stated, unequivocally, that *Roe* was "plainly wrong." Thomas signed on to a similar
Rehnquist dissent that declared *Roe* was "wrongly decided" and
"should be overruled."

That Thomas would express such clear opposition to *Roe* just
eight months after he got to the court put his confirmation testimony on the subject under more scrutiny. This was a man who
couldn't even remember *discussing Roe*? It led his critics to say, told
you so, that all along Thomas had been hiding strongly held antiabortion feelings, even if he would not acknowledge them under
oath before the Senate Judiciary Committee.

To Thomas and his clerks, it seemed like this first term was filled
with more than its share of controversial cases, including an emotionally charged case involving the beating of an inmate. Perhaps as
part of his own therapy, Thomas would sometimes replay the Anita
Hill episode with his clerks. "It was something that came up from
time to time," says Landau, "but more about just how difficult it had
been." It was like being hunted, Thomas confided to his clerks. The
trash he took out at his home had been rifled through, he told them.
It was horrible living through it all.

By the end of that first year, Thomas intimates were eagerly
awaiting a book, *The Real Anita Hill*, by David Brock. They hoped the
book, drawn from an article Brock had written in the *American Spectator*, would severely damage Hill's public image and help restore
Thomas's good name. Brock was developing a reputation as the
right's Bob Woodward, and those close to Thomas eagerly cooperated with him.

Brock's editor flew to Washington to personally deliver an early
copy of the book to syndicated columnist George Will, a Thomas
friend who sometimes takes the justice to baseball games. Will
wrote a blistering column in *Newsweek* on April 19, 1993, in which
he credited Brock with assembling "an avalanche of evidence that
Hill lied—about her career and her relations with Thomas." That
got the pro-Brock/pro-Thomas public relations juggernaut rolling.

The book had an immediate impact at the court. Lewis Powell sent a note to Thomas and included a copy of Will's column, "which is very favorable to you," as he put it. Thomas thanked Powell for the article. "I have learned that if one is honest and fair, things have a way of working out—even though it may not be in this lifetime."

The book, which quickly became a *New York Times* best-seller, was successful in raising questions about Hill's credibility. It also was controversial, its conclusions—chief among them that Thomas was innocent of sexual harassment—widely and bitterly debated. To conservatives, Brock emerged a hero. He had defined Hill, in a phrase widely repeated by her enemies, as "a little bit nutty and a little bit slutty." Not yet thirty, Brock had become, in his own words, a junior member of the capital's conservative elite, treated like a celebrity at parties of the faithful. When he entered a room, conservative commentator Ann Coulter told him, it was like Mick Jagger had arrived. At Brock's book party at the Ritz-Carlton Hotel, Ginni Thomas tearfully embraced him. He was her husband's vindicator.

But the years passed, and a strange thing happened. Brock flipped. He outed the right-wing machinery he had been a party to, describing how he would "twist and turn the facts to advantage my side" and how he was aided in that effort by close Thomas friends and confidantes. In a 2002 book, *Blinded by the Right*, he wrote this about his reporting on Anita Hill: "Every source I relied on either thought Thomas walked on water or had a virulent animus toward Hill." He even claimed Thomas himself helped to discredit a former friend and Reagan appointee, Kaye Savage. In *Strange Justice*, an exploration of the confirmation process that came out a year after Brock's first book, Savage is quoted as telling the authors, Jane Mayer and Jill Abramson, that during a visit to Thomas's bachelor pad in 1982—a time when Anita Hill worked for Thomas—she observed a huge stack of *Playboy* magazines on the floor and centerfolds covering the walls.

Strange Justice, by two prominent *Wall Street Journal* staffers, also had been eagerly anticipated. The pro-Hill camp had hoped the book would unearth more damaging information about Thomas and help validate Hill's allegations. The Thomas camp worried that the book would rekindle the controversy and be a distraction for the justice at the court—"like another cross to bear," as former Thomas law clerk John Yoo put it. When the book arrived in stores, there was a resignation among Thomas intimates that maybe there was no getting past Hill's accusations. Thomas himself was down. "I don't know why people believe these lies," he told Yoo.

Enter David Brock. Assigned by the *American Spectator* to do a review that poked holes in *Strange Justice*, Brock turned to sources who had been helpful to him in his own Anita Hill book. He asked Mark Paoletta, the former White House lawyer and Thomas confidant, for negative information about Savage. Paoletta, according to Brock, posed the question to Thomas.

"Mark told me that Thomas had, in fact, some derogatory information on his former friend Savage; he passed it along to Mark so that Mark could give it to me," Brock wrote in his mea culpa. "Quoting Thomas directly, Mark told me of unverified, embarrassing personal information about Savage that Thomas claimed had been raised against her in a sealed court record of a divorce and child custody battle more than a decade ago. . . . Surely skirting the bounds of judicial propriety to intimidate and smear yet another witness against him, Thomas was playing dirty, and so was I." Thomas, through a court spokesman at the time, declined to comment. But Paoletta told the *Washington Post* that Brock's account was "simply not true. Justice Thomas did not ask me to pass along any derogatory information to David Brock about Kaye Savage."

Blinded by the Right was a 180-degree turn from *The Real Anita Hill*. Brock, who was struggling with his identity—"the peculiar mix of my politics, my profession, and my homosexuality perpetuated my isolation"—had gone from the right's hero to its pariah. And yet there was at least one denizen of the conservative battles who reached out to him, even though she could hardly have been happy about his book. Ginni Thomas left a long message on Brock's

answering machine, he said, saying that she was praying for him:
"We were always friends. I hope we can still be friends." She didn't
want a call back; she just wanted him to know how horrible she felt
for him. Nobody should have his name smeared like Brock's was being smeared in her circles, she said, according to Brock's description
of her message. It was as if she were linking Brock's plight to her
husband's, illustrating again "how politics can destroy people," Brock
recalls. This from the woman who had described her husband's hearings as "spiritual warfare. Good versus evil."

Brock's recantation was an embarrassment to the conservative
movement that had propped him up as a journalistic superstar, but
it had no impact on Thomas's standing. George Will, who was first
to tout *The Real Anita Hill*, dismissed the notion that he had been
bamboozled. Brock or no Brock, he maintained, Hill's allegations
"never seemed plausible about Clarence Thomas." The warriors of
the right were in love with their new justice, and the wounded
Clarence Thomas surely needed their love.

Rush Limbaugh and Clarence Thomas met in 1994. Accompanied
by his fiancée, Marta Fitzgerald, the conservative radio talk show
host arrived late for a dinner party at the Chevy Chase, Maryland,
home of former education secretary William J. Bennett and instantly heard Thomas's trademark guffaw. The justice was telling a
story, and Limbaugh was surprised to find that this deep, hearty
laugh belonged to a man widely thought to be in despair.

During the dinner, Limbaugh noticed how Clarence and Ginni
Thomas never took their eyes off each other, how each beamed
when the other spoke. Limbaugh had met Fitzgerald, a former aer-
obics instructor from Florida, online and now both were about to
embark on a third marriage. Struck by the affection the Thomases
displayed, they sent the couple a note saying their joy was infectious.

After narrowing the choices of marriage sites to California and
Virginia—they wanted privacy, no media attention—Fitzgerald

wondered whether Justice Thomas, a Virginia resident, could perform the ceremony. Limbaugh felt uncomfortable asking—after all,
he barely knew Thomas. He also feared the request might be in poor
taste. Who in the world asks a Supreme Court justice to act as justice of the peace? Limbaugh's initial instincts were right—it was
highly unusual for a Supreme Court justice to preside at a marriage.
According to court lore, the late justice Hugo Black once sent a
memo around to his colleagues instructing them that it was improper to officiate at weddings.

Nonetheless, Limbaugh wrote a carefully worded letter and
faxed it to Thomas's chambers. It took Thomas thirty minutes to reply. He was ecstatic, flattered to be asked, but didn't think he had
the authority to marry anyone. He promised he'd find someone else
who could do the wedding. What Limbaugh didn't realize was that
Thomas was a huge fan who listened to the show religiously and
considered Limbaugh courageous. He gushed about Limbaugh to his
mother, his sister, his friends back in Georgia.

When Thomas didn't get back to Limbaugh and Fitzgerald, they
assumed he had just forgotten about them. In truth, Thomas was
trying to determine if it was proper for him to administer the vows
himself. Two weeks before the wedding date, Thomas surprised
them, saying he could indeed conduct the ceremony. He even offered the use of his home. The Thomases' house sits on a secluded
lot surrounded by woods in Fairfax Station, Virginia, twenty-four
miles from the Supreme Court. Theirs is a quiet neighborhood of
custom brick homes and long driveways, of towering pines and
oaks. The house is nestled so far back from the road that it is not vis-
ible to passersby—a perfect spot for a private wedding.

On the day of the wedding, May 27, Thomas showed up at the office of the Fairfax County clerk of the court and asked to be sworn
in as a civil-marriage celebrant. He told a deputy clerk that Limbaugh was "a very good friend," even though the two men had met
only months earlier. It was a small wedding—just family members,
except for two couples who served as witnesses, Bill and Elayne

Bennett and Mary Matalin and James Carville, the political-consulting odd couple. Matalin and Limbaugh were longtime friends, but Carville, the ragin' Cajun who masterminded Bill Clinton's 1992 campaign, was not exactly in his political element. He mostly remembers sitting out on Thomas's deck "bullshittin' about cooking" with the justice. "They were nice to me at the wedding," recalls Carville. "Clearly they're not my favorite people in politics." In fact, when Limbaugh's devoted audience heard their radio god had invited Carville, many of them were unforgiving. How could he? Why would he?

Whatever grief Limbaugh got for including Carville, it was nothing compared to the criticism Thomas received. The Limbaugh wedding further defined Thomas's image on the court, overtly tieing him to the far right in a way that no other act had done up to that point. For students of court decorum, it was mystifying—even embarrassing—behavior. For Thomas opponents, the wedding became a permanent emblem of their disdain.

"He had Rush Limbaugh's wedding at his house!" the Reverend Al Sharpton boomed through a megaphone after leading four hundred demonstrators to Thomas's neighborhood to protest the justice's voting record on the court. "But today, Clarence, guess who's coming to dinner?!" Thomas's friends seethed at the implications of the disapproval. Larry Thompson, one of Thomas's closest friends, found himself defending his pal but incredulous at the need for doing so. "Somehow, if I'm a black man, I can't be friends with Rush Limbaugh?"

Limbaugh, however, wasn't just any ordinary friend. He was the bombastic epitome of partisan politics, the right's No. 1 on-air flame-thrower. Republican elected officials, awed by his popularity, worshipped at his altar. In 1992, he stayed in the Lincoln Bedroom as a guest of President George H. W. Bush, who personally carried his bags into the White House. When the Newt Gingrich–led Republicans won control of the House in 1994, they showed their gratitude to Limbaugh by making him an honorary member of Congress.

Symbolically, the Limbaugh relationship says something significant about Thomas. Here he is, arguably the nation's most powerful African American, aligning himself with white bomb throwers who otherwise have little contact with blacks and often no empathy for them. Those entrenched in the conservative political firmament see Thomas as one of their own, a rugged individual whose rise they can be proud of because they helped to make it happen. But away from Thomas's presence, some of the same people he laughs and dines with have made hurtful, even idiotic, comments about his race.

In 2005, Bennett, one of the GOP's moral crusaders, said on his radio talk show that "you could abort every black baby in this country and your crime rate would go down." Though he quickly added that such an act would be morally reprehensible, just linking race to crime in this fashion was an astonishing leap for someone of Bennett's stature.

Limbaugh, however, is in a category all his own. He has parodied blacks on his show, speaking in dialect and playing the theme song from the 1970s black sitcom *The Jeffersons.* He once told an African American caller to "take that bone out of your nose and call me back" and referred to Jesse Jackson as "a chocolate chip." In his most controversial racial remarks, Limbaugh suggested during the 2003 pro football season that one of the NFL's top-rated quarterbacks, Donovan McNabb, owed his popularity to his skin color. "I don't think he's been that good from the get-go," opined Limbaugh, who at the time was a commentator on ESPN's NFL pregame show. "I think what we've had here is a little social concern in the NFL. I think the media has been very desirous that a black quarterback do well." The ensuing storm caused Limbaugh to resign.

Could Thomas—an ardent football fan, by the way—really embrace as a friend someone as racially insensitive as Rush Limbaugh? If the justice has cringed at any of Limbaugh's remarks, he has never made that known. Ironically, Limbaugh is exactly the kind of combatant Thomas would normally deplore. Having been excoriated himself for his ideas and wounded in the political arena, Thomas has often derided the take-no-prisoners style of political debate. In a speech a year before officiating at Limbaugh's wedding, he talked about "a principle that seems to be falling out of fashion these days—civility." As Thomas went on to observe, "no good can ever come of treating others badly—whether on account of their race, religion, or gender." Yet when he discovered Limbaugh's syndicated radio program in the summer of 1992, he found someone on the right side of the ideological divide whose vitriol resonated. Thomas couldn't get enough of him. He was so proud of hosting Limbaugh's wedding, in fact, that years later he was still showing off the photos to visiting family and friends from Georgia.

Getting to this point in his ideological journey wasn't easy for Thomas, and he isn't the only one who recognizes that. "It seems to me that the toughest thing in the world of politics to be is a black conservative," says former Republican National Committee chairman Ed Gillespie, who has pushed his party to accelerate its outreach to blacks. In 1994, the same year Thomas was building his friendship with Limbaugh, he spoke publicly of how he had once prayed that his right-leaning views would change so that his opponents' "enmity would evaporate." He had hoped the harangues would ease and he'd no longer be considered antiblack. "I wanted to be liked. I wanted to be popular," he told an audience at the Jesse Helms Center at North Carolina's Wingate College. But his prayers weren't answered, and his beliefs remained the same.

"So my only choice was to stand up for my views or abandon them," he continued, "to turn and run from myself, to abandon my views without being convinced that they were the wrong views. Think of that. If you abandon your views because you are afraid, in essence you have lied to yourself." In Thomas's telling, he went from a self-pitying man to a man of steel. But had he really? The story itself was a type of armor, protecting him from the stress inherent in what he had become—a black outcast who spent an inordinate amount of time explaining himself.

Allen Moore, a veteran congressional staffer who has known

Thomas since they both worked for Senator Danforth more than twenty-five years ago, sees something basic and human in Thomas's allegiance to the right: "People say, 'Why is he hanging around with all of these conservatives?' Because they're the only ones who will have him."

After taking his seat on the court, Thomas went on a kind of conservative thank-you tour that lasted several years. Between November 1991 and April 1993, he paid at least three visits to the Free Congress Foundation, a culturally conservative think tank headed by Paul Weyrich, one of the movement's elder statesmen. In fact, the only public appearance Thomas made in the weeks immediately following his confirmation was on Weyrich's National Empowerment Television satellite network, where he expressed his "deep, deep gratitude" for the way conservatives "stood up for us and the love that you showed for us." The Weyrich Thomas felt indebted to was the same man who had supported tax breaks for racially segregated schools like Bob Jones University.

In 2005, when conservatives were in mutiny over President George W. Bush's choice of Harriet Miers to replace Sandra Day O'Connor on the court, Weyrich would quote Thomas to buttress his position of skepticism. He would say Thomas had once told him that it was important to have not just conservatives on the court but conservatives who have "been through the wars and survived." Weyrich's point: Thomas was one of them and could be trusted in his Supreme Court chair; Miers could not. He also was accessible to them in a way that the barely known Miers, Bush's White House counsel, was not. A persistent campaign by conservative activists and pundits to undermine Miers finally paid off; she withdrew just before her confirmation hearings were to begin.

Remarkably, the arguments used to undercut Miers—that she lacked judicial experience, that she didn't have a brilliant legal mind, that she was nominated for diversity purposes—could easily have been made against Thomas in 1991. But they weren't, at least not by the right. Some of the same conservatives who killed the Miers nomination had led the Thomas bandwagon.

As much as Thomas felt the need to show his gratitude to those who fought for his confirmation, not all of his appearances before conservative groups went smoothly. After speaking at a May 1993 fund-raiser of the Georgia Public Policy Foundation—fund-raisers are taboo for justices under court tradition—Thomas started vetting his schedule with the court's counsel. The vetting, however, didn't alter the thrust of his appearances, which were pretty much confined to those who loved him. This would become his pattern as a justice, and it hasn't changed significantly in sixteen years. He rarely ventures beyond conservative groups and conservative-friendly law schools, the exception being engagements involving schoolchildren.

When Thomas spoke at Concerned Women for America's 1993 convention, he asked that his talk be closed to the media "because he just wants it to be among his friends," according to a convention co-ordinator. The CWA was certainly a good friend, having been one of the strongest backers of Thomas's nomination. In the 1992–93 court term prior to Thomas's appearance at the convention, two cases came before the court that were important to the organization, both of which were argued by a former CWA official. One involved whether civil rights statutes could be used to stop antiabortion protests and the other involved whether a church group could show one of its films on public school grounds. Thomas voted in favor of the CWA position in both cases.

That a conservative jurist would often agree with conservative organizations on legal cases is no surprise. More curious are Thomas's forays into the overtly political realm. Each year the Media Research Center, a conservative watchdog group, holds its "Dis-Honors Awards," a raucous Washington gala at which luminaries of the right savagely roast the so-called liberal media. The center's awards, for the "most outrageously biased" reporting and commentary, are given to network correspondents, anchors, and other journalists who don't show up, of course, and aren't expected to show up. That's what the fun is all about—yukking it up with such conservative stand-ins as Robert Bork and Mona Charen as they mount the stage and accept the awards, with vicious humor, on behalf of the "winners."

In 1999, Julianne Malveaux, one of the left's most unsparing commentators, was the recipient of the "I'm-a-Compassionate-Liberal-but-I-Wish-You-Would-Die Award" for her comment about Thomas on a television talk show. She quipped, "I hope his wife feeds him lots of eggs and butter and he dies early, like many black men do, of heart disease." Malveaux would say later that her remark, however hard-edged, was intended as a joke, not a call for Thomas's death. But to those on the right, it was one of the vilest comments imaginable.

To the astonishment of some in the Monarch Hotel ballroom, Thomas himself picked up Malveaux's award. Soaking up the adulation of a standing ovation, the justice smiled and then spoke: "Normally, we are busy. This is a sitting week [for the court] so we have cases to decide tomorrow morning at 9:30, and I normally spend this night working. . . . But [my wife and I] realized this was such an important occasion that it was time to put aside our personal obligations of the Constitution, the work of the court, our little nephew, and to really attend to this in behalf of one of the kindest, warmest, most sensitive and gracious human beings and a person of generous spirit and, I was almost tempted to say, small-mindedness. I am pleased to accept this on behalf of Suzanne Malveaux and Dr. Atkins." Thomas got the name wrong; *Suzanne* Malveaux is a CNN correspondent. Not missing a beat, the justice went on to take a shot at National Public Radio's Nina Totenberg, one of two journalists to break the story of Anita Hill's allegations. Thomas said he wished Totenberg also could have received a DisHonors prize. "I have finally had the opportunity to have my surgeon remove her many stilettos from my back," he cracked, "and I'd like to return them." In conclusion, Thomas noted that his blood pressure was fine and his cholesterol normal, that he didn't really like fatty foods, and that he was in "wonderful health" as a result of a high-fiber, low-carbohydrate diet. "So I appreciate Ms. Malveaux's concern for me. And perhaps that Atkins Diet can do her some good."

It was a remarkable outing for a Supreme Court justice, proving that for Thomas a rollicking night of partisan bashing was a seduction too hard to resist. Famously thin-skinned—even some of his friends acknowledge this—Thomas has amazing recall for slights and critiques he feels are unfair to him. To deliver a tough assessment that reaches him is to risk forever being locked, unfavorably, in his memory.

During an informal conversation with one of us in 2001, Thomas explained how he had come to view the media as "malicious." He cited an article written nearly twenty years earlier by Ernest Hosendolph, then of the *New York Times*. Thomas nailed the exact date of publication, July 3, 1982. He called the article "the most unfair thing ever written about me" and urged that it be looked up. The story, 982 words, ran on page 5 of the *Times*'s main news section and began this way:

> Clarence Thomas says that, as a youngster growing up in the Deep South in the 1960s and 1970s, he benefited from scholarships and other special programs provided for minorities.
>
> But now, in his new role as chairman of the Equal Employment Opportunity Commission, the 34-year-old Mr. Thomas says he is opposed to aggressive "affirmative action" plans for minorities because they often place young people in programs beyond their abilities, especially in schools.

The piece quoted Thomas extensively but also quoted several critics. By most standards, it was a routine story. Which raises the question: Why would the head of a federal agency feel so injured by such standard journalism? Thomas did not specify—the only certainty is that two decades later this single article had not left his memory.

Myers Anderson, Thomas's grandfather and hero. (Courtesy of Stephen Morton)

Thomas as co-editor of *The Pioneer*, the school newspaper at St. John Vianney Minor Seminary. (Diocese of Savannah)

Thomas playing football with classmates at St. John Vianney. (Diocese of Savannah)

Thomas as the lone black graduate in a group photo of the 1967 St. John Vianney graduating class. *(Diocese of Savannah)*

Thomas's yearbook photo, the College of the Holy Cross, 1971.
(The College of the Holy Cross)

Thomas at the wedding of a friend during his senior year at Holy Cross, April 17, 1971. (*Courtesy of Carolyn White*)

Justice Thurgood Marshall at his desk at the Supreme Court, August 27, 1976.

(Gerald Martineau, the Washington Post)

Thomas and his wife, Ginny, at home, 1991.

(Courtesy of Harry Benson)

Senators John C. Danforth (left) and Strom Thurmond with Thomas, before the start of the tumultuous confirmation hearings, September 10, 1991. (*Harry Naltchayan, the* Washington Post)

Thomas's ceremonial swearing-in on the South Lawn of the White House. Justice Byron White administers the oath as President George H. W. Bush, First Lady Barbara Bush, and Thomas's wife, Ginni, look on, October 18, 1991. (*The George Bush Presidential Library*)

The new justice puffing a cigar just days after his October 1991 confirmation.
(Courtesy of Harry Benson)

Thomas's official Supreme Court portrait.
(U.S. Supreme Court)

Thomas and Ginni at the White House, July 18, 2005.

(*Gerald Martineau, the* Washington Post)

Anita Hill, now a professor of social policy, law, and women's studies at Brandeis University. (*Courtesy of Brandeis University*)

Justice Antonin Scalia answering a question while Justice Stephen Breyer looks on at American University Washington College of Law, January 13, 2005. (*Lucian Perkins, the* Washington Post)

Clarence Thomas and Anthony Kennedy share a laugh with Representative José Serrano, a member of the House Appropriations subcommittee that handles the Supreme Court budget. (*Robert M. Reeder, the* Washington Post)

Keith Hudson, plaintiff in the "cruel and unusual punishment" case decided by the Supreme Court in 1992, one of Thomas's earliest and most controversial opinions. *(Photograph by the authors, 2004)*

School official Kenneth Johnson rallies protestors objecting to Thomas's appearance at an awards ceremony at Prince George's County's Thomas G. Pullen Middle School, June 11, 1996. *(Bill O'Leary, the Washington Post)*

The Reverend Al Sharpton leads several hundred protestors in a two-hour demonstration near Thomas's Virginia home. (*Bill O'Leary, the* Washington Post)

Thomas gets emotional and breaks down before a group of black conservatives at the National Leadership Conference sponsored by *Headway* magazine, September 12, 1998. (*Annie Groer, the* Washington Post)

Emma Mae Martin, Thomas's sister, outside her Pin Point home. (*Courtesy of Stephen Morton*)

Thomas's mother, Leola Williams (center), sister Emma Martin (right), and niece Leola Farmer (left) in front of the Savannah home where Thomas grew up, 2001. (Atlanta Journal-Constitution)

Justice Thomas and his good friend Texas Tech basketball coach Bob Knight, prior to a luncheon at the National Press Club in Washington, September 27, 2004. *(AP photo/Pablo Martinez Monsivais)*

Given Thomas's sensitivities, it's not surprising that he agreed to participate in the DisHonors Awards gala. Having an enemy to fight is what links Thomas and the conservative faithful. "It is permanent warfare," says Craig Shirley, a conservative GOP consultant who was involved in the Thomas confirmation fight. "There's no cease-fire anymore. We're at total war, permanent war."

It is a beautiful October evening in 2003, and Grover Norquist, one of the conservative movement's most influential voices, is in front of his brick duplex on Capitol Hill pushing an old-time rotary-blade lawnmower over a small patch of grass. He is in jeans and a polo shirt, just a couple of hours away from hosting a fund-raiser for Republican congressional leader Roy Blunt of Missouri, when the subject of Thomas is broached.

As head of Americans for Tax Reform, Norquist convenes a weekly forum in Washington that serves as a kind of information and strategy session for the conservative movement. He has known Thomas since the Reagan administration and thought he would have made a great chief justice—before John Roberts was selected. "He maintains the respect of the conservative movement," Norquist says of Thomas.

Just to make sure he is properly understood, Norquist volunteers what he thinks of some of the other justices put on the bench by Republican presidents. Anthony Kennedy? "Universal disappointment in Kennedy, someone who moved to the left upon coming to Washington." David Souter? "He's so consistently rotten." O'Connor? Norquist derisively dismisses her as "the lady," the beneficiary of a Reagan campaign pledge to name a woman to the court. In Norquist's eyes, that was "a very goofy thing to do." (O'Connor would announce her retirement in 2005.) Even Rehnquist, who presided as chief justice for nineteen years before his death in 2005, is given the cool treatment. Norquist viewed Rehnquist as an anachronism or, in his lexicon, "a funny guy. He doesn't appear to be in favor of liberty. He appears to be in favor of police powers. . . . Which is not the modern conservative position."

Scalia and Thomas are the movement's all-stars, the only pure conservatives. And Thomas gets extra credit, Norquist explains, because there is "a recognition that as an African American he gets a whole lot of flak. . . . The left is just nastier to black conservatives than they are to white conservatives. . . . It's harder for him to be hard core than it is for Scalia." And yet Thomas never wavers.

Norquist is a short man with glasses who talks fast, drinks Diet Pepsi, and collects rubber bands, which he displays on the knob of his bookcase. He is so perpetually in motion that the interview winds up in his bedroom, where he keeps a black machete from Malawi and where he is making his bed and putting clothes away before the fund-raiser. (Norquist's reputation would later take a hit as a result of his association with Jack Abramoff, the disgraced former lobbyist who pled guilty to fraud and conspiracy in a scandal that reached the upper ranks of Congress. According to a Senate report issued in 2006, Abramoff funneled payments to Norquist's non-profit Americans for Tax Reform in exchange for Norquist's using his clout in Washington to help Abramoff clients, a possible violation of the group's tax-exempt status.)

It is pointed out to Norquist how ironic it is that the people who love Thomas most are white. The institutions that fete him and the audiences that applaud him as if he were Muhammad Ali are more often than not overwhelmingly white. "That's a problem that there aren't more conservative black guys," Norquist insists. And the reason there aren't more, he continues, is because the Democratic left has succeeded in demonizing Republican conservatives in the black community, "the equivalent of telling black kids that if they study hard they're white. And so they say, 'OK, we won't study.' "

The argument that blacks have been brainwashed by the liberal elite comes across as a heavy dose of condescension. An ongoing problem Republicans have in recruiting and developing more Clarence Thomases is that not enough of them know how to speak to blacks. Blaming African American fealty to the Democratic Party is hardly a winning recruitment strategy.

Thomas, when he isn't playing the part of the aggrieved victim, is actually an excellent ambassador for his side. Sondra Raspberry, a former college instructor and the wife of retired *Washington Post* columnist William Raspberry, happened to get seated next to the justice at journalist Juan Williams's fiftieth birthday dinner party two years ago. She was dreading the table arrangements, for she thought very little of Thomas and loathed his court opinions. As she put it, she was poised to "wring his neck" if the opportunity presented itself. Instead, she was astonished at how much she was drawn to him. "He was so animated." The more they chatted, the more she liked him. And by the time the evening was over, she was ready to cook him a rabbit, which was one subject of their discussion. Tales like this one make Republican operatives salivate, wishing Thomas could be transformed into a more active agent for the party. When Thomas was pitching his memoir to publishers, he made a presentation to Regnery, a small Washington-based house that is a favorite of conservatives. From 2003 to the end of 2005, thirteen books by Regnery's conservative authors made the *New York Times*'s nonfiction best-seller list. Sitting in on the three-hour meeting with Thomas was Greg Mueller, a GOP consultant who was on Regnery's acquisition board. Mueller, who helped run Pat Buchanan's 1996 presidential campaign, was listening to Thomas and thinking that here was a man who didn't belong on the Supreme Court. Not that he wasn't *qualified* to serve on the court but that his skill set could be better utilized on a wide-open stage. As Mueller sees it, Thomas not only has a strong ideological philosophy but knows how to connect with people of different realms.

"I wish I could clone Clarence Thomas and put him in a presidential campaign," Mueller says.

The justice has arrived, and everyone is waiting for him. He is late, but not too late to mingle. The crowd at the Ritz-Carlton Pentagon City hotel in Arlington, Virginia, is a blend of think-tank types, university professors, federal bureaucrats, and conservative activists. Spotting Clarence Thomas, they move in small clusters toward him, slowly, strategically. Some want a personal photo, some an autograph, some just a handshake. Others desire only to linger on the fringes, close enough to watch and overhear. Thomas is always generous to those seeking his attention; he tries never to leave anyone unsatisfied.

He is here this evening, September 23, 2003, as the keynote speaker for a toast to his longtime friend Walter E. Williams, a George Mason University economics professor. Like Thomas, Williams is a well-known black conservative. He has made a living writing provocative weekly newspaper commentaries and appearing on TV and radio programs, including as a substitute host for the *Rush Limbaugh Show*. A sample from a Williams column: "Since black politicians and the civil rights establishment preach victimhood to blacks, I'd prefer that they be more explicit when they appear in public. . . . Were they to be so, saying racists are responsible for black illegitimacy, blacks preying on other blacks, and black family breakdown, their victimhood message would be revealed as idiotic." Known as "the people's economist," Williams is the author of at least six books and more than eighty articles in scholarly journals.

The toast was organized, in part, by his George Mason colleagues; for six years Williams was chairman of the economics department. But as a distinguished roster of toasters—including two Nobel Prize winners—takes the stage and appears via video, it becomes clear this will not be a night to laud Williams's academic achievements. The celebration assumes a remarkable slapstick character, punctuated by racial humor. There are several mentions of Williams's shark-tooth necklace and former Afro haircut and quips that he was once an enforcer for the Black Panthers and preferred to drink his wine from a brown paper bag. There are also repeated wisecracks about Al Sharpton and Jesse Jackson and a description of Williams as "the freedom fighter from the academy." No more than three black dinner guests are in a room of several hundred, not counting Thomas, Williams and his family, and us. Judging by the laughter, most in attendance seem to find the evening hilarious.

Edwin Meese, the former Reagan administration attorney general, says in his tribute that he likes to think of Williams as "the liberals' worst nightmare; that is, an economist with street smarts."

Nobel laureate Milton Friedman, in his videotaped remarks, hails Williams as someone who speaks his mind without equivocation. The noted economist, who would die in 2006, calls Williams one of the foremost proponents of a color-blind society, a line that draws scattered applause.

When Thomas speaks, it is clear he has a relationship with Williams that the other speakers don't. It is as if they are two conservative black soldiers waging a long-term battle for recognition and respect. Thomas recalls initially being inspired by Williams through his writings, on subjects ranging from South Africa to school vouchers, dating back to the mid-1970s. The two first met in 1980 at a "Growth Day" event in Washington—a conservative alternative to the Earth Day celebrations. Through the years, Williams has offered encouragement and unvarnished advice to Thomas, a practice that continues today.

"Dr. Williams, thank you for all your work, your insight, your courage," Thomas says. "You helped to free me from the bondage of group thinking. Your independence gave me courage to assert my own." As an illustration of that courage, Thomas cites Williams's refusing to take a seat in the back of the bus during a Georgia trip to a military base in the 1950s and then declaring himself Caucasian when he reported for duty in Korea, "since whites got better assignments than blacks."

Williams seems overwhelmed by the tributes and at one point says he is unaccustomed to people saying such nice things about him. But what do those nice things amount to? The dominant, feel-good message of the evening seems to be: Walter Williams is black and he's one of us. Not that he's a brilliant economist, an innovator, a future Nobel Prize winner. The conclusion one could easily draw from the toast is that, professionally, Walter Williams is not in the same league as his peers. It is not an evening that focuses on his scholarship. Much of what he is recognized for is his style and personality—the balls to say and write what's on his mind, his cutting wit, and, notably, his fearlessness in taking on conventional black points of view.

In Thomas's eyes, he and Williams are alike. Both worked hard, struggled, became successful in predominantly white environments without the embrace of much of their race. At the very end of his remarks, Thomas mentions *All It Takes Is Guts*, a collection of Williams's columns. "You have guts, my friend," Thomas says. "Thank you for being you and showing those of us who look up to you that the rewards of intellectual independence are far greater than the rewards of ideological or racial orthodoxy."

Four months later, the Walter Williams toast comes up in a conversation with Republican congressman Dick Armey of Texas, the blunt-spoken former House majority leader. Armey, an economist himself, did not attend the toast but is perfectly willing to analyze it. He knows both Thomas and Williams, thinks highly of the former and not so highly of the latter. "I don't normally associate the term *scholarship* with Walter Williams," Armey says. And then this: "Walter Williams doesn't have the keenest of understanding, the depth of thinking, and the quality of work."

Armey, who knows most of the toasters, was not surprised to learn that the celebration unfolded the way it did. "Walter Williams and I spent quite a bit of time together," he says, "and with Walter Williams it's almost a constant discussion about 'I'm a black man in a white man's world.'" It's not just that serious economists don't take Williams seriously as an economist, Armey suggests, it's that Williams has actively exploited his race to create a market for himself in which he is "celebrated as a black conservative free market economist." By contrast, Armey explains, no one would ever think of consigning Thomas Sowell to a black niche. Armey reveres Sowell, an economist at Stanford University's Hoover Institution and a Clarence Thomas mentor. "If you said, 'Dick Armey, come speak at a dinner for Thomas Sowell,' I would be flattered and honored and scared to death I couldn't do it good enough. If you said, 'Dick, come and be part of a statement for Walter Williams,' I would probably decline the offer." (Williams didn't return calls from us requesting an interview for this book.)

It is odd but fascinating hearing Armey dissect the two leading black conservative economists, playing them off each other, holding one in esteem and depicting the other as a self-promoter. The link that connects them all—Sowell, Williams, and Armey—is Clarence Thomas. He has managed to get close to all three, while finding his own place in the conservative kingdom. As Armey sees it, Thomas's ideas and principles are more important to him than his race, and that is a large measure of his appeal and success. "I don't know how color-blind Clarence is with respect to his relationship with the world," says Armey, "but I believe that we are color-blind in our relationship to one another."

CRUEL AND UNUSUAL PUNISHMENT

No case did more to define Clarence Thomas in many people's minds than one brought by Keith Hudson, a prisoner who sued for damages after being beaten by two corrections officers at Angola State Penitentiary in Louisiana. The court's ruling that Hudson's assault amounted to cruel and unusual punishment prompted a Thomas dissent still singled out by his critics as evidence of what they regard as his coldhearted approach to the law.

The dissent, joined only by Justice Antonin Scalia, said that the Eighth Amendment's ban on cruel and unusual punishment did not protect prisoners from beatings by guards unless the prisoners suffered serious injury. Thomas accused the court's seven-justice majority of expanding the Eighth Amendment's protections "beyond all bounds of history and precedent." He called the decision "yet another manifestation of the pervasive view that the federal Constitution must address all ills in our society."

To many legal observers, Thomas's admonition that the federal courts offered no protection for a wide range of social problems had implications far beyond the specific provision at issue in the case. "For Thomas, there are no gray areas and no mitigating factors—one's abstract principles generate a series of categorical judgments that need never yield to a human dimension," former University of Southern California law professor Catharine Pierce Wells wrote in 1993.

The events leading to the case began in the wee hours of October 30, 1983, as Keith Hudson was hunched over the toilet in his prison cell, washing his clothes. If he had learned nothing else in the previous four years he spent at Angola, he knew that washing clothes in his commode left them much cleaner than sending them to the prison laundry. So there he was, busily scrubbing and flushing, when a guard interrupted him.

"Nigger, stop flushing that toilet and go to sleep," ordered Jack McMillian, a guard who is also black.

"I'm in here washing my clothes. I don't know what you're talking about," Hudson shot back.

"Flush that toilet one more time and you're going in the hole," McMillian said.

"I'm washing my clothes," Hudson said. "I live here. You just work here."

McMillian turned away, as he mumbled a warning: "OK, I've got something for you."

Before long, McMillian reappeared outside Hudson's cell with another guard, Marvin Woods. They told Hudson to pack his belongings—he was headed to isolation. They handcuffed and shackled him and led him to a corridor where they shoved him against a wall and began to beat him. "Hold him," McMillian told Woods. "Let me knock his gold teeth out."

Hudson says McMillian harbored a dislike for him because of his well-earned reputation for being a hardheaded prisoner and the fact that he was from New Orleans. McMillian was from Baton Rouge, which in the strange world of Angola made the two natural enemies. The guards went on punching and kicking him "until they got tired," Hudson says.

A third guard, a supervisor named Arthur Mezo, noticed the

commotion but chose not to intervene, other than to warn his two subordinates not to have "too much fun." The beating left Hudson with a split lip, swollen eyes, body bruises, and a cracked dental plate. He was peeing blood. The court record showed that he received no formal medical attention, but he spent most of the next three days curled under his bunk in a fetal position. "That was the only way I was comfortable," he says.

Once his wounds healed, Hudson was determined to seek justice. He was a stubborn prisoner, he admits, who only reluctantly did the farmwork required of prisoners at Angola. ("I ain't reliving slavery," he thought to himself when asked to pick cotton.) He told fellow inmates he planned to take the guards to court. They thought he was crazy. "Everybody said, 'Let it go. They are going to kill you,' " he recalls. "I said, if I die, I'm going to die trying."

An inmate loaned Hudson a book that laid out the basic formats for filing court petitions. Hudson studied it for weeks before filing his case against the guards and the state of Louisiana in December 1983. The suit contained a few misspellings and some bad grammar, but it conveyed Hudson's determination to seek retribution for the beating.

He sought "fifty thousand dollors" in damages and an order to "prohibit further cruelty to myself and other inmates." The case was heard in federal district court four years later. Hudson argued that the beating violated his constitutional rights and he produced two witnesses to back his story. He also told the court that he had suffered "not only mental and physical anguish but a permanent psychological scar for life."

"They had three, four, and five lawyers, and I was sitting over there by myself," Hudson recalls. "It felt like I was stepping over the line. I really didn't know what I was doing." But he was careful to meet the required filing deadlines and to respond to all of the court's requests. That was enough for him to win. A federal magistrate ruled in Hudson's favor, awarding him $800 in damages—a paltry figure that could not be increased because Hudson neglected to ask for punitive damages. Still, the state of Louisiana appealed and a three-judge panel of a federal appeals court reversed the decision in July 1990. The court agreed that Hudson's beating was unreasonable and excessive. But because it caused only what the magistrate had described as "minor injuries" that healed without medical attention, the judges found that Hudson's beating did not rise to the level of cruel and unusual punishment.

With that, Hudson returned to the prison typewriter and pounded out a request to have his case heard by the entire appeals court, "*en banc*." The court denied that request and Hudson exercised his final option, an appeal to the U.S. Supreme Court. "The Circuit Court mustive neglecting to read the entire judgment transcript, because the Magistrate awarded the Petitioner 'actual damages,' and would have awarded the Petitioner 'punitive damages,' but it wasn't stipulated in the Petitioner's 'relief desired,' due the petitioner's lack of knowledge of process and constructing a Civil Action complaint at that time," Hudson wrote in his high court petition.

Virtually every Supreme Court appeal is a long shot because the court agrees to hear only a tiny share—roughly 1 percent—of the eight thousand cases brought before it each year. An appeal from a prison inmate acting as his own lawyer has an incalculably small chance of being heard. But to Hudson's surprise, the court voted to review his case. The legal question it wanted to clarify was whether the use of force against a prisoner might constitute cruel and unusual punishment even if the inmate does not suffer serious injury.

Despite Thomas's well-known conservative credentials, it was a question some people thought he might answer differently from the appeals court. Hudson and Thomas share similar backgrounds: They are both from the "wrong side of the tracks," dark-skinned black men born into poor families in the Deep South. Also, during his confirmation hearings, Thomas left the unmistakable impression that he would bring a unique perspective to court, one that would allow him some level of empathy with criminal defendants. While serving as a judge on the U.S. Court of Appeals for the District of Columbia, he could see from his office window the shackled inmates being brought to federal court on prison buses. As he watched that sad scene unfold before him nearly every day, Thomas said he would remind himself, "But for the grace of God there go I." Maybe, some thought, Thomas would see himself in Keith Hudson.

Oral arguments in *Hudson v. McMillian* were held on November 13, 1991, less than two weeks after Thomas, shaken from his confirmation ordeal, joined the high court. The one-hour argument—a half hour for each side—was one of the final steps in the court's decision making on the case. Representing Hudson at the argument was Alvin J. Bronstein, an American Civil Liberties Union lawyer. By then, all the justices had read Hudson's complaint and pored over the briefs supporting arguments on both sides. Not long after oral arguments, they met in conference, the justices-only meeting where they voted on their decision. Chief Justice William H. Rehnquist was in the majority, so he was responsible for deciding who wrote the majority opinion, which laid out the court's rationale and became the guiding document for lower courts. He assigned the case to Sandra Day O'Connor, who crafted the court's decision.

Soon after oral arguments, it became clear that Thomas was going to dissent. His views on the case startled some court insiders as soon as they began to emerge in draft opinions circulated among the justices. In Justice Harry Blackmun's chambers, there was disbelief. Blackmun was a longtime champion of prisoners' rights and in 1968 had written one of the first federal appellate court decisions declaring brutal treatment of inmates illegal. In a memo to his boss, Blackmun law clerk Jeff Meyer expressed his disdain for an early draft of Thomas's dissent: "My vote for most outrageous line is: 'In my view, if there is anything in this case that would shock our society, it is the notion that a punishment that causes no injury at all or only minor injury, may be deemed cruel and unusual.' " Three weeks later, as Thomas honed his dissent, Meyer assured Blackmun that Thomas raised no legal points worth responding to. He then offered this assessment: "Overall, it's an interesting window into his jurisprudence and view of the scope of the Constitution."

When the Hudson decision was announced the following February, seven of the justices had agreed to reverse the appeals court decision and back Hudson's brutality claim. O'Connor's majority opinion made clear that prisoner beatings might constitute cruel and unusual punishment, even in the absence of serious injury. "When prison officials maliciously and sadistically use force to cause harm, contemporary standards of decency always are violated," she wrote. "This is true whether or not significant injury is evident. Otherwise, the Eighth Amendment would permit any physical punishment, no matter how diabolic or inhuman, inflicting less than some arbitrary quantity of injury. Such a result would have been unacceptable to the drafters of the Eighth Amendment as it is today."

Thomas took a boldly contrary view. The use of force that causes "insignificant harm" to a prisoner may be immoral, torturous, criminal, and even remediable under other provisions of the U.S. Constitution, Thomas said, but it does not constitute cruel and unusual punishment. Then he went further, revealing a willingness to overrule long-settled legal disputes in favor of his understanding of the original intent of the Constitution and legal statutes. This approach would become a hallmark of his work on the court. Quoting court cases from the nineteenth century and citing early English law, Thomas strongly implied a position that he would fully argue in subsequent cases: that "punishment" as contemplated by the framers of the Constitution, had to do only with sentences imposed by judges, not with harsh conditions created by jailers. Thomas questioned whether prisoner mistreatment—from beatings to poor medical care to unsanitary conditions—was the business of the federal courts. He concluded that the court should have rejected Hudson's claim. His was a position that would have reversed decades of court rulings that had slowly increased the legal protections extended to prison inmates.

"Abusive behavior by prison guards is deplorable conduct that properly evokes outrage and contempt," wrote Thomas in his dissent. "But that does not mean it is invariably unconstitutional. The Eighth Amendment is not, and should not be turned into, a National Code of Prison Regulation."

The tone of Thomas's dissent and his refusal to acknowledge the human dimension of the case—he referred to the federal magistrate's finding that Hudson's injuries were "minor," without discussing any details of the beating—left many people, including some of his court colleagues, cold. In her opinion, Justice O'Connor directly challenged Thomas's view: "To deny, as the dissent does, the difference between punching a prisoner in the face and serving him appetizing food is to ignore the concepts of dignity, civilized standards, humanity, and decency that animate the Eighth Amendment." Blackmun was even more pointed in his criticism. In an opinion concurring with O'Connor, he called Thomas's position that an Eighth Amendment claim must be accompanied by serious injury "seriously misguided." Using Thomas's standard, Blackmun said, a whole raft of torture and abuse would lie beyond the reach of the Constitution. "In other words, the constitutional prohibition of 'cruel and unusual punishment' then might not constrain prison officials from lashing prisoners with leather straps, whipping them with rubber hoses, beating them with naked fists, shocking them with electric currents, asphyxiating them short of death, intentionally exposing them to undue heat or cold, or forcibly injecting them with psychosis-inducing drugs," Blackmun said. "These techniques, commonly thought to be practiced outside this nation's borders, are hardly unknown within this nation's prisons."

Blackmun later remarked that Thomas's dissent offered a strong indication of the type of justice Thomas would become on the Supreme Court. "Well, it indicated to me, at least, that here was what appeared to be a fairly conservative approach to some of these things," Blackmun said, with characteristic understatement, when asked about the Hudson case by an interviewer.

Others were less charitable. Alvin J. Bronstein, the ACLU attorney who represented Hudson before the Supreme Court, noting that during oral arguments Scalia had pressed many of the same points made in Thomas's dissent, said that Thomas's work read "almost as though he is a robot being jerked by Justice Scalia." Outside the court, the reaction to Thomas's dissent was no less scathing. A *New York Times* editorial reacting to the dissent called Thomas "the youngest, cruelest justice." In a column written in the style of a letter to a wayward friend, *Washington Post* syndicated columnist William Raspberry called Thomas's dissent "bizarre."

At Angola, meanwhile, Hudson and his fellow inmates cursed Thomas. "The guys were happy for me," Hudson says. "But they were talking about Clarence Thomas. They were calling him Uncle Tom, house nigger, things like that. Some of them were saying, 'I wish he were in here with us.' "

In the immediate aftermath of his court victory, Hudson was featured in a flurry of news reports but otherwise he was still largely invisible to the world, spending most of his time locked away in an isolation cell. He says prison officials received several interview requests for him and turned them down, most often without consulting him. Someone from Harvard University wrote inviting Hudson to visit the campus once he was released from prison in 1992, but he never responded. He also received a call from someone claiming to be a movie producer; he didn't recognize the name so he never returned the call. A woman from New York took a deep interest in him, sending him a sheaf of newspaper clippings and then venturing to Angola for a visit. At the last minute, he refused to see her.

Hudson was released from Angola just months after the Supreme Court's decision, but his life of crime was not over. He was sent back to prison twice more on gun possession and parole violation charges. In 2003, he was released from Orleans Parish prison. Afterward, he held several odd jobs. He caulked windows and worked as a laborer before landing a job cutting grass with the New Orleans Parkway and Park Commission, before Hurricane Katrina left that city in tatters.

Many years after his improbable Supreme Court victory, Hudson remains ambivalent about it. He was happy to win; there is no question about that. But at the same time, he was angry that even his victory seemed to minimize his suffering. "Eight hundred dollars? That was nothing to celebrate," he says. "Everybody was focusing on Clarence Thomas and forgetting how they whipped me in there. Nobody went to jail."

Hudson says he never held much hope that Thomas would side with him. He recalls being glued to the television set in the prison recreation room with about sixty other inmates as the Thomas confirmation drama unfolded. He says the Hill-Thomas controversy divided the inmates much as it did the rest of the country. Many of the inmates sided with Thomas—but he never did. While many aspects of Thomas's story resonated with Hudson—being born into Southern poverty, suffering the indignities of racism, having a father who abandoned him—Hudson believed Thomas would not be sympathetic to someone who ended up in prison. Despite all their similarities, he decided that Thomas was nothing like him, that Thomas did not represent him. The case only proved him right, Hudson says.

Hudson never felt that way about Thurgood Marshall, Thomas's predecessor. Marshall may have been middle class, but the way Hudson saw it, Marshall had something Thomas didn't—the courage to stand up to whites—and that meant a lot. He sensed that Marshall saw himself representing black people on the court—a view Thomas always rejected. A year before the beating that led to his court case, Hudson sent a poem to Marshall from Angola, praising him for holding on to his beliefs at the Supreme Court. He said the piece began, "With these eyes, I have seen the struggle. With these eyes, I've seen the crying of my people."

"I was trying to tell him that I was amazed at his endurance," Hudson says. "I admired him. He stuck with his beliefs about the death penalty being unconstitutional. He was the only black in an isolated situation like that. He kind of blew my mind to be strong like he was to the end." In Thomas, Hudson sees something different. "He is the complete opposite. It is really like a slap in black people's face for him to be up there. If you are up there, you should at least have a sense of compassion for your people."

But to Thomas, none of those factors—Hudson's race, his background, the circumstances of his incarceration—were relevant to the legal question at hand. He also thought those who opposed his view of the case often distorted the facts. "The conclusion reached by the long arms of the critics is that I supported the beating of prisoners in that case," Thomas said in a 1998 speech. "Well, one must either be illiterate or fraught with malice to reach that conclusion. Though one can disagree with my dissent, and certainly the majority of the Court disagreed, no honest reading can reach such a conclusion."

His being the court's only black justice, Thomas has said, should have no effect on how he does his job. "The point that I'd like to stress here is that the court is not a representative body. The court should be the least representative body," he told students at James Madison University in 2001. "That doesn't mean you shouldn't have people from different groups there; I think that's very important. But this is not a representative body. To the extent that it is, then law isn't law. It's not a discipline. It's something that changes based on your pigmentation."

The heated debate ignited by the Hudson case has only expanded into a larger one about Thomas's legal views that still rages. After his confirmation, Thomas had looked forward to the court as a refuge, a calm place in which to recover. Justices disagree; he understood that. But unlike in politics, they do so with civility, symbolized by the handshakes they share each time they meet to decide a case. What *Hudson v. McMillian* demonstrated to Thomas was that it was possible for a single justice to occupy the limelight, as though he were a politician. And to a scarred man who had just departed the political battlefield, this was not a pleasant thought. The lingering controversy over his confirmation made him hesitant to do some of the things other justices did without a second thought. Seven months after taking his seat on the court, for instance, he canceled plans to judge a moot court competition at Seton Hall's law school. He had learned that the school's Women's Law Forum was planning a candlelight vigil to protest his appearance.

Some court observers speculated that Thomas, beaten down by the confirmation process and paralyzed by his inexperience as a jurist, was unduly influenced by his clerks, particularly former Scalia clerk Chris Laudau. At the same time, civil rights leaders grew increasingly disillusioned with him as his unvaryingly conservative judicial philosophy became clearer. "He sides in almost every instance with the powerful over those without power," said Wade Henderson, who then directed the Washington bureau of the NAACP. "It is absolutely no benefit to us whatsoever to have a black face deciding cases that are going directly against the interest of blacks."

Looking back on his first term on the court, the *New York Times* concluded that Thomas was a budding ideologue. "During his first year on the Court, Justice Thomas spoke loudly but not often wisely," the paper opined. "Those who hoped that he would find himself once confirmed more often saw him lose himself in ideology. In this first year, Justice Thomas has failed the test of judiciousness." In the midst of the onslaught, fellow justice Lewis Powell penned a short note to Thomas, urging him to keep his head up:

Dear Clarence,

In recent days the press has not been kind to you. This, of course, concerns you. But criticism goes with being a public figure. As some say, it "goes with the territory." Your colleagues understand this, and so do I.

Best wishes,
Lewis

If the early criticism got Thomas down, he eventually learned to live with it. His freshman term on the court was only a harbinger of things to come. In the years to follow, he would emerge as what many legal scholars call the most conservative justice on the court, the one most consistent in hewing to a strict, unchanging reading of the Constitution. Some legal scholars call Thomas a judicial activist because he argues far more than any other justice for overturning legal precedents, no matter how jarring that could be to society. In Thomas's view, he is simply trying to correct past mistakes and following the path laid by the founding fathers. As the court has swung farther to the right with the confirmation of Chief Justice John Roberts in 2005 and Justice Samuel A. Alito Jr. in early 2006, some conservative activists believe that many of Thomas's views may soon find themselves in the majority. If so, Thomas's approach to the law would be vindicated.

Shortly after delivering a sober commencement address at the Ave Maria School of Law in Ann Arbor, Michigan, Thomas chatted and posed for pictures with some of the fifty-six graduates of the Class of 2004. The posing was done in front of a newly unveiled statue of Sir Thomas More, the Catholic martyr whose courage in the face of death Thomas has called an inspiration. Before long, one of the students at the conservative law school asked about *Brown v. Board of Education*, the monumental 1954 Supreme Court decision to end legal segregation. That ruling was being widely hailed throughout the nation on the occasion of its fiftieth anniversary. Thomas launched into an impromptu lecture, not about *Brown* but about *Plessy v. Ferguson*, the 1896 case that produced the infamous separate-but-equal doctrine. Thomas singled out the lonely dissent of John Marshall Harlan, the only justice to vote against the Plessy decision. "In the eye of the Constitution, in the eye of the law, there is in this country no superior, dominant ruling class of citizens," Harlan wrote. "There is no caste here. Our Constitution is color-blind." Harlan's opinion, as Thomas saw it, was a lesson in perseverance and faith in the Constitution despite widespread ridicule. "It was not reported,"

Thomas said of the dissent. "There were no contemporaneous articles. No law review articles. Just one guy." One guy, he added, whose view eventually was embraced by an entire nation.

It was clear that Thomas sees a lot of himself in Harlan. A minority opinion on the court today can be a majority opinion a generation from now. In his nearly sixteen years as a justice, Thomas has methodically built a record notable for its unwavering conservatism and aggressive challenges to long-standing legal precedents in areas from church-state separation to voting and prisoners' rights.

Like all other judges, Thomas says his actions are defined by the Constitution and the text of laws he is called on to interpret, not by how he feels about the plight of a plaintiff or a particular public policy issue. But unlike many judges, he finds the contemporary context of society all but irrelevant. Instead, he says, he relies on the original intent of the founders. Thomas's former clerks say he strives most for intellectual consistency in his opinions. Sometimes, Thomas explains, that puts helping someone in need or righting an obvious wrong beyond his reach. "There are some opinions—a class of opinions—where something inside you as a human being says, 'Boy, I really need to do something. This just isn't right.' But you have no authority to do anything. That's when discipline is required. As I tell groups of kids when they come to visit me, that it's like watching someone drowning 20 feet below and you only have 10 feet of rope."

That philosophy has been apparent since his earliest days as a justice. In his first year on the court, the justices ruled on a case that placed new limits on the Voting Rights Act of 1965, one of the nation's most fundamental pieces of civil rights legislation. The law allowed many blacks across the South to vote for the first time, paving the way for the election of record numbers of black officials. Given his personal history as a child of segregation, many advocates thought Thomas would support a broad reading of that provision.

The case before the court involved Lawrence C. Presley, the first black commissioner to be elected to a seat in Etowah County, Alabama, since Reconstruction. Historically, the main task of county commissioners was to supervise county road construction and repair projects in their respective districts. After Presley's election, the commission's white majority abruptly decided that the entire body should control all road projects and therefore stripped Presley of power as an individual commissioner. Under the act, political jurisdictions with histories of racial discrimination in elections must clear any changes in election laws with the attorney general or a federal court. Thomas joined a six-person court majority in rejecting the challenge. The change in powers, the majority said, does not have to be cleared by federal authorities. The act, the court ruled, protected black voters against actions that weakened their political power but it did not protect black elected officials against "routine actions of state and local governments."

Presley, who died just months after the court's decision, had supported Thomas's elevation to the court, reasoning that, while Thomas might be conservative, at least he was a black man. But after Thomas's vote in his case, he felt betrayed. "That really hurt him more than the decision," said his widow, Alice Presley. "He would walk around saying, 'I can't believe Thomas voted against me.' "

Thomas's position in the voting rights case is one of many that have cheered conservatives, while causing consternation for much of the civil rights community. Aligning himself with the court's conservative majority, Thomas has supported decisions that scaled back affirmative action, allowed use of public money to send students to parochial schools, and restricted the creation of election districts intended to elevate minorities to public office.

Thomas is the justice most likely to declare federal statutes unconstitutional and, as was stated earlier, to advocate overturning legal precedents. He also is the justice most willing to cast solo votes in pursuit of these aims, making him the justice "most out of step with his colleagues in this area," according to Lori A. Ringhand, a University of Kentucky law professor who wrote a paper on the issue after examining the work of justices between 1994 and 2005.

Ringhand found that Thomas was most likely to vote to invalidate laws he feels violate the First Amendment's protections of free speech and religion, a position shared by many members of the court. Thomas also votes frequently to invalidate statutes he thinks curtail states' rights. This record "stands in considerable tension with the notion—frequently although certainly not unanimously—invoked by political conservatives, that judicial deference is an important part of conservative jurisprudence," Ringhand wrote.

Thomas's rethinking of legal doctrine extends to obscure but important areas of law such as the Constitution's Commerce Clause, which is the basis for a wide range of federal workplace and environmental statutes. Thomas has said the court should consider limiting the clause's reach to its original understanding, which was to allow federal regulation of the movement of goods between states. Given Thomas's emphasis on states' rights, the federal government's regulatory power would be strictly limited to such matters, even as the country—and indeed the world—grows increasingly interdependent. The result would be to invalidate many federal environmental, workplace safety, and civil rights laws, leaving those matters to the states.

As Thomas sees it, most of his colleagues are not willing to go far enough to reconcile the court's work with what he sees as the Constitution's mandate. He thinks they too often are bent on interpreting the laws according to the currents of modern times, rather than according to the timeless words of the nation's founding charter.

Thomas's jurisprudence has made him the toast of conservative activists, who laud his firm legal stands, and the nemesis of liberal activists, who view him as vindictive and narrow in his reading of the law. The irony is that Thomas is the author of few majority opinions in constitutionally significant cases. His unbending approach makes it difficult to assign him opinions in closely contested cases for fear that he might not be able to get other justices to agree with his reasoning and sign on to his often sweeping conclusions. Thomas "has firm views that [the court's swing voters] would be uncomfortable with," says Mark V. Tushnet, a Georgetown University law professor. "If you give him a closely contested major case, he may not end up in the majority."

In his first fifteen years on the court, Thomas's entrenchment made him more a symbol of the growing ideological divide in American jurisprudence than a persuasive force on the bench. He most often finds himself assigned to speak for the court in cases that do not address the great issues of the day—for example, complex regulatory matters and arcane disputes over pension benefits, taxes, and bankruptcy. Cases involving economic issues accounted for 28 percent of the majority opinions Thomas wrote, while they constituted 19 percent of the cases that have come before the court during his tenure, according to a 2004 analysis of Supreme Court decisions by Cornell University's Legal Information Institute.

Thomas seems not to care. This streak of independence—some intimates have called it stubbornness—has coursed through his life. "He's an ornery something—always was," said Eddie Jenkins, his Holy Cross classmate and friend.

On the court's most important cases, Thomas's voice is most often heard in strongly worded dissents and concurrences that he believes one day will become law. It remains to be seen whether that approach will place him on the path of quirky justices whose solitary views never capture the court or in the company of a Harlan or an Oliver Wendell Holmes, one of the greatest justices and an early champion of the legislative authority to prohibit child labor and establish a sixty-hour limit on the workweek.

The membership of the court changed for the first time in eleven years with the addition of Roberts and Alito during the 2005–06 term, making the court unmistakably more conservative. Roberts replaced a fellow conservative in Rehnquist, but a statistical analysis found that Alito was more likely to vote with the court's conservative bloc than was O'Connor, whom he succeeded. Still, it is unclear whether the new justices will be willing to go as far as Thomas in challenging old precedents and knocking down standing legislation.

While many conservatives are wary of governmental power, Thomas has proved himself a strong advocate of sweeping presidential authority—at least in wartime. In the biggest case of the 2005–06 term, the court rejected the Bush administration's plan to use military commissions to try terrorism suspects being held at the naval base at Guantanamo Bay, Cuba. The court ruled that the commissions, which would have permitted hearsay testimony and allowed defendants to be convicted by evidence gained through coercion, were not authorized by federal statute. Moreover, the court majority said, the commissions violated international law. Thomas, Scalia, and Alito dissented from the opinion to rein in the Bush administration's broad view of presidential power.

To underscore his disapproval, Thomas read his dissent from the bench, the first time he chose to do so in his fifteen years on the court. In it, he called the court's decision "dangerous," saying the Geneva Conventions did not cover the detainees at Guantanamo. He also made clear his respect for presidential prerogative. The case, he said, amounted to "an unprecedented departure from the traditionally limited role of the courts with respect to war and an unwarranted intrusion on executive authority."

Since joining the court, Thomas has come under sustained fire from critics who say he lacks compassion.

In 2005, Thomas opposed a court decision finding that the federal law barring sex discrimination in schools and colleges also prohibits school officials from retaliating against those who bring sex discrimination complaints. The court held that the law's protections extended not only to direct victims of sex discrimination but also to those who complain about sex discrimination on behalf of others.

The plaintiff in the case was a male gym teacher, Roderick Jackson, who lost his position as a girls' high school basketball coach in Birmingham, Alabama, after he complained that the girls' team had to play and practice under conditions inferior to those of the boys' team. The law at issue, known as Title IX, requires schools that receive federal money to provide equal opportunities for boys and girls, but it does not actually mention retaliation—a fact cited by Thomas, who said that "Jackson does not claim that his own sex played any role, let alone a decisive or predominant one, in the decision to relieve him of his position." Rather, Justice Thomas went on, Jackson's claim was "founded on the attenuated connection between the supposed adverse treatment and the sex of others."

Courtney Paquette, a 2003 Holy Cross graduate, was among a group of students from the college who met with Thomas in his chambers during her junior year. She says he was showing them "all his stuff"—yearbook, photos—when he pulled out his pocket Constitution. He thumbed through it, stopping to talk about various sections. "This, this, and this. This is what I make decisions on," he told the students. "I don't stray from that."

During his confirmation hearings, Thomas suggested he would be open to legal persuasion and adhere to the law. Many of Thomas's views as a justice, however, are identical to the outspoken and sometimes controversial policy positions he articulated during his years in government. Some observers see consistency in thought, while others see a man more interested in pursuing desired outcomes than considering alternative arguments.

As a Reagan administration political appointee, Thomas opposed the deliberate crafting of election districts that had enabled record numbers of minority representatives to school boards, city councils, state legislatures, and congressional seats across the country. Such redistricting, Thomas argued, treats voting as a group, rather than an individual, right—in the same way that segregation sorted individuals into groups. When the issue reached the Supreme Court in the 1994 case *Holder v. Hall*, Thomas was a justice. In his concurrence with a court majority ruling against a Georgia redistricting plan, Thomas condemned the notion "that race defines political interest." Similarly, Thomas's opposition to affirmative action as demeaning to minorities and problematic under the Constitution was articulated while he served at the EEOC. "I think that preferential hiring on the basis of race or gender will increase racial divisiveness, disempower women and minorities by fostering the notion they're permanently disabled and in need of handouts," he wrote in 1987. Writing in a concurrence to a 1995 ruling establishing tougher standards for justifying federal affirmative action programs, Thomas said: "So-called benign discrimination teaches many that because of chronic and immutable handicaps, minorities cannot compete with them without their patronizing indulgence."

When assigned an opinion or when writing for himself in dissents or concurrences, Thomas has a clerk produce a first draft in consultation with other clerks in the chambers. Thomas then edits or rewrites the draft, often working from his home office. There, according to a family friend, Thomas has a kneeler and before writing opinions he prays. In describing his approach to drafting court opinions, Thomas is quick to say he eschews the flashy, or the evocative, which is a hallmark of some justices, including Scalia. Instead, he tries to focus narrowly on the legal issue at hand. "Someone says I show no personality in my opinions," Thomas has said. "I never thought it was some prose award we were writing for. . . . I read opinions to understand the law, to be led, to be guided. Perhaps it is dry, but it has to be precise, not cute."

Still, Thomas's friends say, his legal approach does not preclude concern for other people. And that concern sometimes makes its way into his opinions. In 1999, for example, he disagreed with a court majority that struck down a Chicago ordinance giving police wide latitude to arrest loitering gang members. In his dissent, he wrote that the law was intended to protect "our poorest and most vulnerable citizens" against the terror of gang violence—even if others worry about giving police too much power to arrest youths who might be innocently hanging out. In a 2005 case, Thomas opposed a court decision clearing the way for the city of New London,

Connecticut, to move ahead with a plan to replace a struggling residential neighborhood with a $350 million commercial project. The court ruled that the Constitution doesn't prohibit local governments from seizing private property for other private uses, so long as it's developed for the public benefit. Thomas dissented, arguing that the decision would only compound the harmful effects that urban renewal projects have had on African American communities through the years. Calling the decision "far reaching and dangerous," he quoted from the *Yale Law and Policy Review*, which called urban renewal synonymous with "Negro removal."

As evidence of his empathy, Thomas's friends also point to the language he used in a dissent from the court's 2003 decision striking down a Texas law banning gay sex. Even though Thomas said legal grounds compelled him to uphold the Texas ban, he called it "uncommonly silly." He concluded: "If I were a member of the Texas Legislature, I would vote to repeal it." Gay rights advocates were unimpressed. Thomas was trying to have it both ways, they said, noting that he also joined a dissent by Scalia, who chastised the court for signing on to "the so-called homosexual agenda."

While Thomas is no advocate for affirmative action, he believes that racism is alive and inescapable. But he feels the government is ill equipped to deal with that reality or to address the legacy of discrimination. The best thing that blacks and other minorities can do, therefore, to improve their circumstance is to become self-sufficient. There are few better symbols of black independence in Thomas's mind than the nation's historically black colleges and universities. Located mainly in the South, where segregation barred blacks from white schools, the nation's hundred-odd black colleges had trained generations of black teachers, doctors, nurses, and other professionals. They achieved what they did despite often being underfunded, working with underprepared students, and coping with second-rate facilities. Through the late 1970s, black colleges produced most of the nation's black college graduates. But with the arrival of desegregation, many black students were lured to better-equipped schools that enjoyed better financial support, leaving many black schools in peril.

United States v. Fordice was a seventeen-year-old suit brought by black plaintiffs in Mississippi, who charged that the state maintained a dual, racially separate system of higher education in which the historically black schools were clearly inferior. Though segregation had long been declared illegal, the state had done little more than say its eight public colleges and universities were open to all students. Mississippi had not moved assertively to desegregate these institutions, the suit alleged. Indeed, many features of segregation remained in place. The state's three black colleges had lower admissions requirements and poorer facilities and offered academic programs available at the five traditionally white public colleges. The result, the suit said, was to discourage white students from considering historically black schools and to channel the majority of black students to the white institutions.

The case was the high court's first dealing with a state's responsibility for dismantling the vestiges of segregation in higher education. The court voted 8–1 to back the plaintiffs' claim that the state needed to do more to desegregate its public colleges and universities, but sent the case back to the lower courts to decide the crucial question of how that should happen. While advocates worried whether schools achieved racial balance as a way of ensuring that black children would have access to first-rate facilities, Thomas believed that racial balance alone did not equate to good schools—a point he would return to in future cases involving school desegregation.

Thomas's deep interest in the topic became clear as Justice Byron White was drafting his *Fordice* opinion for the court. Thomas sent him a three-and-a-half-page memo, going line by line through the draft opinion to suggest changes. "I am not sure that *Brown* itself (as opposed to Green) ordered integration, as opposed to desegregation," Thomas wrote at one point early on. "Could we say instead that *Brown* 'ordered the elimination of racial segregation in public schools'?" Thomas wanted the opinion to make clear that Mississippi's goal should be to eliminate state policies that encouraged racial imbalance rather than to eliminate racial imbalances that grew out of student choices. If black students wanted to attend historically black schools, they should be able to, he said, adding that whites should attend those schools too, but only if the schools are allowed to maintain their historically black identities. In the end, Thomas wrote a concurrence to clarify his position. "It would be ironic, to say the least, if the institutions that sustained blacks during segregation were themselves destroyed in an effort to combat its vestiges," Thomas said.

The ultimate impact of the court's decision remained fuzzy for years. The case was sent to the lower courts, where it lingered more than a decade before a federal appeals court approved a settlement agreement. The deal would funnel more than half a billion dollars in additional money to Mississippi's historically black colleges over seventeen years—so long as the schools each achieved at least a 10 percent white enrollment. But some of the plaintiffs were dissatisfied with that decision, and in 2004 they filed yet another appeal to the Supreme Court, leaving the settlement in limbo.

Still, Thomas's opinion was widely applauded by African American leaders. Howard University law professor J. Clay Smith Jr., who had filed a brief in the case on behalf of an alliance of black colleges and universities and the Congressional Black Caucus, was effusive. "This is a decision that the Warren Court could have written," he said. "The spirit of Thurgood Marshall lives on in this Court."

It was probably the last time that anyone with standing in the civil rights community favorably compared Thomas with his black predecessor on the court—a fact that is never far from Thomas's mind.

11

Marshall's Footprints

The ghost of Thurgood Marshall shadows Clarence Thomas at the Supreme Court. It is hard to escape him. Even in his sixteenth year as a justice, Thomas is burdened by the comparisons. The second black justice is always stacked up against the first. And so the ghost is more like a leaden weight. Thurgood Marshall: the courageous litigator who took on the tormentors of the South, the Joe Louis of legal advocacy, a civil rights legend. Who could walk in those shoes?

Much has been written about Thomas's trampling over Marshall's footprints, of not embracing his legacy. But the two justices are inextricably coupled—bound by race—in ways that are not so commonly known. Though both reached the summit of American jurisprudence, the stories of how they were treated once they got there lend credence to the street axiom that, at the end of the day, a black man is just a black man.

Oddly, Marshall and Thomas are most linked by their opponents' critiques of them. The language and images used to disparage them are strikingly similar: Average lawyer who happened to be in the right place at the right time. Not an intellectual force. More symbol than substance. Both had long, excruciating confirmation hearings that at times turned condescending. Both were said not to be the best candidates for the highest court in the land—not even the best among potential black nominees. Both were dismissed as clones of the dominant figures of the court—Marshall the lackey of William Brennan, Thomas the flunky of Antonin Scalia. Indeed, Thomas and Scalia vote together 90 percent of the time, just as Marshall and Brennan did. But no one has ever suggested that Scalia and Brennan followed the lead of their black brethren. Thomas and Marshall even had their choices of life partners subjected to similar sneers— Thomas for marrying a white woman and Marshall for marrying a woman of Filipino descent.

Both black justices were unafraid to challenge prominent black figures: Marshall took on black militants such as Malcolm X, and Thomas took on civil rights leaders such as Jesse Jackson. Like Marshall before him, Thomas has questioned the emphasis some blacks place on college courses examining one's heritage. Both came to be known as avid storytellers who appreciated a good joke. But the two men sharply disagreed in the way that matters most for Supreme Court justices—on fundamental questions of law and the meaning of the Constitution—and their disagreement bred resentment on both sides. The resentment rarely surfaced publicly and never exploded, decorum being what it is. But there were certainly tense moments. From a distance, Thomas the Reagan administration appointee criticized Marshall when it was in his political interest to do so, and Thomas the Supreme Court nominee praised Marshall when it was in his political interest to do so.

After Thomas was confirmed, he made a round of courtesy calls on the justices and was scheduled for just a short chat with Marshall. But the planned drop-by turned into a two-and-half-hour bull session. Marshall, the court's acknowledged raconteur despite his advancing age, spun tales about his exploits as an NAACP lawyer traveling through the South defending black criminal defendants and filing the lawsuits that eventually drove a stake through Jim

Crow's heart. Thomas has gone on to portray the visit as evidence of their mutual respect, even if Marshall never did.

"Oh, I thought he was wonderful," Thomas said years later when asked about his relationship with Marshall. "You hear things. Again, it reminds me of people in high school who always start things. They're always, 'Oh, you know that guy really doesn't like you.' Or, 'You know what he said about your brother.' There's always one of those guys around. . . . I have nothing but admiration for him and for the decent way in which he treated me and the way in which he treated the institution and, of course, nothing but admiration for what he had the courage to do when he was a lawyer."

The cordial meeting in chambers was misleading. While Marshall loved telling stories and was capable of judicial courtesy, he was not pleased with his successor. He had held firmly on to his seat, despite failing health, only to see it snapped up by a man he could have predicted would go on to oppose many of the things he stood for.

A year after his retirement, Marshall invited his former colleague William L. Taylor to lunch at the office he still kept at the Supreme Court. Marshall and Taylor had known each other since 1954, when Taylor began his legal career with the NAACP Legal Defense and Educational Fund after graduating from Yale Law School. They had celebrated many victories together. But now the two aging civil rights warriors were distressed that the nation seemed to be turning its back on hard-earned advances they had helped bring about. School busing, affirmative action, educational equity—the federal courts seemed to be in retreat on all those issues. Worst of all, Thomas, the nation's only black Supreme Court justice, was helping to lead the rollback.

Taylor and Marshall commiserated and traded tales until late in the lunch when Marshall leaned forward, lowering his voice. "Do you know what they told me about Clarence Thomas?" Marshall asked. "No," Taylor said. "There were ten Negroes in his class at Yale Law School and he ranked number ten." It is unlikely that Marshall could have known that, given Yale's pass-fail grading system and the confidentiality that surrounds student scores. But that Marshall would say it spoke volumes about his feelings toward his court successor.

For his part, Thomas has sometimes allowed that he is actually more a man of the people than Marshall. Thomas told Senator Orrin Hatch's biographer, Lee Roderick, that Marshall would not talk to the common workers at the court. He said Marshall consciously insulated himself from the staff and the public. By contrast, Thomas said he goes out of his way to talk to court employees and chat with school groups and other visitors.

Ironically, when Marshall was elevated to the bench, many critics saw him as an ordinary lawyer in over his head, his civil rights record notwithstanding. This notion was not confined to bigots. Felix Frankfurter, the celebrated Supreme Court justice who had helped start the American Civil Liberties Union, told friends that he considered Marshall unqualified to serve on the appeals court. Opinions of Marshall were equally harsh among some members of the Senate, where his nomination to the U.S. Court of Appeals for the Second Circuit stalled for nearly a year. A Senate subcommittee was assembled to examine bogus charges that he was a Communist sympathizer. In September 1962, after he was cleared, the Senate finally confirmed Marshall, making him the first black American to serve on the U.S. appeals court.

A seat on the court did not shield Marshall from unflattering appraisal. As a judge, he was accused of being overly dependent on his clerks. He was said to need their help to decipher financial cases and other complex legal questions that came before the court. Marshall, supposedly, had expertise only in civil rights.

Things had not changed much by 1967, when Johnson nominated him to the Supreme Court. Yes, there was palpable pride among mainstream black Americans, and much of the press played up the remarkable achievement of the first black man tapped for the nation's highest court. But beneath the cheers lurked questions about Marshall's fitness for the job. The *New York Times* proclaimed Marshall's nomination "rich in symbolism" but went on to say that his work as a lawyer and judge was less than distinguished. The *Chicago Sun-Times* said lawyers would keep a keen eye on Marshall because he had earned a reputation for "laziness" during his career. Joseph Kraft, a widely read liberal-leaning newspaper columnist, opined that Marshall's only qualification for the court was that he was "a Negro . . . not even the best qualified Negro."

The disparagement festered despite Marshall's sterling credentials. During his three and a half years as an appeals court judge, none of the 118 opinions he authored were reversed. From there, he went on to serve as solicitor general, the federal government's representative before the Supreme Court. With his long experience as a judge and a lawyer, President Johnson figured, Marshall would be inoculated against racist charges that he was somehow unqualified. But Johnson miscalculated.

Marshall's nomination languished in the Senate as determined segregationists worked to undermine it. Twenty-four years later, Senator Strom Thurmond of South Carolina would be a vocal supporter of Clarence Thomas's Supreme Court nomination. But when Marshall was nominated, Thurmond did what he could to stop him. In his inimitable Southern drawl, Thurmond quizzed Marshall about obscure corners of the law. "What constitutional difficulties did Representative John Bingham of Ohio see—or what difficulties did you see—in congressional enforcement of the Privileges and Immunities clause of article 4, section 2, through the Necessary and Proper clause of article 1, section 8?" Thurmond asked at one point.

He had company. Some of his Southern colleagues resurrected the canard that Marshall knowingly associated with Communists. Others tried to trip Marshall up with questions about subjects they knew he could not address because they would soon come up before the Supreme Court. It took Johnson's famous powers of coercion for the Senate to confirm Marshall. The vote was 69–11.

Twenty senators simply did not vote, a strategy credited to Johnson, who wanted to get his man on the court while allowing those Southern senators to run for reelection without having to explain a yes vote for Marshall to their constituents. In all, it took Marshall two and a half months to be confirmed. The three previous Supreme Court nominees—Byron White, Arthur Goldberg, and Abe Fortas— had each been confirmed in two weeks or less.

As Marshall fought through the deeply entrenched racism in the Senate to take his historic step up to the high court, an increasingly militant portion of the black population viewed him as a fair-skinned, wavy-haired tool of the establishment. Marshall earned the nickname "Mr. Civil Rights" as a crusading lawyer. But as black rage exploded into riots in cities from Los Angeles to Detroit to Baltimore and Washington, D.C., fewer people seemed to appreciate the revolutionary impact of his work.

Even in the years following the *Brown* victory, there was a small but vocal corps of brothers and sisters who saw Marshall as a sellout. His upbeat, integrationist rap did not go over well among those impatient for change. From time to time, he would bravely take the stage at Harlem's Apollo Theater between the music and comedy shows to give short talks about the legal wars for civil rights. Occasionally, those talks were greeted with boos and bottles tossed from the audience, as if he were some tired Amateur Night act. The critics had multiplied by the time Marshall became a justice. Once, black demonstrators hanged him in effigy. He was also harangued for marrying a woman of Filipino descent, Cecila Suyat, a former secretary for the NAACP. He and Suyat married in 1955, less than a year after Marshall's wife of twenty-five years, Vivian, died of cancer.

Marshall never backed down from his opponents. He had a reverential respect for the law and made no secret of his disdain for the lawlessness of militants. In a 1969 speech at all-black Dillard University in New Orleans, an angry Marshall took aim at black radicals and violent protesters. "I am a man of the law, and in my book, anarchy is anarchy is anarchy," he said. He went on to castigate black people who used race as "an excuse" for not educating their children or taking care of their homes. He questioned the utility of the black studies programs and African culture courses that were being demanded by burgeoning numbers of black students on campuses across the country. "You're not going to compete in the world with African culture alone." Blacks would be competitive, he added, only when they were better educated. His remarks were widely applauded in white newspapers, which urged other black leaders to follow suit.

Clarence Thomas could have given that same speech. In the 1980s and 1990s, in fact, he would make similar remarks and be similarly castigated—especially when he suggested blacks take more responsibility for their own uplift. The importance of education in that process is a theme Thomas has returned to again and again, though clearly he and Marshall would disagree on where individual responsibility ends and government action should begin.

"One out of every six black children between the ages of 14 and 17 years is out of school," Thomas told a meeting of black MBAs in 1983. "Forty-five percent of Hispanics who enter high school leave before graduation. It is no wonder, then, that a frighteningly high number of black and Hispanic adults are functionally incompetent in reading, writing and math skills. They are unable to read want ads; unable to fill out a job application; unable to correctly count their change when they shop."

On black leadership, the sensibilities of Marshall and Thomas sometimes diverged. Marshall, for instance, never understood why people revered Malcolm X. "I still see no reason to say he is a great person, a great Negro," he once told an interviewer. "And I just ask a simple question: What did he ever do? Name me one concrete thing he ever did." Later, he added that Malcolm X "was a bum, hell, he was a damned pimp—a convicted pimp, about as lowlife as you can get." As it happens, Malcolm X was a hero of Thomas's. He saw in Malcolm's nationalism a link to his own do-it-yourself philosophy that originated with his grandfather. During Thomas's early years as EEOC chairman, invoking Malcolm became a convenient rhetorical device in his ongoing war with civil rights leaders. "I don't see how the civil rights people today can claim Malcolm X as one of their own," Thomas told interviewer Juan Williams. "Where does he say black people should go begging the Labor Department for jobs? He was hell on integrationists. Where does he say you should sacrifice your institutions to be next to white people?"

Thomas doesn't mention Malcolm X much these days. But, as we've seen, for years he collected Malcolm's speeches, and as a student at Holy Cross he kept a poster of the one-time Nation of Islam spokesman on his dorm room wall.

Now, that is something Thurgood Marshall would never have done.

As the nation began to celebrate the Constitution's bicentennial in 1987, Supreme Court justices fanned out across the country to give flag-waving speeches praising the wisdom and the foresight of the founding fathers in drafting the nation's charter. It was an occasion for unabashed patriotism and feel-good history. Marshall would have none of it. In a speech before a convention of patent and trademark attorneys in Maui, Marshall said the Constitution was "defective from the start" because it allowed for slavery and did not allow women the right to vote. "What is striking is the role legal principles have played throughout America's history in determining the condition of Negroes. They were enslaved by law, disenfranchised and segregated by law; and, finally, they have begun to win equality by law," Marshall said, adding that the changes could not have been envisioned by the founders. "They could not have imagined, nor would they have accepted, that the document they were drafting would one day be construed by a Supreme Court to which had been appointed a woman and the descendent of an African slave. We the people no longer enslave, but the credit does not belong to the Framers. It belongs to those who refused to acquiesce in outdated notions of liberty, justice and equality, and who strived to better them." Americans, Marshall said, should seek a "sensitive understanding of the Constitution's inherent defects, and its promising evolution through 200 years of history."

The speech provoked an uproar, with many people condemning Marshall's comments as intemperate and racially divisive. Some saw it as yet another sign that the aging justice was losing his grip in the face of declining health and an increasingly assertive conservative bloc on the court. Chief among the condemners was Thomas, then head of the EEOC and one of the highest-ranking African Americans in the Reagan administration. Thomas responded to Marshall in a newspaper commentary. He called Marshall's speech "exasperating and incomprehensible . . . [and an] assault on the Bicentennial, the Founding, and the Constitution itself."

Marshall's speech, in fact, was not the product of momentary pique. Nor was it intended as an assault on the founding fathers or the nation's founding documents. Marshall had spent considerable time thinking his speech over. A former Marshall clerk said his boss ran it by renowned historian John Hope Franklin, who was awarded the Presidential Medal of Freedom in 1995 and wrote the mega-best-selling history of African Americans *From Slavery to Freedom*.

The thought that went into the speech may have been easy to miss given the increasing frequency of angry outbursts from the oft-cantankerous Marshall. In his first few years on the court, Marshall cemented a liberal coalition that supported school busing, temporarily halted the death penalty, expanded prisoner rights, and established a constitutional right to abortion. But the pendulum soon swung in the other direction and by the late 1980s the court liberals were in full retreat. Marshall did not take this well. As the court moved away from its more liberal positions, he grew more irascible.

He confronted his fellow justices in conference and occasionally made shocking public remarks. During a prime-time television interview conducted after David Souter was nominated to replace Marshall's old friend Brennan on the court, Marshall answered a question about President George H. W. Bush by remarking: "It's said that if you can't say anything good about a dead person don't say it. Well, I consider him dead."

On February 13, 1989, Marshall circulated a short, unsigned clipping from the *New York Times* among his court colleagues. Sending it around was yet another in-your-face departure from court decorum. It landed on the justices' desks as the court was scaling back affirmative action programs, and it aptly summarized Marshall's view of the issue. Accompanied by a cover memo reading simply "FYI," the February 7, 1989, clip read, in part:

> The White Team and the Black Team are playing the last football game of the season. The White Team owns the stadium, owns the referees and has been allowed to field nine times as many players. For almost four quarters, the White Team has cheated on every play and, as a consequence, the score is White Team 140, Black Team 3. Only 10 seconds remain in the game, but as the White quarterback huddles with his team before the play, a light suddenly shines from his eyes.
>
> "So how about it, boys?" he asks his men. "What do you say from here on we play fair?"

One former Supreme Court clerk recalls meeting Thomas for the first time during a reception in one of the court's elegant conference rooms. It was early in her clerkship and she was chatting with another clerk when Thomas stepped into the room. "He made a beeline for us the minute he saw us," she recalls. Thomas came over, introduced himself, and peppered them with questions. "He wanted to see exactly who we were," the former clerk remembers. "I almost felt that he knew that I didn't apply to him and he wanted to know why." Indeed, she had not abided by the usual court etiquette, which is to apply to all the justices. Instead, she had applied only to those she could imagine working for: O'Connor, Breyer, Stevens, Ginsburg, and Souter.

Still, Thomas was friendly. Before leaving, he extended an invitation to drop by his chambers sometime and talk. At first, she shrugged the invitation off as a perfunctory gesture. But in the months ahead, Thomas reextended it whenever the two crossed paths in the court's quiet corridors.

"He was friendly in a backslapping kind of way," she says. Finally, she stopped by to chat. The visit lasted for hours. "We had a very long conversation; it was a one-way conversation." At one point, Thomas volunteered that he could stomach civil rights advocates as long as "they didn't just come up here woofing at me," which the former clerk took to mean that Thomas wanted to hear principled legal arguments, not rhetoric. Unprompted, Thomas launched into a discussion of the NAACP Legal Defense and Educational Fund and its role in opposing his appointment to the high court. "He felt a little hurt by how they reacted to the fact that he was taking Thurgood's seat," the former clerk concluded. "But he felt they were not inappropriate in their opposition," given that they confined their critique to the merits of his legal philosophy.

Thomas clearly saw the Legal Defense Fund as an exception. There were all these other black folks who had turned on him, Thomas told the clerk. "He seemed to have this list in his mind of who he liked and who he didn't," she recalls. On the list were many of his black Yale classmates—notably the "pretty people." He felt rejected by them, shunned, Thomas told her. By the time this incredible conversation had ended, she says, "I was left thinking he feels incredibly uncomfortable in his skin. It was almost like a person who didn't feel attractive, who didn't feel accepted. He had different people he blamed for that. . . . It struck me that none of this came out in a narrative way; this person was emoting. He felt he had to explain himself."

And at the end of the day, he told the clerk, there was an over-riding explanation for why many blacks didn't like him now.

"These people are mad because I'm in Thurgood Marshall's seat," Thomas said.

Thomas made it clear by his opinions that the ghost of the great Thurgood Marshall could follow him around all it wanted—the seat was no longer Marshall's. It was his, and he would use it to interpret the law as he saw fit.

In 1993, the court was faced with a case brought by William McKinney, a Nevada prisoner. McKinney said being locked in an eight-by-six-foot cell with an inmate who smoked five packs of cig-arettes a day put his health in jeopardy. He wanted prison officials to do something about it. They wouldn't, so he sued. When the case went before the Supreme Court, it did not rule on McKinney's par-ticular circumstance, but it did say that if prison officials ignored prison conditions that threatened the future health of inmates, their lack of action could form the basis of a cruel and unusual punish-ment claim.

Thomas disagreed, and this time he directly challenged a legal precedent penned by Marshall. Unlike his predecessor, Thomas drew a line separating prison sentences, which he said were addressed by the Constitution, and prison conditions, which he said were not. In his dissent, he criticized the court majority for confusing the two. Beginning with Marshall's 1976 opinion in *Estelle v. Gamble*, he said, the court had willy-nilly expanded the scope of the Eighth Amendment. Prisons are by definition tough—even cruel—places, Thomas said, and the federal courts are not in a position to change that. He cited the most controversial case from his first term to un-derline his point. "In *Hudson*, the court extended *Estelle* to cases in which the prisoner has suffered only minor injuries; here it extends

Estelle to cases in which there has been no injury at all. Because I seriously doubt that *Estelle* was correctly decided, I decline to join the court's holding," Thomas wrote, in a stab at Marshall.

The two justices were also at odds over the death penalty. Marshall, along with Brennan, was arguably the court's most determined opponent of capital punishment. Marshall first grew suspicious of the death penalty when he was a lawyer working in the South in the 1930s and 1940s. Far too often, he saw all-white juries condemn black defendants to death. Other times two suspects charged with the same crime ended up with tragically different sentences, their fates turning on the talents of their lawyers.

Marshall's suspicion of capital punishment hardened into full-scale opposition when he became a justice. In *Furman v. Georgia*, the 1972 case that temporarily suspended the death penalty, the court found that capital punishment as applied then was so capricious and possibly discriminatory that it constituted cruel and unusual punishment. Marshall went further in his concurring opinion, calling capital punishment barbaric and unfit for modern society. "A penalty that was permissible at one time in our nation's history is not necessarily permissible today," he wrote.

For Marshall, this issue had become a passion. He instructed his clerks to pay special attention to last-minute appeals that come to the Supreme Court from inmates facing capital punishment. Most petitions to the high court arrive professionally printed. But petitions from inmates and others too poor to pay printing costs often are typed or handwritten, frequently meriting only cursory attention among the thousands of petitions the court receives each year. "He made it clear that our job was to scour every death penalty appeal for issues that might convince the requisite three other justices to vote to grant [court review]," said Carol Steiker, who clerked for Marshall in 1987. "Justice Marshall's views about the care which death penalty cases demanded can be summed up in the phrase that I watched him write in his big blue marking pen, as he edited a draft of a death penalty dissent: 'A man's life is at stake. We should not be playing games.' "

Marshall not only pushed his clerks to pay close attention to death penalty appeals but also made it a practice to vote to grant every death penalty petition that came to the court.

Each week, a list of executions scheduled across the country is delivered to the Supreme Court justices. Each justice then divides the cases among the clerks, each of whom takes responsibility for following them until the end. Inevitably, lower courts block many scheduled executions. The others rise to the Supreme Court, where each justice is responsible for overseeing cases from particular regions of the country. As an execution date approaches, pleas from an inmate seeking to delay punishment flood the court. Those petitions draw competing arguments from prosecutors. The clerk for the justice assigned to oversee a particular appeal lays out the competing legal issues in a memo circulated among all the justices.

On the night an execution is scheduled, a clerk for each justice is put on what is known at the court as death watch. The clerks often stay in the office into the early hours of the morning sorting through last-minute appeals. They weigh legal arguments and wait while the fateful votes of the justices are rounded up via telephone. If the justices don't agree to hear an appeal and turn down a prisoner's final stay request, the inmate is put to death. The process is always tense and emotional, as the death penalty lays bare in the starkest terms the deep ideological differences separating the justices. Some clerks can barely stand to talk about the issue across ideological lines, for it rubs emotions so raw.

Strictly speaking, death appeals are decided on the legal merits. But the issues are so subjective—was an appellant's claim new? was it substantial?—that, as a practical matter, the appeals often turn on whether or not a justice supports capital punishment.

Thomas does. Two former clerks for other justices say that Thomas almost always votes against death penalty appeals—"reflexively," says one—even in cases that appear to be close calls. "That's just unbelievable—even if you are an ardent death penalty fan," observes the other former clerk. All that is made known outside the court is whether or not an appeal is granted, so that clerk's view is impossible to quantify. But this much is clear: Thomas has proven to be among the justices most reluctant to throw out death sentences that come under Supreme Court review.

He has stood in opposition as the court in the past several years has banned the use of the death penalty against the retarded and juveniles under age eighteen. The court outlawed the juvenile death penalty in a 2005 case, *Roper v. Simmons*, calling it cruel and unusual punishment and saying that a national consensus had developed against the practice. Thomas joined a dissent by Scalia. The opinion scolded the court's majority for acting as if it were the "sole arbiter of our nation's moral standards." Similarly, when the court banned executions of the retarded in a 2002 case, *Atkins v. Virginia*, Thomas joined a dissent by Scalia saying essentially that defendants pretending to be mentally impaired could abuse the ruling.

In 2002, Thomas cast the lone vote against granting a stay of execution to Texas death row inmate Thomas Joe Miller-El, who had challenged his sentence on the grounds that prosecutors systematically excluded all but one black juror in his trial. Eleven blacks were in his jury pool. The high court's decision sent the case back to an appeals court for a hearing. The appeals court decided that prosecutors had valid nonracial reasons for striking blacks from Miller-El's jury and the defendant appealed once again to the Supreme Court.

The Supreme Court again ruled in Miller-El's favor in 2005, and Thomas again was in the minority. By a 6–3 vote, the court held that judges in Texas had improperly discounted evidence showing that prosecutors wrongfully kept African Americans off the Dallas jury that found Thomas Joe Miller-El guilty of murder and sentenced him to death. In his majority opinion, Justice David H. Souter noted that Dallas County prosecutors had objected to two prospective black jurors who were otherwise similar to two whites. He also said prosecutors had used "trickery" in questioning would-be jurors and exercised their right under Texas law to "shuffle" the jury pool, moving blacks to the bottom of the list. Souter added that the Dallas County district attorney's office had, in the years before the Miller-El trial, used a training manual that coached prosecutors to remove potential black, Hispanic, and Jewish jurors because they would be too lenient toward defendants. "It is true, of course, that at some points the significance of Miller-El's evidence is open to judgment calls," Souter wrote, "but when this evidence on the issues raised is viewed cumulatively its direction is too powerful to conclude anything but discrimination."

Thomas disagreed. In his dissent, which was joined by Scalia and Chief Justice William H. Rehnquist, he said that virtually all of the prosecution's peremptory strikes could be accounted for by such nonracial factors as the jurors' reluctance to impose the death penalty. "On the basis of facts and law, rather than sentiments," he wrote, "Miller-El does not merit [victory]."

Thomas also has shown little patience for considering evidence such as a defendant's rough childhood or drug addiction or psychological disorder when penalties are meted out. In 1993, Thomas joined a narrow majority in *Graham v. Collins* that turned down the claim of a Texas inmate who said his jury did not properly consider his troubled childhood when it sentenced him to die for murder. Thomas wrote a separate concurring opinion making clear that a court process that "simply dumps" information about a prisoner's handicap or troubled background onto a jury can lead to arbitrary sentencing and that the victims of arbitrary sentencing often are black. "The power to be lenient is the power to discriminate," Thomas wrote, suggesting as he had in the past that, while one jury might be sympathetic to such claims, another might hold the same evidence against the defendant.

Not that Thomas sees *no* problems with the death penalty. Like his predecessor, Marshall, he worries about the effect of racist juries. But Thomas says the impact of racial bias can be blunted by clear rules delineating when the death penalty should be applied. If courts are to hear whether or not a defendant had a troubled childhood, he says, there should be some mechanism for ensuring that that information is applied the same way for every defendant.

When the Supreme Court reinstated capital punishment in 1976, it required that a defendant's guilt and punishment be decided separately in death penalty cases. This allows juries to weigh factors such as a defendant's age, mental ability, criminal record, or poverty when imposing punishment. Thomas opposes giving jurors such leeway, as it might allow them "to cloak latent animus," he wrote in *Graham*, his most extensive opinion on the death penalty. "A judgment that some will consider a 'moral response' may secretly be based on caprice or even outright prejudice."

Thomas is far more pessimistic about race than Marshall ever was, which is ironic given his insistence on a color-blind view of the law and given his personal history. Thomas has lived most of his life as the only black—or one of a tiny minority of blacks—in overwhelmingly white settings. But almost every step of the way, he has been nagged by doubts and has burned with anger at slights, real and imagined. One bitter lesson Thomas has taken from his experience is that racism is a sad, immutable fact. The sooner black people realize that and gird themselves for that reality, he says, the better off they will be. It is an admonition that he carries into his view of the law.

"Conscious and unconscious prejudice persists in our society," Thomas wrote in concurrence in a 1992 case, *Georgia v. McCollum*. "Common sense and common experience confirm this understanding." In that case, the high court barred criminal defendants from striking potential jurors from a case based on race. The common belief was that white prosecutors abused this power to strike blacks from juries. But Thomas said black defendants would come to "rue the day" the court made the decision, because while peremptory challenges allow white prosecutors to strike blacks from juries in cases involving black defendants, they also allow black defendants to protect themselves from racism by having their lawyers remove white jurors from a case.

Thomas and Marshall also have expressed sharply differing views on the racially flammable issue of affirmative action. Thomas's dissent criticizing the court's 2003 decision upholding the race-conscious admissions program at the University of Michigan Law School began by quoting a speech Frederick Douglass gave to a group of abolitionists in 1865: "What I ask for the Negro is not benevolence, not pity, not sympathy but simply *justice*. The American people have always been anxious to know what they shall do with us. . . . I have had but one answer from the beginning. Do nothing with us! Your doing with us has already played the mischief with us. Do nothing with us!" The dissent came in response to the court's ruling allowing colleges and universities to continue using race as a factor in evaluating potential students—provided the institutions are careful to evaluate individually each applicant's ability to contribute to a diverse student body. Selective schools use the race-conscious admissions practice across the country, and it was challenged as a violation of the Constitution's equal protection guarantees—a view that Thomas shared. Thomas argued in his dissent that the court lacked the courage to overturn race-conscious admissions. He went on to write that the University of Michigan was less interested in the true benefits of diversity than in having the appearance of diversity while preserving an elite law school.

Twenty-five years earlier, Marshall was confronted with the same legal question about the fairness and legality of affirmative action and he came up with the exact opposite answer. Marshall concluded that it was far too late for the nation to achieve justice by simply leaving black people alone. "It is because of a legacy of unequal treatment that we must now permit the institutions of this society to give consideration to race in making decisions about who will hold the positions of influence, affluence and prestige in America," Marshall wrote in support of affirmative action in the court's 1978

Bakke case, which outlawed racial quotas. "For far too long, the doors to those positions have been shut to Negroes. If we are ever to become a fully integrated society, one in which the color of a person's skin will not determine the opportunities available to him or her, we must be willing to take steps to open those doors. I do not believe that anyone can truly look into America's past and still find that a remedy for the effects of that past is impermissible."

Though Thomas reveres Frederick Douglass—his portrait hangs in Thomas's chambers—the justice is selective in quoting him. It's likely that Douglass would have found more in common with Marshall than with Thomas. The nineteenth-century abolitionist and reformer was a committed integrationist who rejected the black nationalist calls for self-reliance. But more significantly, as it relates to the affirmative action debate, Douglass was a fighter who believed America should be held answerable for its sins and forced to correct them.

In powerfully citing Douglass to make his case that blacks did not need a helping hand to get into the nation's best law schools, Thomas omitted key lines from Douglass's 1865 speech. In doing so, he made it seem as if Douglass opposed the kind of meddling that would have included affirmative action. But the omitted text was the advocacy part of the speech in which Douglass challenged the nation to stop crushing the rights of blacks: "Let him alone. If you see him on his way to school, let him alone, don't disturb him! If you see him going to the dinner table at a hotel, let him go! If you see him going to the ballot box, let him alone, don't disturb him! If you see him going into a work-shop, just let him alone—your interference is doing him positive injury."

It was Thurgood Marshall who helped change those conditions forever.

Marshall died on January 24, 1993, at the age of eighty-four. Three days later, his body lay in state in the Supreme Court's Great

Hall. Ignoring the bitter cold, a line of mourners stretched out the door and down the court's marble steps. At times, the line extended partway around the block. All day and into the night, school kids and senior citizens, blacks and whites, police officers, political luminaries, and many more from other walks of life—nearly twenty thousand in all—came to pay their final respects.

Seemingly forgotten were many of the old conflicts. For the moment at least, no one questioned whether Marshall was black enough, whether he was too much of an establishment man, or whether he felt like he was above the masses. In the end, he was celebrated as a civil rights champion, a trailblazing lawyer whose advocacy persisted when he joined the Supreme Court.

As a justice, Marshall continued the legal mission that he began as a lawyer, pushing to expand busing, to equalize school spending across school district lines, to force integration, to institutionalize affirmative action, to broaden human rights—even for prison inmates. But as surely as Marshall's work endeared him to many of the liberal constituents who later opposed Thomas, it made him suspect to those who regard Thomas as a hero. Adding scorn to insult, some who followed his work seem not to have even respected his intellect.

"Justice Thurgood Marshall will be lucky to rank somewhere in the middle of the 105 Supreme Court justices who have served in the United States," conservative commentator Terry Eastland wrote in 1991, shortly after Marshall's retirement. "[He] wrote few opinions of major significance, either for the Supreme Court or in dissent. He was not an intellectual force." William Rehnquist once told an interviewer that, while Marshall was a great legal advocate, he lacked the objectivity of a great jurist. "I don't think he would have been thought of as a great legal thinker," Rehnquist said. "If you are a legal thinker, more or less, you can't just champion the cause of a particular litigant. You have to deal with broader rules of conduct and rules that govern society and figure out how they would affect everybody."

The unflattering critiques of Marshall by Eastland and Rehnquist have a familiar ring. Much the same has been said about Thomas by his detractors: not an intellectual force on the court, not a great legal thinker. "The conventional wisdom about Justice Thomas's first few years on the court was that his opinions were shallow and poorly reasoned, he did little work, and he was a clone of conservative Justice Antonin Scalia with few ideas of his own," said law professor Scott D. Gerber in a sympathetic book about Thomas's jurisprudence.

If Marshall was an advocate for his race while on the court, Thomas has demonstrated he wants no part of that. While awaiting confirmation, he talked about the importance of "diversity" on the court. But as a justice, he most often compares his role to that of a referee who is interested not in the outcome of a contest but only in whether the rules—the Constitution and legal statutes—are closely followed. His legal passions are for individualism, for states' rights, for property rights, for economic liberty, for an unchanging understanding of the Constitution—views historically associated with Marshall's opponents.

As Thomas sees it, there is no way for the nation to compensate for the sins of the past, anyway. What's done is done. The best the nation can do from here on out is to play fair, even if it never has before. It is a view that Marshall never accepted, for he saw it as enshrining second-class citizenship for African Americans and other nonwhites. And it is a view that feeds a sense of betrayal that courses through much of black America when it comes to Thomas. Legally and philosophically, Thomas is certainly no Thurgood Marshall—and he doesn't want to be.

"African Americans have bought into this notion that we need leaders, people to stand up for us," says Donna Brazile, the Democratic consultant and commentator. "And Clarence Thomas is not looking to be a black leader. I'm sure he never applied. He will never fit in Thurgood Marshall's shoes. Those are not the shoes he wants to wear."

12

INSIDE THE COURT

Brian Jones, a young black lawyer and rising star in Republican politics, was at Armand's in Washington getting pizza for lunch when his cell phone rang.

"Don't take that job," instructed Clarence Thomas.

"What job?" asked Jones.

"You know the job I'm talking about. Don't take that job."

Thomas was in no mood to play the coy game. With the rancorous 2000 presidential election finally decided, the buzz was all over town, even in the *Wall Street Journal*, where Thomas read it and believed it: Jones, his longtime protégé, was in line to become assistant attorney general for civil rights. That left Thomas distressed. It was a *black job*, in Thomas's parlance, one that would limit Jones's upward mobility and frustrate him.

That was the route Thomas himself had followed all the way to the Supreme Court—ten months as civil rights chief in President Reagan's Department of Education, nearly eight years as chairman of the Equal Employment Opportunity Commission. One black job after another. But now Thomas was adamantly against that path.

"What time is your interview?" he asked Jones. Informed it was at ten the next morning, Thomas told Jones to be in his chambers at seven. And there Jones was, ready for early-morning career counseling from the lone black jurist on the nation's highest court.

This is the Clarence Thomas rarely glimpsed—the maneuvering mentor and political adviser, a justice who is far more engaged in official Washington than he lets on. From his oak-paneled suite on the court's first floor, Thomas keeps tabs on the capital's gossip, dispenses advice to understudies, chats up commentators, telephones senators. Friends have constructed an image of Thomas as someone who doesn't read newspapers and doesn't follow Washington's public policy debates. But as Senator Charles Grassley, Republican of Iowa, observes, Thomas has a keen interest in some issues that come before the legislative branch. On several occasions, he has gone to Capitol Hill to privately lobby senators to increase pay for federal judges. "It's happened three times that I know of," says Grassley of his meetings with Thomas. "Justice Thomas wanted to give me his views on the judiciary and discuss what he saw were problems in getting good-quality people as judges."

For Thomas, the Supreme Court is not just the preeminent temple of law, where landmark cases are argued and momentous opinions written. It is a secluded, peaceful sanctuary in which to operate, a shield against those who would tear him down. Unlike the other branches of government from which Thomas graduated, where camera crews camp outside your door and leaks can flow like a mighty stream, the court is Thomas's tenured escape from the wars of Washington that nearly destroyed him.

No one bothers him here.

Though his years on the court have been marked by strongly worded dissents and concurrences that prod and provoke but leave him on the margins of influence, inside his chambers he has been an effective spokesman for his ideas, displaying through personal interactions the kind of empathy not often evident in his court writings.

As we've seen, Thomas is perhaps the court's most accessible justice. He is known to spot a group of schoolchildren visiting the court and invite them to his chambers. He debates football with the court police and never looks past the elevator operators and maintenance staff. Students from his alma mater, family members of clerks, strangers he encounters on his cross-country drives in his RV are all familiar guests.

Though he is cool to journalists seeking interviews and others whom he perceives as closed-minded about his views, Thomas is nonetheless curious—even about his provocateurs. According to former Thomas aide Armstrong Williams, the justice expressed a desire to have filmmaker Spike Lee visit his chambers. Thomas was intrigued by Lee's films, especially his early work, such as *Do the Right Thing* and *Malcolm X*. Lee is no fan of Thomas's, however, once stating that if Malcolm X were alive he'd call the justice "a chicken-and-biscuit-eating Uncle Tom."

Visitors are ushered into the carpeted inner office of Thomas's chambers and seated on his leather sofa. On the walls hang framed photos of Booker T. Washington, Frederick Douglass, and Winston Churchill—Thomas's heroes. Resting atop a bookcase is a bronze bust of his late grandfather, the most influential person in his life.

Thomas seems to have an unquenchable thirst for conversation, a need to unburden himself. No meeting with him is ever short. A planned fifteen-minute drop-by invariably turns into an hour, often two, sometimes three, occasionally even four. Guests are stunned that a Supreme Court justice has so much free time. Some find themselves in the awkward position of needing to end the visit because of other appointments; they had not expected to be there so long.

James C. Duff, former administrative assistant to the late chief justice William H. Rehnquist, brought his parents to Thomas's chambers for a quick introduction. Nearly three hours later they were still there, the justice engrossed in their yarns about growing up in a poor county in rural Kentucky. "I wish I could've recorded it," Duff says. "Time just flew by." People who criticize Thomas, adds Duff, extrapolate too much from his judicial philosophy. "The view of him is too one-dimensional."

Not everyone encounters the Thomas the Duffs saw. Some see the brooding, vindictive Thomas. A friend who sees Thomas regularly at the court says the justice keeps a list in his head of who was for and against him during his confirmation hearings. "It hurt him a lot, I'll tell you," says this friend. "And he's still bitter." Thomas retains a special animus for certain civil rights activists and liberal interest groups such as People for the American Way, the Leadership Conference on Civil Rights, and the Alliance for Justice. He blames them, in large part, for the damage done to his reputation.

During sessions in his chambers, Thomas often conveys a man who is undergoing a form of self-therapy. He keeps on his desk a faded yellow statuette of St. Jude, patron saint of hopeless causes. "That's what they called me," Thomas once said, "a hopeless cause." This is the statuette Thomas won in a Latin spelling bee at St. John Vianney Minor Seminary. Some forty years later, he still loves to tell visitors his St. Jude story, of how someone among his white fellow seminarians kept breaking the head off his statuette and he kept regluing it. The story, as he sees it, is an emblem of his resolve.

Others see in Thomas's stories the lingering pain of long-ago struggles and his continuing effort to be better understood. A former clerk for another justice recalls Thomas fetching his St. John's yearbook during her visit. Thumbing through the pages, he pointed out how he was the only black student in his graduating class and grumbled that the school and its students had treated him paternalistically. Thomas "was emoting," says the former clerk. "He felt he had to explain himself."

Class and its relationship to skin color are recurring discussion topics for Thomas. He showed one visitor a boyhood photo of his adult son, Jamal. "Look at how light brown Jamal is," Thomas noted, as if he were gratified Jamal had not grown up like him with the stigma of dark skin. Someone who has worked for many years at the court and was invited to Thomas's chambers for a brown bag lunch recalls the justice characterizing "light-skinned blacks" as his enemies. They never thought he was their equal, Thomas told this visitor.

Most who visit are not anticipating such candor from a justice. Tom Goldstein, a Washington lawyer whose firm devotes itself primarily to Supreme Court litigation, has met most of the justices and declares Thomas "the most real person" of them all. In July 1997, Goldstein stopped by to see a friend who was clerking for the justice and ended up having a two-hour conversation with Thomas. They talked about education, raising children to have exemplary character, and Thomas's judicial philosophy. "The public image of him and the sense you come away with in a one-on-one conversation couldn't be more different," Goldstein said. "And this is from someone who is not a fan of his ideology or jurisprudence. But I am a fan of him personally."

Thomas uses these chamber visits to turn skeptics into converts. He is good at it. Even though he had been a mentor to Brian Jones, Jones's father, a lifelong Democrat, didn't have a high opinion of him. Jones, wishing to allay his father's concerns, took him to see Thomas. They hit it off. They talked basketball, taking turns imitating the famous spin move of former NBA great Earl "the Pearl" Monroe. They talked music and at one point both got up and mimicked the 1970s dance steps of the Temptations.

Jones's father, an insurance executive who worked his way up from the bottom, grew so comfortable with Thomas that he finally blurted out the question he was dying to ask. "What's the deal with Anita Hill? What's the real deal?" Thomas was momentarily caught off balance. He was still mystified by Hill's allegations, he said. He had done "everything he could for this sister." The conversation moved on to how blacks viewed him. As Thomas saw it, whenever he encountered "real, grass-roots black people," he was treated just fine. It was mainly the hoity-toity ones who gave him a hard time. Jones was glad he had taken his father to Thomas's chambers, but the session reminded him of just how scarred Thomas still was.

When Jones arrived for his seven o'clock meeting that morning in the late winter of 2000, he encountered an insistent Thomas who warned him not to risk his career by taking a civil rights job at the Justice Department. "You take that job and you end up fighting for your life every day," Thomas cautioned Jones. "Do you want to wake up every day and fight the [interest] groups?" It was odd advice from a man who had catapulted to the Supreme Court with a résumé of notable "black jobs." But as Thomas tried to explain to Jones: "My generation *had* to do that." His didn't. There were more opportunities now for young black professionals to rise in government through nontraditional avenues.

As it turned out, Jones wasn't offered any job at Justice. He was, however, offered a position as general counsel at the U.S. Department of Education, overseeing a staff of eighty-five attorneys. He accepted.

Thomas was pleased.

The Supreme Court can be a lonely place for a justice. Clarence Thomas had no idea. Getting there was such a huge triumph that the isolation took him by surprise. The work of judges—consulting law books, reading case files, writing opinions—is by its nature solitary. But Thomas had not anticipated such little interaction with his brethren. Justices rarely visit one another, and hardly ever unannounced. Mainly they see one another during their twice-weekly conferences to review cases or when they are on the bench listening to oral arguments, which occur during two weeks of each month from October through April, and then only on Mondays, Tuesdays, and Wednesdays.

The justices also don't have much phone contact, communicating primarily by memo and through their law clerks. The oft-used metaphor that the court is like nine independent law firms especially resonates with Thomas, and not in a good way. Thomas has joked that the communication he receives from colleagues is "usually a letter such as, 'Dear Clarence, I disagree with everything in your opinion except your name. Cheers.' " Jokes aside, Thomas is a social creature, and the court's stiff culture is frustrating at times.

A visitor who joined Thomas for lunch in his chambers not long ago was struck by how lukewarm Thomas seemed about his work life. The visitor had asked a simple question: How was the job going? To which Thomas replied, "Okay." Okay? Some lawyers spend their entire lives dreaming of being nominated to the Supreme Court. The visitor decided to pursue whether Thomas was actually happy as a justice. Would he rather be doing something else? Yes, Thomas said, he'd rather be a small businessman like his grandfather Myers Anderson. He'd rather own something or work with his hands, Thomas told this visitor.

Occasionally Thomas has thought he just doesn't fit in with the other justices. He is not particularly comfortable at official court functions. He is not an opera fan like Ginsburg and Scalia. He doesn't play poker or bridge, and everyone seemed to play bridge—Breyer, Rehnquist, Kennedy, O'Connor. All participated in a rotating, high-powered Washington bridge game. Thomas considered these the hobbies of the ruling class. One of the reasons Thomas never took up golf—Kennedy and Stevens played, as did some of his friends—is because he views golf as a rich man's sport. He likes to curl up in front of his sixty-five-inch color TV and watch football. Until he tore his Achilles tendon in a 1993 pickup game, Thomas regularly played basketball with the clerks in the gym known as the "highest court in the land." He has played less frequently since his injury. "That's how I spent my last hour [as a law clerk], playing him one-on-one," said the six-foot-seven Stephen F. Smith, who clerked for Thomas during the 1993–94 term. "He was quite good."

Though he has boasted he will serve on the court for fifty years, just to outlive his critics, Thomas sometimes sounds like a restless soul. "I'm a lousy career planner," he once said. "I tried to map things out. I was going to be a millionaire by the time I was thirty."

But he kept inching farther and farther away from that goal as he climbed the ladder of government. According to what he told friends, he had not planned to make a career out of the Supreme Court. Robert Foster, a Senate staffer who used to live across the street from Thomas and has known him for more than twenty-five years, recalls a conversation with Thomas shortly after he took his seat on the bench. "Robert, I was only going to stay on the Supreme Court for ten years," Thomas said, "but since they pissed me off, I think I'll stay on for life."

Now, even that pronouncement is in question. Larry Thompson, one of his closest friends and the general counsel at PepsiCo, Inc., says that while he didn't know if Thomas would serve until retirement, "he could be very successful at something other than being a jurist. Knowing him as I do, I don't think he would ever rule anything out totally." Last year, another of Thomas's good friends, J. Michael Luttig, who had repeatedly been on the short list for Supreme Court vacancies, left the federal bench to take a lucrative job as senior vice president and general counsel for Boeing.

In some ways, the high court is the strangest institution in our national government. "To the public at large, the Supreme Court is a remote and mysterious oracle that makes occasional pronouncements on major issues of the day and then disappears from view for months at a time," wrote Linda Greenhouse, the longtime *New York Times* Supreme Court reporter, in a *Yale Law Journal* article. "The nine individuals who exercise power in its name are unaccountable and essentially faceless." They don't hold news conferences to explain their opinions. They rarely respond to criticism—or even to errors made in reporting their rulings. You are not likely to bump into a justice at the Supreme Court, as you might a congressman at the U.S. Capitol. Even though there are only nine of them, justices often go unrecognized at restaurants and social events. A 2004 *Washington Post* poll showed that even Thomas, perhaps the court's most recognizable figure, remained largely unknown to about half of those surveyed.

Justices, for the most part, are not yearning for attention. They give speeches but don't release their public schedules. Thus, it is difficult to track their appearances. Most don't even bother sharing texts of their speeches with the Supreme Court's public information office for posting on the court's official Web site. So sensitive are they about how their words will be interpreted that some justices have actually discouraged universities or organizations from producing transcripts of their remarks.

"In a perfect world, I would never give another speech, address, talk, lecture or whatever as long as I live," wrote Justice Souter in a 1996 letter to his colleague Harry Blackmun. Needling Blackmun, he added: "I know you get a kick out of these things, but you have to realize that God gave you an element of sociability, and I think he gave you the share otherwise reserved for me." True, Souter is the court's most reclusive member. He brings his lunch to work, typically yogurt and an apple, and enjoys the lonely hobby of running—he was once mugged while jogging in his Capitol Hill neighborhood. But even the outgoing Thomas, who gives remarkably self-revealing talks, has questioned whether he should continue making speeches. "Every time we open our mouths, we come close to compromising what we do," he told the Richmond Bar Association.

Under Chief Justice John Roberts, there are indications that the court is slowly moving away from some of its outdated practices. Transcripts of oral arguments, which used to take ten days to produce, are now available online within hours. That said, even with technological improvements—improvements Thomas has championed—the court is still something of an anachronism. Karl Brooks, an associate professor of history and environmental studies at the University of Kansas, was reminded of this several years ago when he was a Supreme Court fellow. The fellows program selects academics, attorneys, congressional aides, and others interested in taking a year off to plow into the work of the federal judiciary. One of the first things Brooks noticed was that the high court dealt almost exclusively in paper, when virtually all federal courts were allowing extensive filings by e-mail. Brooks later noticed something even more astonishing. At a fellows lunch with Chief Justice Rehnquist, the chief smoked four or five cigarettes during his thirty- to forty-minute talk. "Blew me away," Brooks recalled. "You can't go in many buildings of any kind and smoke during working hours." For Brooks, the smoke-out at lunch was an eye-opening illustration that the Supreme Court is separate and distinct from other institutions. "It's a government building, but it's not a government building that operates like any other government building."

The court is wedded to tradition. The justices don their black robes in what is known as the "robing room," a version of which has existed since 1860, when the court was located in what is now the Old Senate Chamber in the U.S. Capitol. The robes are hung in wooden lockers like uniforms. Such traditions foster collegiality, some justices believe. Chief Justice Warren Burger introduced the custom of celebrating justices' birthdays with a group lunch, a toast, and the singing of "Happy Birthday." According to John Paul Stevens, the court's most tenured justice, Thomas has "significantly improved the quality of our singing."

Thomas wants badly to belong, and no other justice speaks more glowingly of the court's traditions, especially its tradition of decorum. "Unlike so much of what we see in a contentious society, at least there, right or wrong, agree or disagree, there is the appropriate solemnity and gravitas to what we do," he told students at Ohio's Ashland University in 1999. "And in a cynical environment, we see no cynicism. Never. Not one drop." Asked about his relationships with other justices, he said: "It is very warm, very respectful. There are no cliques, there are no cabals, there are no little work groups that sneak off and conspire against other people."

This is the Thomas who knows all too well the kind of brass-knuckle infighting that takes place in the executive and legislative branches of government. In fact, he is still somewhat engaged in the skirmishing, regularly representing the Supreme Court in congressional appropriations hearings about the court's budget. But the court is hardly, as Thomas depicts it, a bastion of genteel deliberation, where an unkind word is seldom spoken and lobbying to win the support of justices is frowned upon.

That image was punctured by the 2004 release of the late justice Harry Blackmun's papers, which offer a rare glimpse into the relationship between a junior justice and his senior colleague. Blackmun's files highlight the irreverence, pique, and backstage political maneuvering that the court likes to pretend doesn't exist. Blackmun, who retired in 1994 after twenty-four years on the court, served with Thomas for three of those years. Though they were often on opposing sides of decisions, Thomas had an affinity for Blackmun because of their shared working-class roots. In July 2001, Thomas spoke at the dedication of the Harry A. Blackmun Rotunda in the federal courthouse in St. Louis. He noted that Blackmun was "a modest but unpretentious man" who drove a blue Volkswagen Beetle and would introduce himself to suburban fast-food patrons as "Harry, I work for the government."

A review of Blackmun's papers suggests, however, that he didn't think much of Thomas. He cataloged the bad press Thomas received, made snide remarks about some of Thomas's draft opinions—"pretty bad," he noted of one—and was annoyed by Thomas's most influential mentor, the prickly economist Thomas Sowell. In perhaps the most intriguing correspondence between the two justices, Blackmun sent Thomas a copy of a biting column Sowell had written about Blackmun's announced opposition to the death penalty. "If this were just a case of one vain and shallow old man whom the media have puffed up for their own ideological reasons, it would hardly be worth noticing," Sowell wrote. "But Blackmun is a tawdry symbol of what has gone so wrong in American law over the past few decades." Blackmun must have known how close Thomas was to Sowell when he forwarded the column to his fellow justice. Thomas has publicly referred to Sowell, a senior fellow at Stanford University's Hoover Institution, as "a dear friend" and someone who has had a profound impact on his thinking. Blackmun, nevertheless, in his March 18, 1994, letter to Thomas, said he had never heard of Sowell and proceeded to dress him down. "It is hard for me to understand," Blackmun wrote, "why a responsible University would employ one who dispenses material of this kind." Thomas was embarrassed. Three days later, he responded to Blackmun with a handwritten note, saying he had attempted to contact Sowell but had not yet reached him. "It is upsetting to me to see any friend of mine cause you such distress!" Thomas wrote. "I will speak with him." It's unclear whether Thomas ever spoke to Sowell about the column. (Sowell did not respond to repeated requests from us for an interview.) What is clear, though, is that Thomas's friendship with Sowell endures.

Years later, a former Blackmun law clerk tried to put Blackmun's irritation with Thomas in perspective. Yes, there is a certain collegiality among justices, this person said, but even collegiality has its limitations. "You're in this environment," said the former clerk, "and you have people who are working with you who are, in essence, your enemies."

Law clerks may be the court's most important employees, and yet their role is a mysterious one. They serve as researchers and writers for their justices, advisers, and muses. How much influence they actually exert—or seek to exert—has long been debated. A recent book on Supreme Court law clerks, *Sorcerers' Apprentices*, by political scientists Artemus Ward and David L. Weiden, suggests that clerks are much more than just agents for their justices but they are not the "behind-the-scenes manipulators portrayed by some observers." Ward and Weiden based their conclusions, in part, on the responses of 160 former clerks whom they surveyed. Asked how frequently they were able to change a justice's mind about a particular case or issue, 51 percent of the clerks who responded said seldom, 24 percent said never, and 24 percent said sometimes.

To those seeking to have their cases heard before the Supreme Court, clerks are the first line of review. They appraise the arguments and recommend whether a petition of certiorari (cert petition, as it's known) should be granted or denied. When it comes to how the court will communicate its rulings, clerks are the ones negotiating changes in the language of draft opinions. Acting like ambassadors, clerks from one chamber will pay a visit to clerks from another chamber. Sometimes they cajole, sometimes they barter. As Ward and Weiden posed: "If clerks are constantly networking across chambers to glean information that may be helpful to their justice, lobbying on behalf of their justice, and generally acting as surrogates for their justice in dealings with other chambers, then to what extent do clerks act on their own behalves as opposed to acting on behalf of the justices they are supposed to be representing?"

More than they like to acknowledge, clerks are on the front lines of the court's ideological battles. They scheme, they dish. They are more overtly political and not nearly as reverential as the justices themselves. They have their own private lunchroom and their own social activities—a weekly happy hour, a biweekly excursion to a Chinese restaurant, afternoon basketball games, an annual pie-eating contest.

Tim Wu, now a Columbia University law professor, won the pie-eating contest in 1999, the year he clerked for Justice Stephen Breyer. When he met Thomas that year, at a court reception, he was stunned that Thomas knew all about him.

"You're Tim Wu."

"That's right."

"You clerked for Judge Posner," Thomas said, referring to federal appeals court judge Richard A. Posner.

"That's right."

"You won the pie-eating contest."

"That's right."

"That's amazing," Thomas told him.

Thomas was getting as much of a kick out of Wu's reaction as Wu was getting from the justice's inexplicable knowledge of him. "I have my sources," he told Wu, and then burst into laughter.

Thomas had the gift of a good politician, Wu thought, a way of luring you into his gaze and immediately winning you over.

By court tradition, each justice typically has lunch with each of his colleagues' clerks during the term, though Ginsburg usually hosts a tea in her chambers instead. Thomas is popular in this setting, for he is often the most revealing. He tells stories about his upbringing and his ideological conversion and implores clerks to ask any question on their minds. Some emerge inspired, and others just puzzled.

Thomas especially loves, in Wu's words, to "defeat your expectations of him." He will regale clerks who work for liberal justices with tales from his more radical college years—when he collected Malcolm X's recordings and participated in a civil rights demonstration that turned violent. But then he will go on to dismiss those years as the folly of a foolish youngster. One of his recurring phrases: "Been there, done that."

Ketanji Brown Jackson remembers sitting across from Thomas at lunch with a quizzical expression on her face. She and Wu were in the same class of Breyer clerks. Jackson, who is black, said Thomas "spoke the language," meaning he reminded her of the black men she knew. "But I just sat there the whole time thinking, 'I don't understand you. You sound like my parents. You sound like people I grew up with.' But the lessons he tended to draw from the experiences of the segregated South seemed to be different than those of everybody I know."

Clerks from other chambers often find themselves in discussion about Thomas, as he remains a figure of fascination. In his chambers, Thomas's own clerks are like surrogate sons and daughters. Their loyalty to him is such that they sometimes get emotional trying to defend and protect him. One example occurred in the 1999–2000 term.

On June 28, 2000, the court issued an opinion striking down a Nebraska state ban on a relatively rare abortion procedure in which part of the fetus is delivered into the birth canal before its skull is collapsed. The controversial method, known by its critics as "partial-birth abortion," was a cause célèbre for abortion opponents. So the defeat was a painful one for social conservatives.

Stenberg v. Carhart marked the first time the court had taken up a major abortion case in eight years. Writing for the 5–4 majority was Justice Breyer, who was joined by Justices Sandra Day O'Connor, David Souter, John Paul Stevens, and Ruth Bader Ginsburg. The Nebraska statute, similar to those in thirty other states, was unconstitutional, the court held, as it violated standards already established by the high court in earlier rulings. As Breyer wrote, those "who perform abortions using that method must fear prosecution, conviction, and imprisonment," all of which places "an undue burden upon a woman's right to make an abortion decision."

The principal dissenting opinion was left to Thomas. Given the importance of the case to conservatives, this was considered a high-profile dissent. Thomas's clerks understood the significance of the opportunity. In the politics of the abortion wars, the religious right had used the partial-birth procedure to make a case for how horrifying abortion actually was and, by extension, how cruel abortion-rights advocates were when it came to preserving life. In his dissent, Thomas gave the religious right the kind of language they love, likening partial-birth abortion to "infanticide" and declaring it "so gruesome that its use can be traumatic even for the physicians and medical staff who perform it."

Rehnquist and Scalia readily signed on to Thomas's dissent, but Kennedy did not. Kennedy was an annoyance to conservatives. He had let down Rehnquist eight years earlier when the chief believed he finally had enough votes to overturn *Roe v. Wade* and Kennedy joined Souter and O'Connor in drafting a joint opinion that reaffirmed a woman's right to terminate her pregnancy. Kennedy was considered the turncoat in that case, *Planned Parenthood of Southeast-*

ern Pennsylvania v. Casey. Now, he had seen the light and was on the right side of the voting ledger, as those in the minority viewed it, but Kennedy had decided to go it alone and pen his own dissent. In Thomas's chambers, this was seen as pure grandstanding, not to mention galling.

While draft opinions were still circulating, Kristen Silverberg, one of Thomas's clerks, confronted Jim Bennett, one of Kennedy's, in the clerks' lunchroom, according to an eyewitness, a clerk for a third justice. Silverberg was in tears, berating Bennett and jabbing her finger at him. Why are you guys doing this to us? asked Silverberg, who would later join the Bush White House and become a senior official in the State Department.

Thomas's dissent ended up dwarfing Kennedy's. But Thomas left no doubt as to how he felt about the trouble his colleague caused by joining the *Casey* decision in the first place. That was the original sin, an opinion "constructed by its authors out of whole cloth," Thomas wrote in his dissent. He called the work of Kennedy and the others a product of their "own philosophical views about abortion," adding that "it should go without saying that it has no origins in or relationship to the Constitution and is, consequently, as illegitimate as the standard it purported to replace."

The partial-birth abortion episode is a reminder of how loyal Thomas's clerks are to him. And no justice is closer to his clerks than Clarence Thomas. "Mine are like family," he has said. "You rarely see the other members of the court, but you see your law clerks every day." Thomas has them out to his house for barbecues, and gathers with clerk alums for monthly lunches at Morton's steakhouse in downtown Washington. There, photos of children are passed around and gossip is traded. "We weren't just there as technical assistants," says Stephen F. Smith. "He cared about our lives as people." Another of Thomas's former clerks, who later served in the current Bush White House and is now a successful Washington attorney, says, "If that man told me to walk fifty miles over burning coals, I'd turn around and start walking and wouldn't even ask why."

Thomas's clerks can sometimes get carried away with their devotion. Tales of Thomas's generosity and kindness get elevated to near myth. One Thomas story, passed down from one clerk class to the next, is about how the justice decided to end his cigar-smoking habit. As all of his close friends know, smoking cigars—maduros, *macanudos*, sometimes cheroots—is an extremely important pleasure for Thomas. His financial disclosure reports show gifts of cigars from the likes of Rush Limbaugh. Thomas is sensitive about any public portrayal of his cigar smoking, as former White House aide Fred McClure discovered at a tenth anniversary celebration of Thomas's confirmation. When McClure told Thomas he had seen a Harry Benson photo of him in *Esquire*, glowering, cigar butt in his mouth, looking like a gunslinger, the justice didn't find that too funny. "Ah, I don't read *Esquire*," Thomas grumbled. Still, the justice loved attending the cigar dinners at the private University Club in downtown Washington. And according to *Cigar Aficionado*, which listed Thomas among its top one hundred cigar smokers of the twentieth century, the justice has been an occasional guest at the magazine's "Big Smokes" bashes in the capital. Harvard law professor Charles Fried recalls visiting Thomas in his chambers in 1994 or 1995 and finding his friend already puffing away at 9 a.m. "I should have worn a gas mask to walk into that room," Fried says.

But sometime in 1995, as the story goes, a fifth grader inspired Thomas to quit. Speaking to a group of elementary school kids who were visiting the court from Charlottesville, Virginia, Thomas implored them to do more homework and watch less television. At that point the fifth grader challenged Thomas: Surely, there are things you do that are not good for you. How can you preach to us? Thomas conceded that he enjoyed cigars, even though he knew they were not good for his health. So he offered the boy a deal: "I will never smoke another cigar if you promise me that for one year you will do your homework instead of watch television."

When Thomas returned to his chambers, he handed law clerk Helgi Walker a box of expensive stogies and told her to dispose of them. The following year the same school group returned to the court, and Thomas spotted the boy he had struck a pact with. The boy reported he had really tried hard to uphold his promise not to watch TV. "Well, guess what?" said Thomas. "I haven't smoked a cigar." And Thomas, as the story goes, never smoked another cigar again.

That tale, as recounted by Walker, appears in Ken Foskett's book *Judging Thomas*. Versions of it have appeared elsewhere in print and have been told many times by different storytellers. Thomas himself told a version of the story in a 1997 speech titled "On Faith and Fidelity to the Law." Thomas first referred back to growing up "during a time when one's word was considered one's bond. Indeed, to ask a person to sign a document was considered an insult because the word was superior to any contract." He then segued to his cigars and the boy's television watching. "Though I have no idea if he has kept his word, I am compelled to keep mine," Thomas said. "That compulsion is independent of and not conditioned on the consideration he gave me in return. It was my word, and that is enough."

However well-intentioned Thomas may have been with his promise to the boy, he was not able to keep it. Thomas resumed his cigar smoking, as interviews with friends and family members make clear. "Good cigars, real good cigars," said HUD secretary Alphonso Jackson, when asked about Thomas's tastes. "And I get sick every time I smoke one with him." Abe Famble, Thomas's friend from Pin Point, has a photo from the summer of 2003 in which Thomas is stretched out in a lounge chair on his home deck. He is barefoot, clad in shorts, smoking a cigar.

Thomas's clerks are not always clear-eyed about him, but they are faithful. One year, they pooled their money and bought him a new battery for his RV. They laugh at his puns, however corny. One former clerk recalled that the justice used to keep a bunch of ninety-nine-cent plastic eyeballs in a drawer. They were leftovers from a toy-shopping spree for great-nephew Marky. Whenever Thomas left the office, he'd toss an eyeball to one of his clerks. "You keep an eye on things while I'm gone," he'd say, and then laugh uproariously at his own gag.

Thomas loves to tell stories to his clerks about how his colleagues behave in conference, where the justices meet privately to discuss, and vote on, cases. He used to play a game in the early years where he'd make his clerks guess which way certain justices had voted. Thomas would listen to the guesses and then delight in correcting his clerks when their conventional wisdom was wrong.

Thomas is known for empowering his clerks, for giving them wide latitude. He encourages them to duke it out over cases, and as a result debates in his chambers sometimes get heated. "There weren't physical fights—it didn't reach that level," recalled Chris Landau of his clerkship. "But it got pretty testy."

Unlike most other justices, who assign a single clerk to an individual case, Thomas makes one clerk write a bench memo, typically twenty to thirty pages, outlining the arguments of a case. He then requires his other three clerks to review the memo and comment. Thus, all of his clerks, in the words of one, are "on the hook for every case." Thomas also engages in lengthy discussions with his clerks about cases, sometimes spending hours batting around ideas. This system of rigorous debate and group accountability for the caseload reflects, in the words of one former clerk, Thomas's sense that even in this rarefied world he had to work harder than his colleagues to prove himself "because of the wrong perceptions of who he was and how he got there."

But the process Thomas imposes to hash out cases may contribute to the slowness with which he sometimes delivers his opinions. Thomas's writing speed was something that disturbed Rehnquist and became a factor in which opinions the late chief assigned Thomas, according to former law clerks. And yet, probably more than most justices, Thomas is sensitive to the notion that clerks are the brains behind the black robes.

The question was put to him directly some years ago by a student at Ashland University, a small private school an hour south of Cleveland. The student was in the scholar program at the university's Ash-brook Center for Public Affairs, named after the late Ohio Republican congressman John M. Ashbrook, a prominent conservative. Ronald Reagan personally dedicated the center in 1983, and its speakers have included the leading lights of GOP and conservative thinking—from Dick Cheney to Henry Kissinger to William J. Bennett. The Ashbrook Center represented the kind of safe environment that Thomas typically seeks for his speaking engagements. And so for Thomas, the question from the student was an unusually bold one: How much of your own work do you do? It has been said, the student continued, that the law clerks have a lot of control and power.

Thomas has a quick wit, and if he was startled or peeved he didn't let it show. Like a stand-up comic who had just been given his setup line, he replied: "I think the law clerks are in charge of everything. In fact, I got an allowance from them before I came." But then he got down to the seriousness of the question. "As far as them having power and controlling," Thomas said, "I think that's something that exists in people's minds. We don't spend a lot of time refuting it." He pointed out that he has closely watched the work of his colleagues, and it is consistent. Meanwhile, the clerks change from year to year. "So it can't be the law clerks," he said. "Law clerks are like anybody else—they're employees. There are things you ask them to do."

The law clerks may change from year to year, but Thomas's hiring patterns are pretty consistent—at least ideologically speaking. From the time Thomas came onto the court through the 2002–03 term, twenty-one of the forty-nine clerks he hired had previously clerked for two conservative federal appeals court judges who happen to be close Thomas friends—Laurence Silberman of the D.C. Circuit and the since departed Luttig of the Fourth Circuit.

Thomas's hiring process is intriguing. His interviews of clerk candidates often have little to do with the law or even the duties of clerking. What was college like for you? Do you like sports? How did you grow up? Eric Nelson, who clerked for Thomas in the 1993–94 term, recalls that the justice was particularly interested in Nelson's father, who repaired and installed furnaces and grew up on a Wisconsin farm. Thomas and Stephen Smith spent a lot of time talking about their mutual worship of the Dallas Cowboys and about Smith's two children. Smith, Thomas's first black clerk, had married at nineteen and was a product of Washington's tough Anacostia neighborhood—a fact that especially drew Thomas to him. Smith's father left the family when Smith was eight. The boy grew up taking care of three younger siblings and a mother who had multiple sclerosis. At age eleven, he was doing the family grocery shopping and would often have run-ins with older kids who wanted to take his food stamps. Smith ended up graduating in the top ten of his University of Virginia Law School class and also became a conservative. His philosophy was influenced by his upbringing—his mother, he has said, had a "no-excuses approach" to life, refusing to tolerate laziness and decrying special treatment. Smith declined to participate in a *Virginia Law Review* affirmative action program, for instance, and his résumé made no mention of his race. "That way I know if I get an interview it was on the basis of merit."

Thomas is moved by tales of triumph over adversity, and he forges special bonds with clerks who have struggled. Steven Bradbury, one of Thomas's early clerks, was the first in his family to attend college. His father died when he was a year old; his brother had heart disease and died in 2001. His mother raised her children as a single parent. When Bradbury introduced Thomas to his mother, a lifelong Democrat, the two connected. Thomas would later tell his clerks that he wanted to write opinions "that Steve's mom could understand." Long after Bradbury's 1992–93 clerkship ended, Thomas continued to inquire about her. She died in 2003. "It was a significant part of my experience with the justice," says Bradbury, who went on to head the Justice Department's Office of Legal Counsel and become a leading proponent, as Thomas has been on the court, of granting the president broad power to fight the war on terrorism.

What Thomas doesn't like are clerks who have "drivel" on their transcripts—courses without intellectual heft, in his judgment. Chances are good that if you've taken women's studies, Afro-American studies, and those "Law and" courses, you won't be clerking for Thomas. Some years ago, Randy Jones, then president of the National Bar Association, came to visit Thomas. Among the subjects on Jones's mind was the dearth of black law clerks at the high court, which Thomas attributed more to class than to race. Jones, like numerous others who have engaged Thomas one-on-one, found himself drawn to the justice. But he was unsettled by Thomas's seeming disdain for the study of one's own history and cultural heritage. The Supreme Court, Thomas told Jones, required "forward thinking," and he worried that women and people of color were too easily pigeonholed already.

"It's not that I'm against the advancement of the race," Thomas said, "it's that our strategy for advancement has got to change."

Jones wasn't the first to be lectured by Thomas on the limitations blacks impose on themselves and the importance of choosing one's studies wisely. When Cedric Jennings was ushered into Thomas's chambers in March 1995, he was a high school senior headed to Brown University. He had been featured in a *Wall Street Journal* series that captivated Thomas. Raised by a single mother in a difficult southeast Washington neighborhood, Jennings was another inspiring example of succeeding against the odds. His high school, Ballou, was one of the worst in the city, and violence and drugs were minefields he had to negotiate. Yet Jennings excelled magnificently in this environment, fending off the low achievers and their ridicule to earn a top spot on his school's honor roll.

When he came to see Thomas, he was struck by how short and muscular the justice was and that his hair wasn't combed. He also was perplexed by Thomas's counsel. Jennings was proud he had received a scholarship to an Ivy League university, but Thomas, wearing a frown, questioned the choice of Brown. "You're going to be up there with lots of very smart white kids," Thomas told him, "and, if you're not sure about who you are, you could get eaten alive." Thomas went on: "No doubt, one thing you'll find when you get to a school like Brown is a lot of classes and orientation on race relations. Try to avoid them. Try to say to yourself, I'm not a black person, I'm just a person. You'll find a lot of so-called multicultural combat, a lot of struggle between ethnic and racial groups—and people wanting you to sign on, to narrow yourself into some group identity or other. You have to resist that, Cedric. You understand?"

Thomas spent more than two hours mentoring Jennings that day, but the two have not spoken since. Jennings went on to graduate from Brown, get a master's degree from Harvard, and become a social worker. Meanwhile, journalist Ron Suskind won a Pulitzer Prize for a *Wall Street Journal* series on Jennings's struggles and expanded it into a critically acclaimed book, *A Hope in the Unseen*. The book brought even more fame to Jennings, who has sometimes wondered why Thomas never followed up with him. Maybe the justice was disappointed in him for not taking some of his advice, like the suggestion Jennings contact the Horatio Alger Association of Distinguished Americans, which helps students with hardships. "I've been tempted to call him," Jennings said. "But I don't know what I would say." Jennings had always been appreciative of Thomas's kindness—no one of Thomas's stature had ever reached out to him—but "I could never have seen him as one of my mentors. Maybe he wanted that."

Unknown to Jennings, Thomas did not like Suskind's book, at least not the part that chronicled the visit to his chambers. Several years ago, Thomas was mingling with guests at a reception when a young black researcher for the Cato Institute, a Washington think tank with a libertarian bent, approached him. The young man said he had read *A Hope in the Unseen* and was fascinated by the exchange between Thomas and Jennings. He asked Thomas to elaborate. All lies, Thomas responded sharply, the writer made up the whole thing. Thomas's jaw tightened. He was clearly irritated but didn't specify why. All he had tried to do was help Jennings, Thomas said, and for that he got burned.

Suskind says he met with Thomas for three hours in his chambers, going over in great detail every single Jennings remembrance about his session with the justice. Thomas was more than forthcoming. Suskind would ask if something Jennings told him was accurate, and Thomas would typically reply: "You bet. Here's more." Informed by one of us that Thomas had disputed the book version of their meeting, Jennings was incredulous. "Are you kidding? That's odd. Wow. Why would he say that?" Suskind had depicted the meeting exactly as it happened, Jennings said.

It seems likely that Thomas was hurt, if not embarrassed, by how the book presented him. And his way of expressing his disappointment was to denounce the entire work. Maybe after spending so much time with Jennings and then Suskind he had expected to see himself portrayed more plainly as a role model trying to assist a promising black student, instead of the complicated, tortured justice with his dark warnings about race. "He struck me," Jennings said, "as somebody who has been hurt a lot and is still trying to find himself." Thomas had told Jennings, just as he had told Randy Jones, that in hiring law clerks he looked for those who were proficient in "the maths and the sciences, real classes, none of that Afro-American studies stuff," according to Suskind's book. "If they've taken that stuff as an undergraduate, I don't want them."

The court's spotty record of hiring minority clerks is an ongoing concern among Capitol Hill lawmakers, especially Democrats such as Representative José Serrano of New York, a member of one of the congressional committees that annually review the Supreme Court's budget. Almost every year, Serrano spars with the justices who are sent to represent the court, one of whom is usually Thomas. Thomas, however, always seems to play the supporting role, not the lead. It was Justice Anthony Kennedy who did most of the talking during a House Appropriations subcommittee hearing on St. Patrick's Day in 2004. And thus it was Kennedy whom Serrano put on the griddle over the court's outreach and hiring. "Every year we discuss this and every year you tell us how qualified we are, and nothing seems to happen," scolded Serrano, a former chairman of the Congressional Hispanic Caucus. Kennedy tried his best to explain that recruitment exists and that minority law students "know they have a right to be there" at the top law schools. But he also noted the realities of a tough competition—Kennedy himself gets five hundred applications each year for four clerk slots. Serrano was unimpressed. Thomas tried to help, suggesting that many qualified law clerks could be found outside the traditional Ivy League law school pool. But the problem, Thomas continued, is that unless minority kids get funneled into appellate court clerkships they will never make it to the Supreme Court. That's just the way the system works. It's not "like General Motors hiring," Thomas emphasized. There is a prescribed route to ascension, and you don't get to the highest court without an apprenticeship at the rung below.

Thomas doesn't talk much about his own record of hiring minority clerks, which is hardly impressive. But he *is* proud of the women he has nurtured. During a recent conversation with the justice, a former Thomas clerk noted that her Washington law firm had hired several of the justice's female clerks. Thomas beamed. The women who clerked for Thomas were known to be tough and feisty. One, Margaret Ryan, had been a marine officer and ran marathons. Another, Laura Ingraham, went on to become a hard-hitting radio and TV commentator. "If I were going into war and there were a shortage of firearms," Thomas quipped, "I'd give them to my male clerks because the women don't need them."

Through 2002, 27 percent of Thomas's clerks had been female, putting him in the middle of the pack among his colleagues in hiring women. In the past five years his numbers have improved—six of the sixteen clerks he has hired for the court terms 2003–04 to 2006–07 have been women. Thomas's reliance on his clerks—and his faith in them—is rooted in trust. When you're dealing with sensitive matters, he has said, you can't have clerks "who are just plain ol' dishonest, who are keeping notes, who plan to leak things, who are talking to people about it. I don't talk to my wife about these things, and she's my best friend."

Thomas's concern about betrayal stems, of course, from personal experience, most notably the events surrounding the disclosure of Anita Hill's allegations of sexual harassment. But Thomas also is aware of the central role clerks have played in divulging court secrets. Bob Woodward and Scott Armstrong's 1979 book, *The Brethren*, has become the standard for inside-the-court reportage. But among justices and other court loyalists, it is exactly the kind of work they hope never gets repeated.

The Brethren revealed the maneuvering and politicking that take place in the consideration of cases, and the backbiting among justices, who emerge in this account as a less than noble lot. According to the book's introduction, more than 170 former law clerks cooperated. Even though five of the nine justices also talked to Woodward and Armstrong, it was the former clerks who were held most responsible for the damage done to the institution. An infuriated Justice Byron White quietly tried to determine which of his own former clerks had shared information with them, and he vowed never to have lunch with clerks from other chambers again.

Then, in 1998, Edward Lazarus whipped up another storm at the court with his own insider's account, *Closed Chambers*. The book was based in part on his clerkship ten years earlier with Justice Harry Blackmun, and it turned Lazarus into a pariah among court insiders who believed he had violated a basic tenet: You don't divulge what you learn, hear, and see as a court employee. In describing his book, Lazarus wrote: "Others have written about the epidemic of partisanship and lack of character in our government's elected branches and the cycle of recrimination and disaffection it has created. This book is about the creeping of that toxic combination into the delicate ecosystem of the Supreme Court." The book put succeeding clerk classes under even greater scrutiny. While telling us he had "a very clear conscience about all of this," believing he had been care-

ful not to cross an ethical line, Lazarus acknowledged that a consequence of his book was that the court had gone to great lengths "to
pressure law clerks not to reveal *anything*." (When clerks come to
the court they pledge to honor a written code of conduct that includes a lifetime vow of confidentiality.)

What constitutes a violation of confidentiality remains open to
interpretation. A 2004 *Vanity Fair* article by David Margolick, Evge-
nia Peretz, and Michael Shnayerson detailed the behind-the-scenes
skirmishing over the *Bush v. Gore* recount case. Based largely on the
views of clerks to liberal justices, it caused a lot of teeth gnashing
at the court and among court alumni. More than ninety prominent
attorneys and former Supreme Court law clerks submitted a statement to *Legal Times* condemning the anonymous clerks who cooperated in the article for "conduct unbecoming any attorney or legal
adviser working in a position of trust." Among those who signed the
statement was former Thomas clerk Erik Jaffe, who likened clerk
cooperation in the *Vanity Fair* article to "stealing my diary."

Thomas detests clerk leaks, and he is careful about whom he
takes into his confidence. "I don't want people walking around making me feel uncomfortable," he said. "I like people who are alive,
who have energy, who believe in something, who have good work
habits, who know how to take criticism, who know how to give
constructive criticism, who are mature, who are self-starters, and
who are fun to be around." He hasn't had much to worry about with
his clerks. In fact, they have been his biggest defenders and protec-
tors after they leave him—writing law review articles and newspaper commentaries and showing up on C-SPAN to counter what they
consider misperceptions about him in the public mind. A number of
them agreed to be interviewed for this book, some without Thomas's
knowledge.

One big mystery about Thomas lingers. Why is he so silent on the
bench? Not even his "family" of loyal clerks can put that question to
rest.

13

SILENT JUSTICE

Several years ago Savannah's Beach High School took a bus trip to Washington. The students toured area colleges and Smithsonian museums and made their way to the Supreme Court on a morning when the justices were hearing arguments in a case.

The four-story Supreme Court building is stately and imposing, with its fluted Corinthian columns and white Vermont marble that gleams in the sun. Visitors cross a wide plaza that faces the Capitol, climb a set of steps, and enter the main entrance through a pair of 6½-ton bronze doors. The courtroom itself, which is located in a section of the building constructed to resemble a Roman temple, has a forty-four-foot-high ceiling, and the justices sit behind a wing-shaped bench made of Honduran mahogany.

Jeannie Sanders, an English teacher at Beach High and one of the trip's chaperones, had attended high school with Clarence Thomas and was eager to see him in action. Jim Crow–era children of Savannah's black Catholic schools like Thomas and Sanders (who was Jeannie Polite back then), were a close-knit bunch. They understood they had received a privileged education compared with what was available in the segregated public schools. While Sanders had been unhappy with Thomas's voting record on the court, she was proud of his accomplishments. Her pride came with a cost. Being one of Clarence Thomas's St. Pius classmates meant you were often teased unmercifully back home: *You all thought you were so much better than everybody else, and look what your good Catholic institution produced— Clarence Thomas, brainwashed.*

Sanders, a stylish woman with a fondness for crossword puzzles, trained her eyes on Thomas. "He sat back in his chair and looked up at the ceiling the whole time, playing with his pencil," she remembers. At one point, a fellow teacher whispered to her: "Didn't you go to school with him? What's wrong with him?" Again, Sanders's pride kicked in. "He's thinking," she replied to her colleague. But inside, Jeannie Sanders was fuming. "I was so mad at him."

The disappointment she felt that day, the embarrassment, has stayed with her. She can't understand why Thomas never spoke, never asked a question, why he seemed so disengaged from what was taking place before him. Those who come to the Supreme Court to listen to oral arguments for the first time are often struck, as Sanders was, by Thomas's nonparticipation. His silence has become one of his signature characteristics as a justice and a subject of ongoing fascination—both in the legal community and among the public at large.

At times during oral arguments, there has been an informal betting pool among law clerks: Will Thomas ask a question today? By tradition, clerks who have worked on the case the justices are hearing sit in chairs opposite the press pews. But other clerks scatter throughout the courtroom or grab a spot in the reserved hallway behind the bench. Sometimes they carry on quietly among themselves, a kind of running color commentary on the proceedings. When Thomas's voice is heard, there is usually surprise, if not shock, which one former clerk described this way: "Thomas? Thomas? Did he ask a question?"

The silence has taken a toll on Thomas's reputation. It has even led clerks for other justices to wonder whether Thomas is just not as bright as some of his colleagues. Or, perhaps, just intellectually lazy. As one former Breyer clerk put it, in preparing for oral arguments "you have to work your way all the way through the case to decide what the big questions are. . . . I think he's giving himself a break by not asking questions, unfortunately."

Thomas's fellow justices don't hold that view. They understand that the quality of a justice's work doesn't turn on participation in oral arguments. They also know court history. Justice William O. Douglas, for example, would stack books in front of him during oral arguments, hiding his face behind the pile so he could do other work—like draft an opinion. William Brennan didn't ask many questions during arguments and neither did Thurgood Marshall in his later years. "There is no correlation between who's the most talkative and who has the most influence," says Supreme Court scholar David Garrow, who points out that if you listen to tapes from arguments in the fifties, sixties, and seventies, the court was much quieter than it is now. "I just think it's sort of bad manners that they're yukking it up, seemingly almost every day."

That Thomas hardly ever asks a question in this environment is seen by some as another sign that he doesn't belong. His colleagues recognize that he gets more scrutiny than any other justice, and some wish that he wouldn't give his critics ammunition to use against him. Antonin Scalia and Stephen Breyer, justices who are close to Thomas, have privately urged him to speak more from the bench, as have some of his friends outside of the court.

"Listen, I can't figure it out. . . . But he doesn't talk and I don't know why it is," says Harvard law professor Charles Fried, who has been friends with Thomas for nearly twenty-five years. "I have a guess, but it's only a guess and I've never spoken to him about it." Fried got to know Thomas during the Reagan administration, when Fried was solicitor general and Thomas was EEOC chairman. Fried believes Thomas's silence on the court is linked to his bitter confirmation hearings. It was a painful period for Thomas, fraught with confrontation. As a result, Thomas is wary of further confrontation, which explains, in Fried's mind, why he won't accept Fried's invitations to speak at Harvard. He wants to avoid such showdowns. And to Thomas, squaring off with an advocate in a quick-draw public session—with his colleagues constantly interrupting—is tantamount to confrontation. That's Fried's analysis. "I think it's a shame, I think it's a pity," he says. Fried has argued many times before the high court, both as solicitor general and as a private attorney. He believes Thomas would benefit from participating in the public debate at the court. "It'd be good for him," Fried says. "Because I think that when you get into that it affects you and maybe it changes you a little bit . . . and he would learn from it."

Thomas, however, identifies with the late Harry Blackmun on this subject. Blackmun thought too many of his brethren were in love with the music of their own voices. To make his point, he'd gleefully tally how many questions colleagues asked during an argument. In two cases argued in 1993, according to Blackmun's notes, Ruth Bader Ginsburg asked a combined forty-eight questions, followed by Scalia's thirty-three and Souter's eighteen. Blackmun himself followed the advice that Hugo Black offered him soon after Blackmun joined the court in 1970: Go for the jugular in writing opinions, "but don't agonize in public."

"If you don't ask many questions," Black counseled his junior colleague, "then you will not ask many foolish questions."

Thomas sometimes cites Blackmun when trying to deflect queries about participation in oral arguments. During a judicial conference in St. Louis, a questioner noted that Thomas was one of the least active, if not *the* least active, justice on the court. The questioner wondered what that reflected about Thomas. "It reflects that Justice Blackmun left the court because he was the least active before," Thomas quipped, adding: "I think it's much to-do about nothing. People yak, yak, yak."

Thomas has suggested there is a certain amount of grandstanding in the yakking. When a questioner at a Richmond Bar Association gathering asked him about the possibility of televising oral arguments, Thomas said it was a bad idea. "People act strange when a camera is on them." The court was "fairly quiet" when he joined it in 1991, Thomas continued. "Now we look like the *Family Feud*."

Scalia, who has been on the court for twenty years, accepts blame—or maybe that's credit—for creating what the experts call a "hot bench." He is the most amusing justice and the best practitioner of the rapid-fire grilling justices give advocates while carrying on a robust debate among themselves. During one oral argument in 2006, Scalia said he was reminded of the movie comedy *My Cousin Vinny*, about two teenage boys from New York who wind up in jail on charges of first-degree murder while traveling in the South. Unable to afford an attorney, they call on a cousin who took six tries to pass the bar exam and has never taken a case to trial. The real-life case heard by the court, *United States v. Gonzalez-Lopez*, involved a Missouri federal judge's decision to prohibit a drug defendant from having the California lawyer of his choice. Instead, the defendant was left with a St. Louis attorney who had never argued a criminal case and went on to lose the defendant's. The U.S. Court of Appeals for the Eighth Circuit invalidated the conviction, ruling that the Missouri judge had improperly excluded the first lawyer, a decision that merited automatic reversal of the conviction. At the oral argument, Deputy Solictor General Michael Dreeben argued that it was wrong to automatically reverse the conviction without an inquiry to determine whether the rejection of the first lawyer had really affected the outcome of the case. Who was to say the second lawyer wasn't competent? At this, Scalia scoffed. "I don't want a competent lawyer," he boomed. "I want a lawyer who will get me off. I want a lawyer who will invent the Twinkie defense." The Twinkie defense—that too much sugar intake diminishes mental capacity—was used effectively by a psychiatrist testifying for defendant Dan White, the San Francisco County supervisor who shot and killed his colleague Harvey Milk and San Francisco mayor George Moscone in

1978. White ended up being convicted of manslaughter instead of the more serious charge of murder.

Scalia loves to make spectators at the court laugh and to catch those who argue before the court off guard. Not that he has much regard for the advocates. They are inconsequential, Scalia has told people, more like puppets. The justices are really communicating to, and trying to influence, one another. But don't feel sorry for the advocates. Experienced, savvy litigators welcome the barrage of questions—that's how they figure out the concerns of justices, who's in play and who's not. Thus, they can tailor their arguments on the spot. It looks like dodgeball in there, but it's really more like speed chess.

Sometimes the advocates are awful, and if they are they will get eaten alive, not to mention become the butt of wisecracks in the back corridor when the justices depart from the bench. The inexperienced sometimes succumb to the pressure of environment—they get flustered, flub the names of justices. There are too many voices to discern, there is too much impatience from the bench. This is the part of the process Thomas can't stand. A former Thomas clerk said it is the jarring interjections from colleagues that really inhibit him in asking questions. "He doesn't like getting interrupted," says this former clerk. "He likes to ask follow-ups."

Scalia has no problem holding the floor and asking follow-ups. Right there with him is his good friend and ideological counterpoint and opponent Ginsburg, whose impact on the court was felt as soon as she arrived in 1994. She became the subject of news reports for her outspokenness during oral arguments. At one point, Rehnquist received a letter from a fellow Wisconsinite, attorney Priscilla Ruth MacDougall, urging him not to listen to complaints from other justices about Ginsburg's relentless interruptions. "If Justice Ginsburg has questions to ask, they are unquestionably worthy of being asked," MacDougall wrote, attaching to her letter a *Milwaukee Journal* gossip column headlined, "Madame Justice Needs a Lesson in Manners." MacDougall's advice to Rehnquist: Give each justice a minimal time allotment for questions. If more time is needed, a justice can ask colleagues to yield. This is the way it works in Congress.

What Rehnquist thought of that advice is unclear, but his views on oral arguments were well defined long before MacDougall's letter. Unlike Thomas, Rehnquist believed there was value in the exchanges generated by a justice's persistent questions. "Questions," Rehnquist wrote in his book *The Supreme Court*, "may reveal that a particular judge has a misunderstanding about an important fact in the case, or perhaps reads a given precedent differently from the way in which the attorney thinks it should be read. If the judge simply sat silent during the oral argument, there would be no opportunity for the lawyer to correct the factual misimpression or to state his reasons for interpreting the particular case the way he does."

The current chief justice, John Roberts, also is a fan of oral arguments, having been among an elite corps of private attorneys who specialized in Supreme Court appearances. Before being named to the U.S. Appeals Court for the D.C. Circuit in 2003, he had won six of ten cases he argued at the Supreme Court over a period of five court terms. Roberts was known for his meticulous study habits, which included holding several "moot court" practice sessions in the weeks leading up to an argument and rehearsing to himself the lines he would use on justices.

So while Thomas may be lukewarm about oral arguments, both of the chief justices he has served under have believed strongly in the importance of the argument sessions.

Thomas has contributed to the mystery surrounding his silence by giving varying explanations for it. "I do enjoy listening to oral arguments," he told the Arkansas Bar Association in 1998. "I think you can win or lose your case at an argument." On the other hand, he has said, justices are quite familiar with a case by the time it reaches the argument phase—having read the opposing briefs—and not much new is learned in this forum. He has said he wants to be polite to the advocates by not interrupting them. "I think if we invite a person in, we should at least listen to what he has to say." He has said that because so many of his colleagues are active questioners, "usually, if you wait long enough, someone will ask your question." He has also harkened back to his childhood to explain his silence, illustrating again that his feelings of inferiority as a teenager are still living with him at the Supreme Court.

Speaking to a visiting group of students at the court in December 2000, Thomas gave his most detailed and emotional response to date for his reticence at oral arguments. The question was put to him by a sixteen-year-old boy, and Thomas addressed him directly. "There's no reason to add to the volume," Thomas began, in a session televised by C-SPAN. "I also believe strongly, unless I want an answer I don't ask things. I don't ask for entertainment, I don't ask to give people a hard time." But Thomas quickly segued to what he described as "a more personal reason" for his silence.

> When I was sixteen, I was sitting as the only black kid in my class, and I had grown up speaking a kind of dialect. It's called Geechee. Some people call it Gullah now, and people praise it now. But they used to make fun of us back then. It's not standard English. When I transferred to an all-white school at your age, I was self-conscious, like we all are. It's like if we get pimples at sixteen, or we grow six inches and we're taller than everybody else, or our feet grow or something; we get self-conscious. And the problem was that I would correct myself mid-sentence. I was trying to speak standard English. I was thinking in standard English but speaking another language. So I learned that—I just started developing the habit of listening. And it just got to be—I didn't ask questions in college or law school. And I found that I could learn better just listening. And if I have a question I could ask it later. For all those reasons, and a few others, I just think that it's more in my nature to listen rather than to ask a bunch of questions. And they get asked

anyway. The only reason I could see for asking the questions is to let people know I've got something to ask. That's not a legitimate reason in the Supreme Court of the United States.

Deconstructing Thomas's silence has become something of a legal parlor game and an exercise in pop psychology. One theory is that his quiet on the bench speaks to an insecurity. Unlike most of his colleagues, who had been stars as either litigators or law school professors, Thomas doesn't have much experience with the back-and-forth of debating points of the law. He did serve a two-year stint in the Missouri attorney general's office, arguing appellate cases for the state. But that was right out of law school some thirty years ago. It could be that Thomas is just not comfortable performing in the high-stakes, point-counterpoint setting of a Supreme Court oral argument. To use an analogy, it is possible to be a terrific journalist but not terrific on *Meet the Press* or *Crossfire*. Some journalists are just uneasy—or unskillful—in that kind of forum. "Justices are not Larry King types—they're not performers," says William H. Webster, a retired judge and former FBI director who got to know Thomas during the Reagan administration. "The fact that he doesn't ask a lot of questions is not a reflection on him."

John Yoo, a former Thomas clerk who remains close to the justice, says his former boss's reticence can be chalked up to stubbornness. He's prepared to ask questions, Yoo maintains. He just refuses to be cowed into doing anything and sometimes adopts the opposite behavior to make a point. Yoo, a University of California at Berkeley law professor, is someone Thomas listens to. He came to national prominence in recent years as a principal architect of the most controversial—and contested—legal positions adopted by the Bush administration to fight the war on terror, positions Clarence Thomas supported at the Supreme Court. As a Justice Department lawyer, Yoo argued that the U.S. Constitution gives the president virtually unfettered authority during wartime (terrorism being a new kind of war). This authority, in his view, includes the right to authorize warrantless eavesdropping on communications originating or ending in the United States, despite a federal law barring such activity. But Yoo's most provocative opinion was contained in an August 1, 2002, memo that argued that the administration did not have to abide by federal antitorture laws. To be classified as torture, the memo stated, an interrogation method would have to cause lasting psychological damage or suffering "equivalent in intensity to the pain accompanying serious physical injury, such as organ failure, impairment of bodily function, or even death."

As for Thomas's nonparticipation in oral arguments, Yoo believes that if other justices asked fewer questions, Thomas would probably ask more. "He's very stubborn," Yoo says.

Tom Goldstein, a Washington attorney who specializes in arguing before the Supreme Court, is as mystified as most others about Thomas's muted voice. It can't be that he is uncomfortable engaging the advocates, Goldstein surmises. "There is some bad advocacy up there, and I could see him picking apart some advocates." And if it is confrontation he seeks to avoid, why not just ask helpful questions, plain questions in search of clarity? "Whatever it is," Goldstein concludes about Thomas's silence, "it is something deep."

Watching Thomas in the courtroom is like being at a sporting event and fixing your sights on a player who, although important, is not central to the action. The fullback who never gets the ball. The power forward who never scores. Many who come to witness an oral argument, like scouts who zero in on an athlete, come to study Thomas.

He thumbs through a legal brief in the case, leans back in his chair, then sits upright, inspects his nails, rubs his chin, stares at his hands, rubs his neck, removes his glasses, puts them back on. Sometimes he gazes off into the distance. Occasionally, his eyes settle on someone in the audience, but not for long. He never seems poised to pipe up and cite section 4 of the Clayton Act, for example. Whatever he is thinking, however he is feeling, uninterested is what he often conveys.

During oral arguments on October 8, 2003, in the case of *Raytheon v. Hernandez*, Thomas looked bored, which was surprising given his EEOC background and the nature of the case. Joel Hernandez, a former Raytheon technician who had lost his job because of continued alcohol and cocaine usage, was trying to get it back after turning to religion and getting himself clean. At issue for the court was whether the Americans with Disabilities Act requires employers to consider rehiring rehabilitated former employees who have been terminated for violating drug-free workplace rules.

At one point, Thomas sat back in his chair and covered his eyes with his hand, prompting a television producer in the press gallery to write a note to a colleague. "Is Thomas asleep?" The correct answer: No.

In observing Thomas, what are most intriguing are his conversations. Not that you can hear them. The talking that Thomas does from the bench is of the whispery kind with the justice seated next to him, Stephen Breyer. Breyer plays the perfect consigliere. He nods slowly, he nods rapidly. He leans in close and whispers back. Sometimes he initiates the whispering. Sometimes they laugh at each other's whispers. To the uninitiated, this ongoing routine— easy to pull off because each justice can control his own voice amplification—looks strange. Or just plain rude. It is the kind of public behavior that Thomas's grandfather would never have tolerated. Not paying attention? Whispering to your buddy while someone else is talking?

Not even a decision of the court triggers an automatic halt to the Thomas-Breyer chatterfest, as was evident on the morning of December 2, 2003. That's when Justice Souter, at the start of the court's public session, announced the court had ruled unanimously, in *United States v. Banks*, that it was constitutional for police to wait no more than twenty seconds before using a battering ram to enter a drug suspect's apartment. As Souter explained the ruling from the bench, Thomas and Breyer were in their own private colloquy. Whatever Thomas needed to tell Breyer, it apparently couldn't wait two minutes.

Though the two are fond of each other—both are known around the court for being approachable and unpretentious—Breyer is not completely comfortable with the public role he occupies as Thomas's confidential sidekick at oral arguments. Breyer has told people privately that he and Thomas sometimes peer into the audience and see something funny and the sight just prompts them to laugh together. Their constant inaudible discussions, he has said, are most often about life's insignificant moments. "You ever watch *Seinfeld*? *Seinfeld* was about nothing," Breyer once explained. "That's what we talk about—nothing."

The arrangement is stranger for Thomas than it is for Breyer. Thomas is the one seen jawing away off mic while rarely offering a contribution to the official proceeding. Breyer, on the other hand, is an oral-argument Jedi. A former Harvard law professor, he ruminates aloud, citing obscure legal cases and posing hypothetical scenarios with a dry wit that places him second only to Scalia in entertainment value. He is the court's other accessible intellectual.

Until 2006, when Samuel Alito joined the court and forced a change in seating arrangements—seating is done by seniority—Breyer was to Thomas's immediate left and on the right side of the bench facing the public. Now, Breyer is to the right of Thomas and on the left side of the bench facing the public, the side where the press sits. In both configurations, Justice Kennedy has been Thomas's opposite seatmate. But the two rarely confer. Thomas feels more kinship to Breyer, those who know both men say.

To take in an oral argument is a privileged experience. There are fourteen weeks of arguments, in two-week intervals from October to April. The court typically hears thirty-minute presentations from attorneys on each side of a case, two cases per morning on Mondays, Tuesdays, and Wednesdays, with the occasional afternoon session. Public seating is limited, on a first-come, first-served basis. In major cases, long lines form in the wee hours of the morning.

When eleven students from Benjamin Banneker High School in Washington, D.C., arrived for oral arguments on October 6, 2003, they were tremendously excited. All were high achievers enrolled in a constitutional law class as part of the Marshall-Brennan Constitutional Literacy Project sponsored by American University's Washington College of Law. Taught by Kate De Govia and Kat Fotovat, the class studied Supreme Court cases involving children, schools, and student rights. The kids—ten black and one Latino—had ambitions to become doctors, lawyers, ambassadors, computer moguls. They already had excelled beyond the walls of Banneker, winning a national moot court competition.

The case before the Supreme Court that October morning was *Castro v. United States*; a federal inmate serving a drug sentence was trying to win the right to a new trial. But the real object of student interest was Clarence Thomas. Months earlier, he had come to Banneker in an appearance broadcast by C-SPAN. After finishing his formal talk, after the camera crews had left, Thomas lingered for ninety minutes chatting with students, posing for photos, and shaking hands.

But the Thomas the Banneker class saw at oral arguments did not resemble the engaging, garrulous justice who had come to their school. The students were befuddled. They watched a mum Thomas rock in his chair, lean back, and stare at the ceiling. "I thought he was meditating," recalled senior Ayotunde Akinola. As other justices vigorously questioned the lawyers presenting their arguments, the students became transfixed by Thomas's body movements. "He kind of took the attention, even though he didn't mean to, because you're trying to figure out what he was doing," said another senior, Parris Bourne. "He was spinning around in his chair like a child," recalled Erica P. Boykin, who was planning to study international affairs and economics in college. "I was disgusted to the point of being appalled."

A few students were willing to give Thomas the benefit of the doubt. "What if he feels he understands everything?" suggested Crystal Kemp, whose dream was to become a corporate attorney. Maybe he didn't need to pay close attention to the arguments in that case, she said. Or, as Bourne posed: "Maybe he stayed up all night reading the court case—he was tired." Still, it felt odd and uncomfortable watching him. "Weird," as Boykin put it. "Because if you know people are going to be watching you, you'd think you should try to make yourself presentable."

It is likely that Thomas couldn't care less. And by the time the students left the Supreme Court that day, some of them had come to that conclusion as well. "He figures he has a lifetime appointment," Kemp surmised. She could just imagine what he was thinking: *I'm Clarence Thomas. You can't stop me*.

14

Scalia's Clone?

The maître d' led Justice Antonin Scalia to the only table set in a dimly lit back room of Washington's A. V. Ristorante, a family-style restaurant located, until it closed in July 2007, two miles and a world away from the marbled majesty of the Supreme Court. They knew the justice well here, even where he liked to sit—always the seat against the wall. Awaiting him was a bottle of Montepulciano d'Abruzzo, a modest-priced wine from central Italy. His favorite.

The neighborhood around the restaurant had been scruffy for as long as anyone could remember. But lately it had gone upscale, with pricey condominiums, offices, and the city's mammoth convention center rising nearby. Amidst this makeover, the A. V. remained as it always was, decidedly old-school. Outside, the place was partially clad in Formstone. A slightly worn awning with the green, white, and red of the Italian flag led patrons to the front door. Inside, the walls were paneled, the wooden tables were laminated, and the food was garlicky.

Scalia had been coming here for half a century, beginning when he was a Georgetown University undergraduate. The restaurant seemed to connect Scalia with his immigrant roots and he encouraged others at the court to dine here. Thomas's former clerks used to hold their monthly reunion lunches with the justice at the A. V. because some of them liked the pizza. But Thomas worried that the restaurant's location, on the fringes of D.C.'s business district, was a bit inconvenient, so the gatherings were moved to a steakhouse in the heart of the city's business hub.

The A. V. may not have been centrally located but Scalia rarely had lunch, and certainly never pizza, anywhere else. He liked to split a large anchovy pie. While known to meet with reporters on occasion, Scalia is not a fan of the press, which he believes often oversimplifies the work of the court. He once made headlines for ordering federal marshals to confiscate the tape recorders of two journalists taping a speech he delivered in Mississippi. But over three pizza lunches at the A. V., he discussed his relationship with Thomas, who is frequently compared with Scalia, and most often unfavorably.

The two are regarded as the court's most conservative members, and their partisans say they are the two justices most loyal to the Constitution's original intent. But there is no doubt that Thomas is often cast as the follower and Scalia the leader. "Scalia's clone" is the moniker that stuck to Thomas during his early years on the court, and it has been a difficult tag to shake.

"It's a slur on me as much as it is a slur on him—like I'm leading him by the nose," Scalia says. "It's a slur on both of us. I don't huddle with Clarence and say, 'Clarence this is what we're going to do.' Really, it ticks me off." This "slur," Scalia believes, is an extension of the "hatred and animosity" generated against Thomas during his confirmation fight. "It's either racist or it's political hatred," Scalia says.

At seventy, Scalia exudes the energy of a younger man. His thinning hair is lustrous black, and his complexion is flushed. When Thomas joined the court, Scalia knew they shared the same approach to the law. Scalia, the incumbent, so to speak, and the one with the outsize personality, feared some would come to view Thomas as his sidekick. "I was worried about that all along," he says.

An only child born in Trenton, New Jersey, and reared mostly in

Elmhurst, Queens, Scalia was raised a strict Catholic. His father, an exacting and intellectually minded professor of Romance languages at Brooklyn College, came to the United States from Sicily as a teenager. His mother, the daughter of Italian immigrants, was an elementary school teacher. He attended Xavier High School, a Jesuit military academy in lower Manhattan, often toting his French horn on his subway commute to school. Nino, as his friends and fellow justices call him, graduated at the top of his class at Xavier, just as he did later at Georgetown and then Harvard Law School. It was at Harvard that he also began to stand out for his conservative views.

By the time President Ronald Reagan appointed Scalia to the Supreme Court in 1986, he was widely viewed as a future leader of the court's right wing. Sure enough, Scalia has developed into an intellectual legal force and a conservative darling. His sharp-edged questions from the bench and combative but carefully reasoned legal opinions are legendary. Not to mention his quick wit. At the same time, Scalia has become captive of his own unbending legal views. When he served on the Court of Appeals for the District of Columbia, some liberal clerks disparaged him as a "Ninopath" for what they saw as his obstinacy on almost every issue. The nickname appears not to have followed him to the Supreme Court, but the trait that inspired it certainly has.

He speaks bluntly in public and in his scholarly writing, then backs up his views in his court opinions. In a 1979 law review article attacking race-conscious affirmative action programs, Scalia wrote: "My father came to this country when he was a teenager. Not only had he never profited from the sweat of any black man's brow, I don't think he had ever seen a black man." If that was the case, he reasoned, why should a black man be given any advantage in business or school over someone like his father—or anyone in the same position? Affirmative action is inherently discriminatory, Scalia says, and his legal opinions on the subject have never wavered from that standard.

Similarly, he sees no federal right to abortion, declaring flatly that there is no basis for it in the Constitution. He has voted repeatedly to uphold the death penalty, arguing that its implementation was clearly envisioned by the framers, not just for heinous murderers or national traitors but also for the perpetrators of most any felony. If people want to eliminate the death penalty, he says, they ought to petition their state legislatures and Congress, not the courts.

For Scalia, legal compromise is not an option. He does not spend a lot of time away from oral arguments trying to influence the views of his court colleagues. Doing so, he says, is futile. As for those who believe his my-way-or-the-highway attitude alienates colleagues, Scalia is dismissive. "I don't think anybody would have joined any more of my opinions if I had been sweeter," he says. Thus, he has little to contribute to the flurry of memos that move between chambers as the language of court opinions is being negotiated. "I can't trade," he explains. "I have nothing to trade."

That inflexibility leaves Scalia to convey his views mainly by lobbing explosive dissents and concurrences into the legal fray. His hope is that his ideas will be adapted by a new generation of lawyers and judges who will move them into the mainstream. He cherishes his role in this process, even if by definition it means he is in the minority. "I'm writing my dissents for the law schools. I like to make them pizzazzy," he says, adding: "It's more fun than writing in the majority."

He believes that Thomas feels much the same, that they are adherents to a noble cause, swimming against the tide to change legal culture. If Scalia was once alone on the court's far-right wing, Thomas has provided regular company since joining in 1991. Like Scalia, Thomas has rock-hard notions about the law that most often—but not always—put the two justices on the same side of cases that come before the Supreme Court.

Thomas was visibly spent from his confirmation hearings during his first months on the court, and legal observers noted that his early opinions closely resembled those of Scalia. The two cast identical votes on the first thirteen cases in which Thomas participated.

Also, the man seen as Thomas's most influential clerk, Chris Landau, formerly worked for Scalia. That evidence led some commentators to conclude that Thomas did no more than follow Scalia's direction. The supposition has infuriated Thomas for years. "I think Thomas is basically in Scalia's pocket," Bruce Fein, an associate deputy attorney general in the Reagan administration, observed in 1994. During his first thirteen years on the court, Thomas voted with Scalia 92 percent of the time, the highest correlation between any two sitting justices.

Writing about Thomas after his second year on the court, black syndicated columnist Carl T. Rowan noted that Thomas had cast court votes that made it harder for blacks and other minorities to be elected to Congress or file employment discrimination lawsuits. It was foolish to think that the court's lone black justice would ever "come home" and adopt views shared by what Rowan saw as the mainstream of black America. "You look at Justice Thomas's voting record in his two terms on the Supreme Court and you see no reason to even hope that this man who succeeded Thurgood Marshall will ever be anything other than a clone of the most conservative justice, Antonin Scalia," Rowan said.

It is Rowan whom Thomas blames most for perpetuating the "Scalia clone" image, and the mere mention of the late columnist's name still riles him. But this perception of Thomas wasn't confined to the realm of public commentary. In the insular world of the court itself, some law clerks began to believe that you could figure out where Thomas would end up on a case simply by knowing Scalia's position.

One of the first cases Thomas heard as a justice, for example, involved a cross burning on the lawn of a black family in St. Paul, Minnesota. The issue before the court was whether a city ordinance banning the display of symbols that are racially or religiously offensive was compatible with the First Amendment's free speech protections. In their preliminary vote at conference, the justices unanimously agreed that the law was too broad and should be struck down as a violation of the Constitution. But as they worked to hash out an opinion, deep ideological divisions emerged, and Thomas, the only black justice, seemed to be lining up with the faction that would sharply limit such laws. Molly McUsic, a clerk to Justice Blackmun, wrote to her boss: "CT is still out, but based on past behavior it is a fairly safe bet that he will join AS." Her prediction proved correct. Thomas—and three other justices—did indeed join Scalia's majority opinion that governments cannot outlaw acts such as cross burnings simply because of their hateful implications. "Let there be no mistake about our belief that burning a cross in someone's front yard is reprehensible," Scalia wrote in the 1992 decision. "But St. Paul has sufficient means at its disposal to prevent such behavior without adding the First Amendment to the fire."

Interestingly, a more confident Thomas took a different posture on a similar case a decade later. The issue before the court in 2002 involved a Virginia law that made it a felony for any person to burn a cross in public or on someone else's property. The law hinged on a provision presuming that all such cross burnings were by definition intended to intimidate. As an attorney for the state defended the law during oral arguments, Thomas stunned the court by breaking his usual silence during oral arguments and emotionally invoking the terrible legacy of cross burning while urging the attorney defending the law to make his argument even stronger. "Aren't you understating the effects . . . of a hundred years of lynching?" Thomas asked. "This was a reign of terror, and the cross was a sign of that. . . . It is unlike any symbol in our society. It was intended to terrorize a population."

Thomas's words made national news, in no small part because of his personal story of growing up black in segregated and racially hostile Georgia. The irony was that since joining the court Thomas had made it a point to call his life experience, and his black skin, irrelevant to his job as a justice. His emotional words proved powerful, as they inspired similar expressions of outrage from other justices.

Scalia, for one, observed that black people would rather see a rifle-toting man in their front yard than a burning cross. The comments from the other justices prompted widespread speculation that Thomas had swayed the court to his view that the law should be upheld. But he hadn't. Despite the justices' empathetic comments, they struck down the portion of the Virginia statute that categorized all cross burnings as threats. That definition was too broad for the court, but not for Thomas.

In the end, he dissented.

"In my view, whatever expressive value cross burning has, the legislature simply wrote it out by banning only intimidating conduct undertaken by a particular means," Thomas wrote. "A conclusion that the statute prohibiting cross burning with intent to intimidate sweeps beyond a prohibition on certain conduct into the zone of expression overlooks not only the words of the statute but also reality."

When confronted with the criticism that he is a Scalia clone, Thomas most often bristles and dismisses it as uninformed, a cheap way for his ideological opponents to diminish him. Around the court, he and Scalia are known to joke about it, with Scalia himself playfully calling Thomas his clone. But beyond the laughter, the suggestion that he is anybody's lackey clearly hurts. And when Thomas talks about it publicly, there is often a bitter edge. "Of course, Nino Scalia is my leader and I don't move unless he tells me what to do," Thomas told the Palm Beach County Bar Association in 1997, his words dripping with sarcasm. Some Thomas defenders see a pattern in the criticism of the justice—all of the attacks, they say, are intended to make him seem not as bright as his peers, not as competent. This perception of unworthiness, they say, underlies the oft-repeated appraisal that Thomas's court opinions are not up to snuff.

There is no doubt that the constant digs affect Thomas—not only in his own mind but also in how others perceive him. When Chief

Justice William H. Rehnquist's diagnosis of cancer was announced at the start of the court's 2004–05 session, it touched off rampant speculation about whom President George W. Bush would appoint to replace him. Bush had made headlines during the 2000 presidential campaign when he pointed to both Thomas and Scalia as the justices he most admires, and many assumed that the two would be at the top of the president's list to succeed Rehnquist. Some Washington pundits, noting that Scalia seemed to be popping up at more public events than usual after disclosure of Rehnquist's cancer, became convinced he was campaigning for the job. But privately Scalia told people that he was ambivalent about the prospect, because it would force him to alter his style. "It's hard to be a shin kicker if you're chief justice," he says.

The talk of Scalia or Thomas being named chief justice caught the ear of incoming Senate minority leader Harry M. Reid, a Nevada Democrat and key figure in the confirmation of Bush's judicial appointments. As far as Reid was concerned, Scalia would have made an acceptable nominee for chief justice. Allowing that he often disagrees with Scalia on individual cases, Reid said he still could support Scalia for chief justice because he is "one smart guy." But for Reid, Thomas was another matter. "I think he has been an embarrassment to the Supreme Court," he said. The conjecture proved inconsequential when Bush nominated John G. Roberts Jr. to replace Rehnquist after the chief justice's death in the summer of 2005. Having briefly considered elevating Thomas, the president had ruled him out for political and other reasons.

Charles Fried, the courtly Harvard law professor who got to know Thomas while serving in the Reagan administration, says he understands what it must feel like for his friend to be dismissed as inconsequential. It's like people are saying to him: "Hey, this guy is black. He can't possibly be doing this good work. He must be a ventriloquist puppet." Thomas is not the first justice to suffer such judgments. In *The Brethren*, Bob Woodward and Scott Armstrong report that clerks took to calling Justice Thurgood Marshall "Mr. Justice

Brennan-Marshall" because he often trusted and followed his friend "on the detailed, technical questions of legal scholarship."

The unflattering comparison between Thomas and Scalia adds a layer of complexity to their generally warm relationship. On one level, Scalia is the justice who feels closest to Thomas, both ideologically and personally. Not only do they often vote together, but they also are known to commiserate with each other in one or the other's chambers when court decisions don't go their way. Scalia, who enjoys escaping Washington to hunt duck and quail, has offered to take Thomas on some of his excursions. Thomas has declined the invitations because he is afraid of snakes.

Despite their alliance, the two have sharply contrasting public personas and personal styles. Thomas is, as we've seen, reticent during oral arguments. He prefers watching sports in the family room of his home to going out on the town and is reluctant to open himself to public scrutiny. Scalia, meanwhile, is an opera aficionado who was an extra in a 1994 production of Strauss's *Ariadne auf Naxos*. He is known to entertain partygoers by sitting down at the piano and banging out a few tunes, and he seems to bask in the unique semi-celebrity that comes with being a Supreme Court justice. He also enjoys jousting with critics who summon the nerve to challenge him.

After delivering a lecture on the relationship between foreign law and U.S. judicial opinions at the American Enterprise Institute, a Washington think tank, in February 2006, Scalia agreed to take questions, so long as they related to his talk. When the queries strayed off topic, he refused to answer.

"I don't think it's relevant and I am the one answering the questions," he said, after an inquiry about the war on terror.

When another pesky questioner who was sitting up front referred to him as "Anton," Scalia quickly corrected him.

"An-ton-in."

Undeterred, the man continued with a rambling statement. "As the nation begins to fall apart and as Dick Cheney runs on the hunt . . ."

"Apart from insults, do you have a question?" Scalia interrupted.

"Yes," the man said. "That . . ."

"Questions don't begin with 'that,' " Scalia interjected.

"What does a question begin with?"

"Not 'that,' " Scalia said, as the microphone was taken from the man.

Scalia continued on, joking that he would take questions from the back, since all the "bad guys" seemed to be sitting up front. Not long after, the man started to shout out comments from his seat, until finally Scalia signaled for staffers to evict him. They took hold of the man's arm and led him to the door.

"Don't use force," Scalia urged, and the workers released the man as he walked out.

Thomas almost never mixes it up with his detractors in public forums. Subject himself to hostile questioning? That is not in Thomas's nature. On the rare occasion that he is unexpectedly challenged, his responses are usually terse.

A popular legal Web site calls Scalia "the strong man of the Supreme Court," a reference not only to his brain power but also to his pugnacious style. He can be unsparing when attacking those who stake out opposing legal positions. Not even fellow justices are off limits. Scalia publicly upbraided Justice Sandra Day O'Connor during a 1988 case in which the Supreme Court upheld a Missouri law banning state workers and public hospitals from taking part in abortions. O'Connor agreed with the decision, but she would not yield to pressure from Scalia to cast the decisive vote that would have overturned the right to abortion affirmed in *Roe v. Wade*. Scalia saw her refusal as a failure of both logic and courage—and he said so. Repeatedly naming O'Connor in his own concurrence—a shocking departure from common court courtesy—Scalia bemoaned the fact that the court had missed a chance to settle the abortion issue once and for all. "Justice O'Connor's assertion . . . that a 'fundamental rule of judicial restraint' requires us to avoid reconsidering *Roe*, cannot be taken seriously," he wrote.

Thomas also is no fan of judicial half measures, and he has advocated overturning a broad array of Supreme Court precedents, including *Roe*. But it would not be Thomas's instinct to challenge another justice by name, certainly not in the text of an opinion.

Their styles may clash at times, but Scalia and Thomas are close allies when it comes to ruling on cases that come before the court. In large part, they often vote alike because they share an allegiance to originalism, a form of legal interpretation that attempts to adhere to the precise words of the Constitution and legal statutes. Originalists believe the meanings of those documents were locked into place when they were written. If the death penalty was common when the Constitution was written, how could it now constitute cruel and unusual punishment? they ask.

"When two justices are similar in their constitutional approaches, it is not surprising they would agree," says Geoffrey Stone, a constitutional law professor at the University of Chicago Law School. "Those justices who tend to have more extreme views than their colleagues, whether on the right or on the left, will tend to vote together."

However evenhanded originalism sounds in theory, in practice it produces what is best described as conservative legal outcomes. Originalists unfailingly find race-conscious affirmative action illegal, the death penalty constitutional, and the idea of a constitutional right to privacy that protects abortion and homosexual rights bogus. For the originalist, there is no room in the law for layering in the contemporary social context.

Proponents of originalism discuss it almost as if it were an unchanging mathematical axiom, and they are scornful of the more liberal view that the Constitution is a living document whose meaning evolves with the times. "If you don't use the original meaning of the text as your criterion to decide a case, what do you use?" Scalia asked in a 1999 speech to the Jewish Council for Public Affairs. "You will find there is nothing to use except your own prejudices. For the non-originalist, every day is a new day. You wake up and think, 'I wonder what is unconstitutional today?' "

Even with all their legal similarities, the contours of Thomas's jurisprudence—and subtle differences with Scalia—have grown clearer through the years. Thomas is far bolder than Scalia about extending his line of thinking to its logical conclusion, regardless of the disruptive effects a ruling would have on the laws guiding American society. Thomas has called for overturning more court precedents than any of his colleagues. Through the years he has written minority opinions calling into question court decisions allowing widespread application of federal environmental, civil rights, gun control, and workplace laws and regulations. If Thomas had his way, such measures would be wiped off the federal books and would become the sole purview of states.

Thomas shocked legal observers in 2004 with his concurrence in a case challenging the words "under God" in the Pledge of Allegiance. The court refused to strike the phrase from the pledge, but its decision rested on a technicality. The court ruled that Michael Newdow, the San Francisco Bay–area atheist who challenged the pledge, did not have the proper standing to bring the case. Thomas also voted to reject Newdow's position, which had been upheld by a lower court, but he insisted on going further. Writing alone, he said that the constitutionally mandated separation of church and state applied to the federal government but not to individual states— a startling position that would allow New York, for example, to declare Catholicism its official faith or Utah to recognize the Mormon Church as its state religion.

Such unconventional and sweeping views have prompted Scalia to observe that Thomas does not believe in *stare decisis*, the Latin term that refers to the respect for precedent. Following previous court decisions is an important legal concept that allows for continuity and predictability in the law, which are essential for businesses and other institutions to operate. Scalia says he regularly yields to that reality—even when he thinks the court took a wrong turn in the past. But precedent is far less important to Thomas. For him, whatever virtue lies in the continuity of the law is trumped by the need to follow what he sees as the correct interpretation of the Constitution.

"I'm more willing to let sleeping dogs lie," Scalia says.

Of course, not every legal precedent is just or even desirable. It required reversing court precedent, for example, for the court to strike down school segregation in the historic 1954 case *Brown v. Board of Education*. The decision reversed the high court's ruling more than a half century earlier in *Plessy v. Ferguson*, the case that made "separate but equal" the law of the land.

Scalia generally is more skeptical of government authority and executive powers than Thomas. The two parted ways in a key 2004 case that helped define how President Bush is waging the U.S. war on terrorism. The case involved Yaser Hamdi, a dual citizen of the United States and Saudi Arabia detained by the U.S. military after being captured in Afghanistan, where he allegedly was fighting for the Taliban. Scalia agreed with the court's position that the federal government did not have the right to hold Hamdi indefinitely without a court hearing. Thomas was the court's lone dissenter, taking an expansive view of presidential prerogative and concluding that Hamdi's indefinite detention "falls squarely" within the war powers of the president. In the end, Hamdi was not charged and was allowed to return to Saudi Arabia after surrendering his U.S. citizenship.

Thomas and Scalia are both considered strong defenders of free speech. Scalia has voted to defend flag burning as protected by the Constitution, but Thomas's positions are often more absolute, making him among the court's staunchest defenders of the First Amendment. The first time that Scalia and Thomas openly clashed in the text of an opinion was in a 1995 First Amendment case, *McIntyre v. Ohio Board of Elections*. The issue before the court was whether a state law banning the distribution of anonymous campaign literature violated the First Amendment. The court said that it did. Thomas agreed with the decision but not with the reasoning of the justices on his side. He wrote a solo concurrence saying that the court had ignored the central question in the case: whether the framers of the Constitution believed the First Amendment protected anonymous political leafleting. Citing examples from history, including the anonymous publication of the *Federalist Papers*, Thomas argued that the framers had intended for leafleting to be covered under the First Amendment. Scalia disagreed. In his dissent, he said Thomas had misconstrued the historical record, which he said was unclear on the matter.

"We use the same approach to the law," Scalia explains. "But that approach doesn't always produce the same answers."

The bond shared by Thomas and Scalia goes beyond their jurisprudence or their commitment to conservative principles. They also share a religious connection: they are both observant Catholics. And while there are now five Catholics on the Supreme Court, with the recent addition of Roberts and Samuel A. Alito Jr. (Anthony Kennedy is the other), Thomas and Scalia remain the two justices who talk most openly about their faith.

Scalia was raised a Catholic by his Italian immigrant parents and he never strayed. He went from his Jesuit high school to the Catholic Georgetown University. As he worked his way up through the legal profession, the father of nine has never been shy about proclaiming his faith. Typical is a 1996 speech he delivered at an event sponsored by the Christian Legal Society at the Mississippi College School of Law. Scalia offered an impassioned defense of his faith, urging Christians to stand strong in the face of a modern world that he said dismisses them as fools. "We are fools for Christ's sake," Scalia told the group, which is dedicated to integrating biblical principles with the law. "We must pray for the courage to endure the scorn of the sophisticated world." With his typical biting wit, he added: "The wise do not believe in the resurrection of the dead. It is really quite absurd. . . . So everything from Easter morning to the Ascension had to be made up by the groveling enthusiasts as part of their plan to get themselves martyred."

For Thomas, the faith journey has at times been tortured. Born into a Baptist household, Thomas was a grade schooler when he converted to Catholicism after going to live with his grandfather. Catholic schools and a year of seminary followed. But Thomas left the church in 1968, bitter about the racism he saw among his fellow seminarians and, by extension, in the church. Twenty-eight years later, spurred on by his confirmation battle, he returned to Catholicism, regretful that he had ever left. "The drubbing I took during the 1980s on matters such as affirmative action and other racial issues assured my return to the very same faith that I had abandoned in a fit of passion," he told a group of Catholic lawyers and judges. "Though there is much unspent passion, it is only through faith that I can accept trespasses against me."

During his years of estrangement, Thomas went to the occasional church service. And by the time his grandparents died in 1983, it was not unusual for him to begin his workdays by attending morning Mass. After Thomas married Ginni, the couple attended services at the three-thousand-member Truro Episcopal Church, a northern Virginia congregation known for its antiabortion activism and flamboyant worship style, which included members who spoke in tongues and offered prophecies.

By the time she met Thomas, Ginni had been through her own spiritual sojourn. At one point, she was active in the Cult Awareness Network, a group that spread the word about what it called "destructive" cults, before a series of lawsuits put it out of business in 1996. She joined the group after her experience in Lifespring, a self-awareness group she joined in the early 1980s. Lifespring was founded a decade earlier and had attracted 300,000 members with its promise to help adherents find the key to personal growth. Along the way, there were complaints that members were "programmed" to recruit more followers and make financial contributions. Ginni had parted ways with the group by the time she met Thomas.

"I had intellectually and emotionally gotten myself so wrapped up with this group that I was moving away from my family and friends and the people I work with," she told the *Washington Post*. She also told the newspaper that she was confused and troubled by some of Lifespring's methods, including a session at which members stripped down to bikinis and bathing suits and stood in a U-shaped formation making fun of one another's bodies and posing pointed sexual questions to one another. Lifespring officials said Ginni took some of their practices out of context.

At Truro, the Thomases seemed happy and were outspoken about the central role of religion in their lives. They both discussed the confirmation battle in terms usually reserved for religious allegory, with Thomas implying that it was retribution for past sins. They also credit their religious faith for guiding them through that ordeal. "I watched in horror as people who claimed to be on the side of some greater good tore at my very soul," Thomas said. "But unlike in my youth, I found strength by running toward God, not away from Him. This way, the burdens of unfairness and frustration become an opportunity to be virtues."

Before joining the court, Thomas developed a close relationship with Scalia's son Paul, who went on to become a priest in Virginia. Thomas had written a letter of recommendation in support of Paul's application to Holy Cross. When it became clear that Paul wanted to be a priest, Thomas assured him that he would attend his ordination—not as a fallen Catholic but as a practicing one. He kept his word. Paul became a priest in May 1996 and Thomas was there. A month later, Thomas made public his recommitment to Catholicism during a speech at Holy Cross, telling fellow alumni that he had reclaimed the "precious gift" of his faith. "It was a joy to receive my first communion in St. Joseph Chapel this afternoon," he said.

He and Justice Scalia are among the government and political leaders (including Senator Edward M. Kennedy) who regularly attend Mass at St. Joseph's, a Catholic church within walking distance of the Supreme Court. On Sundays, Thomas goes to St. Andrew the Apostle Catholic Church, a two-thousand-plus-family parish in Clifton, Virginia. "He's an exemplary Catholic," says Father Jerome Fasano, the church's pastor. "And an inspiration to us the way he practices his faith."

U.S. appeals court judge Alex Kozinski got a glimpse of how much Scalia loves pizza from the A. V.—and maybe also a glimpse of the qualities that undergird Scalia's approach to the law—back when he was chief judge of the United States Claims Court in Washington. The two agreed to have lunch in Kozinski's office, and Scalia laid down one condition: The pizza had to be from the A. V. Kozinksi, a self-styled pizza snob, complied, only to be disappointed. "It wasn't so great," he said. "The cheese was thin, the tomato sauce a bit too tart, and the crust slightly on the soggy side. The pinnacle of pizzadom it was not."

A month later, Kozinski had another occasion to share pizza with Scalia. This time he decided to surprise his friend with a pie from Vesuvio's, which before closing in 1996 was widely regarded as home of the best pizza in Washington. "To be candid, a side-by-side comparison of an A. V. Ristorante pizza and a Vesuvio's pizza would be like putting Pee-wee Herman into the ring with Muhammad Ali," Kozinski said. Scalia felt otherwise. When he saw that lunch was not from the A. V., he made no attempt to hide his displeasure. "I won't eat it," Scalia said. And he was serious.

When Scalia says he wants pizza only from the A. V., that's what he means. Kozinski saw that as an apt metaphor for Scalia's work as a justice. A hardheaded justice with big, compelling ideas, Scalia has often set the terms of debate on the court, even if many of his arguments do not galvanize a consensus, Kozinski said. "Scalia's influence will grow and continue to be felt for a very long time because of the sheer volume and force of the ideas he puts out, term in and term out," he observed back in 1990. "To fault Scalia for having failed to garner a consensus on a lot of issues is like blaming a farmer because he has not yet collected a harvest while he's still busy sowing seed. The fact is a body of law can't be changed overnight."

On this point, Thomas is happy to be closely allied with Scalia, as he sees his role on the court in much the same light. Asked about his influence on his colleagues, Thomas said: "It's overrated how much you persuade other people. You do the best job you can. They are bright people. They have their oaths. They have their consciences. And they make their decisions."

At the end of our final lunch with Scalia—as usual, not a slice of pizza left behind—the justice mentions an intriguing group dynamic. There are more Italian Americans who are liberal than conservative, he notes, "but they're all proud of me."

If only this were true for Thomas among African Americans, whose love or loathing of the justice is more likely than not to be divided along ideological lines. From his perch, Scalia finds this hard to understand. "I hope you can put him in the proper perspective," he urges us. "He is an extraordinarily talented man who came up from nothing. From *nothing*," he emphasizes. "It's just a shame what's happened to him."

15

THE QUIET, ANONYMOUS LIFE

Behind the wheel of his forty-foot RV, Clarence Thomas couldn't be happier. The '92 Prevost motor coach has a bedroom in the back, plush gray leather chairs, a kitchen, satellite television, and a computerized navigational system. "It's a condo on wheels," he has said—a condo from which he observes the nation and, when he chooses, engages with fellow citizens. He is drawn mostly to small towns and RV campgrounds, national parks, and historic landmarks. Thomas has told friends he has never had a bad experience traveling by motor coach. Away from the urban centers, he often encounters people who don't recognize him or don't care that he's a Supreme Court justice. He loves to pull into a Wal-Mart parking lot in jeans and deck shoes, a cap pulled over his head. Plopped outside the vehicle in a lawn chair, he can sit for hours, chatting up strangers about car waxes and exterior polishes, sipping lemonade.

"When he's out on the road in his bus," says a close friend, "it's like he's off the record with himself."

Not that he's usually alone. Each summer, Thomas's boyhood friend Abe Famble and Famble's wife, Odessa, come to visit from Pin Point. They rent a van and bring with them Thomas's mother and stepfather, his sister, Emma Mae (at least most years), and his cousin Isaac Martin. They spend a week relaxing and reminiscing. Thomas relishes this yearly ritual. They barbecue on his deck. They stay up late at night playing cards—I Declare War—in the kitchen. They stop in at the Supreme Court gift shop. They go to the outlet malls. They plan day trips to historic sites.

"When we get there," observes Famble, "he lets the whole world go and deals with us."

One summer, they took a road trip to Luray Caverns, a popular tourist attraction in Virginia's Shenandoah Valley. Another summer it was to Gettysburg, where they toured Civil War battle sites. The much-loved center of attention on many of these trips is Marky, the great-nephew who changed the lives of Clarence and Ginni. Marky arrived in 1997, not long after the Thomases decided against having a child of their own—a disappointing decision for Ginni. Thomas already had a teenage son from his first marriage by the time he and Ginni got married, and his career was on the rise. He didn't have the inclination or the time, he felt, to raise another child—especially given the demands of being a judge. And then something unexpected happened. Thomas's sister brought some of her grandchildren— Thomas's great-nieces and nephews—to the annual family visit to Virginia in the summer of 1997. One of them was a precious five-year-old with the fair skin and curly hair typical of children of mixed unions. Ginni and Clarence fell in love with Marky, who happened to be the product of a biracial marriage like their own.

The boy's father, Mark Martin, was Emma's son. He was in jail on a second probation violation related to a 1995 conviction for dealing crack cocaine. The boy's mother, Susan Martin, a Head Start teacher, had her hands full. She was raising on her own little Mark, his two sisters, and a fourth child from another relationship. The five of them lived in a public housing development in Savannah.

After family members left that summer, the Thomases discussed the idea of little Mark's coming to live with them. Soon they were pitching the idea to Emma Mae and Marky's parents. Thomas explained that the boy would have the best of everything—his own room, a private school education, lots of extracurricular activities. He could give to Mark what his grandfather had given to him at about the same age—a chance to grow and thrive. He could give him, from the wide windows of a condo on wheels, an opportunity to see the world—or at least a relaxed, unfettered view of America that Thomas never saw as a child and that he cherishes as an adult.

When they made their offer to raise Mark, the Thomases suggested they could take in Marky's sisters as well. But that was too much for their mother, Susan. Losing Marky would be difficult enough. "The feeling was that boys would be harder to teach," recalled Mark Martin, who, as we noted earlier, is now serving thirty years in prison on drug charges. "The girls would be easier. . . . We just decided to let him take Marky." The requisite custody papers were drawn up, and the Thomases drove to Savannah to pick up Marky right before Thanksgiving of 1997. Parting with her son was difficult, though, and Susan Martin cried and cried. In January 1998, a Savannah judge made it official: Clarence and Virginia Thomas were now the legal guardians of six-year-old Mark Martin.

Those who were close to Thomas saw how he poured himself into new fatherhood. He altered his Supreme Court schedule, leaving work early enough to wait in the school pickup line with the other parents. He gave Marky extra homework to help improve his reading and math skills. He was just as vigilant with Marky in sports, especially basketball. Thomas made him put his right hand behind his back so he would be forced to learn how to dribble with his left hand. Soon he was good enough to play on an AAU select team. Now fifteen, he attends a Catholic high school in Potomac, Maryland, and is becoming increasingly more independent. He spent much of last summer at a camp away from the Thomases.

With or without Mark, there will always be plenty of road trips. When trying to convince Ginni that buying a motor coach was a good idea, Thomas took out a map of the United States. He drew boxes around the locations where his fellow justices owned vacation homes. Then he drew a box in the center of the map and added wheels to it. Unlike his colleagues' getaways, he suggested to Ginni, their vacation home could be mobile. Growing up, he had never ventured beyond three counties in Georgia. A touring bus would allow him to visit anyplace in the country, at his own pace, with complete privacy. "I used to wonder where all of those cars traveling down Highway 19 were going," he has said. "Now, I know."

With his coach, Thomas can be spontaneous. Sometimes, he just picks up and goes. The experience "gives me a chance to think unlike anywhere else," he told his Florida RV buddy Earl Dixon. Thomas jokes that when he hits the lottery, he'll upgrade: newer coach, bigger engine. Same solitude.

Isolation, it seems, suits him now. He doesn't like crowds or fusses. He won't come to the reunions of his black classmates at Holy Cross and Yale, and he spurns the invitations of a black federal judges' group. They reach out to Thomas, but he thinks these occasions present too much hassle. He likes to work in his yard, tend to his flowers, watch sports on television, listen to country music. Sometimes paranoia consumes the justice. He won't get TiVo, he has told people, because Big Brother can track you that way. The uncertain threat of terrorism frightens him. "He's scared as hell like the rest of us," says pal Abe Famble, who has discussed the matter with him.

Except for occasional small dinner parties with close friends and chili get-togethers he cohosts with Dana Rohrabacher, a Republican congressman from California, Thomas isn't much for socializing. Most of his time away from work is spent doing things with Mark. The worst part about being a Supreme Court justice, he has said, is the loss of anonymity. He misses being able to walk across a campus without being accompanied by federal marshals or to shop at Sam's and have no one whisper or stare. He was in the checkout line at a neighborhood Cosco once and a cashier wouldn't take his check. She told Thomas that it was store policy to accept only checks that included street addresses, and his had a P.O. box number. So she asked for his street address. "I can't give it to you," Thomas said, not explaining that he was a Supreme Court justice and the P.O. box was for security reasons. The cashier held her ground—can't accept it—and said Thomas would have to take up the matter with a manager. The manager looked at the check, looked at Thomas, immediately recognized him. He apologized. "Have a nice day," he told the justice. That his position would generate even a small commotion at a checkout line is bothersome to Thomas.

Some of his longtime friends have observed that he has become more reclusive, less available to them. "As a Supreme Court justice he is not as accessible to us as he used to be," says Steve Urbanczyk, an attorney and Holy Cross graduate who belongs to an informal lunch group that includes Thomas.

The quiet space afforded by his RV too often eludes him. The public's constant fascination with him, as though he were an archaeological find, clearly discomfits Thomas. "Sometimes this enterprise of trying to understand him gets blown out of proportion," explains a former Thomas law clerk. "Have you ever thought of what it would be like to have hundreds of people out there trying to figure you out?"

Thomas can't fathom why he is the subject of such unending curiosity. In a handwritten note to journalist Ken Foskett in fall 2002, Thomas wrote: "I do not understand this interest in me. At bottom, I merely tried to do as my grandfather advised: make the best of the hand that had been dealt me. Perhaps some are confused because they have stereotypes of how blacks should be and I respectfully decline, as I did in my youth, to sacrifice who I am for who they think I should be."

But for Thomas, as for most other public figures of his stature, there is no escaping critical attention. As Father John E. Brooks, the former Holy Cross administrator who has maintained a relationship with Thomas, puts it: You can either engage the debate about you or decide it doesn't matter. What Thomas seems to have chosen is to become a prisoner of that debate. "He's in the stockade all by himself," says Brooks.

Thomas's friendships are key to understanding him. His relationships—with the college basketball coach, the RV aficionado, black judges appointed by Democrats—are more eclectic than most realize. He is drawn to survivors and iconoclasts, to those who have succeeded against long odds and to those he believes have been misunderstood. One of them is Dick Armey.

Armey's fishing hole is somewhere off I-66, west of the nation's capital, in rural Virginia. Armey won't disclose the location—that's his secret. When you fish with Armey, as Clarence Thomas does, the congressional leader turned lobbyist provides everything. "I provide the equipment. I provide the lures," Armey says. He and Thomas meet at Denny's for breakfast before dawn and then drive and drive, and drive some more, until they get to the turnoff.

Thomas is not a big fisherman. "Didn't even hook his worm up properly," Armey recalls of their first time out, "and yet he out-catches me all day long. On top of that, he keeps count." Tallying one's haul aloud is a kind of fisherman's trash talk, and Thomas marveled at being able to outfish his more experienced host.

It was during one of their fishing forays that Armey gave Thomas the nickname Clyde. "It just started one day. . . . I don't know, I just started calling him Clyde." Thomas embraced his nickname, even sending Armey a can of chili from the Washington restaurant Clyde's. But Thomas's protective wife, Ginni, was immediately suspicious. She wanted an explanation. "I think it's a natural instinct for a woman who loves her husband to say, 'Hey, I wanna know what's going on here?' if she sees something irregular like me calling him Clyde," Armey says, laughing.

It was Ginni who introduced him to Thomas back in 1986 when she was just dating the future justice. Armey knew Ginni from "the wars," as he put it, a reference to the legislative battles conservatives waged on Capitol Hill. Armey was then a junior congressman from north Texas and Ginni lobbied Congress on labor issues for the U.S. Chamber of Commerce. Later, she was put in charge of congressional relations for the Labor Department. In 1993, Armey hired her away as a senior policy coordinator for House Republicans. Following the 1994 elections that swept Republicans into power for the first time in forty years, Armey was elevated to majority leader and tapped Ginni to be his liaison to committee chairmen.

In many ways, Armey acknowledges now, it was a thankless job. Committee chairs resented her interference in their work, viewing her as a proxy for House leaders—specifically Armey—who wanted to control them. "I don't think she was treated well," Armey says. Meanwhile, behind Ginni's gentle, sunny demeanor was a sharp partisan edge that angered Democrats and at times embarrassed Republicans. In 1996, she helped gather material on Clinton administration scandals for House Republicans to use on the campaign trail until word of the program leaked out, prompting the GOP to end it. An April 1996 memo Ginni wrote, sent to House committees, was illustrative of her style. The memo asked for "examples of dishonesty or ethical lapses in the Clinton administration" and "anecdotes that amplify these areas," according to a *Wall Street Journal* report.

It was the kind of blatant political appeal that a more savvy staffer wouldn't dare put in a memo that could surface publicly. Which hers did. Two weeks later, when Democratic congressman Jim Moran of Virginia noticed Ginni in the audience at a hearing into the Clinton White House travel-office firings, he turned indignant. Moran insisted on knowing why "Mrs. Clarence Thomas in that bright blue dress" was in the room, adding that he smelled "a political witch hunt."

This public insult was too much for Ginni, and she later confronted Moran on a House elevator. Holding a copy of the book *Everything Men Know About Women*, in which all of the pages are blank, Ginni told Moran: "This book is about you." Thomas was amused by the dustup. He left his wife a playful voice-mail message in which he sang from the song "Devil with a Blue Dress On."

Humor aside, it would be difficult to recall a more politically active Supreme Court spouse than Ginni Thomas. She has written at least two *Wall Street Journal* op-ed articles in the past five years denouncing Democrats for opposing Republican judicial nominees. On September 9, 2003, she appeared on the CNBC television show *Capitol Report*, after President Bush's choice for a federal appeals court vacancy, Miguel Estrada, withdrew his name from consideration. Senate Democrats had succeeded, procedurally, in blocking his nomination from going forward, arguing that Estrada was another example of Bush's effort to populate the federal judiciary with extreme ideologues. This was enough to rile Ginni, who was not just director of executive branch relations for the conservative think tank the Heritage Foundation but also the wife of a man who had been through a judicial war that she would never forget. "The hard left has hijacked the confirmation process for judges," she told the CNBC hosts, "and it's got to stop."

Though Thomas had some obvious things in common with Armey—both were unafraid to speak their mind, both had a strong religious foundation, Armey had employed Thomas's wife—their relationship really evolved at the fishing hole. "You get these quiet periods when you're fishing," explains Armey. "You get a little meditative." On one such occasion, a thought occurred to Armey and he turned toward Thomas. "Clarence, I'm just sitting here thinking. Now, here I am, just a poor kid out of Cando, North Dakota, in Virginia fishing with a Supreme Court justice." Responded Thomas: "You know, I was just sitting here thinking that here I am, just a poor kid out of Georgia, out here fishing with the majority leader."

The friendship between Thomas and Armey may have developed through fishing, but it tightened because of the "tattoos" they shared—Armey's term for the labels others brand you with that can't be removed. Like Thomas, Armey also was accused of inappropriate sexual behavior. In his case, three female former students alleged that he made improper advances when he was a professor at North Texas State University. And like Thomas, he was humiliated publicly by a media disclosure. In 1995 Armey referred to the openly gay Democratic congressman Barney Frank of Massachusetts as "Barney Fag" on a radio program. At first he denied what was clear to journalists who listened to the tape; then he said that the reference was unintentional, the result of getting tongue-tied. He apologized to Frank. But the episode is now part of his biography. "I'm stuck with it," Armey says, in the way that Thomas is stuck with Anita Hill's allegations of sexual harassment. Both blamed the media for these tattoos.

Armey, however, has an axiom that has helped him handle his tattoos: *You can't hurt a man who don't give a damn*. "Actually, I developed that out of economics," he explains. "There's an instrument we use called the 'indifference curve,' which I've pondered on for years. And I thought, indifference can be a very beneficial emotion. So I have actively cultivated indifference in my life. I'm probably one of the few people in the whole world that has ever done that. And it's just born out of my study with that one instrument, which I found quite fascinating. And then I adopted it. So for me, my point is: Pain is inevitable and suffering is optional. If you're hurting me, I can just choose to not give a damn. And then it doesn't hurt anymore."

Armey has tried his "indifference curve" rationale on Thomas without success. Thomas pretends not to care about the damage Anita Hill's allegations did to his reputation, but he does care. "Oh, yeah, I think he cares intensely," says Armey. "It bothers him. It's hard not to care how people feel about you."

Armey didn't understand the depth of Thomas's pain until a conversation some years ago in Thomas's home. As Armey remembers it, "Clarence was ragging on me" about running for president. "I said, 'Well, Clarence, then all right, I'll go get me elected president. And then after I'm president, when the opportunity presents itself, I'm going to make you the chief justice.' He said, 'Nope, no, you won't.' And I said, 'Why not? You wouldn't want to be chief justice of the Supreme Court?' He said, 'No, because I would have to go through a confirmation process, and I'll never let them do that to me again.' "

That the wounds from the Anita Hill experience were still severe enough to curtail Thomas's ambition surprised Armey, now a senior policy adviser for the DLA Piper law firm and chairman of Free-domWorks, a conservative grassroots organization. "I thought that was remarkable," he says.

What also surprised Armey was a detour Thomas took during a trip to North Dakota. The justice had been invited to speak at a University of North Dakota Law School commencement in Grand Forks and decided to extend his stay. Armey's sister got a call from the marshal's office informing her that Thomas wanted to tour Cando, population 1,342. It was a 107-mile drive from the law school, but Thomas wanted to see where Armey grew up and have a meal with some of his family members. Thomas didn't want any attention, so he asked that the visit be kept hush-hush. The justice stayed overnight at the Sportsman Motel and had breakfast at Armey's sister's house—he loved the venison sausage—and returned to Grand Forks to catch his plane. To this day, Armey, who knew nothing of the visit beforehand, remains touched that Thomas went out of his way to see Cando. "I always thought that was kind of a neat deal," Armey says, "that he took enough interest in me and where I came from."

When Bob Knight was invited to address a National Press Club luncheon several years ago, he asked that Thomas be included on the dais. In Knight, perhaps the most controversial coach in college basketball history, Thomas sees a man of principle whose values always place the student above the athlete. His success on the court has not been compromised by cheating off the court. Knight also, however, has a long record of violent outbursts that include hurling a chair across the court during a game and allegedly assaulting a police officer in Puerto Rico while serving as coach of a U.S. team. In 2000, Indiana University essentially said enough is enough and fired its longtime coach for allegedly grabbing a freshman by the arm and publicly dressing him down. Thomas views Knight as a strict disciplinarian, much like Thomas's grandfather, who didn't believe youngsters should be coddled, either.

Now at Texas Tech in Lubbock, Knight got into a heated altercation with the university's chancellor at a grocery store in 2004, an episode that threatened Knight's standing at the school. Thomas happened to be in Lubbock visiting the law school and Knight at the time. Though he didn't actually observe the incident, Thomas later told visitors at a private Supreme Court reception that he had offered to come to Knight's defense. According to these visitors, Thomas went on to say that he and Knight got along so well because both distrusted the media. Thomas believes that the media magnify Knight's controversies, which then tend to overshadow all the good he does. Same thing happens to him, Thomas believes. The coach came under fire again in 2006 for putting his hand on a player's chin.

It is not surprising that Thomas enjoys the company of sports figures. He is a huge fan, especially of college and pro football and of college basketball—not to mention NASCAR. "I would l-o-o-ove to be the NFL commissioner," he once said. Relationships in sports develop easily for Thomas. When Dallas Cowboys owner Jerry Jones learned that Thomas was an ardent Cowboys fan, he invited Thomas to a game. That was sixteen years ago. Since then, Thomas has watched games from Jones's box in Dallas and with the owner during Cowboys-Redskins games in Washington. After one Cowboys victory in D.C., Thomas left the stadium with Jones and Prince Bandar bin Sultan, who at the time was the Saudi Arabian ambassador to the United States. They went to Bandar's home to celebrate. The Cowboys made sure Thomas was kept up to date on the team. Early on, the organization set him up with a subscription to the weekly team newsletter and began regularly sending him news clippings that detailed injuries, lineup changes, features on key players—this before the Internet made such a service obsolete. What most in the Cowboys organization didn't know is that Thomas's love for their team was fueled by his disdain for the Washington Redskins, the team he grew up watching because it was the closest NFL team to Savannah at the time and Skins games were sometimes broadcast in Georgia. Thomas soured on the Skins because they were the last team in the NFL to sign a black player, he has told friends. At the invitation of Jones, Thomas has addressed the Cowboys several times before and after games. Following the Cowboys' 1993 Super Bowl victory, Thomas was guest speaker at the private ring presentation ceremony.

"He is easy, real easy to talk to," says Jones of their relationship. "I do admire him."

Thomas and another NFL owner became good friends through the Horatio Alger Association of Distinguished Americans, whose members range from Billy Graham to Colin Powell, from Oprah Winfrey to Wayne Gretzky. It annually awards more than $5 million in college scholarships to young people who have overcome great obstacles. Thomas often encourages youngsters he meets to apply for the scholarships and now hosts the annual awards dinner at the Supreme Court.

Each year the association presents its Horatio Alger Award, which comes with a lifetime membership, to outstanding leaders who have succeeded in spite of adversity. Thomas received the award in 1992, his first full year on the court and one of the roughest periods of his life. Also receiving the award that year was H. Wayne Huizenga, owner of the Miami Dolphins.

Huizenga had the kind of self-made story that appealed to Thomas. Growing up in Florida, Huizenga watched his father's building business fail and his parents divorce. Living with his mother, he drove a truck and pumped gas after school to help with expenses. He left college to work with a friend who owned a garbage collection company, but he went on to build three *Fortune* 500 companies. Thomas

and Huizenga hit it off, and it wasn't long before the justice was attending Dolphins workouts and speaking to the team. In 2005, when
he visited the training facility to help Huizenga hand out Horatio Alger scholarships to students, the Dolphins were nowhere to be found.
He had addressed the team before the 2004 season, and they had gone
4–12. "You can tell what I did for their season," Thomas quipped. "I
ruined them. . . . Notice they didn't have the team out here today."

It is striking how quickly Thomas can develop a meaningful relationship with someone and confer his trust.

Thomas met Earl Dixon in April 2001 as the justice was getting
his customized Prevost motor coach serviced in San Antonio, Florida.
Dixon was at the facility holding a meeting as president of the
Marathon Coach Club, a group of RV enthusiasts. The men talked
and exchanged phone numbers. Weeks later, Thomas called to say he
was returning to north-central Florida in his Prevost. Dixon, the
owner of a pest-control company and a former Florida state legis-
lator, invited Thomas to park his coach at the Big River RV park in
Welaka. That night they grilled catfish, swapped stories of "growing
up hard" in the South, as Dixon puts it, and watched the NBA play-
offs. And that's how a chance encounter blossomed into a close
friendship. Now, Dixon says, they talk "pretty frequently," and Thomas
even hosted a dinner for Dixon's Marathon Coach Club at the
Supreme Court.

According to Thomas's 2002 financial disclosure report, Dixon
and his wife, Louise, made a $5,000 "educational gift" to Marky,
Thomas's great-nephew. Dixon had met Mark and was moved by
how Thomas had assumed the boy's upbringing a year or so before
Mark's father was sentenced to federal prison. "I don't know what
the justice's salary is," Dixon explains of his gift, "but I know how
expensive schooling is and I have the means and I really wanted to
see a young man like Marky succeed."

In 2006, associate justices earned $203,000 annually, but Thomas has never been among the wealthier of his colleagues. In fact, Thomas said he still had outstanding student loans when he took his seat on the court in 1991. He was elated to receive a $1.5 million advance from HarperCollins for his memoir, the most he had ever been paid for work in his life. Still, Thomas was hardly a pauper when Dixon offered his $5,000 gift. At first, Thomas was worried about the propriety of the donation, as Dixon recalls, but he agreed to accept it if the contribution was deposited directly into a special trust for Mark. Thomas wrote Dixon a long thank-you note.

Thomas tends to guard his relationships closely and takes exception when friends divulge information that he views as private. Insiders can quickly become outsiders.

Clint Bolick, a loyal Thomas aide at EEOC, was one of the trench fighters in the confirmation battle. Thomas is godfather to Bolick's son. But after a 1993 *New Yorker* article on Thomas was published, Bolick found himself on the outs. In the article, Bolick recalled Thomas's saying: "One of the happiest days of my life was when I cancelled my *Washington Post* subscription." And in the same paragraph, the article's author, Jeffrey Toobin, wrote that Thomas called Bolick to "congratulate him" shortly after his op-ed pieces in the *Wall Street Journal* "helped precipitate the downfall of Thomas's law-school classmate Lani Guinier, whom President Clinton had nominated to head the Justice Department's Civil Rights Division." Thomas and Guinier had been close at Yale. The appearance that he had privately supported Bolick's campaign to brand her a "quota queen" for her civil rights views undoubtedly embarrassed Thomas. He conveyed his unhappiness to Bolick. "I was heartsick that I had inadvertently caused hurt to someone I intensely admire," says Bolick, describing how he downed two or three shots of vodka to ease his anguish.

What Thomas can't seem to abide is anything that hints at disloyalty, at least in his mind. Just cooperating in an article like Toobin's would qualify, as it portrayed Thomas as angry, wounded, and politically motivated—all images he rejects.

Bolick's experience is hardly unique. Glenn Loury recalls Thomas's reaction when he encouraged him to cooperate in a separate *New Yorker* profile, this one to be written by Henry Louis Gates Jr., the Harvard University scholar. Loury got to know Thomas well during the early 1980s, when Loury was the first black tenured economics professor at Harvard and Thomas was chairman of the EEOC. Both were rising black conservative stars. Gates had a reputation for doing thought-provoking pieces on race and for not having an agenda. So when he asked Loury if he'd mind approaching Thomas about an interview, Loury thought nothing of it. Loury, now a Brown University economics professor, was surprised when Thomas "conveyed a certain disappointment in me" just for querying him. "What are you doing asking me that?" Loury recalls Thomas saying. "I thought you knew better than that."

Their relationship was never the same, according to Loury, who later had a much-publicized split with the political right (a 2002 cover story in the *New York Times Magazine* detailed his ideological conversion). So maybe that compounded Thomas's ire. All Loury knows is that his daughter, a young attorney in Washington, badly wanted to meet Thomas. Thomas promised a meeting and told Loury to set it up with his administrative assistant, Loury says. But Loury called, and called again, and never got a return call. He doesn't quite understand what happened between them. He and Thomas no longer speak. "Maybe I pissed him off somewhere down the line," Loury says.

As cold as Thomas can be to those who disappoint him, he has gone out of his way to help some who have least expected his support. Among the most telling of his relationships are those he has cultivated with black judges, most of whom are Democrats. On several occasions, Thomas has telephoned Republican senators or otherwise intervened on behalf of stalled African American judicial nominees. One of them was his Yale Law School classmate Eric Clay. Thomas helped unclog his nomination by President Clinton to the federal bench; Senate Republicans had bottled it up. Thomas also came to the aid of another black Clinton appointee, federal district court judge Henry H. Kennedy Jr. His nomination to the federal bench in May 1997 met resistance from Republicans and languished for nearly four months. Exercising his influence to assist black Democratic judges runs counter to the Thomas caricature and often confounds those who are beneficiaries of his goodwill. They expect to see one of the images they have heard about—the rigid ideologue, the neutered justice disconnected from his race, Antonin Scalia's lapdog. Instead, they discover a much more complex man, who cannot be easily categorized.

"It was totally baffling to me," federal district court judge Victoria A. Roberts says of her visit to Thomas's chambers in June 1998. "I didn't know how to take it." Here she was, a black woman who had been nominated to the federal bench in Michigan by President Bill Clinton, and she couldn't get a hearing. Republicans had held up her nomination for a full year. The reason? As president of the black lawyers association in Detroit, Roberts had actively opposed the 1987 Supreme Court nomination of former federal judge Robert H. Bork, one of the right's judicial icons. That was reason enough for retribution a decade later, Roberts was told.

Roberts was sent to Thomas by Damon Keith, a senior judge on the Court of Appeals for the Sixth Circuit and a Thomas friend. Keith, who had been appointed by President Jimmy Carter, talked Roberts up to Thomas: first black president of the state bar, managing partner in a major law firm, someone of integrity. Thomas agreed to see her.

Roberts changed her flight plans because of the Thomas meeting, arriving in Washington a day before her hearing. She spent nearly an hour in Thomas's chambers. He told her how he grew up listening to Motown artists and rattled off tunes by the Temptations, the Marvelettes, and Smokey Robinson and the Miracles. "I was very comfortable with him, to my surprise," Roberts says. About fifteen to twenty minutes into the conversation, Thomas abruptly stopped, Roberts recalls. "I have spent longer talking to you than I talked to President [George H. W.] Bush when my name was submitted to the bench," he told Roberts. "To this day, I'm still not certain why or how I got this nomination."

Thomas said he wanted to help Roberts. If Damon Keith was vouching for her, that was good enough for him. "The Republicans should not be surprised that President Clinton would nominate a person to the bench who would oppose Bork," Thomas said, according to Roberts. "If you can assure me that you can be fair, I'll make some calls."

Keith recalls Thomas's phoning him and saying: "You can tell her she'll be confirmed. I've talked to Orrin Hatch and Trent Lott." Lott, the Mississippi Republican who was Senate majority leader at the time, says he had "a faint recollection" that Thomas might have called him, adding: "I would hope that he would feel free to call if he had some information about a nominee that would be helpful." Hatch, the former Republican chairman of the Judiciary Committee and a close Thomas friend, says the story "sounds familiar" but he can't recall details. All Roberts knows is that after her hearing a Republican counsel to the Judiciary Committee approached and said: "We've heard from Justice Thomas, and you won't have any more trouble." And she didn't. On June 26, 1998, by unanimous consent, Victoria Roberts was confirmed by the Senate.

At conferences of black lawyers and judges, she has told the story of Thomas's involvement, sometimes drawing raised eyebrows and perplexed looks. "He has, in his own way, helped me and others like me," Roberts reflects. "And we're on the bench, and we're making decisions that may be very contrary to those he may make." Still, whenever Thomas's name comes up among her colleagues, "it's never good."

"He's a complicated person," she says. "Very puzzling to me."

Of all the Thomas critiques over the years, there is only one that
Thomas himself has fully embraced. Titled "Native Son: Why a Black
Supreme Court Justice Has No Rights a White Man Need Respect,"
it was written by the late Edith Efron and published by *Reason* magazine in February 1992. It was so dead-on that Thomas recommended it to friends as a way of understanding him. Nearly a
decade later, the article had not left his consciousness when he met
Efron's editor by chance after a speech in Washington. No one else,
Thomas told Virginia Postrel, had been able to see so clearly into his
mind. Efron was a self-described libertarian and one-time associate
of Ayn Rand's whose eclectic writing career included stints with the
New York Times Magazine and *TV Guide*.

In assessing what the confirmation hearings had done to Thomas,
Efron reread *Native Son*, the tragic 1940 novel by Richard Wright,
whose work had a major influence on Thomas. "I would have to put
him number one, numero uno," Thomas once told an interviewer.
"Both *Native Son* and *Black Boy* really woke me up. He captures a lot
of the feelings that I had inside that you learn how to repress." In
Thomas, Efron saw a man "who had been stereotyped out of existence and who was controlling a violent anger at what was happening to him" before a Senate panel deciding his fate. *Native Son*
provided the context for understanding that anger:

> One finds many things relevant to Thomas and to his roots and
> his lifelong concerns in this book. But in this particular con-
> text, one finds one crucial thing—his limits. The one thing
> Thomas would not, could not, permit, whatever else might be
> at stake, the one stereotype that it would be downright danger-
> ous to paste on him, leaps out from those pages.
>
> *Native Son* is the story of Bigger Thomas, a defiant, terrified,
> sensitive black tough, a chronic delinquent trapped for life in a
> white world where he dreams of experiencing connectedness
> to others but cannot. He gets a job as a chauffeur for a rich
> white family. Entirely by accident—there is nothing equivocal

about this—he suffocates their daughter with a pillow when she is dead drunk. In terror that he will be charged with murdering her, he burns her body in a furnace. It does not occur to him that he will automatically be charged with raping her and that he has burned the evidence that he did not. One lie leads to another, one crime to another, and eventually the young Bigger Thomas becomes the object of a 5,000-man police hunt that combs every inch of the segregated slum in which he is trapped. Eventually he is caught; he is defended by two white communists; their efforts fail; and Bigger is found guilty—guilty, above all, of the two crimes he has not committed, the rape and the murder of the white girl.

The parallels between the narratives of Bigger Thomas and Clarence Thomas are far from perfect, but the justice has always identified with Wright's roiling, misunderstood character.

As inspiring as Thomas can be, it is striking how many of his speeches contain tales of woe. In thinking about this trait in Thomas, we are reminded of an observation Paul Newman made about acting to film director Robert Benton. An interviewer had said to Newman: "You must love acting to work as hard at it as you do." And Newman replied: "No, all of this is about how much I didn't want to go into the sporting goods business." The point, suggested Benton: "It's not always that we're running toward something. It's what we're running away from."

Even on joyous occasions, Thomas can resemble a man who is still fleeing something awful. Elaine Cassel captured this in a May 19, 2003, piece in the political newsletter *CounterPunch*. She had just read news coverage of a Thomas commencement address at the University of Georgia Law School and was struck by how familiar his remarks sounded. Four years earlier, Thomas had been the commencement speaker at her daughter's law school graduation at George Mason University in Virginia. "It was a somber, self-pitying speech that left many of the thousands of attendees squirming in their seats," Cassel wrote. "Apparently Thomas has only one speech—one that recounts his hard life in Pin Point, Georgia, his 'crushing' experience of graduating from Yale Law School (pity the poor man who has to go to Yale) without one offer to work in the law firm of his dreams—a firm in Atlanta or Savannah, Georgia."

Cassel, an attorney who also teaches law and psychology at Marymount University, sees in Thomas "the epitome of a selfish man, a narcissist to the core. The man you invite to a party whose presence hangs like a dark cloud over the fun that would be." As for Cassel's daughter, Courtenay Brinckerhoff, she graduated at the top of her law school class while working, raising two children, and attending classes from 6 to 10 p.m. Brinckerhoff was singled out by Thomas for her achievement under difficult circumstances. ("How can you maintain an A average, have a full-time job, and have a family? That's beyond me.") But in Brinckerhoff's eyes, Thomas's speech was a downer on an otherwise uplifting day. "It was kind of depressing," she said. "It seemed to me, here's a person who had made it to the ideal place that any of us would want to make it to, and obviously he had some hurdles. But it was not the speech you would have expected from someone who had made it to that point. . . . It wasn't a feel-good, go-out-and-conquer-the-world speech."

Thomas believes there are lessons to be learned from struggle—to him, recounting his struggles *is* inspiring. During a visit to the Virginia Home for Boys, Thomas encountered a hyperactive child who had trouble concentrating. The boy had never sat still longer than ten or fifteen minutes, he told Thomas. "It's hard in school," the boy said. "I know it," replied Thomas, "but it's hard for me."

Havenwood is perfectly suited for Clarence Thomas. It is a tranquil development of large lots and custom brick homes in Fairfax Station, Virginia, close enough to downtown Washington that the commute is not difficult, but far enough away to feel pleasantly secluded. If he could only take a helicopter to work, Thomas told a court visitor, he would live even farther out. Most of the homes have long driveways. And some houses, including Clarence Thomas's, as was noted earlier, can't be seen from the street. At Havenwood's entrance is a sign that lets visitors know this is a private road, residents and guests only, no soliciting. Landscaped median strips line this main road, which ends in a cul de sac. According to local realtors, houses in the development, which was built in the early 1990s, sell for upwards of $1.5 million. Not that there is much turnover. "People pretty much come out here and stay out here," says Diane Lenahan, who runs the local Wolf Run Realty.

The area has plenty of horse trails, and nearby is where the Battle of Bull Run was fought during the Civil War. Thomas feels at home in his neighborhood, which is predominantly white. He is regularly seen at Davis's general store, down the street from his home. He always speaks to the cashiers. Fifteen minutes away are several strip malls, where Thomas also is frequently spotted. In nearby Burke, Virginia, is his favorite barbecue joint. And four miles from his home is the quaint town of Clifton, where the Thomases buy fresh-cut blossoms and sometimes dine at the rustic Heart in Hand, which gained notoriety many years ago as the place where first lady Nancy Reagan would lunch with George Will. The restaurant also was used in the opening scene of the movie *Broadcast News*.

Ginni is more active in the neighborhood than her husband, participating in cookie bakes and homeowners' association meetings, according to neighbors. Often she has Marky with her. And if Marky isn't with her, he's with Thomas, whom friends say has been reenergized by raising an impressionable boy. "It seemed like it turned back the clock ten years on his life," said former Thomas clerk Stephen F. Smith, whose own children used to go to school with Marky.

There was no guarantee the arrangement would work. Back in the late 1980s, as we recounted earlier, Emma Mae had sent her oldest son, Clarence, to live with his uncle. But the boy had not liked the Washington area and asked to come home.

Marky, however, didn't seem to have the same adjustment problems as young Clarence had. He excelled in school, took up golf, became a Harry Potter fan. Each summer, he returns to Savannah to spend time with his mother and grandmother. His relationship with his father, though, is complicated. Big Mark calls his son once or twice a month from the federal correctional facility in South Carolina to which he was transferred. The Thomases send him copies of Marky's report cards. Marky writes him letters, and Big Mark ponders the possibility of one day resuming his role as father. "I think about it every day," he says.

For now, Clarence Thomas is fulfilling that role. Sometimes when the justice gives a speech at some out-of-the-way location, there's Marky in the audience. It's not uncommon to hear Thomas warm up the crowd with a Marky story. One of his favorites is the time Mark was explaining to someone his biracial parentage. "He said that he was both black and white when asked what his race was, and that meant that he was Italian," Thomas told Hillsdale College in Michigan, to much laughter. "So much for the Census Bureau."

Traveling the open road was something Thomas never got a chance to do when he was a kid. Now, he gets to share the experience with Mark. It is essential to his happiness. "The RV world gives me a chance to balance things out," Thomas has said. "It allows me a sense of freedom."

16

EXPECTATIONS

Henry Louis Gates Jr. is explaining why black Americans expect so much of their greatest achievers, expect them to represent the entire race, expect them to pass the test of authenticity. It's a long, complicated conversation that winds its way through history, touching down in all sorts of places. Before long Gates is linking Henry James and Black History Month, segueing from stocking caps to Walt Whitman.

He is laying the framework for comprehending Clarence Thomas.

Gates has the scraggly beard and wire-framed glasses of the prototypical scholar but the mien of a soul brother who not only knows his history but also knows how to talk some serious shit. Formerly the chairman of Harvard's African and African American Studies Department, Gates became a celebrity intellectual, building a dream team of race thinkers at the world's most prestigious university while writing provocative articles for the *New Yorker* and spearheading television documentaries. He is now director of Harvard's W.E.B. Du Bois Institute for African and African American Research, a new perch for him. Gates has personal experience with this topic expectations, as almost every African American high achiever does. He was skewered for a 1992 *New Yorker* piece that called out black anti-Semitism and for a PBS documentary that cited the role of Africans in the slave trade.

"But the thing is, so what? I mean, it's the truth," Gates says, without a squirm of discomfort. "I'm a scholar, not a cheerleader." Bravado duly expressed, he adds: "But it's still painful."

The question of legitimacy—Are you black enough? Are you black in the right way? Whom do you owe for your success?—has percolated in black communities for more than a century. The question is as much about class as about race.

Even during slavery, the class stratification among blacks was far more complex than the house niggers–field niggers divide that is most commonly referenced in popular culture. In *Unchained Memories*, the book version of the HBO documentary, Rosa Starke, a South Carolina slave, broke down how slaves saw themselves: The top class was the house servants (butlers, maids, nurses, chambermaids, cooks); then came the carriage drivers, gardeners, carpenters, barbers, and stable men. Next were the wagoners, blacksmiths, and slave foremen, then the slaves who tended to the cows and took care of the dogs. "All dese have good houses and never have to work hard or git a beatin'," according to Starke. Lower down in the pecking order were the wheat cradlers, the corn threshers, and the cotton gin feeders. And the lowest of the low were the common field hands. Back then, of course, the pecking order was imposed by overseers who had the whip and the law on their side.

Today, the overseers are dead. But the divide that exists between the educated and the uneducated, between those who can afford the accoutrements of success and those who can't afford dinner, has become perhaps the biggest barrier to racial solidarity. And the schisms among African Americans that are based on economics, occupational status, and social rank are more pronounced than ever.

"We're all black," says Gates, "but we have greater class division than we've ever had."

It's February 2004 in Los Angeles, a brilliantly sunny day on the University of Southern California's campus. Gates's class-division point is on dramatic display at, of all things, a hip-hop summit. The summit is the brainchild of hip-hop entrepreneur Russell Simmons, part of a larger project to register new voters and harness the potential political power of this generation of rap-music-loving, MTV-video-watching young people. In theory, this summit and others held in cities across the country would connect the rappers and rap moguls with the folks in the 'hood. In theory, there should be a natural synergy between the guardians of street culture and those living out the realities of the streets. But not today in USC's packed auditorium on the same weekend as the National Basketball Association All-Star Game.

As it turns out, the folks from the 'hood have some tough questions for the cultural caretakers, who are crunched together on the overcrowded stage and adorned in all the trappings of street success—authentic pro sports jerseys and enough platinum-and-diamonds to draw envy from a distance. The caretakers include not only rappers but music and movie producers, athletes, and other celebrities. The rap cats, those with the greatest swaggers, get hit with the hardest questions: How much of your personal money are you reinvesting in the community? What is hip-hop doing to resolve the real-life street conflicts that lead to violence, which the rappers then hype on their recordings? Why isn't this summit being held at a community center in South Central Los Angeles or Watts, somewhere in the 'hood rather than on this richly endowed campus?

The rappers are defensive, the forum grows testy, and it isn't long before an actual punches-thrown fight seems imminent. And logical. The presence of a Nation of Islam security force forming a protective ring around the stage doesn't help matters. Nor does the moderator, the unskillful Reverend Ben Chavis Muhammad, who keeps cutting off questioners.

"Instead of working against us, work with us," begs Damon Dash, CEO of Roc-A-Fella Records, the label founded out of a car trunk from which Dash and rap icon Jay-Z sold CDs on Brooklyn's streets and ended up multimillionaires. "What you're saying is right," Dash tells the community folks, "but you're attacking the wrong people." The plea of Dash and the rest of the rap collective boils down to this: We're new to success, first-generation tycoons still feeling our way. We haven't sorted out the inherent tension between prosperity and responsibility. But we're here, we're trying. "Take that aggression you have and take it outside the culture and attack *them*," Dash urges. By *them* he means whichever white, mainstream culprits rile the soul. But please, don't blame hip-hop.

Just as the summit is about to get out of hand, the wisest woman in the room takes the microphone and asks for calm and puts the whole thing in perspective. "Cut that music off," instructs Cynthia Mendenhall, aka Sista, a respected Watts community leader who was instrumental in brokering a truce between rival L.A. gangs. "You don't hear what we hear," she tells the assembled panel. "You don't represent me. . . . I just got paid yesterday. I'm broke today. . . . We not mad at ya'll. Bring it to the 'hood.

"Ya'll flossin' at the mic," Mendenhall continues, using the street vernacular for styling. "Don't none of ya'll live where I live." Her neighborhood just buried another child for trying to buy a loaf of bread, she says.

And then Mendenhall gets even tougher, taking aim at the false machismo that gets so many black men hurt, jailed, or killed. Don't sell toughness, she implores, don't market prison as a stripe of manhood, like it's a gold medal or something. "Tell a nigga you got raped in prison," Mendenhall insists. "Tell the kids the truth." Sweeping her hand across the auditorium, she looks back toward those seated behind her as the applause builds to a crescendo. Some of the kids in the audience are black USC students. Some on stage have formal educations. "Some of you have made it to college," she says, "and our kids haven't made it across the street."

Mendenhall is a hit, of course. She cools the heat at the meeting, which is abruptly adjourned, and the Reverend Chavis, Damon Dash, and most of the other celebs quickly scurry into the sunlight . . . and their waiting luxury cars.

It's not just party identification or ideology that earns you an up-braiding in black America. Clarence Thomas, take heart. Not even the hip and the popular—not Will Smith, not Oprah Winfrey—are exempt from a sort of racial auditing, though that fact is lost in most debates about black authenticity.

Ernie Barnes, arguably the nation's best-known contemporary African American painter, says: "Black people get pissed off when I paint white people. It's like they own me. Like I belong to them."

Virtually every black professional has had his or her race credentials challenged at some point—whether at the neighborhood barbershop or in the company cafeteria, though not usually in the pages of major newspapers and magazines. In that respect, Thomas experiences a public isolation that overshadows whatever personal hell is lived by the obscure black Merrill Lynch exec. But the questions hounding Thomas are deeper still. They are really questions of identity. Do you *see* yourself as black? Are you black in your soul? Is it possible to identify with the common struggles and culture of black Americans without the group identifying with you?

Thomas's black identity is indeed important to him, based on what he has said publicly and told friends privately. But many African Americans simply don't believe him. In part, that's because Thomas has so much curmudgeon in him that his guard often goes up even when no fight exists. He seems obsessively wary of racial traps, worried that he will be put in a box reserved solely for black skin. And that's an intolerable thought for a man who sees boxes as anathema. So whatever racial pride Thomas feels is overshadowed by this greater need not to be typecast, which is a synonym for limited, which is a synonym for inferior.

A student at Ashland University, an overwhelmingly white private school in Ohio, asked him to comment on the hyphenated American. Was it helpful or divisive to maintain this form of ethnic identification? "Well, I don't know," Thomas said, a little uncomfortable with the question. "I am black, I'm an American, and I'd sort of like to keep it that way. . . . I don't hyphenate where I'm from. I really don't get into that debate very much. It's not something that I found particularly useful."

Thomas was asked another race-related question at this same gathering in 1999, this one about the pressures of being black in public life. He mentioned an essay in the *Washington Post* that challenged whether District of Columbia mayor Anthony Williams was black enough. "Now, when last have you seen an article that says somebody is not white enough?" Thomas responded. "Or you've seen an article that says somebody is not woman enough? It makes no sense, but those things can be said. They're easy attacks."

So easy they often are targeted at Williams, an awkward man who wears ill-fitting suits and bow ties, more budget-crunching nerd than natural politician who opted not to run for reelection in 2006. He can't shoot hoops or adroitly dance the electric slide, though he's never embarrassed by his effort. Unlike Thomas, who handles most criticism in extremes—either angry rebellion or feigned disinterest—Williams is willing to engage in dialogue with his critics, rarely losing his balance when challenged on his blackness.

Thomas is no Tony Williams. At Ashland University, the justice went on to hurl his own attacks at the anonymous people who harbor "those assumptions" about what it means to be black and are "real snide and cynical" about their perspective. And when you're shooting in the dark at unspecified enemies, it's easy to keep discharging rounds of fire. By the time he had finished, Thomas had likened these unidentified attackers to slave owners.

"I wanted to go and get them a couple of overseers and about 2,000 acres," he said.

And just like that, Thomas had drawn an absurd link between the difficult but routine challenges that public figures must weather and the most oppressive and vile chapter in American history.

Sometimes, Thomas hunts ants with grenades.

He is not, he surely must know, the first hall-of-fame black figure in this discomfiting position.

It's fashionable now, for example, to celebrate the work of Zora Neale Hurston. Her novel *Their Eyes Were Watching God* has become a literary classic. But when Hurston was alive she was often criticized for her close ties to white patrons, and her work was picked apart by her peers as too neutered for the times. And her political views? Those were difficult to label but routinely lambasted. In attempting to explain how blacks were better off in the South than in the North—they had all that whites had, including their own hotels and nightclubs—Hurston told an interviewer in 1943: "In other words, the Jim Crow system works." Her comment prompted an uproar from black leaders such as NAACP chief Roy Wilkins, who accused her of spouting "vicious nonsense" to sell books. "Now is no time for tongue-wagging by Negroes for the sake of publicity," Wilkins wrote in a newspaper commentary. "The race is fighting a battle that may determine its status for fifty years. Those who are not for us, are against us."

Unlike some of her contemporaries—notably Richard Wright, who was and remains the most influential writer in Clarence Thomas's life—Hurston was not drawn to the rage-and-rebellion narrative. She knew blacks to be, as she wrote in a 1938 essay, people who "love and hate and fight and play and strive and travel and have a thousand and one interests in life like other humans." This is a sentiment Thomas would wholeheartedly embrace today to rebut critics who subscribe to narrowly circumscribed notions of blackness.

Marcus Garvey is another revered figure whose standing among black Americans is more complicated than is often recalled by the T-shirt hawkers. His Universal Negro Improvement Association was at one time the largest, most prosperous black organization in the world. In his heyday, during and after World War I, Garvey was a charismatic leader whose majestic parades and messages of economic and political self-determination resonated with blacks. But he had his flaws. When he reached out to the Ku Klux Klan as a kindred spirit on the question of keeping the races separate, he crossed the line. The Jamaican-bred Garvey seriously underestimated the hatred American blacks had for the Klan and watched his support erode because of the blunder. Beset by managerial problems and debt, he was convicted of mail fraud in connection with the stock sale of his steamship line. A campaign to win his release from prison was successful, but Garvey was deported back to Jamaica and barred from returning to the United States. As popular as Garvey was, he often came under fire from other respected black organizations and leaders—notably the NAACP and W. E. B. Du Bois. This is a familiar position, historically, for blacks in leadership positions.

Jesse Jackson and Al Sharpton found themselves out of sync with most African Americans after they criticized the 2002 film *Barbershop* for its playful ridicule of civil rights matriarch Rosa Parks. As every black man who has ever gotten his hair cut in a black barbershop knows, nothing and nobody is off limits in the shop. That singular fact was validated by the overwhelming backlash against Jackson and Sharpton after their critiques. They thought, erroneously, that they would be applauded for standing up for the blood, sweat, and tears of the civil rights movement, as embodied by Parks's courageous refusal to give up her seat on a public bus in 1954. But what they discovered is that sometimes funny is just funny. And dumb is dumb.

Harvard's Gates remembers taking his father to the movie. His father couldn't wait to go. "He said anything Jesse and Al Sharpton are pissed off at must be good, must be funny," Gates recalls. "So we went, and I laughed my behind off."

Gates enjoys holding court and loves company. He insists that visitors call him "Skip," which is what everyone calls him. On his desk is a Colin Powell bobblehead doll. "I like Colin Powell," he says, smiling, though this was before the war in Iraq and before the United States facilitated the ouster of Jean-Bertrand Aristide, the democratically elected president of Haiti whose wife Gates hosted a breakfast for at Harvard. Which is to say, before the venerable Teflon Powell watched his rep take a beating even in black America, putting him closer to Clarence Thomas than he had ever wanted or expected to be.

"But there are a zillion historical precedents for Clarence Thomas," Gates continues, "and I'm not talking about Booker T. Washington." Washington, of course, is always mentioned in connection with Thomas, who has Washington's portrait hanging in his chambers. But unlike Thomas, Washington created a black institution (Tuskegee) and had a huge black following.

The tradition of black conservatism, to which Thomas is now the most prominent heir, can be traced back to Jupiter Hammon, a Long Island slave and pioneering black literary figure. He is often considered the founding father of black conservatism. He urged slaves not to rebel but to transcend their condition, to focus not on physical bondage but on living a Christian life. "If God designs to set us free," Hammon exhorted New York slaves in 1787, "he will do it in his own time; but think of your bondage to sin and Satan, and do not rest until you are delivered from it."

Many of those not commonly thought of as conservatives— Frederick Douglass, A. Philip Randolph, Louis Farrakhan—sometimes embraced conservative ideas. Even Du Bois, whom Thomas sometimes cites in his Supreme Court opinions, was labeled a conservative in his later years. After many years of angrily squaring off against Booker T. Washington—the symbol of protest versus the symbol of accommodation—Du Bois in 1934 severed ties with the NAACP he cofounded and argued for the preservation of segregated black institutions. Thus, almost two decades after Washington died, Du Bois, ironically, had moved closer to the thinking of his nemesis.

Over time, enough room was created on the black conservative spectrum to accommodate not only the Jupiter Hammons but militant nationalists like Malcolm X, an early influence of Thomas's, back in his "radical days" at Holy Cross, as he likes to say. It was then that Thomas first read *The Autobiography of Malcolm X* and began collecting the recorded speeches of the black Muslim leader. In Malcolm, Thomas saw a perfect strain of conservatism: He preached self-reliance, thought white liberals were condescending, and considered black leaders who pushed for integration wrongheaded. These are Thomas's views even today, though hardly anyone would call him a modern-day Malcolm X. In fact, he now dismisses the protests of his collegiate era as immature, infuriating fellow black Holy Cross alums who think Thomas either is playing politics or has developed a convenient case of amnesia.

Thomas likes to argue that it's not the message that's under assault but the messenger, and that if people would just debate his ideas he'd have no problem with them. "We have an interesting race sometimes," Thomas said in a 1994 speech. "It is the only race that will evict those who are smart, those who are successful." He went on: "If you are too smart, too successful, know too much, do too well, then you can't be black anymore. You lose touch. This is the only race where it is a shame to be knowledgeable. It is a shame for someone to know calculus. That doesn't make any sense to me. Then during Black History Month we say we discovered mathematics."

That speech was delivered at Tuskegee University, a historically black college founded by Booker T. Washington. Here, Thomas's provocative take on blacks and education was greeted with applause by black college students. Perhaps Thomas should try this more often—engage those who are not already converts. But Thomas is uncomfortable debating his ideas; rarely will you find him in a forum where his critics get to challenge him and he gets to challenge them.

J. Clay Smith, a Howard University law professor, recalls that when Thomas came to Howard some years ago he arrived with two "bodyguards," as Smith puts it, and seemed strangely uncomfortable. Especially for a black man. Chief Justice William Rehnquist had come to Howard with one of his law clerks, and Justice Sandra Day O'Connor had come alone. After Thomas spoke, questions to him had to be filtered through the dean. Smith thought: You don't have to be afraid of *us*.

Thomas's allies often praise him as courageous just for holding to his views under such duress. But if he were really fearless, he would more resemble George S. Schuyler, the most influential black conservative for much of the twentieth century. Schuyler didn't give a hoot what people thought of him or his ideas, didn't wring his hands in despair as Thomas often does. A protégé of H. L. Mencken's, he became the first black journalist to reach national prominence. But Schuyler was much more than a journalist. He was an irreverent social critic, a cutting satirist, a prolific novelist, and an unapologetic observer of America's racial condition. He started his career on the far left and ended it on the far right. Though he was ostracized and isolated by mainstream black organizations, he never shrank under the weight of criticism or provocation.

Schuyler welcomed wars of words and always held his own— whether it was in print against Langston Hughes in 1926 or on the radio against Malcolm X and James Baldwin in 1961. His novel, *Black No More*, described by the writer Ishmael Reed as "the most scathing fiction about race written by an American," hilariously probed the question of what would happen if blacks became white through a scientific treatment. Even the serious W. E. B. Du Bois, who was incisively caricatured in the book, thought it was funny. Not that Schuyler was always right or always smart. When he wrote a commentary attacking the awarding of the Nobel Peace Prize to Martin Luther King Jr. in 1964, it turned him into an outcast in black communities. "Dr. King's principal contribution to world peace has been to roam the country like some typhoid-Mary, infecting the mentally disturbed with the perversion of Christian doctrine, and grabbling lecture fees from the shallow-pated," Schuyler wrote. And that wasn't even his harshest stuff.

Schuyler died lonely and alone in New York's Manhattan Hospital in 1977. He was eighty-two, having lived a life on his own terms.

Gates is asked why there is such livid reaction to Thomas, such disappointment, in many black quarters. He starts with context: "We haven't had people in leadership positions for very long. . . . So of course we have, broadly speaking, a great concern for something we might call racial accountability. But nobody's quite sure what racial accountability is. . . . I mean, there's not like a Nielsen meter monitored to every black household in America. . . . But I think we're like every other emerging ethnic group, that when the representatives get up there like the Irish or the Italians or the Jewish people, we want them to protect our larger group interest in the face of discrimination against, respectively, the Irish, Italians, or Jewish people. I think that's perfectly reasonable."

In a lecture at Brandeis University in 2001, Justice Ruth Bader Ginsburg noted that the first five Jewish justices—she was the sixth—all saw the law "as protector of the oppressed, the poor, the minority, the loner," as evident in their life's work. The first of them, Louis Brandeis, appointed to the court in 1916 by President Woodrow Wilson, was sometimes referred to as "the people's attorney" when he was practicing law. He helped establish the pro bono tradition in this country, spending half his time on public interests. Even so, when he was nominated the initial reaction among Jews was tepid, in part because of a belief that Brandeis was not truly Jewish and that there were many other Jews better qualified for such a historic appointment. Raised in a home absent of formal religion, Brandeis was not a practicing Jew and adopted his Jewish identity late in life, primarily through Zionism. None of that, however, granted him any exemptions from anti-Semitism, as his detractors quickly made plain. One of his fellow justices, the intolerable James McReynolds, was so openly anti-Semitic that he would get up and leave the room whenever Brandeis spoke in conference.

Whatever their larger contributions to the court, most of the Jewish justices have not been afraid to represent themselves as Jews. In 1943, after the court abruptly overturned an opinion Felix Frankfurter had written three years earlier, he reminded his colleagues in an angry dissent that "one who belongs to the most vilified and persecuted minority in history is not likely to be insensible to the freedoms guaranteed by the Constitution." And Arthur Goldberg once said: "My concern for justice, for peace, for enlightenment, stem[s] from my heritage."

Though the Brandeis appointment established de facto a "Jewish seat" on the court, that tradition is now a mothballed relic; two of the last four justices named to the court, Ginsburg and Breyer, are Jewish, but no one characterizes their seats that way. Thomas is not given that luxury. As only the second African American justice, he is seen by almost everyone to occupy the "black seat" held by Thurgood Marshall for twenty-four years. Until there's more than one African American on the court—there were two Jewish justices as early as 1932—Thomas almost assuredly will remain a symbol.

As successful as black Americans have been in overcoming first slavery and then Jim Crow, it's doubtful many would speak as confidently about their group's status in the twenty-first century as Justice Ginsburg did about Jews in the United States. She and other Jews, she said, "face few closed doors and do not fear letting the world know who we are."

As Gates points out, "For most of us, contemporary black history starts in 1969 with the onset of affirmative action." That led to the expansion of educational and job opportunities, the growth of the black electorate, the enlargement of the black middle class, and more representation in the power structures of the nation. But African Americans are only a generation removed from the beginnings of this process, "and we're still working it all out." Inferior schools, a disproportionate number of black men in prison, and racial dispar- ities in wealth and income are among the problems that weigh on many African American families. Opportunity is like a salve that treats inequity—and so the discussion comes around again to affir- mative action.

Thomas clearly feels that too much weight has been piled on his back, and unfairly so. "Does a black man instantaneously become 'in- sensitive,' a 'dupe,' or an 'Uncle Tom' because he happens to disagree with the policy of affirmative action?" is a question Thomas once posed to students at Mercer University Law School. Gates says Thomas fails to grasp the significance of affirmative action, espe- cially for those who have made it. He calls it the contemporary equivalent of the Emancipation Proclamation. "The civil rights movement has been boiled down to one big issue for most black people," Gates says. "It's not welfare reform, it's not jobs, it is affir- mative action. That is what's left of the civil rights movement." He likes to use himself as an example: Gates was one of six blacks at Yale when he entered in 1966. The Class of 1973 had ninety-six blacks. "How come all these black people got in after '69 who weren't in before 1969? . . . The answer is two words: affirmative action."

Gates says he will always defend Thomas's right to be conserva- tive, to believe whatever he wants to believe. But he wonders why he's so bitter. "Justice Thomas has chosen to make a stand on that one issue," says Gates of affirmative action. "I mean, what did he ex- pect? It's like riding on an anti–gay marriage platform in Greenwich Village or in Provincetown. . . . You're going to be surprised when people are angry at you?" But the justice has to be himself, Gates concludes, for that's all he really can be. "I don't think there's one way to be black."

Nobody exemplifies this idea better than Clarence Thomas, who in nearly sixty years of living has worn his blackness in numerous ways: as a poor, abandoned child awed by the stern, illiterate grand- father who took him in; as a teenager wounded by teasing about his dark skin; as a confused college student who collected recordings of Malcolm X's fiery speeches; as the darling of white conservatives who summoned the phrase *high-tech lynching* when his seat on the Supreme Court was about to slip away.

Today, Thomas wears his blackness like a heavy robe that both ennobles and burdens him. The problem of color is a mantle he yearns to shed, even as he clings to it.

Like the rest of America, he may never escape.

EPILOGUE

Clarence Thomas sat silently amid the drama playing out on the final public session of the Supreme Court's 2006–2007 term. At stake was the ability of public schools to consider race when making school assignments, and passions were flaring on both sides of the court's deepening ideological divide.

As the justices handed down what was widely regarded as their most important racial decision in a decade, three of the nine read their opinions from the bench—the rough equivalent of a shouting match in the decorous world of the high court. Some justices saw the ruling as ratification of the colorblind principles upholding the landmark *Brown v. Board of Education* decision. Others saw it as an abandonment of *Brown*'s integrationist aspirations.

Through it all, Thomas said nothing—as he almost always does. But there was no need to. He had already made himself heard where it mattered most, as part of the five-justice majority that ruled the race-conscious school admissions programs in Louisville and Seattle violated the Constitution's Equal Protection Clause. The decision prompted civil rights leaders and school officials to predict that the court's decision in *Parents Involved in Community Schools v. Seattle*

School District No. 1 would sharply curtail what officials could do to achieve some semblance of racial balance in the nation's public schools.

In an impassioned dissent, Justice Stephen G. Breyer said the court's decision "announces legal rules that will obstruct efforts by state and local governments to deal effectively with the growing re-segregation of public schools."

But that rationale was brushed aside by Chief Justice John G. Roberts Jr.'s plurality opinion. "Before *Brown*, schoolchildren were told where they could and could not go to school based on the color of their skin," Roberts wrote. "The school districts in these cases have not carried the heavy burden of demonstration that we should allow this once again—even for very different reasons." He added: "The way to stop discrimination on the basis of race is to stop dis-criminating on the basis of race."

Those words had to be music to Thomas's ears. They reaffirmed a view he has stated repeatedly in school integration, affirmative ac-tion, and other race cases through his first sixteen years on the high court. The fact that the nation's public schools are becoming more racially isolated is of little concern to Thomas, who has long doubted the educational value of school integration. As he sees it, the principle of colorblindness—other than in the most tightly de-fined circumstances—is paramount.

"Racial imbalance is not segregation, and the mere incantation of terms like resegregation and remediation cannot make up the dif-ference," Thomas wrote in a concurrence, before adding, "If our history has taught us anything, it has taught us to beware of elites bearing racial theories."

We have heard one question perhaps more than others since the publication in April 2007 of the hardcover edition of *Supreme Dis-comfort. Is there a chance that Justice Thomas will change? Are there any signs that he is changing now?* It is not an unreasonable query, given the history of the Supreme Court and the liberties afforded by life-time tenure. Many justices have adjusted their views, some radically. Earl Warren, William Brennan Jr., and John Paul Stevens were all Republican appointees and they all turned out to be more liberal than advertised, disappointing their sponsors. The most striking example of a justice changing his ways is Hugo Black, the former Ku Klux Klansman who became a strong supporter of civil rights during his thirty-four years on the court.

But when it comes to Thomas, change does not seem to be in the equation. "I ain't evolving," Thomas was quoted as telling his clerks early in his tenure. So far, he has been true to his word. Rather than Thomas moving closer to the court's mainstream, the court's mainstream is moving closer to Thomas's conservative positions.

The addition of Roberts and Justice Samuel A. Alito Jr. has undeniably shifted the court to the right, to the delight of social conservatives and the consternation of liberal activists. The court's new lineup meant that there were four solidly conservative votes on most issues—Roberts, Alito, Scalia, and Thomas—with Justice Anthony Kennedy emerging as the court's new swing voter. Remarkably, Kennedy was in the majority in all twenty-four 5–4 cases the court decided during the 2006–2007 term.

More often than not, Kennedy swung to the right. During the term, the court not only limited the ability of school districts to use race-conscious means to pursue school integration, but it also restricted the free-speech rights of students, struck down portions of the McCain-Feingold campaign finance law, and restricted campaign advertising by interest groups including unions and corporations. The court also upheld a federal law banning so-called partial-birth abortions. In each of those cases, Thomas was part of the five-vote conservative bloc that voted for those decisions. And where he differed with his conservative brethren, it was most often to stake out a more extreme position.

In *Gonzales v. Carhart*, the court reversed an earlier ruling and for the first time found legal a ban on a specific abortion method. Seven years earlier, the court had struck down an almost identical Nebraska law. "The government may use its voice and its regulatory authority to show its profound respect for the life within the woman," Kennedy wrote in the court's majority opinion. Kennedy justified the ban on the controversial procedure for ending midterm pregnancies by arguing that other abortion procedures are still available.

Thomas, while agreeing with the decision, added a one-paragraph concurrence that made it clear that he sees no federal right to abortion whatsoever. "I write separately to reiterate my view that the Court's abortion jurisprudence, including *Casey* and *Roe v. Wade*, has no basis in the Constitution," Thomas wrote.

Thomas again advocated a more conservative position than his colleagues in *Morse v. Frederick*. The case was brought by Joseph Frederick, a student who unfurled a banner reading "Bong Hits 4 Jesus," as he and other students stood on the street watching the Olympic torch pass by their Juneau, Alaska, school on its way to the 2002 Winter Games. The school's principal suspended Frederick for the demonstration, calling the banner an endorsement of marijuana use. Frederick sued, calling the suspension a violation of his First Amendment rights.

The high court ended up supporting the suspension in a narrowly crafted decision clarifying the rights of schools to allow officials to punish speech or demonstrations that may "reasonably be viewed" as promoting illegal drug use. But Thomas wrote a concurrence suggesting that the court should have issued a more sweeping ruling. "In my view, the history of public education suggests that the First Amendment, as originally understood, does not protect student speech in public schools," Thomas wrote.

Thomas was even more dismissive when it came to the student's legal claim. "Frederick assets a constitutional right to utter at a school event what is either gibberish or an open call to use illegal drugs," the justice wrote. "To elevate such impertinence to the status of constitutional protection would be farcical."

Just as Thomas's jurisprudence is unchanged, so too is his demeanor. The silent justice still almost never talks from the bench. A story by McClatchy Newspapers said that in the 218 hours of oral argument the court held between October 2004, when the Supreme Court began identifying individual justices on oral argument transcripts, and May 16, 2007, Thomas spoke a grand total of 281 words. He did not speak from the bench at all during the 2006–2007 term. By contrast, Breyer, the most talkative justice, rattled off nearly 35,000 words between January and May 2007, the story said.

Thomas has been no less taciturn with us. Another question often raised with us by those curious about Thomas is: *What does he think of your book? Have you heard from him?*

As it happens, we have—sort of. We sent the justice a signed copy of our book, accompanied by a short note assuring him that we had done our best to tell his story fairly and accurately. Not long afterward, a padded envelope from the U.S. Supreme Court arrived at the *Washington Post*. Inside of it was the opened mail bag, the book, and the note we had sent to the justice. Also enclosed was a typed message on an embossed card from the justice's chambers. It was signed by Thomas's secretary, Dorothy Barry.

It read: "This book is being returned to you at the request of Justice Thomas."

AUTHORS' NOTE

The first time either of us encountered Justice Thomas was in July 2001 at the Eighth Circuit Judicial Conference in St. Louis. He was approached at a reception where he was helping to dedicate the rotunda of a new federal building. In the receiving line, an introduction was made.

Thomas said he had received the first of our two letters requesting an interview for a *Washington Post Magazine* article. "Very kind letter. I wish you all the best. Good luck."

This would become a pattern over the next four years, long after our magazine profile had been published and we turned our attention to a book on the justice. One or both of us would approach Thomas at receptions, dinners, speeches, congressional hearings, wherever the possibility of a chat existed. He was always cordial. Pleasantries would be exchanged, followed often by casual conversation. While these brief conversations veered from the raising of his son, Jamal, as a single parent to his quest not to be pigeonholed by race, they almost always included some harsh critique of the media. The media are "malicious," he said on one occasion. "You're in a tough business."

Thomas once had wanted to be a journalist himself, he noted, but now he distrusted journalists more than any other group of professionals. They lie, and they are deceptive, he said. Nothing personal, he would always add.

While there was great value in observing Thomas as he spoke to different audiences and interacted personally with individuals, our ultimate aim was to convince him to participate in our project through formal interviews. There was reason to be hopeful, we thought. During that first encounter in St. Louis, Thomas seemed to have a need to be heard and understood. One night, bone-tired and clasping a bottle of almost-finished Evian, he continued to chat away as he waited for an elevator to carry him to his room.

On February 26, 2003, he attended an annual black-tie dinner hosted by the American Enterprise Institute, one of Washington's premier think tanks. Skipping the ballroom dancing, Thomas shook hands and hugged his tablemates and said his good nights. As he headed up a short flight of steps toward a curtained exit where security awaited him, one of us tapped him on his shoulder: Congratulations, Mr. Justice, on your forthcoming memoir. Looking forward to reading it. And now a question: Would you consider meeting with us to talk about our own book, under any ground rules you choose?

Sure, if he were still chairman of the EEOC, Thomas replied. He used to have reporters visit him all the time back in the Reagan administration years, he said. But the media abused that relationship, squandering their access and turning against him. "I think I'll pass, buddy. But good luck. I wish you luck."

How much of Thomas's reluctance to engage us was personal—and how much of it was professional—was becoming difficult to appraise. We knew firsthand that his wife, Ginni, had not liked our magazine profile, especially its racial focus. We also knew that the justice was no fan of the so-called liberal *Washington Post*, though he had lots of company in that regard.

The pursuit of a Thomas interview quickly became an intricate chess game. We wrote six letters to the justice, none of which got a response. At least a dozen Thomas friends said they had spoken to the justice—or offered to speak to him—on our behalf. They included housing and urban development secretary Alphonso Jackson, Republican Senate staffer Barbara Ledeen (a close friend of Ginni's), former deputy attorney general Larry Thompson, former federal appeals court judge J. Michael Luttig, commentator Armstrong Williams, and Justices Stephen Breyer and Antonin Scalia. Steven Bradbury, a former Thomas law clerk and now a senior Justice Department lawyer, urged us to "be persistent and nag him." We did. But ultimately our persistence didn't matter. Thomas chose not to cooperate.

This book is the product of several hundred interviews with people who have known, observed, or interacted with Thomas during the course of his life, including many who had never before spoken with a journalist and are providing their accounts for the first time. The interviews include more than forty with former Supreme Court law clerks and other former and current employees of the court.

Thomas's mother and sister, the father of his first wife, and relatives of his late father granted us extensive interviews on multiple occasions. Thomas's nephew, whose son the justice is raising, gave us an exclusive interview from prison. Former president George H. W. Bush answered our questions by e-mail.

While most of our interviews were conducted on the record, a number of them were not. Some sources with key insights into Thomas would speak to us only if their names were not used, either because of the sensitivity of their professional positions or because Thomas would not approve.

Anyone interested in studying Thomas would do well to follow the long paper trail he has left in more than thirty years of public service. His ideas, political views, and legal philosophy are revealed in hundreds of speeches, court opinions, and other writings, which we exhaustively combed. In addition, we watched countless hours of videotaped Thomas appearances, courtesy of the C-SPAN Archives in West Lafayette, Indiana. In reviewing the annual financial disclosure reports justices are required to submit, we learned much about Thomas's associations and interests.

Material found at other archives also proved invaluable. The papers of former justices Harry A. Blackmun and Thurgood Marshall, stored at the Library of Congress, were especially useful in helping us understand the relationships between justices and the culture of the Supreme Court, as were the papers of former justice Lewis F. Powell Jr., housed at Washington and Lee University School of Law. We also utilized the collections at the College of the Holy Cross, the presidential libraries of Ronald Reagan and George H. W. Bush, the Hoover Library at Stanford University, the Catholic Diocese of Savannah, and the Bull Street Library in Savannah.

The Senate transcripts of Thomas's Supreme Court confirmation hearings provide a unique verbatim account of the most tumultuous period of his life. We also are grateful to Nan Aron and the Alliance for Justice for giving us complete access to their files. Others involved in the confirmation battle—on both sides—made available contemporaneous memos, research papers, and other personal files. Notable among them were former Democratic Senate aide Ricki Seidman and Republican Senate staffer Robert Foster, a Thomas friend.

Now, to the matter of Thomas's colleagues. We had never covered the Supreme Court beat and were not known to any of the justices. So we decided it would be best to try to approach them in person about Thomas. We caught up with Scalia in a Washington hotel lobby as he was about to dash into a Federalist Society dinner. He agreed to meet us for lunch, which led to another lunch and then a third lunch, and finally to his agreement to put selective portions of our conversations on the record.

Breyer was buttonholed for a lengthy chat at a private Howard University Law School luncheon and again, for a shorter talk, following a Stanford alumni event. He seemed supportive of our project and expressed a desire to see an exploration of Thomas beyond the caricature. But apparently he didn't get very far with Thomas.

Responding to a follow-up letter we sent him, Breyer said he thought it best to "stick to my general rule and not provide special remarks about my colleague."

We understood the unofficial court code, even if none of the justices were willing to spell it out for us in plain language: They would talk to us only if authorized by Thomas. Scalia had been the exception. Justice Ruth Bader Ginsburg, whom we're told has a warm relationship with Thomas, ignored our first letter. After our second letter, she sent word through a mutual friend we enlisted that she would consent to be interviewed only if Thomas asked her to. The same veiled scenario occurred with Justice Anthony Kennedy. Tracked down at a Library of Congress reception, he was friendly and welcoming and his cooperation seemed possible. He promised to get back to us. He never did. Chief Justice William Rehnquist was more formal—and certainly more efficient than his colleagues—in dealing with us. He responded to our first letter in less than two weeks and concluded with a lament about his beloved but disappointing Green Bay Packers. While he declined our interview request, he invited us to submit written questions. So we did— eighteen in all, on everything from how opinions are assigned, to the court's public image, to what Thomas brings to the institution. Rehnquist reviewed our questions and decided he wouldn't take any of them. "These questions seem to be simply a written form of what would otherwise be an interview, which I had earlier declined," he wrote in a letter dated February 25, 2004. "That is not to say that they are not perfectly legitimate questions from your point of view, but just as I did not want to do an interview I do not care to answer them."

On May 17, 2004, we tried one last time to change Rehnquist's mind. He had just finished speaking at an American Law Institute forum and was walking slowly across the hotel lobby. A limo was waiting for him outside. Greetings and a handshake were exchanged. Were there really *no* questions he felt he could answer? Not even about the workings of the court? "Sorry to disappoint you," the chief said. "What I said in my letter is what I meant." Rehnquist would be hospitalized with thyroid cancer five months later and die the following year.

While researching this book, we could never quite make up our minds whether Thomas was actively or passively opposing our project. On the one hand, we figured Thomas couldn't be working too hard to thwart us, given that so many of his close friends, family members, and former law clerks had granted interviews. On the other hand, we periodically encountered people like Ted Olson, the former solicitor general and a close Thomas friend. He kept saying he would do an interview but needed to speak with Thomas first. We probably checked in with Olson a dozen times. But we could never pin him down for an interview. So we wondered: Was Thomas throwing the rock and hiding the hand? Was he just pretending to be indifferent about our book?

We never got an answer from Thomas himself, but we did get one from Justice John Paul Stevens. His candor about his colleague from Pin Point, Georgia, was refreshing. "I asked him if he wanted me to talk to you," Stevens said when approached at a judicial conference in Chicago. "And he said no."

That Thomas declined to be interviewed for this book didn't make him less fascinating to us. It made us work even harder to try to understand and explain him, and we are enormously indebted to all those who helped us in that pursuit.

ACKNOWLEDGMENTS

The *Washington Post*, our professional home, encouraged this project every step of the way, and for that we owe an enormous debt of gratitude. We offer a special shout-out to former managing editor Steve Coll, who cleared the way for us to pursue it. We know Steve could not have worked that bit of magic without the backing of CEO Don Graham, publisher Bo Jones, and executive editor Len Downie, all of whom nurture an atmosphere of enterprise and excellence that make the newspaper a special place in American journalism. When Phil Bennett took over as managing editor he immediately embraced the project. We are grateful for his unflagging support and for his newsroom leadership.

This book sprouted first as a *Washington Post Magazine* piece, then grew into a two-day series before reaching maturity. Thanks to the editors who nourished it along the way: Glenn Frankel, T. A. Frail, Tom Shroder, and Jeff Leen. Also, we appreciate the patience of our bosses and colleagues (and former colleagues) who tolerated our leaves, leave extensions, days worked at home, and other maneuvers that proved necessary to writing this book. Foremost on that list are Liz Spayd, John Harris, Michael Abramowitz, Maralee Schwartz, Peter Baker, Scott Vance, and Jim VandeHei.

From the beginning, our sunny agent, Andrew Blauner, never wavered in his belief in us and this book. Our editors at Doubleday could not have been better. The brilliant Bill Thomas understood the idea for the book right away and helped his first-time authors think more deeply about their subject. Katie Hall counseled us through the book's early days. And Gerry Howard—with his wisdom, sharp eye, and considerable forbearance—guided the project home. Katie Halleron: we owe you.

We were fortunate to receive the help of some talented researchers along the way. John Imbriglia was first among equals. He not only mined documents, distilled court opinions, and summarized innumerable speeches, but he also provided some first-rate reporting and much-needed encouragement, particularly in the project's early, foggy days. Margot Williams, formerly of the *Post*, helped us amass a wealth of information on Justice Thomas. A hearty thanks also to Amy Jennaro and Lizzie Hogan, who provided quick, sound research on the law and other topics; their work was critical. Drew Johnson-Skinner, Mike Tunison, and Justin Britt-Gibson also pitched in with valuable research.

Veteran Supreme Court reporters Joan Biskupic and Charles Lane graciously responded to our never-ending stream of queries and offered sage counsel that helped to demystify the cloistered world that is the Supreme Court. We thank them for their knowledge and friendship.

The Woodrow Wilson International Center for Scholars, led by Lee Hamilton, provided a home away from the newsroom during part of our leave. Philippa Strum, the center's insightful legal scholar, was especially helpful. The Hoover Institution at Stanford University provided us several fellowships in a beautiful setting, and for that we are appreciative. We also are indebted to Dean Kurt L. Schmoke and the Howard University School of Law for offering workspace and numerous sounding boards on the law.

Thanks to professors Barbara Feinman Todd of Georgetown University and Stephen Wermiel of American University's Washington

College of Law for identifying researchers and providing other assistance. We would like to credit Cornell University's Legal Information Institute for helping us understand and quantify the work of the court. We are grateful to Susan Swain, Robin Scullin, and Robert Browning for allowing us unlimited access to the C-SPAN Archives. We are much obliged to Aubrey Immelman, an expert in developing personality profiles of public figures, for his study of Clarence Thomas. We also benefited from several conversations with Wendell Williams, a clinical psychologist in the Washington, D.C., area. A nod also to John Jacob, the archivist at the Lewis F. Powell, Jr. Archives, for his guidance. We owe a special thank-you to Kathy Arberg and the staff in the Supreme Court's public information office.

Thanks also to Joe Elbert, Vanessa Barnes Hillian, and Erica Lusk of the *Washington Post* photo staff for their help and generosity, as well as to Jennifer Beeson of the *Post* magazine.

Our many friends and advisers buoyed us along the way. While it is impossible to mention everyone, please know you are all treasured. Sunni Khalid, Jerry Bembry, Herb Lowe, Wil Haygood, Craig Ferguson, Emmett Thomas, Lonnae O'Neal Parker, Ann Gerhart, Marcia Davis, Robert Pierre, Vanessa Williams, Hamil Harris, Milton Coleman, Bob Kaiser, Rick Atkinson, Margo Hartso, Jabari and Liana Asim, Joe Davidson, Shannon Wiggins, Barry Fletcher, Mireille Grangenois, Steve Holmes, and Leonard "Doc" Haynes are among those who provided needed counsel and encouragement.

We could not have gotten this far without our parents—Doris and George Hill; Beryl and Stanley Fletcher. They have always stood by us, and we owe them everything. Hugs also to Geraldine Britt and Jimmy Nickson.

And Leisa "Boo" Merida, you are the best.

Above all, thanks to our amazing, supportive wives, Donna Britt and Gale Fletcher, and to our children, Skye Merida, Darrell Britt-Gibson, Justin Britt-Gibson, and Mike and Candice Fletcher. This book would not have been possible without our families' incredible patience, encouragement, and love.

NOTES

1991, found that 47 percent of blacks surveyed believed Clarence Thomas and 20 percent believed Anita Hill. A *Los Angeles Times* poll published the same day found that 31 percent of blacks polled thought that Anita Hill's allegations were definitely or probably true, compared with 52 percent who thought they were probably or definitely false; the same survey found that 35 percent of blacks were "certain" in their belief of Thomas's version of events, compared with 9 percent who were "certain" of Hill's version.

18 Emerge, *a since-departed*: Interviews with former *Emerge* editors and a spokeswoman for *Ebony*.

20 *A special strain of animus*: Interview with Eric Ferrer.

20 *"The appropriate word is venom"*: Interview with Brent Bozell.

21 *"My grandfather—that's the guy that got me out"*: *Reason* interview, November 1987.

22 *The audience cheered with pride*: Videotape of speech, *Headway* National Leadership Conference, September 12, 1998, C-SPAN Archives.

23 *"Life is not worth living"*: Ibid.

24 *Debra Dickerson, a gifted writer*: Interview with Debra Dickerson.

24 *Of all the slights*: Family members and friends, including Leola Williams and Lester Johnson, told us the library controversy deeply affected Thomas.

24 *It seemed like a no-brainer*: Interview with Harlan Crow; copy of Thomas's financial disclosure form for calendar year 2001.

25 *Thomas followed the flap*: Conversation reconstructed by Lester Johnson.

26 *In May 2003*: Interview with Keith Burchfield.

26 *Ben Carson, a renowned brain surgeon*: Interview with Ben Carson, who reconstructed his conversations with Thomas. Information about the Horatio Alger Association of Distinguished Americans was taken from the group's Web site.

27 *Thomas is not naïve*: Interview with Ralph Boyd Jr.

28 *Early in Thomas's tenure*: Interview with Eddie Jenkins.

28 *But after his most famous turn*: Ibid.

29 *Apparently softened by the letter*: Ibid.

29 *"After all the yelling and screaming"*: Interview with William Coleman.

30 *This is the same Donna Brazile*: Several interviews were conducted with Donna Brazile about her relationship with Clarence Thomas.

31 *"It's never too late"*: Interview with Kweisi Mfume.

31 *Even Fred McClure*: Interview with Fred McClure.

31 *He made himself available*: We interviewed a number of lawyers and judges, including D'Army Bailey, to reconstruct what went on behind the scenes of Thomas's 1998 appearance at the National Bar Association. Michael A. Fletcher also covered the event for the *Washington Post*.

2 : THE PIN POINT MYTH

35 *It's possible to miss this speck*: We made three trips to Pin Point, attended
    church services there, hung out at a Pinpoint Hall fish fry, watched
    Thomas's mother and a friend pick crabs, and interviewed the key people
    who have been involved in Thomas's life and the life of the community.
    This chapter is based largely on their firsthand accounts and our own
    observations. Unless otherwise indicated, all quotations are from the
    authors' interviews.

39 *One of the dealers was Clarence Thomas's nephew*: Mark Elliot Martin's
    criminal history is detailed in documents obtained from U.S. District
    Court, Southern District of Georgia (Savannah), and Superior Court of
    Chatham County (Georgia). We also interviewed Martin by phone on
    December 12, 2003, when he was in the Federal Correctional Institution
    in Coleman, Florida.

39 *On August 19, 1998*: Keith Paul, "Drug Investigation Results in Arrests,"
    Savannah Morning News, August 20, 1998.

46 *It wasn't long before the marriage unraveled*: Leola Williams discussed her first
    marriage with us. We learned more about M. C. Thomas through
    interviews with his family members, notably his niece Ethel Thomas. His
    funeral program lists his birth date as August 28, 1930, which would put
    his age at death in conflict with the age listed on his marriage license.

47 *"I just wanted to get out of the country"*: Andrew Peyton Thomas, *Clarence
    Thomas* (San Francisco: Encounter Books, 2001), p. 55.

3 : THE SAVANNAH REALITY

52 *The 500 block of East Henry Street*: Michael A. Fletcher reported on this
    event as it happened.

53 *"I got teased about my hair"*: Speech, Tuskegee University, November 18, 1994.

56 *"His life wasn't no struggle"*: Interview with Charlie Mae Garrett.

56 *"Personally, I thought he was rich"*: Interview with Marion Poole.

56 *"Why did my mother choose"*: Thomas, *Clarence Thomas*, p. 64.

57 *"And my daddy looked at me"*: Interview with Leola Williams.

57 *Anderson walked off the porch*: Ibid.

58 *"He was probably the biggest ice and wood man"*: Interview with Sam Williams.

58 *"Oh, Myers was middle class"*: Interview with Prince Jackson.

59 *"My grandparents weren't educated"*: Speech, Thomas Pullen Middle School in
    Landover, Maryland, May 1996.

59 *the "Mother Church" for Savannah's black Catholics*: Research into the history
    of St. Benedict the Moor Catholic Church and the school it operated was
    conducted at the headquarters of the Diocese of Savannah.

59 *"Segregation had really ruined the [public] schools"*: Interview with Bill Haynes.

60 *After Myers Anderson*: Interview with Floyd Adams Jr.

60 *"Yes, we were to be what they called mannerable"*: Speech, Mercer University
    Law School, May 1, 1993.

61 *By the time he began St. Pius X High School*: Speech, Tuskegee University, November 18, 1994.

61 *"Back then they used to call it checking"*: Ibid.

61 *Led by W. W. Law*: The Ralph Mark Gilbert Civil Rights Museum and local historian Charles J. Elmore were helpful in sorting out Savannah's civil rights history.

63 *"Some people may have made jokes"*: Interview with Philip W. Cooper Jr.

63 *"As you went down the caste system in Savannah"*: Interview with Orion Douglass.

64 *"You had the black elite"*: Ken Foskett, *Judging Thomas* (New York: William Morrow, 2004), p. 61.

65 *In a 1994 speech*: Thomas gave this speech—on November 10, 1994, at Wingate College in North Carolina—as a favor to Senator Jesse Helms.

65 *This was the same Jesse Helms who stated*: Jack Betts, "The Same Old Jesse Helms Can't Face Up to Race," *Charlotte Observer*, October 20, 1996; Paula Schwed, "Helms Calls King's Legacy 'Division—Not Love,' " United Press International, October 3, 1983.

66 *"People love to talk about conflicts interracially"*: Foskett, *Judging Thomas*, pp. 61–62.

66 *According to a St. Pius survey*: Diocese of Savannah files.

67 *After a study of the city's Catholic schools*: "Consolidation for Catholic High Schools," *Southern Cross* [Diocese of Savannah newspaper], February 12, 1970. The Benedictine headmaster quoted is Father Aelred Beck.

67 *"It broke my heart to see St. Pius close"*: *Southern Cross*, April 10, 1997.

68 *"I was a stray dog"*: Ibid.

68 *Oddly, Chisholm and Thomas never discussed what it felt like*: Interview with Richard Chisholm.

69 *"I cannot begin to tell you"*: Clarence Thomas, "Remembering an Island of Hope," *St. Croix Review*, December 1986.

70 *Thomas's white classmates don't remember*: Interviews with Steve Seyfried and several other white seminarians.

72 *"Having had to accept my blackness"*: Speech, National Bar Association, July 29, 1998.

73 *One of the explanations Thomas has given*: Ken Foskett, "Trials of Life: Racism Wasn't Only Challenge," *Atlanta Journal-Constitution*, July 2, 2001. Father William Coleman, who was running a charity in Mexico, said of Thomas's dialect back then: "It was pretty much unintelligible to a standard English speaker."

4: MYERS, LEOLA, AND EMMA

75 *Clarence Thomas took this photo*: Details about the photo from interview with Leola Williams.

76 *"My grandfather would be an anachronism"*: Speech, Ohio Northern University, April 7, 1994.

76 *His sister, a dropout*: Interviews with Emma Mae Martin and Thomas friends to whom he has confided his disappointment in his sister.

77 *"A few years before he died"*: Speech, Ohio Northern University, April 7, 1994.

78 *He remembers Anderson railing about rock 'n' roll*: Speech, Acton Institute, May 5, 1994.

78 *"He seemed totally unmoved and undaunted"*: Ibid.

78 *Anderson was the product of an adulterous liaison*: Foskett, *Judging Thomas*, p. 33.

78 *"In Savannah, all you hear"*: Interview with Leola Williams.

79 *He was not an absolute ace at everything*: Interview with Bill Haynes.

80 *"the shit beaten out of them"*: Jane Mayer and Jill Abramson, *Strange Justice* (Boston: Houghton Mifflin, 1994), pp. 38, 364.

80 *His wife, Christine*: The portrait of Christine Anderson is based on interviews with Leola Williams, Ethel Thomas, Sam Williams, and Prince Jackson; several Clarence Thomas speeches; and Anderson's funeral program. See also Foskett, *Judging Thomas*, p. 42.

83 *"I turned where the hopeless and the lonely turn"*: Thomas, *Clarence Thomas*, p. 232.

83 *Asked if he would have been proud of Clarence*: Interview with Sam Williams.

83 *Leola Williams has a small office*: We conducted three interviews with Clarence Thomas's mother for this book, one of which was at Candler Hospital.

85 *He wrote letters to his relatives*: Interviews with Ethel Thomas and Monique Thomas-Morgan, Ethel's daughter, who shared a letter Thomas wrote to her.

86 *"If you can put up with my momma"*: Interview with Leola Williams.

87 *"his mother dumped him and his brother on the grandfather"*: Mayer and Abramson, *Strange Justice*, p. 37.

88 *Thomas apologized to his sister*: Interviews with Emma Mae Martin and Armstrong Williams. (We conducted four separate interviews with Thomas's sister for this book—two at her home in Pin Point and two at the Bethesda Home for Boys, where she works.)

90 *"He was pretty disgusted with his sister"*: Interview with Fletcher Farrington.

5 : "Radical" Times

95 *"Just like others"*: Speech, Conception Seminary College, September 7, 2001.

95 *"I used to make that walk"*: Ibid.

98 *His first roommate*: John Lancaster and Sharon LaFraniere, "Growing Up Black in a White World," *Washington Post*, September 8, 1991.

98 *They sat quietly*: Foskett, *Judging Thomas*, p. 90.

98 *"That's good; I hope the SOB"*: Speech, College of the Holy Cross, March 24, 1984.

98 *"I've run into too many rednecks"*: Thomas, *Clarence Thomas*, p. 108.

100 *But at Conception, his classmates named him*: Lancaster and LaFraniere, "Growing Up Black in a White World."

100 *"The reaction of a lot of people"*: Interview with Frank Scanlon.

100 *"That has been painful"*: Speech, Conception Seminary College, September 7, 2001.

101 *"It all seemed so pointless"*: Speech, College of the Holy Cross, February 3, 1994.

101 *"He was crying"*: Interview with Leola Williams.

102 *"Just as Richard Wright's"*: Speech, College of the Holy Cross, February 3, 1994.

102 *"I filled it in"*: "Clarence Thomas '71: 'Old Man Can't Is Dead,' " *Crossroads*, March–April 1984.

103 *"When I got to"*: Ibid.

104 *Black students accused*: College of the Holy Cross Archives.

104 *A survey of Holy Cross*: Student Survey on Racial Attitudes, College of the Holy Cross Archives.

104 *"My new dormitory"*: "Clarence Thomas '71: 'Old Man Can't Is Dead.' "

104–5 *"Thomas said Siraco*: Ibid.

105 *"He never talked"*: Interview with Tom Lawler.

106 *I felt alienated"*: Joanne Sadowski, "Thomas Recalls Lonely Days," *Crusader*, March 30, 1984.

107 *"The more Holy Cross people"*: College of the Holy Cross Archives.

108 *"In case I get"*: Interview with James Millet.

108 *"There were some things"*: Interview with Gordon Davis.

109 *"We broke his Afro comb"*: Interview with Eddie Jenkins.

109 *"A lot of black students"*: Interview with James Terry.

109 *At Holy Cross football games*: Interview with Dhafir Jihad.

113 *The Ambush home was always open*: Interview with Nelson Ambush.

114 *"I don't know about you guys"*: Interview with Clifford Hardwick, who recalled Thomas's comments.

114 *"What would I tell"*: Speech, College of the Holy Cross, February 3, 1994.

6: THE MAKING OF A CONSERVATIVE

124 *"This thing about how they"*: Juan Williams, "A Question of Fairness," *Atlantic Monthly*, April 1987.

124 *"We never talked"*: Interview with Abraham Goldstein.

125 *"Thomas, as he told it"*: Interview with Jeffrey Zuckerman.

125 *"We had to sort of pull ourselves up"*: "Classmates: 'Clarence is Just Clarence,' " *National Law Journal,* July 15, 1991.

125 *Coleman, who also worked*: Interview with Clarence Martin.

126 *"You had to prove yourself"*: Juan Williams, "Black Conservatives, Center Stage," *Washington Post*, December 16, 1980.

127 *"He dressed like"*: Interview with Quintin Johnstone.

128 *"I didn't belong"*: Foskett, *Judging Thomas*, p. 123.

129 *"He was into"*: Interview with Henry Terry.

129 *"He did porn"*: Interview with Dan Johnson.

129–30 *"Indeed, we would have been hypocrites"*: Michael Wines, "The Thomas Nomination; Stark Conflict Marks Accounts Given by Thomas and Professor," *New York Times*, October 10, 1991.

131 *"I think that Clarence was very disappointed"*: Interview with Lester Johnson.

132 *"I went to law school"*: Williams, "A Question of Fairness."

133 *"Danforth wanted somebody"*: Interview with Guido Calabresi.

134 *When they heard about his job*: Speech, University of Georgia School of Law, May 17, 2003.

134 *"I couldn't get a job"*: Speech, *Headway* National Leadership Conference, September 12, 1998.

134–35 *"He was totally engaging"*: Interview with Michael Doyle.

135 *"I was concerned"*: Interview with Drew S. Days III.

136 *"People notice that"*: Interview with Marvin Krakow.

7: METEORIC RISE

138 *"He was an impressive"*: Interview with Margaret Bush Wilson.

140 *"The problem I have"*: Speech, *Headway* National Leadership Conference, September 12, 1998.

140 *"His feeling was"*: Interview with Michael Middleton.

140 *"He was very strong"*: Interview with Neil Bernstein.

143 *"pouring half a glass of water"*: Interview with Bill Kauffman. "Clarence Thomas," *Reason*, November 19, 1987.

143–44 *"He has predicted much"*: From Thomas's speech at *Headway* magazine's National Leadership Conference, September 12, 1998.

144 *"Patricia Roberts Harris and I"*: "Blacker Than Thou II," *Washington Post*, February 14, 1981.

148 *"I was almost apologetic"*: Senate Judiciary Committee, "The Nomination of Clarence Thomas to Be Associate Justice of the Supreme Court of the United States," 102nd Congress, 1st sess., September 20, 1991, p. 8.

148 *"Let's face it"*: Ibid.

150 *"I'm Clarence Thomas"*: Sharon LaFraniere, "Despite Achievement, Thomas Felt Isolated; Rebuffs Stung Emerging Conservative," *Washington Post*, September 9, 1991.

151 *"If I ever went to work"*: Juan Williams, "Black Conservatives, Center Stage," *Washington Post*, December 16, 1980.

151 *"It was clear from lunch"*: Interview with Juan Williams.

153 *"Displayed on his desk:"* Interview with Michael Middleton.

154 *"I don't fit in with whites"*: Kim Masters, "EEOC's Thomas: Ready to Sing a Different Tune," *Legal Times*, December 24–31, 1984.

155 *"That was Kathy's idea"*: Interview with Nelson Ambush.

155 *"Kathy was quiet"*: Interview with Alphonso Jackson.

156 *"Love her, love her"*: Interview with Leola Williams.

157   *First, his cab driver*: Speech, Labor and Employment Law conference, April
       25–26, 1984.

158   *When Thomas dismissed*: Thomas, *Clarence Thomas*, p. 266.

161   *"I must confess"*: Memo from Clarence Thomas to Edwin Harper, Ronald
       Reagan Library.

162   *"Don't tell me"*: Williams, "A Question of Fairness."

162   *"I understand—Clarence"*: Interview with William Bradford Reynolds.

163   *"Think about this"*: LaFraniere, "Despite Achievement, Thomas Felt Isolated;
       Rebuffs Stung Emerging Conservative."

163   *"Is there some way"*: Interview with Ken Masugi.

164   *"What offends me"*: Masters, "EEOC's Thomas: Ready to Sing a Different
       Tune."

165   *"But he was so nice"*: Laura Blumenfeld, "The Nominee's Soul Mate;
       Clarence Thomas's Wife Shares His Ideas. She's No Stranger to
       Controversy, and She's Adding to His," *Washington Post*, September 10,
       1991.

167   *"Clarence was first discussed"*: Interview with William Bradford Reynolds.

170   *"The politics of the situation"*: Ibid.

8: WHO LIED?

171   *"He was ambivalent about the process"*: Interview with J. Michael Luttig.

171   *John Sununu strongly favored naming the first Hispanic*: Ann Devroy and
       Sharon LaFraniere, "Danforth's Backing Was Key to President's Choice of
       Thomas," *Washington Post*, July 3, 1991.

172   *Richard Thornburgh, though he liked Thomas, had warned*: Ibid.

172   *the panel would give Thomas the lowest rating*: The American Bar Association
       Standing Committee on the Federal Judiciary, which interviewed a
       thousand people in reviewing Thomas's entire legal career, deemed him
       "qualified" for the Supreme Court but short of its highest rating of "well
       qualified." Two of the committee's fifteen members concluded Thomas
       was "not qualified." The ranking was an embarrassment to the Bush
       administration and it placed Thomas at the bottom of Supreme Court
       nominees evaluated by the ABA dating back to the Eisenhower
       administration. As a measure of the rarity of a "qualified" rating, eighteen
       of the twenty-three nominees assessed by the ABA's panel since 1955
       received unanimous "well qualified" ratings. "To reach the well qualified
       standard," Ronald Olson, chairman of the committee, told us, "one has to
       be among the very most prominent members of our profession."

173   *He was tired and overweight*: The section on Marshall in this chapter is
       derived largely from Juan Williams's *Thurgood Marshall* (New York: Three
       Rivers Press, 1998). We also interviewed several former Marshall law
       clerks.

175   *A series of carefully orchestrated lunches*: Gary Lee, "Nominee Thomas Finds
       No Middle Ground," *Washington Post*, August 9, 1991.

175 *White House strategists even culled*: Memo for Mark Paoletta, Bill Lucas, and Michael Calhoun, through Ron Kaufman, from Meghan Flaherty, July 18, 1991 (Re: "Black Attorneys within Administration"), George Bush Presidential Library.

176 *Thomas had confirmed his "blackness"*: Interoffice Memorandum, Washington Bureau, NAACP, July 29, 1991, draft minutes of meeting with Thomas.

177 *considered it just a PR gimmick*: Interview with Leola Williams.

177 *he would later serve more than three years in prison*: Craig Schneider, "Fugitive Ex-Senator Nabbed in the Bahamas," *Atlanta Journal-Constitution*, April 5, 2003.

178 *George Kassouf had been investigating Thomas for two years*: Interview with George Kassouf.

179 *Aron did not think it was appropriate*: Interviews with Kassouf and Nan Aron.

179 *how uncomfortable he was with personal matters*: Mayer and Abramson, *Strange Justice*, p. 229.

180 *"He was coached"*: Interview with C. Boyden Gray.

181 *Ricki Seidman, an influential staffer*: According to a chronology of Anita Hill's contacts with the Senate provided by Seidman, Seidman first called Hill on September 5, 1991. Seidman called again on September 8 and Hill stated she wanted to discuss the sexual harassment issue but was leaving town. On September 9, Seidman called again and Hill told her of the alleged sexual harassment by Thomas. Seidman suggested she talk to Metzenbaum staffer James Brudney. On September 10, Brudney called her.

181 *"Oh, my God"*: Interview with Fred McClure.

182 *"Anita? You can't"*: Mayer and Abramson, *Strange Justice*, pp. 246–47.

182 *"She's lying about me"*: Interview with Thomas friend who asked not to be named.

182 *confiding in an old law school chum, Gary Phillips*: Mayer and Abramson, *Strange Justice*, pp. 224–25.

183 *he was a mess*: The most authoritative account of Thomas's emotional condition during the confirmation process is in John C. Danforth's *Resurrection* (New York: Viking, 1994). Danforth conducted interviews in late 1991 and early 1992 with the principal players on Thomas's side, including Thomas himself and his wife, Ginni. We relied heavily on *Resurrection* in this chapter to explain Thomas's state of mind and how those in his inner circle were dealing with him.

183 *"His anger is gone"*: Danforth, *Resurrection*, p. 104.

183 *"I feel like someone has reached up inside"*: Ibid.

183 *Allen Moore thought there must have been something*: Ibid., p. 103.

184 *"I don't want to talk about it"*: Ibid., pp. 103–4.

184 *How uplifting these friends were*: Ibid., p. 105.

184 *"like something was inside of him"*: Ibid., p. 106.

184 *The contortions on the floor*: Ibid.

184 *"He had one foot in the grave"*: Interview with Abe Famble.

184 *Thomas's sister, Emma, wondered why*: Interview with Emma Mae Martin.

185 *"I'm not a psychic"*: Interview with the Reverend Henry Delaney.

185 *Thomas assisted him in getting funding*: Interviews with Delaney and Clint Bolick.

186 *"the danger of perjury"*: Danforth, *Resurrection*, pp. 108–9.

186 *"Clarence," he instructed, "you cannot lie"*: Ibid., p. 109.

187 *senior officials who wanted to ditch Thomas*: Interview with C. Boyden Gray.

188 *Michael Crichton, the novelist*: Interview with C. Boyden Gray.

188 *"I have been wracking my brains"*: All testimony cited in this chapter, verbatim or paraphrased, is taken directly from the official printed record of the Senate Judiciary Committee hearings (U.S. Government Printing Office, 1993) or *The Complete Transcripts of the Clarence Thomas–Anita Hill Hearings*, ed. Anita Miller (Chicago: Academy Chicago Publishers, 1994) unless otherwise noted.

191 *"not a spur-of-the-moment comment"*: Arlen Specter, *Passion for Truth* (New York: William Morrow, 2000).

192 *an idea that was "remarkably parallel"*: Danforth, *Resurrection*, p. 61.

192 *"Could he have used other words?"*: Interview with Fred McClure.

192 *"he was playing the [race] card"*: Interview with Herbert Kohl.

193 *Biden, Democrat of Delaware, said almost a year after the hearings*: Florence George Graves, "The Other Woman," *Washington Post*, October 9, 1994.

195 *"I personally found that strange"*: Interview with Hank Brown.

197 *"thoughts of inconsistencies, ambiguities"*: Timothy M. Phelps and Helen Winternitz, *Capitol Games* (New York: Hyperion, 1992), p. 220.

197 *denigrated Holmes by quoting*: Ibid., pp. 220–21. Alliance for Justice report, "Judge Thomas: On the Record."

199 *Danforth's wife, Sally, believed Thomas should take a polygraph*: Danforth, *Resurrection*, p. 181.

200 *"battling for the court of public opinion"*: Interview with Larry Thompson.

200 *"Is it about a polygraph?"*: Danforth, *Resurrection*, p. 182.

200 *"No, I will not take a polygraph test"*: Ibid.

200 *Thomas's close friend Laurence Silberman*: Ibid.

200 *"you might go down because of this"*: Ibid.

200 *"That was never anything I was worried about"*: Interview with Larry Thompson.

201 *"I didn't think he would be like he is"*: Interview with John Breaux.

202 *Clyburn says he deeply regrets his decision to vouch for Thomas*: Interview with James Clyburn.

203 *"And when he said race was not a factor"*: Interview with Arlen Specter.

204 *"Arlen, you're not really going to vote for Clarence Thomas"*: Interview with Nan Aron.

205 *When Specter encountered Thomas in the Senate dining room*: This encounter and an account of Specter's interview with Thomas appear in Specter's *Passion for Truth*. Specter elaborated on these events, and his views of Thomas, in two interviews with Kevin Merida.

206   *he "wouldn't object" if someone wanted to reopen an investigation*: Graves, "The Other Woman."

207   *"No, why would I?"*: Interview with Alan Simpson.

208   *"If you go back and put the worst slant"*: Interview with Orrin Hatch.

208   *"unbelievable, that anybody could be that perverted"*: *Complete Transcripts* of Hill-Thomas hearings.

208   *"When it's all said and done"*: Interview with C. Boyden Gray.

209   *"Clarence, what do you think of all this?"*: Interview with Alan Simpson.

209   *"Isn't it something"*: Ibid.

9 : THE AFTERMATH

210   *"Getting the heck beaten out of you"*: C-SPAN Archives, profile of Thomas, April 3, 2001.

210   *"you're facing one of the toughest jobs"*: Interview with Chris Landau.

211   *"I administered the oath at this time"*: Memorandum to the Conference, Chambers of the Chief Justice, October 23, 1991, Lewis F. Powell, Jr. Archives, Washington and Lee University School of Law.

211   *"You are here now"*: Thomas speech, Forum Club of the Palm Beaches, December 19, 1997.

212   *"You will not be surprised to find that the work"*: Ibid.

212   *"When I arrived, I had no staff"*: C-SPAN Archives, profile of Thomas, April 3, 2001.

212   *"On your first day, you show up and you know nothing"*: Ibid.

213   *"Surely they must have been aware of Roe against Wade"*: Harry A. Blackmun Papers, Library of Congress.

214   *Tom Jackman was surprised by a phone call*: Interview with Tom Jackman.

214   *The story recounted a Kafkaesque drama*: Tom Jackman, "The Wrong Man's Sex Arrest Leads to Nightmare Journey," *Washington Post*, November 8, 1999.

215   *She'll never forget a dinner for Thomas*: Interview with Malena Cunningham.

216   *"The past year has been, to say the least, a challenge"*: Copy of letter, August 24, 1992, provided by Dhafir Jihad.

217   *Thomas was mentioned in 32,377 newspaper stories*: Scott Douglas Gerber, *First Principles* (New York: New York University Press, 1999), p. 3.

219   *"It was something that came up from time to time"*: Interview with Chris Landau.

220   *Lewis Powell sent a note to Thomas*: Lewis F. Powell, Jr. Archives, Washington and Lee University School of Law.

220   *"I have learned that if one is honest and fair"*: Ibid.

220   *conservative commentator Ann Coulter told him*: David Brock, *Blinded by the Right* (New York: Crown Publishers, 2002), p. 118.

220   *Ginni Thomas tearfully embraced him*: Ibid., p. 120.

221   *"some derogatory information"*: Ibid., pp. 242–43.

221   *Brock's account was "simply not true"*: Howard Kurtz, "Author Says He Lied in Book on Anita Hill," *Washington Post*, June 27, 2001.

221 *Ginni Thomas left a long message on Brock's answering machine*: Interview with David Brock.

222 *"spiritual warfare. Good versus evil"*: *People*, November 11, 1991.

222 *"never seemed plausible about Clarence Thomas"*: Interview with George Will.

222 *Rush Limbaugh and Clarence Thomas met in 1994*: The account in this chapter of how Limbaugh and Thomas met, and how Thomas came to host Limbaugh's wedding and officiate at it, is largely drawn from the "Unofficial Summary of the Rush Limbaugh Show" for June 3, 1996, by John Switzer (jswitzer@limbaugh.com). Switzer writes he has no connection to Limbaugh or the show. In addition, we consulted news reports of the wedding and interviewed James Carville, who attended.

223 *Hugo Black once sent a memo around*: Tony Mauro column, *Recorder*, June 9, 1994.

223 *He gushed about Limbaugh*: Interviews with Leola Williams, Emma Mae Martin, and Abe Famble.

223 *He told a deputy clerk that Limbaugh was "a very good friend"*: Mauro column, June 9, 1994.

224 *"He had Rush Limbaugh's wedding at his house!"*: Timothy M. Phelps, "Justice's Views Assailed," *Newsday*, September 13, 1995.

224 *"Somehow, if I'm a black man"*: Interview with Larry Thompson.

225 *"you could abort every black baby"*: Michael A. Fletcher and Brian Faler, "Bennett Defends Radio Remarks," *Washington Post*, October 1, 2005.

225 *He has parodied blacks on his show*: Leonard Shapiro, "Limbaugh Quits TV Job under Fire," *Washington Post*, October 2, 2003.

225 *"I don't think he's been that good from the get-go"*: Ibid.

226 *"no good can ever come of treating others badly"*: Speech, Mercer University Law School, May 1, 1993.

226 *"the toughest thing in the world of politics to be is a black conservative"*: Interview with Ed Gillespie.

227 *" 'Why is he hanging around with all of these conservatives?' "*: Interview with Allen Moore.

227 *Weyrich would quote Thomas*: Dan Balz, "Right Sees Miers as Threat to a Dream," *Washington Post*, October 3, 2005.

228 *When Thomas spoke at Concerned Women for America's 1993 convention*: Jeffrey Toobin, "The Burden of Clarence Thomas," *New Yorker*, September 27, 1993.

228 *Each year the Media Research Center*: Information on the "DisHonors Awards" in this chapter comes from the MRC Web site and our firsthand observations at three dinners. Thomas's appearance viewed on videotape.

231 *"It is permanent warfare"*: Interview with Craig Shirley.

233 *"I wish I could clone Clarence Thomas"*: Interview with Greg Mueller.

233 *The justice has arrived*: Everything recounted about the Walter Williams toast, September 23, 2003, was observed by us.

236 *"I don't normally associate the term* scholarship *with Walter Williams"*: Interview with Dick Armey.

10: CRUEL AND UNUSUAL PUNISHMENT

238 *"For Thomas, there"*: Catharine Pierce Wells, "Clarence Thomas: The Invisible Man," *Southern California Law Review*, November 1993.

239 *Hudson says McMillian*: Interview with Keith Hudson.

242 *In a memo*: Harry A. Blackmun Papers, Library of Congress.

242–43 *Three weeks later*: Ibid.

247 *"The conclusion reached"*: Speech, National Bar Association, July 28, 1998.

247 *"The point that I'd like"*: Q & A session, James Madison University, March 15, 2001.

248 *"During his first year"*: "Justice Thomas, the Freshman," *New York Times*, July 5, 1992.

248 *"Dear Clarence"*: Lewis F. Powell Jr. to Clarence Thomas, February 27, 1992, Lewis F. Powell, Jr. Archives, Washington and Lee University School of Law.

250 *"There are some opinions"*: Speech, John M. Ashbrook Memorial Dinner, February 5, 1999.

251 *"That really hurt him"*: David G. Savage, "In the Matter of Justice Thomas: Silent, Aloof and Frequently Dogmatic, Clarence Thomas' Judicial Persona Emerges," *Los Angeles Times Magazine*, October 9, 1994.

251 *Thomas is the justice*: Lori A. Ringhand, "Judicial Activism: An Empirical Examination of Voting Behavior on the Rehnquist Natural Court," *Constitutional Commentary*, Spring 2007.

252 Thomas "has firm views": Interview with Mark V. Tushnet.

256 *"Someone says I show"*: Speech, John M. Ashbrook Memorial Dinner, February 5, 1999.

259 *"This is a decision"*: Linda Greenhouse, "The Supreme Court: Court, 8–1, Faults Mississippi on Bias in College System," *New York Times*, June 27, 1992.

11: MARSHALL'S FOOTPRINTS

262 *"Oh, I thought he was wonderful"*: Remarks, National Center for Policy Analysis, September 9, 1999.

262 *Taylor and Marshall commiserated*: William L. Taylor, *The Passion of My Times: An Advocate's Fifty-Year Journey in the Civil Rights Movement* (New York: Carroll Graf, 2004), p. 28.

263 *Felix Frankfurter*: Williams, *Thurgood Marshall*, p. 307.

264 *But beneath the cheers*: Ibid., pp. 12–13.

264 *In his inimitable Southern drawl*: Ibid., p. 336.

265 *"I am a man of the law"*: Ibid., p. 344.

267 *"What is striking"*: Thurgood Marshall, Remarks, San Francisco Patent and Trademark Association, May 6, 1987.

269 *"It's said that if you can't say"*: "Marshall: Brennan Is Irreplaceable," *Washington Post*, July 27, 1990.

269 *"The White Team and the Black Team"*: Thurgood Marshall Papers, Library of Congress.

272 *For Marshall, this issue*: Carol Steiker, "Did You Hear What Thurgood Marshall Did for Us?" Eulogy, Memorial Service, February 22, 1993.

279 *"Justice Thurgood Marshall will be lucky"*: Terry Eastland, "Only a Footnote, but a Monumental One; A Middling Justice Is Best Honored for His Heroic Work at the Bar, Leading to the Brown Ruling," *Los Angeles Times*, June 28, 1991.

279 *"I don't think he would have been thought"*: Williams, *Thurgood Marshall*, p. 402.

280 *"The conventional wisdom"*: Gerber, *First Principles*, p. 25.

280 *"African Americans have"*: Interview with Donna Brazile.

12: INSIDE THE COURT

281 *"Don't take that job"*: Interview with Brian Jones.

282 *he has gone to Capitol Hill to privately lobby senators*: Interview with Charles Grassley.

283 *Nearly three hours later they were still there*: Interview with James C. Duff.

285 *"The public image of him"*: Interview with Tom Goldstein.

285 *mimicked the 1970s dance steps of the Temptations*: Interview with Brian Jones.

287 *"Dear Clarence, I disagree"*: Speech, Palm Beach County Bar Association, February 7, 1997.

287 *"That's how I spent my last hour"*: Interview with Stephen F. Smith.

288 *"I was only going to stay on the Supreme Court for ten years"*: Interview with Robert Foster.

288 *"I don't think he would ever rule anything out totally"*: Interview with Larry Thompson.

288 *"To the public at large"*: Linda Greenhouse, "Telling the Court's Story: Justice and Journalism at the Supreme Court," *Yale Law Journal*, April 1, 1996.

288 *A 2004* Washington Post *poll*: Asked for their opinion of Thomas, 51 percent of respondents said they didn't know or hadn't heard enough about him; 22 percent had a favorable opinion, 10.5 percent an unfavorable opinion, 16 percent a mixed opinion.

289 *"In a perfect world, I would never give another speech"*: Harry A. Blackmun Papers, Library of Congress.

290 *the chief smoked four or five cigarettes*: Interview with Karl Brooks.

290 Thomas has "significantly improved the quality of our singing": David E. Graham, *San Diego Union-Tribune*, April 8, 2004.

290 *"And in a cynical environment, we see no cynicism"*: Q & A session, Ashland University's Ashbrook Center for Public Affairs, February 5, 1999.

293 *"You're Tim Wu"*: Interview with Tim Wu.

297 *"I will never smoke another cigar"*: Foskett, *Judging Thomas*, p. 301.

298 *"Good cigars, real good cigars"*: Interview with Alphonso Jackson.

299 *"There weren't physical fights"*: Interview with Chris Landau.

300 *twenty-one of the forty-nine clerks he hired*: Our analysis based on clerk lists provided by the Supreme Court public information office.

301   *"That way I know if I get an interview"*: Details of Smith's upbringing are gleaned from Brooke A. Masters, "D.C. Child Leapt from Depths of Welfare to Top of Class," *Washington Post*, May 17, 1992.

301   *"It was a significant part of my experience"*: Interview with Steven Bradbury.

302   *"It's not that I'm against the advancement of the race"*: Interview with Randy Jones.

302   *When Cedric Jennings was ushered into Thomas's chambers*: The account of Jennings's dealings with Thomas is based on Ron Suskind's *A Hope in the Unseen* (New York: Broadway Books, 1998) and interviews with Jennings and Suskind.

303   *All lies, Thomas responded*: We witnessed the exchange at the reception, which took place before a Walter Williams toast, September 23, 2003.

304–5 *"Every year we discuss this"*: From Kevin Merida's notes on the House Appropriations subcommittee hearing, March 18, 2004.

305   *"If I were going to war"*: Interview with former Thomas law clerk who asked not to be named.

305–6 *"who are just plain ol' dishonest"*: Q & A, Ashland University, February 5, 1999.

306   *Even though five of the nine justices*: Reaction to *The Brethren* is drawn from David Garrow, "The Supreme Court and *The Brethren*," *Constitutional Commentary* 18, no. 2 (2001), and Dennis J. Hutchinson, *The Man Who Once Was Whizzer White* (New York: Free Press, 1998).

307   *"walking around making me feel uncomfortable"*: Q & A, Ashland University, February 5, 1999.

13: SILENT JUSTICE

309   *"He sat back in his chair and looked up at the ceiling"*: Interview with Jeannie Sanders.

309   *an informal betting pool among law clerks*: Interviews with former law clerks who spoke only on condition they not be named.

310   *led clerks for other justices to wonder*: Ibid.

310   *"I just think it's sort of bad manners"*: Interview with David Garrow.

310   *"Listen, I can't figure it out"*: Interview with Charles Fried.

311   *In two cases argued in 1993*: Harry A. Blackmun Papers, Library of Congress.

311   *"If you don't ask many questions"*: Philippa Strum, "Change and Continuity on the Supreme Court: Conversations with Justice Harry A. Blackmun," *University of Richmond Law Review* 34, no. 1 (2000).

311   *"It reflects that Justice Blackmun left the court"*: Kevin Merida and Michael A. Fletcher, "The Lonely Stand of Clarence Thomas," *Washington Post Magazine*, August 4, 2002.

312   *"People act strange when a camera is on them"*: "Justice Thomas to Reduce Speeches," Associated Press, May 20, 2000.

313   *"If Justice Ginsburg has questions to ask"*: Copy of letter to Rehnquist in the Harry A. Blackmun Papers, Library of Congress.

314   *Roberts was known for his meticulous study habits*: Joan Biskupic, "Lawyers
       Emerge as Supreme Court Specialists," *USA Today*, May 16, 2003.

314—15 *"I think if we invite a person in"*: Alice Marie Beard's Web site, April 22,
       2000. Beard was among fourteen law students who met with Thomas in
       his chambers.

316   *"Justices are not Larry King types"*: Interview with William H. Webster.

316   *chalked up to stubbornness*: Interview with John Yoo.

317   *"There is some bad advocacy"*: Interview with Tom Goldstein.

319   *"You ever watch* Seinfeld?": The source is someone with direct knowledge of
       Breyer's comment who asked not to be identified.

320   *When eleven students from Benjamin Banneker High School*: The section about
       Benjamin Banneker High School and its trip to the court is based on
       interviews with students, teachers, and the school principal.

14: SCALIA'S CLONE?

323   *"It's a slur"*: Interview with Antonin Scalia.

324   *In a 1979 law review article*: Ruth Marcus and Susan Schmidt, "Tenacious
       after Staking Out a Position; Supreme Court Nominee's Views Attuned to
       Reagan Era Conservative Philosophy," *Washington Post*, June 22, 1986.

326   *"I think Thomas is basically"*: Joan Biskupic, "Scalia, Thomas Stand Apart on
       the Right; Supreme Court Conservatives Challenge Majority's View of the
       Law," *Washington Post*, June 24, 1994.

326   *"You look at Justice Thomas's voting record"*: Carl T. Rowan, "Thomas Is Far
       From 'Home,' " *Chicago Sun-Times*, July 4, 1993.

327   *Molly McUsic, a clerk to Justice Blackmun*: Harry A. Blackmun Papers, Library
       of Congress.

329   *But for Reid*: Rick Weiss, "Reid: Democrats Will Fight on Key Issues,"
       Washington Post, December 6, 2004.

329   *Charles Fried, the courtly Harvard law professor*: Interview with Charles Fried.

332   *"When two justices are similar"*: Interview with Geoffrey Stone.

335   *"We are fools for Christ's sake"*: Joan Biskupic, "Scalia Makes the Case for
       Christianity; Justice Proclaims Belief in Miracles," *Washington Post*, April
       10, 1996.

337   *"I had intellectually and emotionally gotten"*: Marc Fisher, "I Cried Enough to
       Fill a Glass," *Washington Post Magazine*, October 25, 1987.

338   *"It wasn't so great"*: Alex Kozinski, "My Pizza with Nino," *Cardozo Law Review*
       12 (1991).

15: THE QUIET, ANONYMOUS LIFE

340   *"It's a condo on wheels"*: Thomas's quotation and details about his Prevost are
       in *RVIA Today*, the newsletter of the Recreational Vehicle Industry
       Association, September 2001.

341   *discussed the idea of little Mark's coming*: Details of how the Thomases
       became the legal guardians of Marky come from interviews with his

father, Mark Martin, and his grandmother, Emma Mae Martin. His
mother, Susan Martin, declined to be interviewed.

342 *Soon he was good enough to play*: Details about Marky's activities and
interests come from family members and Thomas friends.

343 *"I used to wonder where all of those cars"*: *RVIA Today*.

344 *"not as accessible to us as he used to be"*: Interview with Steve Urbanczyk.

344 *"I do not understand this interest in me"*: Foskett, *Judging Thomas*, epilogue.

344 *"He's in the stockade all by himself"*: Interview with Father John E. Brooks.

345 *"I provide the equipment"*: Details about the Armey-Thomas relationship are
drawn from two interviews with Armey.

346 *"Mrs. Clarence Thomas in that bright blue dress"*: Details about Ginni Thomas's
congressional work and her confrontation with Representative Jim Moran
come from Edward Felsenthal and David Rogers, "Devil with a Blue Dress
On," *Wall Street Journal*, April 25, 1997.

350 *"I would l-o-o-ove to be the NFL commissioner"*: Sarah Talalay, "Justice Thomas
for Commish?" *South Florida Sun-Sentinel*, May 15, 2005.

350 *Thomas left the stadium with Jones*: Interview with Jerry Jones.

352 *"You can tell what I did for their season"*: Talalay, "Justice Thomas for
Commish?"

352 *Thomas met Earl Dixon in April 2001*: Researcher John Imbriglia conducted
several interviews with Earl Dixon on his relationship with Thomas.

353 *Bolick found himself on the outs*: Marc Fisher, "The Private World of Justice
Thomas," *Washington Post*, September 11, 1995.

353 *"I was heartsick"*: Interview with Clint Bolick.

354 *"What are you doing asking me that?"*: Interview with Glenn Loury.

354 *Thomas has telephoned Republican senators*: Interviews with six sources who
have direct knowledge of Thomas's involvement on behalf of black
judicial nominees.

355 *"It was totally baffling to me"*: Interview with Victoria A. Roberts.

355 *Roberts was sent to Thomas by Damon Keith*: Interview with Damon Keith.

356 *"You can tell her she'll be confirmed"*: Ibid.

356 *"a faint recollection"*: Interview with Trent Lott.

356 *the story "sounds familiar"*: Interview with Orrin Hatch.

357 *"Both* Native Son *and* Black Boy *really woke me up"*: Bill Kauffman,
"Interview with Clarence Thomas," *Reason*, November 1987.

358 *an observation Paul Newman made about acting*: Robert Benton, interviewed
by journalist Donna Britt.

359 *"the epitome of a selfish man"*: Interview with Elaine Cassel.

359 *Thomas's speech was a downer*: Interview with Courtenay Brinckerhoff.

360 *where the Thomases buy fresh-cut blossoms*: Details about the Thomases'
neighborhood and their life there come from interviews with friends,
merchants, and neighbors and from direct observation.

361 *"He said that he was both black and white"*: Remarks, Hillsdale College
inauguration of its president, September 9, 2000.

361   *"The RV world gives me a chance"*: Remarks, *RVIA* awards luncheon, June 7, 2004.

16: EXPECTATIONS

362   *Henry Louis Gates Jr. is explaining*: We conducted two interviews with Gates for this chapter.

364   *It's February 2004 in Los Angeles*: Kevin Merida was at the hip-hop summit and reported firsthand.

366   *"Black people get pissed off"*: Interview with Ernie Barnes.

367   *"I am black, I'm an American"*: From Thomas's speech at Ashland University.

368   *"In other words, the Jim Crow system works"*: Valerie Boyd, *Wrapped in Rainbows* (New York: Scribner, 2003), p. 365.

368   *"Now is no time for tongue-wagging by Negroes"*: Ibid., p. 366.

368   *She knew blacks to be*: Ibid., p. 311.

370   *The tradition of black conservatism*: *Black Conservatism*, ed. Peter Eisenstadt (New York: Garland Publishing, 1999), p. xv.

370   *"If God designs to set us free"*: Ibid.

371   *"We have an interesting race sometimes"*: Speech, Tuskegee University, November 18, 1994.

371–72   *he arrived with two "bodyguards"*: Interview with J. Clay Smith.

372   *"the most scathing fiction about race"*: Ishmael Reed, introduction to George S. Schuyler, *Black No More* (New York: Modern Library, 1999).

373   *Ginsburg noted that the first five Jewish justices*: Justice Ruth Bader Ginsburg, "From Benjamin to Brandeis to Breyer: Is There a Jewish Seat?" Louis D. Brandeis School of Law at the University of Louisville, February 11, 2003. Most of the material on Jewish justices, including Brandeis and Arthur Goldberg, is taken from that lecture. See also Robert A. Burt, *Two Jewish Justices* (Berkeley: University of California Press, 1988).

375   *"Does a black man instantaneously become 'insensitive' "*: Speech, Mercer University Law School, May 1, 1993.

SELECTED BIBLIOGRAPHY

Biskupic, Joan. *Sandra Day O'Connor: How the First Woman on the Supreme Court Became Its Most Influential Justice*. New York: Ecco, HarperCollins Publishers, 2005.

Boyd, Valerie. *Wrapped in Rainbows: The Life of Zora Neale Hurston*. New York: Scribner, 2003.

Brock, David. *Blinded by the Right: The Conscience of an Ex-Conservative*. New York: Crown Publishers, 2002.

————. *The Real Anita Hill: The Untold Story*. New York: The Free Press, 1993.

Cooper, Phillip J. *Battle on the Bench: Conflict Inside the Supreme Court*. Lawrence: University Press of Kansas, 1995.

Danforth, John C. *Resurrection: The Confirmation of Clarence Thomas*. New York: Viking, 1994.

Debolt, Margaret Wayt. *Savannah: A Historical Portrait*. Gloucester Point, Va.: Hallmark Publishing Company, 2001.

Eisenstadt, Peter (editor). *Black Conservatism: Essays in Intellectual and Political History*. New York and London: Garland Publishing, 1999.

Ellison, Ralph. *Invisible Man*. New York: Random House, 1947.

Elmore, Charles J. *Savannah, Georgia*. Black America Series. Charleston, S.C.: Arcadia Publishing, 2002.

Foskett, Ken. *Judging Thomas: The Life and Times of Clarence Thomas*. New York: William Morrow, 2004.

Gates, Henry Louis, Jr., Spencer Crew, Cynthia Goodman. *Unchained Memories: Readings from the Slave Narratives*. (Based on the HBO documentary.) Boston-New York-London: Bulfinch Press, 2002.

Gerber, Scott Douglas. *First Principles: The Jurisprudence of Clarence Thomas*. New York: New York University Press, 1999.

Hill, Anita. *Speaking Truth to Power*. New York: Doubleday, 1997.

Holzer, Henry Mark. *The Keeper of the Flame*. Bangor, Maine: Madison Press, 2006.

Hutchinson, Dennis J. *The Man Who Once Was Whizzer White: A Portrait of Justice Byron R. White*. New York: Free Press, 1998.

Irons, Peter. *A People's History of the Supreme Court*. New York: Penguin Books, 2000.

Jeffries, John C., Jr. *Justice Lewis F. Powell, Jr.: A Biography*. New York: Charles Scribner's Sons, 1994.

Joyner, Charles, Muriel and Malcolm Bell, Jr. Savannah Unit, Georgia Writers' Project, Work Projects Administration. *Drums and Shadows: Survival Studies Among the Georgia Coastal Negroes*. Athens: Brown Thrasher Books. University of Georgia Press, 1940, 1986.

Kalman, Laura. *Abe Fortas: A Biography*. New Haven and London: Yale University Press, 1990.

Lazarus, Edward. *Closed Chambers: The Rise, Fall, and Future of the Modern Supreme Court*. New York: Penguin Books, 1999.

Leak, Jeffrey B. *Rac[e]ing to the Right: Selected Essays of George S. Schuyler*. Knoxville: University of Tennessee Press, 2001.

Maroon, Fred J. and Suzy Maroon. *The Supreme Court of the United States*. Lickle Publishing, in cooperation with the Supreme Court Historical Society, 2002.

Mayer, Jane and Jill Abramson. *Strange Justice: The Selling of Clarence Thomas*. Boston: Houghton Mifflin Company, 1994.

Miller, Anita (editor). *The Complete Transcripts of the Clarence Thomas–Anita Hill Hearings: October 11, 12, 13, 1991*. Chicago: Academy Chicago Publishers, 1994.

Morrison, Toni (editor). *Race-ing, Justice, En-gendering Power: Essays on Anita Hill, Clarence Thomas, and the Construction of Social Reality*. New York: Pantheon Books, 1992.

Ogletree, Charles J., Jr. *All Deliberate Speed: Reflections on the First Half Century of Brown v. Board of Education*. New York and London: W.W. Norton & Company, 2004.

Onwuachi-Willig, Angela. "Just Another Brother on the SCT: What Justice Clarence Thomas Teaches Us About the Influence of Racial Identity," University of Iowa College of Law: *Iowa Law Review*, Vol. 90, 2005.

Phelps, Timothy M. and Helen Winternitz. *Capitol Games: Clarence Thomas, Anita Hill, and the Story of a Supreme Court Nomination*. New York: Hyperion, 1992.

Rehnquist, William H. *The Supreme Court*. New York: Alfred A. Knopf, 2001.

Scalia, Antonin. *A Matter of Interpretation: Federal Courts and the Law*. Princeton: Princeton University Press, 1997.

Schuyler, George S. *Black No More*. New York: Modern Library, 1999.

Smith, Christopher E. and Joyce A. Baugh. *The Real Clarence Thomas: Confirmation Veracity Meets Performance Reality*. New York: Peter Lang Publishing Inc., 2000.

Sowell, Thomas. *Black Rednecks and White Liberals*. San Francisco: Encounter Books, 2005.

————. *Race and Culture: A World View*. New York: Basic Books, 1994.

Starr, Kenneth W. *First Among Equals: The Supreme Court in American Life*. New York: Warner Books, 2002.

Suskind, Ron. *A Hope in the Unseen: An American Odyssey from the Inner City to the Ivy League*. New York: Broadway Books, 1998.

Taylor, William L. *The Passion of My Times: An Advocate's Fifty-Year Journey in the Civil Rights Movement*. New York: Carroll & Graf Publishers, 2004.

Thomas, Andrew Peyton. *Clarence Thomas: A Biography*. San Francisco: Encounter Books, 2001.

Ward, Artemus and David L. Weiden. *Sorcerers' Apprentices: 100 Years of Law Clerks at the United States Supreme Court*. New York: New York University Press, 2006.

Williams, Juan. *Thurgood Marshall: American Revolutionary*. New York: Three Rivers Press, 1998.

Woodward, Bob and Scott Armstrong. *The Brethren: Inside the Supreme Court*. New York: Simon and Schuster, 1979.

Wright, Richard. *Native Son*. New York: Harper & Brothers, 1940.

INDEX